W9-DDW-295

TOLERATION AND ITS LIMITS

NOMOS

XLVIII

NOMOS

Harvard University Press

I	*Authority* 1958, reissued in 1982 by Greenwood Press

The Liberal Arts Press

II	*Community* 1959
III	*Responsibility* 1960

Atherton Press

IV	*Liberty* 1962
V	*The Public Interest* 1962
VI	*Justice* 1963, reissued in 1974
VII	*Rational Decision* 1964
VIII	*Revolution* 1966
IX	*Equality* 1967
X	*Representation* 1968
XI	*Voluntary Associations* 1969
XII	*Political and Legal Obligation* 1970
XIII	*Privacy* 1971

Aldine-Atherton Press

XIV	*Coercion* 1972

Lieber-Atherton Press

XV	*The Limits of Law* 1974
XVI	*Participation in Politics* 1975

New York University Press

XVII	*Human Nature in Politics* 1977
XVIII	*Due Process* 1977
XIX	*Anarchism* 1978
XX	*Constitutionalism* 1979
XXI	*Compromise in Ethics, Law, and Politics* 1979
XXII	*Property* 1980
XXIII	*Human Rights* 1981
XXIV	*Ethics, Economics, and the Law* 1982
XXVI	*Marxism* 1983
XXVII	*Criminal Justice* 1985

XXVIII *Justification* 1985
XXIX *Authority Revisited* 1987
XXX *Religion, Morality, and the Law* 1988
XXXI *Markets and Justice* 1989
XXXII *Majorities and Minorities* 1990
XXXIII *Compensatory Justice* 1991
XXXIV *Virtue* 1992
XXXV *Democratic Community* 1993
XXXVI *The Rule of Law* 1994
XXXVII *Theory and Practice* 1995
XXXVIII *Political Order* 1996
XXXIX *Ethnicity and Group Rights* 1997
XL *Integrity and Conscience* 1998
XLI *Global Justice* 1999
XLII *Designing Democratic Institutions* 2000
XLIII *Moral and Political Education* 2001
XLIV *Child, Family, and State* 2002
XLV *Secession and Self-Determination* 2003
XLVI *Political Exclusion and Domination* 2004
XLVII *Humanitarian Intervention* 2006
XLVIII *Toleration and Its Limits* 2007

NOMOS XLVIII

Yearbook of the American Society for Political and Legal Philosophy

TOLERATION AND ITS LIMITS

Edited by

Melissa S. Williams

and

Jeremy Waldron

NEW YORK UNIVERSITY PRESS • *New York and London*

NEW YORK UNIVERSITY PRESS
New York and London
www.nyupress.org

Library of Congress Cataloging-in-Publication Data
American Society for Political and Legal Philosophy. Meeting (2004 :
Atlanta, Ga.)
Toleration and its limits / edited by Melissa S. Williams and Jeremy
Waldron.
p. cm. — (Nomos ; 48)
Papers presented at the annual meeting of the American Society of
Political and Legal Philosophy in Atlanta, Ga., on January 2–3, 2004.
Includes bibliographical references and index.
ISBN-13: 978-0-8147-9411-1 (alk. paper)
ISBN-10: 0-8147-9411-4 (alk. paper)
1. Toleration—History. 2. Religious tolerance. 3. Toleration—Political
aspects. I. Williams, Melissa S., 1960– II. Waldron, Jeremy. III. Title.
HM1271.A54 2008
179'.9—dc22 2007037276

New York University Press books are printed on acid-free paper,
and their binding materials are chosen for strength and durability.

Manufactured in the United States of America
10 9 8 7 6 5 4 3 2 1

CONTENTS

PREFACE

MELISSA S. WILLIAMS

The essays collected here, in this forty-eighth volume of NOMOS, emerged from the annual meeting of the American Society of Political and Legal Philosophy (ASPLP) in Atlanta on January 2 and 3 of 2004, which was held in conjunction with the annual meeting of the Association of American Law Schools. Our topic, "Toleration and Its Limits," was selected by the Society's membership.

The current volume includes revised versions of the principal papers delivered at that conference by David Heyd, Steven D. Smith, and Ingrid Creppell. It also includes essays that developed out of the original commentaries on those papers by Glyn Morgan, Rainer Forst, Kathryn Abrams, Andrew Sabl, Glen Newey, and Noah Feldman. Jeremy Waldron and I extend our sincere thanks to each of these authors for the thoughtfulness of their original contributions, their work in revising the pieces for publication, and their patience through all the delays in bringing this volume to press.

Toleration has a rich tradition in Western political philosophy. Much of the discussion at the conference recurred to this tradition in exploring the philosophical nuances of the concept of toleration and the scope and limits of toleration in contemporary liberal democratic societies. In order to make explicit the debt of contemporary philosophical reflection to that tradition, we solicited a number of additional essays for the present volume that revisit some of the tradition's key figures. We are grateful to Michael

A. Rosenthal, Alex Tuckness, Rainer Forst, and Glyn Morgan for writing the original—and very illuminating—studies of Spinoza, Locke, Bayle, and John Stuart Mill that appear here. Many thanks as well to Jeremy Waldron for his provocative piece on Hobbes, which fills out the historical section of the volume.

Toleration is a principle that has become so fixed a feature of liberal democracy that we are in danger of embracing it too uncritically. We therefore also thought it salutary to include a piece that takes a more critical perspective on the concept of toleration and its usage in political discourse. Wendy Brown's powerful analysis helps to remind us of some of the dark side of toleration, and we want to express our appreciation for her willingness to contribute it to this volume.

There are other dimensions of the theory and practice of toleration that deserve scholarly attention. In particular, we are conscious of the non-Western traditions of toleration, especially in Islam, Buddhism, and Confucianism, which it would have been revealing to juxtapose to the Western tradition represented here. But New York University Press has already been more than generous in allowing us to publish as many pieces as are included here, and so we have to hope that the worthy project of developing such a comparative study of toleration will soon find its champion.

The editors at New York University Press, and particularly Gabrielle Begue, Ilene Kalish, and Despina Papazoglou Gimbel, have been unfailingly supportive of this volume and of the NOMOS series despite frustrating delays in production. On our own behalf and on behalf of the Society, we wish to express our deep gratitude for the Press's ongoing support for the series and the tradition of interdisciplinary scholarship that it represents.

We also wish to thank the officers of the ASPLP for their leadership and loyalty to the NOMOS series. In particular, Jacob Levy, its Secretary-Treasurer, has demonstrated a steadfast commitment to our joint enterprise. He is an exemplar of the professionalism, responsibility, care, and intellectual engagement that has sustained the ASPLP for its fifty years. All of us who are affiliated with NOMOS and the ASPLP owe him a profound debt of gratitude for much more than his excellent fiscal management.

As Managing Editor, Genevieve Fuji Johnson also bears a vast share of the responsibility for keeping the NOMOS series alive and in good health. Her organizational skill, good judgment, efficiency, and keen intelligence have been crucial to every stage of the process, from organizing the conference to offering editorial input to preparing the manuscript for publication. Were it not for her dedicated work—which she has carried out through the completion of her doctorate and into her appointment as Assistant Professor of Political Science at Simon Fraser University—we would be much further behind with the series. It is a privilege to work with her.

Rinku Lamba, who is completing her Ph.D. in Political Science at the University of Toronto, has also provided critical assistance during the production phase of the volume. Many thanks are due to her as well. Thanks also to Tobold Rollo for preparing the index.

Finally, I want to express my personal debt of gratitude to Jeremy Waldron. In taking on the role of co-organizer of the conference and co-editor of this volume, he may have been more generous than he initially intended despite his generous nature. His wealth of knowledge, critical eye, even-handedness, and lively intelligence have all made it a delight to work with him throughout; and his patience and magnanimity have been a great personal support as we finally brought the volume to a close.

MELISSA S. WILLIAMS
Toronto, April 2007

CONTRIBUTORS

LAWRENCE A. ALEXANDER
Law, University of San Diego

KATHRYN ABRAMS
Law, University of California, Berkeley

WENDY BROWN
Political Science, University of California, Berkeley

INGRID CREPPELL
Political Science, George Washington University

NOAH FELDMAN
Law, New York University

RAINER FORST
Political Science, Johann Wolfgang Goethe-Universitt

DAVID HEYD
Bioethics, National Institutes of Health, and Philosophy, Hebrew University

GLYN MORGAN
Government, Harvard University

GLEN NEWEY
Politics, University of Strathclyde

MICHAEL A. ROSENTHAL
Philosophy, University of Washington

ANDREW SABL
Government, Harvard University, and Public Policy and Political Science, University of California, Los Angeles

STEVEN D. SMITH
Law, University of San Diego

ALEX TUCKNESS
Political Science, Iowa State University

JEREMY WALDRON
Law, New York University

MELISSA S. WILLIAMS
Political Science, and Centre for Ethics, University of Toronto

INTRODUCTION

JEREMY WALDRON AND
MELISSA S. WILLIAMS

1.

The American Society for Legal and Social Philosophy has never in its first half-century devoted a volume in its NOMOS series to the theme of toleration. One might have expected such a book in the early years when the NOMOS volumes addressed some of the classic issues: authority, community, responsibility, liberty, justice, equality, representation, political obligation, and the public interest. Toleration, after all, is one of the defining topics of political philosophy—historically pivotal in the development of modern liberalism, prominent in the writings of such canonical figures as John Locke and John Stuart Mill, and central to our understanding of the idea of a society in which individuals have the right to live their own lives by their own values, unmolested by the state so long as they respect the similar interests of others. The relevance of the topic straddles our three constitutive disciplines. Toleration has been central in the history of early modern and modern political theory; it is a testing ground of great analytic interest for various philosophical characterizations of state's function in relation to morality; and in constitutional law, it presents itself as a way of thinking abut First Amendment rights such as the free exercise of religion and the wall of separation between church and state. One would have expected a volume on this before now. We will not speculate as to why toleration has been so conspicuously absent from the NOMOS series. But we are very glad that at this late stage we have been able to make up the deficit with a fine collection of papers addressing the topic in an intriguing variety of ways.

2.

The theme of toleration would have been a good choice for a past volume of NOMOS, but it undoubtedly remains a fitting topic for our times. If the "circumstances of toleration" should be understood as the existence of a plurality of religious faiths with varying degrees of power to oppress one another, then arguably those circumstances obtain as pertinently today as during the sixteenth- and seventeenth-century wars of religion that gave way to the European tradition of religious toleration. The rise of fundamentalist and jihadist Islamic movements is one of the most striking phenomena of modern world politics. It has transformed the politics of the Middle East and thus also the politics of the global oil economy, and after the terrorist attacks of September 11, 2001, it has convulsed the security politics and legal and political systems of countries such as the United Kingdom and the United States. Even before 9/11, some political scientists talked openly of a "clash of civilizations": Islam versus the broadly liberal West.[1] Even if one embraces the "clash of civilizations" thesis against its many critics, the parallels to the early modern period might encourage the conclusion that now, once again and more than ever, we need to revisit the doctrines of toleration that were so instrumental to a European peace.

Others talk, perhaps more plausibly, of a clash within Western liberal democracies between mainstream political culture and minority religious and cultural communities, with particular focus on Muslim minorities. This sort of talk has become quite common in political theory and political commentary in Europe, where it is galvanized not only by worries about war and terrorism, but also by ongoing controversies about the social integration of immigrants from former colonies, many of whom are Muslim. While most non-Muslims in Western democracies continue to express attitudes of toleration or acceptance of Muslim minorities post-9/11, one might think it overgenerous to characterize contemporary dynamics as expressing a strong climate of toleration. *L'affaire du foulard* in France—which in the name of universalist republicanism and *laïcité* resulted in a government decision to ban students from wearing the *hijab* in public schools—lay in the background of the street riots in Paris in 2005.[2] The murder in 2004 of Dutch filmmaker Theo van Gogh by a Dutch-born Muslim of Moroccan descent heightened an open and ongoing confrontation between liberal secularists (and feminists) and Muslim communities in the Netherlands.[3] In 2005, the Danish newspaper *Jyllands-Posten* published cartoons depicting Mohammed, violating the Islamic proscription of graphic depictions of the prophet, and it did so with a conscious intention of provoking controversy. The cartoons proved more provocative than the editors foresaw, generating angry demonstrations throughout the Muslim world, violent attacks on Danish and Norwegian embassies, and the loss of human life—in addition to heated debates over the limits of toleration and the proper exercise of rights of freedom of expression.[4] The birthplace of liberal toleration does not, in such times, inspire triumphalist praise for its achievements in securing the conditions of stable pluralistic democracy.

Thus we may have some reason to question the progressivist story of liberal modernity which begins with the discovery of toleration and ties it to the emergence of constitutionally limited government, the recognition of individual rights, and the spread of democracy. In one strand of that story, modernization—both political and economic—was meant to go hand in hand with secularization, the shift to a rational basis of politics and economy and away from religion as an important foundation of political life. Processes of secularization and individualization are supposed to be good news for toleration because they can lessen the religious passions that produce the desire to repress other faiths. Indeed, on some definitions of toleration (as putting up with what one disapproves) they render toleration itself obsolescent. Yet the global reach of modernization through capitalism has not produced a withering away of religion. True, there has been a decline of religious belief in Europe, though over the last two decades this decline is actually quite modest, and in some countries—notably Italy and Denmark—people have actually become more religious.[5] American exceptionalism holds true: Americans are significantly more religious than Europeans. Almost 60 percent of the U.S. population reports that religion plays a "very important" role in their lives, compared with 33 percent in the United Kingdom, 27 percent in Italy, and 11 percent in France.[6] And American religiosity shows no signs of decline. More broadly, though, recent empirical research suggests that modernization has two competing effects on religiosity: to the extent it increases affluence and well-being through economic development, it weakens religious belief, but to the extent it increases cultural-religious diversity (through migration), it is associated with heightened competition between religious groups and intensified religiosity in general populations.[7] So we need not look to the rise of religious fundamentalism, whether Christian or Islamic, to be persuaded that toleration as a response to religious pluralism remains a highly relevant construct.

For good reason, then, there continues to be very lively interest in the issues relating to toleration in each of our three constituent disciplines. A number of important monographs and volumes of essays have been published in the last ten years or so that indicate the issue of toleration is very much alive.[8] The core philosophical questions concerning the meaning of toleration continue to be debated, and new issues arise as new generations of scholars pursue the topic and connect it to other controversies in jurisprudence, political theory, and political philosophy.

3.

What is toleration? The richness of the Western intellectual tradition of toleration flows in part from the fact that the answer to this question is deeply disputed. One source of disputation over the meaning of toleration is the question: Who or what is the agent of toleration, and what is its object? At the core of the traditional discussion, toleration is understood as a way of characterizing the appropriate relation between the state, on the one hand, and various religious beliefs, practices, and ways of life held and followed by members of society, on the other. The state tolerates a set of beliefs and practices if it does not attempt to change or suppress them or impose penalties for holding or following them, even though it does not endorse them (indeed, even though at some level it may oppose them). In this volume, David Heyd questions the premise: to see the state as the principal agent of toleration, he argues, is to lock us into an outmoded understanding of toleration as an act of royal grace, an image of toleration that may have been appropriate enough for the monarchy of the *ancien régime* but is ill-suited to a modern democratic state grounded in the rule of law according to principles of impartial justice. What the modern state owes its citizens is not toleration but justice, and toleration properly understood is a matter not of politics but of private morals.

Others insist on the essential political relevance of toleration, while rejecting the view that toleration is best understood as a vertical relationship between the state and its subjects or citizens. With different emphases and diverse accounts of the moral psychology of toleration, a number of our contributors—Rainer Forst, Kathryn Abrams, Glyn Morgan, Andrew Sabl, and Ingrid Creppell—agree that toleration is best understood as a horizontal relationship between citizens in their public identity to one another, and of citizens' churches, mosques, synagogues, congregations, and other religious and ethical associations to one another. Citizens acting individually or in groups tolerate one another if they refrain from interfering with one another's practices or beliefs, even when they are convinced that these are wrong. In a pluralistic democracy, these authors argue, an attitude of toleration is a necessary support to citizens' capacity to understand themselves as engaged in a project of shared self-rule grounded in egalitarian respect.

On some conceptions, toleration represents a concession or indulgence by an established state church or a majority religious group: it does not take advantage of its dominant position to suppress the beliefs and practices of non-conforming groups. But many find this conception of toleration condescending and unsatisfactory. On a more ambitious approach, toleration requires the state to refrain altogether from establishing any official faith, tolerant or non-tolerant: it should simply stay out of the business of religion. Belief and worship are things that should be left to the citizens as private matters. And citizens, for their part, should regard the beliefs and practices of those of other faiths as none of their business, strictly the business of those who hold and follow them.

If there is a common theme here it is the image of a pluralist society in which men and women of differing beliefs go proudly about their own business, living their lives in accordance with their own values or the religious teachings that they find convincing and congenial, and gathering with like-minded people so that they can avow these beliefs and follow these practices openly in the company of others. This attractive image of religious pluralism is compatible with a very weak form of religious establishment (of the sort one sees in modern Britain, for example); it is certainly compatible with there being majorities and minorities on religious matters and with some majority being predominant in the society. But a case can be made that under circumstances of weak establishment and/or social predominance, toleration is precarious and the attractive pluralism that we have imagined will inevitably be haunted by the worry that at any time predominance could turn into domination and weak establishment pave the way for more aggressive claims by the state. Defenders of toleration therefore often make the stronger claim that the law should be entirely neutral on matters of religion, that there should be a wall of separation between church and state, and that freedom of worship and belief should be regarded as a human right and secured at the national level by a constitutional guarantee.

On most traditional approaches, toleration is compatible with the tolerating entity (the state, churches in their relation to one another, or citizens in their relation to one another) holding the view that the beliefs or practices being tolerated are in themselves wrong or undesirable. Some philosophers even maintain that toleration makes no sense apart from some such view: if we didn't think the beliefs or practices in question were wrong, the issue of tolerating them would not arise. (In this volume, Lawrence A. Alexander calls this "the paradox of toleration.") Whether or not this is part of the meaning of toleration, there is a further question about whether toleration places limits on the holding or expression of such critical views. It may do so in the case of the state: the strong position described a moment ago might have the consequence that the state and its officials should express no view whatsoever on religion or on any particular religion (let alone act on any such view). For churches and citizens, of course, such a requirement would defeat the very purpose of toleration, which is to secure room for the holding of particular religious views which necessarily as part of their truth claim involve the view that other religious beliefs are mistaken. It may, however, be part of an ethic of tolerance—the virtue associated with toleration—to moderate these views, at least in the public realm, and limit oneself to their being expressed sensitively and respectfully.

There may also be an argument, either on the basis of the toleration ideal or as an independent matter of civility in liberal politics, for refraining from citing one's religious views in political argument. We know that even if religious views are not themselves embodied in laws, they may be relevant in principle to the debates that citizens have about what their laws should be. Citizens have to reach a view on what do about such issues as abortion, euthanasia, the regulation of sexuality, social justice, the regulation of war, and so on. On issues like these, religious arguments are among the most powerful considerations that can be cited for positions on one side or another of the debates that citizens face (positions which in themselves would involve no affront to toleration if they were enforced); and it may be tempting for people to form pressure groups or even political parties to ensure that these religious considerations are given proper attention in political debate. People must be able to pursue what they take to be the important implications of their beliefs; that itself seems to be part of the tolerationist ideal. On the other hand, if we take the strong view that religion should be utterly separate from the politics of a society, then there may be a case for requiring people not only to refrain from demanding that religious views be enforced, but also to refrain from demanding that *anything* be enforced if the only grounds for that demand are religious.

Here as elsewhere, we find that toleration can sometimes seem to be at war with itself. In order to protect religious freedom, we have to place some limits on religious expression. That in itself is not a criticism, for on no conception is the duty of toleration unlimited. On no conception is the freedom which religious toleration protects absolute. Obviously, toleration restricts the practice of punishing heretics and apostates and it may even have to restrict expressions of the belief that heretics deserve to be burned and apostates deserve assassination, even when these are not necessarily followed by action. Beyond that, religiously inspired practices which are dangerous or beliefs which are seditious or disruptive of a tolerant social order are not to be tolerated. Usually, however, suppression or penalization of these views and practices proceeds on the basis of descriptions that have nothing to do with their religious character: they are penalized because they involve killing, not because they involve human sacrifice; because they involve extortion, not because they involve compulsory tithing; because they undermine democracy, not because they look forward to the rule of the saints; or because they involve attacks on other people's property or liberty, not because they involve vigorous evangelization. Figuring out these limits is sometimes quite difficult, for banning an action under a non-religious description may make it impossible for some people to practice their faith—and there is a question whether this is something that should be taken into account when lawmakers are debating what are otherwise the entirely non-religious merits of a legislative proposal. As we lay down rules for the prevention of cruelty to animals, for example, should we consider the impact that these may have on practices of ritual slaughter associated with various religions? Or is a state fulfilling its duty of toleration if it just concentrates on the non-religious merits of the regulation, unconcerned with their religious impact? These are some of the issues and antinomies that arise in the core discussion of toleration as it has been traditionally conceived.

4.

How one responds to these and other questions about the character, the extent, and the limits of toleration depends of course on the case one makes for it. Toleration is not a self-justifying idea. It is a demanding principle that requires us to check and inhibit what might otherwise seem natural ways of pursuing what we value or what we think important in life. We have to have good reason for doing this. Some, like Steven D. Smith in his essay in this volume, argue that there is no neutral justification for toleration that can stand apart from the values that we are committed to. An ultraliberal theory of toleration based on a commitment to neutrality goes nowhere, if only because toleration itself has to rest on ideals that the liberal cannot be neutral about. We hold a principle of toleration (if we do), not because values don't matter, but because values like peace, diversity, autonomy, or the integrity of individual conscience matter more than (say) the religious values that we might be inclined to uphold through the agency of state and law.

Toleration as self-restraint, whether in the expression of religious beliefs or in the open criticism of them, stands in contrast to a view of a politics of public reason in which citizens openly share the reasons, including the religious or cultural reasons, for their positions on controversial matters of public policy. Kathryn Abrams paints this contrast by distinguishing "forbearant" toleration in which one keeps one's disapproval of others to oneself, from "engaged" toleration, in which one actively strives to understand the other's belief from the standpoint of the other, even if in the final analysis one is not persuaded to agree with the other about religious or moral judgments. Like Anna Elisabetta Galeotti in her argument for a strong connection between toleration and recognition,[9] and Ingrid Creppell in her arguments for the centrality of identity to the robust practice of toleration,[10] Abrams argues that non-interference with others is inadequate to the challenges of egalitarian democracy under circumstances of deep pluralism and social diversity. What we need, instead, is a politics of active listening oriented toward mutual understanding.

Questions of toleration are thus inextricable from current issues in both law and political philosophy. In law, the place of religion in a liberal society continues to be a matter of considerable discussion among constitutional scholars. In the United States, issues of religious toleration are framed by the twin guarantees of non-establishment and the free exercise of religion. A number of important constitutional questions explore the tension between these two: to opponents of religion (or of a particular religion), the leeway granted to religious institutions often approaches establishment, while to many of those who hold religious commitments, the aversion from anything that might conceivably be regarded as state affiliation can tend to suppress their freedom to practice their religion, especially their freedom to do so in public. Tangled issues like this crop up in the debate about school vouchers (allowing parents in effect to spend some of their tax dollars that would otherwise go to public schools on the fees charged by religious schools): is this a matter of equal freedom and ensuring that religious parents are not burdened with having to pay twice for the education of their children, because they choose not to send them to public schools?

There is a similar tangle of issues in regard to the possibility of religious exemptions from generally applicable laws that are not in the first instance motivated as attacks on religion. In a notable pair of decisions in the 1990s, the U.S. Supreme Court rejected the position that the enforcement of narcotics laws against the sacramental use of peyote in Native American religious ceremonies and the enforcement of historic preservation ordinances against a Catholic diocese seeking to modernize a church building called for strict scrutiny as a burden on the free exercise of religion.[11] The decisions were very controversial, partly because they were unprecedented, partly because the second of them struck down (at least as applied to the states) legislation passed by Congress—the Religious Freedom Restoration Act—attempting to impose a more stringent reading for constitution's free exercise guarantee. Justice Scalia defended the decisions on the ground that allowing any grater ambit for free exercise would unduly impair the operation of the modern welfare/regulative state:

> The rule respondents favor would open the prospect of constitutionally required religious exemptions from civic obligations of almost every conceivable kind—ranging from compulsory military service, to the payment of taxes, to health and safety regulation such as manslaughter and child neglect laws, compulsory vaccination laws, drug laws, and traffic laws, to social welfare legislation such as minimum wage laws, child labor laws, animal cruelty laws, . . . environmental protection laws, and laws providing for equality of opportunity for the races. The First Amendment's protection of religious liberty does not require this.[12]

Opinions may differ about the implications of what Justice O'Connor called the court's "parade of horribles."[13] There is no doubt, however, that Justice Scalia is right: the greater the scope for religious liberty, the greater the constraint on the regulatory state. What we see here is the considerable difficulty in pursuing a strong tolerationist line against a background in which whole areas of ordinary life—"things indifferent," in John Locke's language—are now all subject to state regulation for the sake of health, safety, or educational or environmental values.

Recent political philosophy also links centrally to themes of toleration. One issue that has assumed a new prominence concerns the place of religious claims in political deliberation. In *Political Liberalism,* John Rawls argued that political positions (at least on basic justice and constitutional essentials) should not be argued for on the basis of comprehensive moral, philosophical, and religious conceptions. Instead citizens should do their best to argue publicly on the basis of a common stock of ideas accessible to all.[14] This is an indirect application of one particular conception of toleration—a conception that looks for a politics in which all religious elements have been banished from the public realm. But naturally enough it has also led to a debate about whether this is reasonable and about whether there are moral positions that do not admit of a public secular formulation or defense.

Connected with this, we find that there are continuing debates in political philosophy about the application of tolerationist ideas to more general questions of ethics and culture. In the 1970s, philosophers debated the idea of the state being neutral not just between religions but more generally between conceptions of the good or individual conceptions of what made life worth living.[15] Ethical toleration was thought to be as important as religious toleration. The idea was that conceptions of the good were just as important to individuals as their religious views, that a society in which a plurality of conceptions of the good was followed would be no less stable, no less viable than a religiously pluralist society, that the demands of justice could be established without relying on any conception of the good; the law and state should therefore confine themselves to justice and morality and not seek to make individual citizens ethically more virtuous people or to give them meaningful lives, any more than it sought on the traditional conception to promote piety or modes of public worship. This antiperfectionist extension of the toleration idea opened up debates about the functions of the state, the relation between state and community, and the separability of various strands of normative thinking (the right and the good, for example).

Some of these debates about ethical perfectionism and liberal neutrality, which flourished mainly in the 1970s and 1980s, have continued into the present. In 1986, Joseph Raz published *The Morality of Freedom,* which gave a new depth to discussions of perfectionism and neutrality in liberal theory. Raz's view was a challenging one: he argued that nobody can sensibly value autonomy except to the extent that it is exercised in pursuit of activities that are themselves of value.[16] If this is true then autonomy cannot be cited directly as a value supporting toleration, because toleration is characteristically presented as an argument for not interfering with choices that we have reason to regard as bad or wrongheaded. If someone thought that a particular religious belief was repugnant, or if someone thought that religious belief in general was demeaning and misconceived, then it would be difficult for them to make an argument that respect for individual autonomy required us to tolerate it. Certainly the doctrine of liberal neutrality is hard to defend on Raz's account.[17] Still, Raz's position is consistent with the idea of a plurality of values, and if one also accepts his view that the choice of (say) one way of life sometimes involves regarding other ways of life as unworthy (even though they are not appropriately regarded as unworthy by anyone who chooses to follow them), then there may be room for a traditional notion of toleration, based on respect for individual autonomy, within the context of Raz's overall perfectionism. The relationship between respect for moral autonomy and the practice of toleration is thematized in the present volume by several of our contributors, including David Heyd, Glen Newey, Rainer Forst, and Glyn Morgan.

Another concern of these essays is how we should understand the appropriate *object* of toleration, a question that may be distinguished from debates over the agent or the moral psychology of toleration. We mentioned the extension of the toleration argument from religious views to conceptions of the good generally. A similar extension, though in a slightly different direction, involves culture and issues of cultural rights. In the classic Lockean picture, the state in a religious plural society distances itself from the beliefs and practices of any particular religion. But pluralism has many forms: one of its most striking forms in the modern era is the multicultural character of modern Western societies—partly as a matter of endogenous diversity (including religious diversity) and partly as a result of immigration. In a multicultural society, different groups follow (or seek to follow) different rules and customs in a whole range of areas of life besides religion including language, health care, neighborhood relations, family structure, and the education of children. As such, culture confronts head-on the activities of an activist welfarist regulatory state: it is competing directly in the same business of regulating the texture and detail of everyday life. On the other hand, the bearers of cultural practices are often unwilling to give them up, not (as in the case of religion) because they see them as crucial to the salvation of their souls, but because they regard the practices as an indispensable part of their identity. Law and legal theory have had to come to terms with this clash, as we have seen. But political philosophers (and political theorists) have also sought to make sense of the identity claims involved here, and to find ways of reckoning the importance of cultural claims with an overall matrix of justice and rights.[18]

We may value toleration of a diversity of cultural practices, but not every culture we tolerate values toleration, either in its relation to other cultures or (more alarmingly) in relation to the beliefs and practices of its own members. A culture (or a religion, for that matter) is seldom the same to all those whom it claims as its members. Individual men and women may be related problematically to a culture or a religion by their own ambivalence, or by their membership in an internal minority, by the fact that they may also have a foot in another religious or cultural camp—something which is almost inevitable in the circumstances of a modern multicultural society, where allegiances and memberships overlap and cut across one another. People may be related problematically to "their own" culture or religion by the oppressive place to which it assigns them: as a number of feminist writers have noticed, this is particularly true of women.[19] Toleration of a culture can easily shade over into indulging that culture's own intolerant oppression of those within its power.[20] But there is a paradox in any solution, because culture (the very thing that is being tolerated) is likely to come equipped with its own definition of what is and what is not oppressive, a definition which challenges the conceptions of oppression that are used by those liberals who want to place limits on toleration in this regard.

5.

Debates over the philosophical logic of toleration, its moral psychology, and its appropriate agents and objects have shaped the Western tradition of liberal thought since the early modern period. Before turning to a discussion of that tradition, though, it is important to notice that toleration is not a uniquely Western doctrine. Islam has its own deep traditions of doctrinal and philosophical reflection on the justification and limits of toleration.[21] Buddhism, one of the world's oldest ethical traditions, offers not only rich philosophical resources for justifying toleration but the oldest exemplar of a political regime of toleration, in the rule of the Emperor Ashoka over India in the third century B.C.E.[22] And notwithstanding recent debates over "Asian values" and their support for benign authoritarianism, as in Lee Kwan Yew's Singapore, Confucianism contains abundant philosophical resources for a defense of individual moral autonomy of the sort that supports toleration.[23] We deeply regret that the constraints of an already-full volume preclude us from including a conversation with non-Western traditions of toleration. Such a conversation would be a worthy—and timely—contribution to our understanding of toleration.

The Western tradition of political and philosophical writings on toleration, however, is amply rich and multi-faceted to reward focused study. There is plenty for modern commentators to argue about, just in order to find out what lines of argument were actually being pursued by key figures, let alone how these arguments play out in the arrays of issues that actually concern us today. It is not possible to identify any one single line of canonical justification. Many aspects of the Western canon's diverse arguments for and against toleration are explored in the essays by Rainer Forst, Michael A. Rosenfeld, Alex Tuckness, and Glyn Morgan in this volume, on the classic writings of Bayle, Spinoza, Locke, and Mill.

This has proved particularly true of John Locke, whose *Letter Concerning Toleration* is probably the best-known of the classic defenses of toleration. Locke scholarship—particularly in regard to his political and religious arguments—has deepened immeasurably over the last forty years,[24] and modern discussions of the *Letter Concerning Toleration* reflect this. Locke pursues a number of separable and overlapping lines of argument, some of them specifically Christian, some of them based on a liberal conception of the proper function of the state, some of them pragmatic based on a specific doctrine about the nature of genuine faith and the inability of coercion to produce genuine belief, some of them based on reciprocity and a consideration of what turning the tables on a dominant Christian majority might involve.

Alex Tuckness points out that the way in which Locke defended his position on toleration against actual opponents in the Second, Third and incomplete Fourth *Letters Concerning Toleration* differs somewhat from the way he proceeded when he was responding only to imagined objections to the line he was taking in the first *Letter.* Tuckness argues that the later letters reveal the pressure Locke felt from the criticisms of Jonas Proast and others, so far as the argument about the inability of coercion to produce true belief was concerned. He thinks that under this pressure, Locke revealed that the argument he really thought important was a universalization argument: we cannot understand how a Christian magistrate has the authority to enforce the true (Christian) religion, without deriving it from a more general principle that *any* magistrate has the authority to enforce true religion as he understands it. Authorizations of this kind can only be conferred in general terms and the way they are applied in particular societies necessarily turns on the reasoning of those entrusted with political power. So, Locke argues (according to Tuckness), if we balk at the prospect of legitimate enforcement of (say) Islam at the hands of a Muslim prince against his Christian subjects, we must also resist the prospect of the enforcement of Christian religion (or any particular Christian doctrine) against those who do not accept it. We must resist the claimed authority wholesale; there is no room in the circumstances of politics for resisting it in some cases (those where we think the prince is right) and not others.

Locke's arguments for toleration are perhaps the best-known in the liberal canon, though Tuckness has done us a service by revealing their complexity and by exploring a line of Lockean argument that has been unjustifiably neglected. Michael A. Rosenthal and Rainer Forst do similar service in focusing our attention on the arguments, respectively, of Locke's near-contemporaries

Baruch Spinoza and Pierre Bayle—arguments that are not as well known now, though they were equally important in the seventeenth and eighteenth centuries. Both Rosenthal and Forst relate the tolerationist thinking of the philosophers they study to the arguments of Locke's famous *Letter*.

Michael Rosenthal argues that Spinoza pursued a more sophisticated version of the view about the relation between coercion and true belief which, as we have seen, Locke held but which (on Tuckness's account) he felt pressure to give up. Locke held that belief was not subject to the will; but Spinoza held that the will and the intellect were inseparable and the will could not operate upon belief in any way that was independent of the intellectual processes by which belief was determined. Like Locke, Spinoza had to confront the objection that even if force cannot work directly to produce true belief, it may have indirect efficacy in that regard. His answer, according to Rosenthal, rests on a subtle but compelling theory of the internal economy of the intellect. Belief represents not just an output of the mind, but a certain sort of equilibrium among the complex elements of which the intellect is composed. The fact that some aspect of one's believing a certain proposition is affected by fear or compulsion—for example, the fact that one had the experience of being compelled to read the books that taught that that proposition was true, rather than coming upon them in the normal course of epistemic life—that fact affects the nature and quality of the "belief" that results and may undermine its stability as well as its proper relation to other beliefs that one holds. In this sense, force may be incapable of producing genuine belief, even when it is used only indirectly.

Rainer Forst's discussion of Bayle also takes the Proast-Locke controversy as its point of departure. Locke's vulnerability to Proast's argument for indirect coercion revealed the danger, for the tolerationist position, of the absence of an independent moral argument for the wrongness of state interference with religious belief. Locke was prepared to appeal to specifically Christian arguments at this point.[25] But as Forst argues, Locke's argument remains a "permission" conception of toleration, in which the governing authority chooses not to exercise its superior political might to suppress the religious views of a minority it judges to be wrong in its religious beliefs. At most, on Tuckness's reading of

Locke as offering an argument from the perspective of the universal legislator, Locke has a "coexistence" view of toleration, in which magistrates understand that the power of ruling may not be in their hands forever, and that there is therefore a prudential reason for tolerating incorrect religious faiths for the sake of avoiding conflict. Neither version of toleration, however, expresses respect for the dissenting religious believer. According to Forst, Bayle is the first theorist of toleration to ground it in a principle of mutual respect among equals. Contrary to many interpreters of Bayle, Forst argues that his defense of toleration is not based on a skeptical stance toward religious truth claims. Rather, Bayle navigates the tensions between faith and reason by maintaining that faith is not against reason, but goes beyond it. Faith offers answers to questions on which reason must remain silent, and reason can neither confirm nor refute the claims of faith. "Reasonable faith knows that it is *faith*; hence it does not compete with reason on reason's terrain—and vice versa" (102). Within Bayle's view, then, it is possible to affirm that another's religious faith is reasonable, while also maintaining that it is fundamentally wrong. Bayle's morality of mutual respect and epistemic restraint undergirds a conception of toleration that is more far-reaching than that of any of his contemporaries, extending equally to atheists, Catholics, Jews, Muslims, and all the others who lay beyond the limits of toleration drawn by Locke. The limits of toleration, according to Forst's Bayle, are drawn not by the content of belief but by the believer's propensity to uphold the public peace and to forswear the temptation to try to force conscience.

The other thinker whose work is canonical in the area of toleration is John Stuart Mill, though in Mill's case we are dealing with a more general argument that has implications for the toleration debate, rather than an argument (like those of Spinoza, Bayle, or Locke) that address religious toleration directly.

Glyn Morgan is interested in the view of social relationship that underpins Mill's defense of the toleration of diverse individual life-styles in *On Liberty*. The potential for individual liberty to serve its progressive purpose depends not only on *what* we tolerate but also on *how* we tolerate. Indifference, detachment, or polite self-restraint should not be mistaken for progressive tolerance, which requires a sort of censorious acceptance: a willingness to let others know precisely and pointedly why one thinks they are deeply mistaken, at the same time that one refuses to interfere with their actions. Of course the harm principle defines the limit of toleration so understood. We must not tolerate actions that harm others in their most fundamental interests. But there are many objectionable actions that fall short of such harm, including harms to oneself and to one's moral character, and it is a moral failure—what Mill calls "selfish indifference"—to refrain from expressing our disapproval in such cases. Toleration must be reconciled with our duty to shape one another's character for the better, and to foster the progress of moral understanding by exchanging critical arguments with those with whom we disagree, on matters of individual conduct as well as public policy. The prospects of democracy itself depend upon the improvement of the moral character of individuals through exchanges of this sort. Only our interests in security from serious harm can justify the coercion of the state, but a society committed to the equal security of all—a truly progressive society—should not cultivate a culture of excessive permissiveness toward groups that undervalue the equality and freedom of all their members.

Spinoza, Locke, Bayle, and Mill—these are not the only philosophers of toleration in our tradition. Toleration has also had its defenders in twentieth century political philosophy. So, for example, religious freedom is one of the basic liberties secured under John Rawls's two principles of justice as fairness: Rawls argues that persons behind the "Veil of Ignorance," which he uses as a heuristic to figure out the impartial demands of justice, would not take chances with their liberty by acknowledging any principle that allowed for the enforcement or suppression of religious views: "Even granting . . . that it is more probable than not that one will turn out to belong to the majority (if a majority exists), to gamble in this way would show that one did not take one's religious or moral convictions seriously."[26] The moral and political philosophy of Immanuel Kant is also a major source of insight into the values that underpin toleration, particularly the value of autonomy. And Kant's work in this regard continues to be a major point of orientation in contemporary debates. (It has to be said, however, that there is an important difference between the idea of moral autonomy that is so crucial for Kant's moral philosophy and the ideal of personal autonomy that he seems to be invoking when he writes that "[n]o one can coerce me to be happy in his way (as he thinks of the welfare of other human beings); instead each may seek his happiness in the way that seems good to him.")[27]

There is also in this volume an essay on Thomas Hobbes, but that is not a discussion of an argument *for* toleration; it is the presentation of an argument on the other side. Hobbes made an argument for erastianism, an argument that the state continues to have an important role to play in orchestrating public worship. It is usually thought that Hobbes opposed liberal toleration for secular reasons: the need for peace and conflict resolution in religious matters and the need to defuse religiously based objections to the exercise of civil authority. Jeremy Waldron shows, however, that Hobbes also pursued a religious argument for the state's role in these matters. The whole society, as much as any other entity, is required to worship, placate, and propitiate God, and there is something offensive to God in that regard, Hobbes reckons, in the uncoordinated mish-mash of religious observances that one finds in the practices of a tolerant pluralistic society. This provides a salutary reminder that the image of pluralism, mentioned at the beginning of section 2 of this Introduction, is necessarily appealing to everyone.

6.

Besides the refreshment of arguments in the canon of political thought that we have already discussed (in the papers by Forst, Tuckness, Rosenthal, and Morgan), one of the things that is most striking about our essays is the presentation of a number of different images of toleration. At the beginning, we alluded to an image of a pluralist society—a society in which men and women of differing beliefs go proudly about their own business, living their lives in accordance with the religious teachings that they find congenial, but each taking little interest (positive or negative) in anyone else's religious or spiritual affairs. They care about their own beliefs; they simply don't care about those of anyone else; they have different and more important things to preoccupy themselves with in their relations with others. It is the image of toleration that one gleans from Voltaire's famous observation on the

London Stock Exchange: "Go into the Exchange in London, . . . and you will see representatives of all the nations assembled there for the profit of mankind. There the Jew, the Mahometan, and the Christian deal with one another as if they were of the same religion, and reserve the name of infidel for those who go bankrupt."[28] Amongst the many purposes toleration can serve, we should not lose sight of the fact that it is good for the business of capitalism.

That's one image of toleration—toleration as detachment—and it is attractive to many. We would like to end this introductory essay by sketching out three other pictures of toleration that emerge from the contributions to this volume.

One alternative image emerges mainly as a foil, for the various presentations; it is not the sort of toleration favored by any of our authors. It is toleration as restraint exercised *de haut en bas*: someone in a privileged position (a state official, for example, or a comfortable member of a religious majority) tolerates beliefs and practices that are in some sense beneath him. In this picture, the demands of toleration are unilateral and asymmetrical: toleration is a one-way relationship from high to low. Argument for toleration is a matter of persuading the powerful or privileged figure that it would be undignified, or irrational, or counterproductive, or just unkind not to let others hold and practice their own religions. We appeal to his interests—the interests of the dominant figure—and persuade him that his own statecraft discloses no reason to persecute or suppress. (As many of our authors note, John Locke's theory is often interpreted as arguing in this spirit.) Or, if we appeal to the interests of those who are tolerated, we do so only to the extent that they are taken on board in the sentimental economy of the privileged figure. He feels for their predicament and their vulnerability, and he ought to show mercy on them by not pursuing, in religious matters, the advantage given to him by his superior power or authority.

As we said earlier in this Introduction, toleration conceived in this way can easily seem insulting to those on the receiving end. Wendy Brown's essay emphasizes this perception of asymmetry: "The pronouncement, 'I am a tolerant man,' conjures seemliness, propriety, forbearance, magnanimity, cosmopolitanism, universality, the large view, while those for whom tolerance is required take their shape as improper, indecorous, urgent, narrow, particular, and often ungenerous or at least lacking in perspective" (408). Brown is particularly interested in how this asymmetry plays out also on the matrix of civilized/uncivilized. Societies which describe themselves as tolerant regard this as an attribute of civilization: those whom they tolerate are lower in the scale of civilization and those they have to deal with who will not tolerate other religions are barbarians, beyond the pale (and so paradoxically may have no claim to the benefit of the toleration that defined who was civilized in the first place). Brown's thesis reminds us that tolerance has not always been regarded as a virtue—not just from the perspective of those who would like to see religion enforced but also form the perspective of those who have no interest in that, but are interested in the way we present ourselves in our relations with others whose views and practices are unfamiliar to use. People have talked of "repressive tolerance,"[29] and we must not assume, just because toleration is the liberal virtue *par excellence,* that it is immune from criticism in itself or as part of the general critique of liberalism.

The advantage of this image of toleration *de haut en bas* is its realism: it acknowledges the realities of power and orients its normative arguments to what is likely to convince the holders of power, rather than simply giving vent to the resentment of the powerless. A second alternative, which may also pride itself on its realism, is Glen Newey's picture of toleration as *murality*—as a matter of building walls around and within a political community to contain and limit antagonism. Newey is skeptical about conceptions of toleration that require the deep sharing of values like autonomy and integrity. He believes that we find a better (certainly a more viable and realistic) grounding for toleration in the Hobbesian ideas of peace and security. A community whose members recoil from the prospect of civil war will look for any structures and arrangements that avoid endemic religious conflict. It is conceivable that they will aim to set up an erastian sovereign of the sort that Hobbes envisaged (though in the short term the effort to do so is likely to make matters worse not better). Most likely they will look for ways of defusing religious conflict, separating the potential combatants, and establishing some sort of *modus vivendi* between them. As the saying goes, good fences make good neighbors: if one can set things up so that differing religious sects are, so to speak, walled off from one another and walled off too from the prospect of gaining control of the state, then it may be possible to contain and limit their antagonism. The walls of Newey's murality are partly a matter of separation, partly a matter of guarantee, and they define a sort of toleration that is pursued not for the sake of any moral ideal but for the sake of what he calls an "unquiet but not murderous" form of coexistence.

Toleration as murality takes seriously the lethal ground on which increasingly, in many parts of the world, religious conflicts are played out. It looks for any means of reducing that lethal potential, whether those means answer to the traditional depiction of toleration and whether or not they can be supported by the values that traditionally have been though to underpin toleration. One of the most controversial features of Newey's conception is that it offers no guarantee up front about the shape of tolerant social and legal arrangements: they may involve a recognizable scheme of constitutional guarantees, they may involve an Ottoman-style millet system, they may involve suppression of evangelism or even apostasy, or they may even involve carefully limited forms of religious competition. We do not decide these matters a priori, he argues, but in light of what is necessary in a particular historical and social environment to keep the peace.

Some will say that this image therefore betrays the promise of liberal toleration, because that tradition looks forward to a particular kind of approach to religious pluralism, not just any old structures for containing religious antagonism. They may say that Newey is entitled to doubt whether the liberal toleration is necessarily effective in securing peace, but that should not be the same as defining "toleration" so that it covers any arrangement which proves effective in that regard.[30]

Newey's murality was put forward in this volume as a direct challenge to Ingrid Creppell's image of toleration as mutuality, and it is with this more optimistic and more idealistic picture of toleration that we will end. Creppell's vision of toleration as mutuality also presented itself as a revisionary conception: it is an alternative, for example, to the *de haut en bas* picture that, as we noted earlier, emerges from the Lockean argument. Toleration, Creppell argues, is about relationship, but it is better conceived as a symmetrical two-way relationship, rather than a one-way dispensation administered from a position of power. I tolerate you as you tolerate me: the toleration relationship is to be understood in the first instance as a relation of respect among equals.

It is crucial to Creppell's conception that toleration is not expected to exist in a relational vacuum. In a modern multi-faith and multi-cultural society, the members of various groups are bound together by all sorts of common concerns. There is, to be sure, the common concern for security that Newey emphasizes. But there is also the common search for justice and fair terms of cooperation generally, even in matters that don't involve religion. There are elements of mutual aid and common loyalty that drives us to look out for each other and work together to create and maintain structures of care for matters of common concern. Creppell's view is that this panoply of relatedness is not just the upshot of self-interested individual behavior. As she puts it, there is a will to relationship: "the institutions and ethos of politics itself must be valued for more than strategic purposes" (316). But if this will to relationship is present anyway in the fabric of social life, then toleration can be understood as an integrated aspect of it, not as something that has to be argued for as an entirely fresh relationship, as it were among strangers. True, we are separated to some extent by our differing religious beliefs. But in the last analysis, she says, "we come down to the question of why would those who believe fundamentally different things desire to live in a society together?" (349). Since they evidently do desire to live together in something more than muted antagonism, we can take the shared and reciprocal concern and respect that characterizes that will to relationship as a basis for thinking through this potentially divisive issue of the attitude we take to each others' religions. If we address the matter on this basis of mutuality, Creppell reckons, we will see how to argue for toleration and the arguments we use will have the advantage of being not *ad hoc* but fully integrated into the ideals that underpin every aspect of our relationship in liberal society.

Where does this leave us? Should we understand toleration as a pragmatic solution to the evils of religious conflict, or as an expression of a moral-practical ideal grounded in universalistic principles of egalitarian respect and impartiality? Perhaps, as Noah

Feldman argues in his essay in this volume, we should not allow ourselves to be pressed into a dichotomous choice. Yes, human beings are motivated by narrow and partisan self-interest. Instrumental justifications of toleration, as securing the peace that is a necessary condition for the fulfillment of our other ends, can be highly effective in motivating us to resist the impulse to pursue our interests violently. But we are also moral beings, and as such disinclined to sustain, indefinitely, political orders that we cannot affirm as basically just. Toleration is useful, but we care about it because we also believe that it is moral.

7.

Toleration becomes an issue when societies that were once monolithic communities of faith and value split on these questions into different sects and parties or when individuals and families who previously lived in separate communities of faith and value come together in a single social and political environment. The canon of Western liberal thinking on toleration emerged in the early modern period when these processes were just beginning in Western Europe and North America. The problem has not gone away, nor despite the best efforts of those early modern theorists has it been solved. On the contrary it is as urgently in need of solution now as it has ever been, for as well as increasing diversity and the effects of travel and immigration, there is a sense now that we share a world where the question of toleration is posited not just as an issue for states, for their local laws and constitutions, but for humanity as a whole.

NOTES

1. See Samuel Huntington, *The Clash of Civilizations and the Remaking of World Order* (New York: Simon and Schuster, 1998). There is some excellent discussion of the Huntington thesis in the essays by Wendy Brown and Steven D. Smith in this volume.

2. For a critical analysis connecting the Paris riots to French traditions of republicanism as a "*mission civilatrice,*" see Yvonne Yazbeck Haddad

and Michael J. Balz, "The October Riots in France: A Failed Immigration Policy or the Empire Strikes Back?" *International Migration* 44(2): 23–34 (2006).

3. Ian Buruma, *Murder in Amsterdam: The Death of Theo van Gogh and the Limits of Tolerance* (London: Penguin Books, 2006).

4. For a fulsome discussion of the issues, see Tariq Modood, Randall Hansen, Erik Bleich, Brendan O'Leary, and Joseph H. Carens, "The Danish Cartoon Controversy: Free Speech, Racism, Islamism and Integration," *International Migration* 44(5): 3–62 (December 2006).

5. Neil Nevitte and Christopher Cochrane, "Individualization in America and Europe: Connecting Religious and Moral Values," *Comparative Sociology* 5(2–3): 203–31 (2006).

6. See "Among Wealthy Nations, U.S. Stands Alone in its Embrace of Religion," Pew Global Attitudes Project Report, December 19, 2002, available at http://pewglobal.org/reports/display.php?ReportID=167.

7. Thorleif Pettersson, "Religion in Contemporary Society: Eroded by Human Well-being, Supported by Cultural Diversity," *Comparative Sociology* 5 (2–3): 231–57 (2006).

8. See, e.g., Anna Elisabetta Galeotti, *Toleration as Recognition* (Cambridge: Cambridge University Press, 2005), Ingrid Creppell, *Toleration and Identity: Foundations in Early Modern Thought* (London: Routledge, 2002), and Michael Walzer, *On Toleration* (New Haven: Yale University Press, 1999). For edited volumes, see Catriona McKinnon and Dario Castiglione (eds.), *The Culture of Toleration in Diverse Societies: Reasonable Toleration* (Manchester: Manchester University Press, 2003), Susan Mendus (ed.), *The Politics of Toleration in Modern Life* (Edinburgh: Edinburgh University Press, 1999), and David Heyd (ed.), *Toleration: An Elusive Virtue* (Princeton: Princeton University Press, 1998).

9. Galeotti, *Toleration as Recognition.*

10. This volume, and in Creppell, *Toleration and Identity.*

11. See *Employment Division v. Smith,* 494 U.S. 872 (1990) and *City of Boerne v. Flores,* 521 U.S. 507 (1997).

12. *Employment Division v. Smith,* op. cit., 888–89 (Scalia J., for the court).

13. Ibid., 902 (O'Connor J., concurring).

14. See John Rawls, *Political Liberalism,* rev. ed. (New York: Columbia University Press, 1996), 10, 213–14.

15. See Ronald Dworkin, "Liberalism," in Stuart Hampshire (ed.) *Public and Private Morality* (Cambridge: Cambridge University press, 1978). See also the papers in Robert Goodin and Andrew Reeve (eds.), *Liberal Neutrality* (London: Routledge, 1990).

16. Joseph Raz, *The Morality of Freedom* (Oxford: Clarendon Press, 1986), 417: "[A]utonomous life is valuable only if it is spent in the pursuit of acceptable and valuable projects."

17. Ibid., 110 ff.

18. See Charles Taylor, *The Ethics of Authenticity* (Cambridge: Harvard University Press, 1991) and *Multiculturalism and "The Politics of Recognition"* (Princeton: Princeton University Press, 1992), Will Kymlicka, *Liberalism, Community, and Culture* (Oxford: Oxford University Press, 1989) and *Multicultural Citizenship* (Oxford: Oxford University Press, 1995), Chandran Kukathas, *The Liberal Archipelago* (Oxford: Oxford University Press, 2003), and Jacob T. Levy, *The Multiculturalism of Fear* (Oxford: Oxford University Press, 2000). See also the essays in Avigail Eisenberg and Jeff Spinner-Halev (eds.), *Minorities within Minorities* (Cambridge: Cambridge University Press, 2005).

19. See, e.g., Susan Moller Okin, *Is Multiculturalism Bad for Women?* (Princeton: Princeton University Press, 1999), Seyla Benhabib, *The Claims of Culture* (Princeton: Princeton University Press, 2002), and Ayelet Shachar, *Multicultural Jurisdictions* (Cambridge: Cambridge University Press, 2001).

20. For a vivid account of how this plays out in a strongly tolerant society, see Unni Wikan, *Generous Betrayal: Politics of Culture in the New Europe* (Chicago: University of Chicago Press, 2001).

21. See, e.g., the title essay by Khaled Abou El Fadl, and critical responses, in Joshua Cohen and Ian Lague (eds.), *The Place of Tolerance in Islam* (Boston: Beacon Press, 2002), Sohail H. Hashmi, "Islamic Ethics in International Society," in Sohail H. Hashmi (ed.), *Islamic Political Ethics: Civil Society, Pluralism, and Conflict* (Princeton: Princeton University Press, 2002), esp. 167–69.

22. For an overview of Ashoka's regime of toleration and its legacy, see Amartya Sen, *Human Rights and Asian Values* (New York: Carnegie Council on Ethics and International Affairs, 1997), 19–23. Sen also discusses the tolerant Islamic regime of the Moghal emperor Akbar in the sixteenth century. See also his discussions of Ashoka and Akbar in *The Argumentative Indian* (London: Penguin, 2005), 12–19, 287–91.

23. See, e.g., Joseph Chan, "Moral Autonomy, Civil Liberties, and Confucianism," *Philosophy East and West* 52(3): 281–310 (2002).

24. See Peter Laslett's introduction to John Locke, *Two Treatises of Government* (Cambridge: Cambridge University Press, 1988). See also John Marshall, *John Locke: Resistance, Religion and Responsibility* (Cambridge: Cambridge University Press, 1994) and Richard Ashcraft, *Revolutionary Politics and Locke's "Two Treatises of Government"* (Princeton: Princeton University Press, 1986).

25. See the discussion in Jeremy Waldron, *God, Locke, and Equality: Christian Foundations of Locke's Political Thought* (Cambridge: Cambridge University Press, 2002), 210–11.

26. John Rawls, *A Theory of Justice* (Cambridge: Harvard University Press, 1971), 207.

27. "On the Common Saying: That May Be Correct in Theory but It Is of No Use in Practice," in Immanuel Kant, *Practical Philosophy,* translated and edited by Mary Gregor (Cambridge: Cambridge University Press, 1996), 277, at 291. See also Jeremy Waldron, "Moral Autonomy and Personal Autonomy," in John Christman and Joel Anderson (eds.), *Autonomy and the Challenges to Liberalism* (Cambridge: Cambridge University Press, 2005), 307.

28. François Marie Arouet de Voltaire, *Philosophical Letters* (New York: Macmillan, 1961), 26.

29. See Herbert Marcuse, "Repressive Tolerance," in Robert Paul Wolff, Barrington Moore, and Herbert Marcuse, *A Critique of Pure Tolerance* (Boston: Beacon Press, 1965).

30. On the relative weight of peace and other moral considerations within liberal toleration, see Melissa S. Williams, "Tolerable Liberalism," in Avigail Eisenberg and Jeff Spinner-Halev (eds.), *Minorities within Minorities* (Cambridge: Cambridge University Press, 2005).

PART I

TOLERATION IN THE WESTERN CANON OF POLITICAL PHILOSOPHY

1

HOBBES ON PUBLIC WORSHIP

JEREMY WALDRON

I

We usually assume that the difference between Thomas Hobbes and John Locke on the issue of religious toleration is explained by Hobbes's greater concern about the danger to civil peace posed by religious disagreement. Both thinkers agree that there is no point trying to use civil laws to govern personal faith or belief.[1] "Faith," writes Hobbes, "hath no relation to, nor dependence at all upon, Compulsion, or Commandment" (L 42: 342).[2] It is not under voluntary control and therefore not something that an individual can alter in response to any "promise of rewards or menaces of torture" (L 42: 343).[3] But they disagree on the relation between religious views and political disturbance. Though Locke accepts that measures must be taken against any view that teaches that civil law is not to be obeyed, he does not think very many religions will have this consequence:

> . . . no Sect can easily arrive to such a degree of madness, as that it should think fit to teach, for Doctrines of Religion, such things as manifestly undermine the Foundations of Society . . . because their own Interest, Peace, Reputation, every Thing, will be thereby endangered.[4]

Hobbes, by contrast, sees the connection between religious belief and subversion as endemic. Since religion is partly about eternal sanctions, it poses a standing danger to the use and effectiveness of civil sanctions to maintain order and peace in society. People quite rightly believe that God's command is to be preferred to the command of anyone else including their sovereign, and so it is of the utmost concern to the sovereign what his subjects believe God's commands to be (L 43: 403). True, the sovereign cannot control those beliefs directly. But he can control them indirectly by controlling their sources and in particular by controlling what people are taught to believe by those who hold themselves out as experts on God (L 42: 372). Locke is notoriously equivocal about the possibility and utility of this sort of indirect thought-control.[5] Mostly he seems to believe that it is unnecessary and that the main source of political disturbance is not a proliferation of uncontrolled views about what God commands but competition for the privilege of establishment and the resentment of those believers whose faith and practice are not accorded full toleration.[6] We may surmise that, had he known of Locke's view, Hobbes would have thought it naïve and dangerous. A sovereign cannot neglect the supervision of the opinions that are taught in his realm, for "in the well governing of Opinions, consisteth the well governing of men's Actions, in order to their Peace, and Concord" (L 18: 124). Hobbes thinks it pretty clear that the civil power needs to control the appointment of spiritual pastors, and supervise and license their activities, and this amounts in effect to establishing a national church.

II

The argument that derives the sovereign's authority over teachers and doctrines from the need to keep peace and maintain respect for civil law is an important theme in Hobbes. But it is not the only case he makes for religious establishment.

In this chapter, I will examine a quite separate line of argument based on the requirements of what Hobbes calls "Publique Worship." This argument has nothing to do with the sovereign's responsibility to keep the peace. It concerns the intrinsic importance of uniformity in religious practice and is based on some interesting philosophical observations about the role of convention in action and language.

The argument I want to consider has not been discussed very thoroughly in the voluminous literature on Hobbes and religion.[7] Hobbes devotes a lot of attention to it in *Leviathan* (Chapter 31) and *De Cive* (Chapter 15) but his commentators have not. I am not sure why this is. Perhaps it is because the argument is difficult to reconcile with the general view that Hobbes does not take religion very seriously. It is often thought that most of Hobbes's political theory can be read as though the rumors are true, that it was written by an atheist.[8] But not this part of Hobbes's theory. The premise of the argument about public worship is that *God is to be worshipped* by all persons, natural and artificial.[9] Without uniformity, Hobbes argues, without established forms of liturgy and religious practice, God cannot be worshipped by a commonwealth. Such worship as there is will be an unordered and confusing mélange of private individual and sectarian practices and that *in itself* will be an affront to God and a problem for society quite apart from any threat to the peace that it involves.

Commentators know that Hobbes devotes the whole second half of *Leviathan* to scriptural and ecclesiastical matters. And many of them get very excited about this, tracing in detail his views on basic theological doctrine, ancient Israel, early church history, the papacy, and so on.[10] But the general tenor of these discussions is that Hobbes's doctrinal, scriptural, and ecclesiastical theology is primarily defensive: He is combating the claims and pretensions of others (particularly Roman Catholics), which might tend to unsettle the state.[11] To put it another way, most of Hobbes's argumentation about religion is perceived as having been premised on the *social* significance of the prevalence of certain religious beliefs. Whether in his view of natural religion in Chapter 12 of *Leviathan*, or his view about religious conflict, or his view of the subversive implications of papism, Hobbes can be read as saying, "Some people believe X (about God or about the mission of the church); this is likely to have effect Y in society; therefore the sovereign has to do Z (pander to credulity, prevent conflict, make sure everyone knows that Roman Catholic orthodoxy is false, etc.)." But his discussion of public worship cannot be read in that way. The argument is not "some people believe X; therefore, the sovereign has to do Z," but rather "X is the case; therefore, the sovereign has to do Z." And X, as I have said, is an explicitly religious premise about the necessity of worship, put forward affirmatively by Hobbes in his own voice.

Yet another way of putting this is to say that Hobbes's argument about the requirements of public worship is not an argument about civil religion, if by "civil religion" we mean religion which "is a part of humane Politiques" (L 12: 79),[12] religion set up by statesmen "with a purpose to make those men who relyed on them, the more apt to Obedience, Peace, Lawes, Charity, and civill Society" (L 12: 79).[13] Hobbes certainly believes in civil religion and would have been in favor of a national church even had he not accepted the argument about public worship that I am going to discuss. But there is more to religion than civil religion, i.e. religion established for purposes which independently are purposes of the state. The argument about public worship *adds* to Hobbes's conception of the functions of the state: The state's function is not just to keep the peace, but to coordinate worship so that uniform honor to the Almighty can be offered in the name of the whole commonwealth. Maybe non-uniform worship will also be socially inflammatory. But Hobbes's position is that whether it is socially inflammatory or not, non-uniform worship falls short of what God requires of us as an organized community.

III

The premise of Hobbes's account of public worship is a premise of natural law. Hobbes's account of natural law has two parts. The first, set out in Chapters 14 and 15 of *Leviathan,* explains the natural law duties we owe to one another. The second part, set out in Chapter 31, concerns "what Praecepts are dictated to men, by their Naturall Reason onely, without other word of God, touching the Honour and Worship of the Divine Majesty" (L 31: 248).

That humans are required to worship God is, for Hobbes, beyond dispute. God rules over us by virtue of His enormous power: "[t]o those . . . whose Power is irresistible, the dominion of men adhaereth naturally" (L 31: 246–47). He has commanded us to worship Him, but even if He had not commanded it, it would be an overwhelmingly prudent thing to do (which is more or less what a natural law obligation amounted to in Hobbes's theory):[14]

> the worship we do him, proceeds from our duty, and is directed according to our capacity, by those rules of Honour, that Reason dictateth to be done by the weak to the more potent men, in hope of benefit, for fear of dammage, or in thankfulnesse for good already received from them. (L 31: 249–50)

Worship is a way of showing that we esteem God, that we think "as Highly of His Power, and Goodnesse, as is possible" (L 31: 248), and that we are ready to obey Him. In our worship, we also indicate our lack of hubris, i.e. our readiness to accept that our own enterprises cannot compete with God's. Worship, says Hobbes, is similar to the way reason requires us to act towards any overwhelming superior, that is, to anyone whose power is so much greater than our own that it makes no sense to test our strength against his. In these circumstances, what reason requires is for us to praise, flatter, and bless the one who is our superior, to supplicate to him, thank him, pay attention to him and obey him, defer to him, speak considerately to him, and so on—all of which "are the honour the inferior giveth to the superior."[15]

Worship, then, is "an outward act, the sign of inward honour; and whom we endeavour by our homage to appease, if they be angry or howsoever to make them favourable to us, we are said to worship."[16] The internal aspect of worship is just the attitude of esteem, humility, and readiness to serve that the action is ultimately supposed to convey. The external aspect, however, consists of words, actions, and gestures. Acts of worship often involve describing God, attributing to Him various properties and attributes, such as "infinite," "eternal," "most high," "good," "just," "holy," etc. These terms—vague (like "good"), superlative (like "most high"), and negative (like "infinite")—really do not express much determinate meaning. But that is not a problem, says Hobbes, for their aim is to convey admiration and humility (L 31: 251). They are to be understood as speech acts of prostration not description, "for in the Attributes which we give to God, we are not to consider the signification of Philosophicall Truth, but the signification of Pious Intention, to do Him the greatest Honour we are able" (L 31: 252).[17] By the same token, it is appropriate for our words or worship to be embellished with music and other forms of ornamentation (L 31: 252); we should not complain that such embellishment distracts from the propositional content of our speech, because the words of worship are, as Hobbes puts it in an early work, "rather oblations than propositions."[18] Their propositional content is secondary to what we should think of as the prostrative illocutionary force of our utterances.[19] Non-verbal actions can also be signs of worship, and Hobbes offers, as examples of actions that naturally conveyed the sort of respect that worship requires, things like standing rather than sitting, kneeling, lying prostrate, and so on (DC 15: xi: 189).

The examples just given are of things which naturally convey honor.[20] But there are also things that fulfill this function in non-natural ways. These are drawn from among the "infinite number of Actions, and Gestures, of an indifferent nature" (L 31: 253), things which in themselves do not convey any unequivocal meaning so far as honor is concerned.[21] Hobbes calls worship expressed in this way "Arbitrary Worship" (L 31: 249). The first category of arbitrary worship comprises forms "such as hee requireth, who is Worshipped" (L 31: 249): God might instruct us to worship Him in a way that would not count as a form of worship if He had not specifically required it. The others are actions and practices established as a result of human decision. We might decide that it is proper for men to remove their hats while in church, even though hat-wearing or hat-doffing has no inherent significance, and even though the contrary rule could as easily have been adopted. Hobbes's general position with regard to this category is that anything which is *taken to be* a form of worship *is* a form of worship, unless it has a natural significance that indicates the contrary (DC 15: xviii: 197).

But taken to be a form of worship *by whom?* Here Hobbes is a little ambiguous (and, as we shall see in the next section, this ambiguity has some consequences for his theory). Sometimes he talks of signs of worship "such as the Worshipper thinks fit" (L 31: 249). But he quickly moves to a more social and spectatorial perspective:

> Worship consists in the opinion of the beholders: for if to them the words, or actions by which we intend honour, seem ridiculous, and tending to contumely; they are no Worship; because no

> signes of honour; and no signes of Honour; because a signe is not a signe to him that giveth it, but to him to whom it is makes; that is, to the spectator. (L 31: 249)

In response to this, we might say that the signs used by the individual worshipper are intended for the benefit of God, not for the benefit of the on-lookers. But Hobbes's account of worship is continuous with his account of honor (L 10: 63–69), and he sometimes toys with lines of thought that suggest that honor is not a two-person relation between honorer and honoree, but essentially a three-person relation between A (the person doing the honoring), B (the person who is honored), and C (an onlooker, who is supposed to be impressed by the honoring). Honor, Hobbes implies, is a matter of A offering to B signs which any other person, C, looking on will understand as signs of high regard:[22] "there is no sign but whereby somewhat becomes known to others, and therefore is there no sign of honour but what seems so to others" (DC 15: xvii: 196). This comes close to implying that there can be no such thing as private (secret) worship. In fact, Hobbes does not quite say that; he says there can be private acknowledgement of God's power using *natural* means of honor.[23] (But certainly there is a strand of Hobbesian thought which, to our ears, sounds almost Wittgenstenian: In respect of arbitrary worship, how can any single individual *in secret* establish that given word or sign conveys honor?)[24]

So it seems that forms of arbitrary worship other than those established by God's command are necessarily conventional—that is, they involve the establishment of meanings among groups of persons. The obvious analogy here is the establishment of linguistic meaning generally. We will pursue this in section V, where we will scrutinize Hobbes's claim that the relevant meanings have to be established by a sovereign in order to make public worship possible. Before reaching that, however, we should pause to consider Hobbes's account of the *obligatory* character of public worship.

IV

We have spoken of the human obligation to offer worship to God. Few early modern defenders of toleration question this.[25] The

striking and distinctive thing about Hobbes's position is that the obligation to worship applies to *all* persons, artificial as well as human individuals. It applies, presumably, to families and businesses.[26] It applies in particular to the artificial person formed when people agree to subordinate themselves to a sovereign—this agreement being "more than Consent, or Concord; it is a reall Unitie of them all, in one and the same Person" (L 17: 120).[27]

The commonwealth considered as a person is bound by the law of nature.[28] Though the power of the Sovereign is "as great, as possibly men can be imagined to make it" (L 20: 144), still it pales by comparison with the irresistible power of God. So the premise Hobbes uses for the individual human duty of worship applies here too, only now we are to read the first person plurals of Hobbes's formulation ("we" and "our") collectively rather than distributively:

> the worship *we* do him, proceeds from *our* duty, and is directed according to *our* capacity, by those rules of Honour, that Reason dictateth to be done by the weak to the more potent men, in hope of benefit, for fear of dammage, or in thankfulnesse for good already received from them. (L 31: 249–50; my emphasis)

Accordingly, Hobbes concludes that there is public worship, as well as private worship: "Publique, is the worship that a Commonwealth performeth, as one Person" (L 31: 249).

V

What is public worship supposed to involve? In some cases its requirements are ordained by divine positive law. This is true of the worship of ancient Israel. In other cases, they are established by those who have general charge of the public realm. Worship is a form of honor, and the sovereign controls public honor: "[I]n Commonwealths . . . he, or they that have the supreme Authority, can make whatsoever they please, to stand for signes of Honour" (L 10: 65). To honor men, the public power establishes titles, offices, coats of arms, and other ornaments. These have the meaning that the public power determines they should have (L 10: 65). And the same is true, Hobbes says, of the public honoring of God.

Of the various actions and gestures that might be used in worship, "such of them as the Common-wealth shall ordain to be Publicly and Universally in use, as signes of Honour, and part of Gods Worship, are to be taken and used for such by the Subjects" (L 31: 253). And subjects are also to follow the lead of the sovereign in choosing the words that are used for public worship: "[T]hose Attributes which the Soveraign ordaineth, in the Worship of God, for signes of Honour, ought to be taken and used for such, by private men in their publique Worship" (L 31: 253).

This amounts to a pretty "extreme conventionalism in regard to religious practice,"[29] and evidently it is a conventionalism that is intended to leave little or no room for individual or sectarian dispute. Objecting to one liturgy or the other, or objecting to use of masculine pronouns in referring to God, or objecting to some rule about whether men cover their heads in church, scarcely makes sense, on Hobbes's account, because these forms of word and gesture have only the meaning they are stipulated to have in public worship.

To what extent is Hobbes's conventionalism about worship derived from his general conventionalism about names and language? He presents it as a consequence of the more general conventionalism:

> And because words (and consequently the attributes of God) have their signification by agreement and constitution of men, those attributes are to be held significative of honour that men intend shall so be; and whatsoever may be done by the wills of particular men, where there is no law but reason, may be done by the will of the Commonwealth by laws civil. And because a Commonwealth hath no will, nor makes no laws but those that are makes by the will of him or them that have the sovereign power, it followeth that those attributes which the sovereign ordaineth in the worship of God for signs of honour ought to be taken and used for such by private men in their public worship. (L 31: 253)

But the matter is complicated in two ways.

First, elsewhere in his philosophy, Hobbes seems to take a less social view of linguistic conventions. Tom Sorell has suggested that for Hobbes the imposition of names is in the first instance a solitary activity: "A single speaker simply takes a sensible mark and in affixing it to an object, makes it into a reminder for himself of a conception raised by the object."[30] This tends to cast doubt on the need for anything like social convention, let alone sovereign prescription, and it corresponds to the suggestion we noted earlier that sometimes Hobbes is prepared to think of honor (and worship) as consisting of whatever the individual worshipper thinks about the words and gestures he is using. In fact, Hobbes vacillates on this at the linguistic level, and sometimes talks about naming and meaning in more social terms: "the remembrance of the names or appellations of things, . . . is, in matters of common conversation, a remembrance of pacts and covenants of men made amongst themselves, concerning how to be understood of one another."[31] If we follow Hobbes in that line of thought, we might find it easier to put his theory of language to work in his theory of public worship.

The second difficulty, however, is that even if we focus on the social version of Hobbes's conventionalism, it is not at all clear (from what Hobbes says in other contexts) that the establishment of meanings is to be regarded as a matter of "what the Soveraign ordaineth" (L 31: 253). Hobbes seems to go along with the biblical account of the origins of language. God got the ball rolling and "instructed Adam how to name such creatures as he presented to his sight," and Adam and his posterity took over the process and added more names and different kinds of names (L 4: 24–25).[32] After the catastrophe at Babel, men dispersed into various groups and each group reinvented naming and formed its own language. So far, so good. Hobbes then makes the point that, if the peoples of the earth had not (re)invented language, civil and political life would have been impossible. That tells us that language is not a product of political life or sovereign stipulation or the social contract; it is a precondition of it, according to Hobbes. Since there cannot be sovereignty without language, linguistic meaning in groups of people cannot depend on sovereign prescription.[33] Language establishes itself from the bottom up, not from the top down.

So there has to be a *special* reason why the sovereign determines the attributes of "publique worship." Hobbes's general conventionalism about language will not do by itself, because it is social not political conventionalism. One possibility is that although languages can come into existence without political stipulation, still political stipulation might be necessary for language to be created specifically *for* a political group. Although a language like English may be spoken all over the place and might have emerged just as a general practice among various people, a language *for England*—that is, for the purposes of public worship by this particular commonwealth—might not be able to be established so casually.

Another possibility (connected with this) has to do with the type of speech act that public worship is supposed to involve. Earlier we noted Hobbes's view that language, as used in worship, is used primarily in a non-constative way.[34] Now it is crucial to Hobbes's overall theory that consensus in the evaluative use of language cannot be expected to emerge as an informal social matter (even if descriptive meanings can). Humans are just the sorts of creatures that plunge into dissensus when they start commending or condemning things (L 17: 119). Since worship involves commendation of a sort, it is an area of language-use which requires extraordinary coordination, and that may be the coordination that only sovereign stipulation can provide.[35]

VI

So, "there is a *Publique*, and a *Private* Worship" (L 31: 249). What is the relation supposed to be between the two in a Hobbesian commonwealth?

Hobbes seems torn. On the one hand, he says that private worship is free and that it should not be controlled by the laws so long as it is conducted by individuals "in secret" (L 31: 249). That is consonant with the view of private faith with which we began. On the other hand, he appears to think that any worship that takes place in the sight of others takes on an inherently public aspect: "Private [worship], is in secret Free; but in the sight of the multitude, it is never without some Restraint, either from the Lawes, or from the Opinion of men" (L 31: 249).[36]

The point here seems to be that a publicly visible diversity of forms of individual worship is liable to detract from the sense that worship is being offered to God *by the commonwealth.* "[S]eeing a

Commonwealth is but one person, it ought also to exhibit to God but one worship" (L 31: 252) and Hobbes infers from this that "those actions that are done differently, by different men, cannot be said to be a Publique Worship" (L 31: 252–53). Substantively, the problem is that with a diversity of practice, worship cannot be said to be shared:

> if each Man should follow his own reason in the *worshipping* of God, in so great a diversity of worshippers, one will be apt to judge anothers worship uncomely, or impious; neither will the one seem to the other to honour God. (DC 15: xvii: 196)[37]

It seems to follow then that if public worship does not supersede private worship, we will undercut the impression that we want to give to God that, as a Commonwealth, we are prepared to honor Him. "[W]here many sorts of Worship be allowed . . . it cannot be said there is any Publique Worship, nor that the Commonwealth is of any Religion at all" (L 31: 253). The result will be that there is at least one person, the Commonwealth, that is not worshipping God and—since the well-being of the Commonwealth is vulnerable to God's displeasure and crucial to the well-being of individuals—that is foolhardy and dangerous to the society and everyone in it.

So, to conclude Hobbes's argument: The commonwealth needs public worship and since people need the commonwealth, they must do what is necessary to make public worship possible. They must give up the use of their private reason, at least so far as publicly visible worship is concerned, and "transferre their Right of judging the manner of Gods worship on him or them who have the Soveraign power" (DC 15: xvii: 196).[38] This, then, along with the argument about civil peace that we discussed in section I, is the basis on which Hobbes lays the foundation for a national church.[39]

VII

There is one obvious objection to the theory of public worship, to which Hobbes seems very sensitive. He wonders "[w]hether it doth not follow, that the City must be obeyed if it command us directly to affront God, or forbid us to worship him?" (DC 15: xviii: 197). What happens when the demands of individual conscience conflict with the prescriptions of public worship? As we have already seen, part of Hobbes's answer to this objection is that, if the matter is unclear or controversial, then the subject should defer to the sovereign's stipulation, for what *can* (at a pinch) be stipulated as a mode of honoring God *should* be regarded as such if the sovereign prescribes it (DC 15: xviii: 197).[40]

But what if the subject cannot see how the actions or words prescribed by the sovereign can be anything other than insulting to the Almighty? Is he still required to participate? Hobbes's answer differs as between *De Cive* and *Leviathan*. In *De Cive* he suggests that disobedience is sometimes appropriate. No one has a natural right to insult God or neglect his worship, and therefore no one can be deemed to have transferred to the sovereign a right to command that this be done (DC 15: xviii: 197). Of course, taking this line may lead to unjust punishment, and any Hobbesian conclusion that the punishment is unjust may be ineffectual. But that is not an objection to this line of response: As John Locke observed in a similar context,

> There are two sorts of Contests amongst men, the one managed by Law, the other by Force. . . . You will say, then, the Magistrate being the stronger will have his Will, and carry his point. Without doubt. But the Question is not here concerning the doubtfulness of the Event, but the Rule of Right.[41]

Leviathan, by contrast, takes a more authoritarian line. The subject should not think he is required to make himself a martyr in this sort of case. Hobbes argues that martyrdom is a very limited vocation, and not required of anyone except a witness to the resurrection (L 42: 344–45). The better policy is for the subject to comply with the sovereign's command and console himself with the thought that he is not personally answerable to God for the insulting nature of the public worship he participates in, because

> whatsoever a Subject . . . is compelled to in obedience to his Soveraign, and doth it not in order to his own mind, but in order to the laws of his country, that action is not his, but his

> Soveraigns; nor is it he that in this case denieth Christ before men, but his Governour, and the law of his countrey (L 42: 344).

Now actually, as A. P. Martinich points out (at the end of one of the few discussions of Hobbes's theory of public worship by a modern commentator), this second line is a little disingenuous, since elsewhere it is Hobbes's position, not that the subject attribute the problematic action required of him to the sovereign, but that the subject adopt *as his own* the view that the sovereign hath commanded: "[E]very subject is by this institution author of all the actions and judgments of the sovereign instituted" (L 18: 124).[42] If the sovereign says we are to trample the image of Christ,[43] then the gist of Hobbes's general position is that we are to treat that as being done in our name and as our responsibility, not as something we can dissociate ourselves from. In maintaining the contrary in Chapter 31 of *Leviathan,* Hobbes seems to be playing fast and loose with this theory of the proper attribution of actions done in the name of the public, simply to evade the force of the obvious objection.

VIII

The difficulty to which Martinich draws our attention—the difficulty about who the action of worship should be attributed to when the sovereign's commands as to worship are obeyed—also points us to a deeper problem in Hobbes's account. If public worship—worship by the commonwealth—is necessary, why is it not sufficient for this worship to be carried out by the sovereign *on his own* as representative of the whole society? The sovereign, we know, has "the right to present the person of [us] all" (L 18: 121).[44] So why can't he be our high priest for the purpose of public worship, and attribute his own words and gestures to the whole community, leaving us (as individuals) to their own devices? Why does public worship require any action by the ordinary subject at all? Sure, the sovereign's actions will be attributed to the subject, and that may itself be a burden to sensitive consciences; but to this sort of conscience, it will not be nearly as much of a burden as the subjects' actually having to perform the actions and gestures of worship prescribed by the sovereign.

Hobbes comes close to acknowledging this in *De Cive* when he writes that "the actions done by particular Persons, according to their private Reasons, are not the Cities actions, and therefore not the Cities worship; but what is done by the City, is understood to be done by the command of him, or them who have the Sovereignty" (DC 15: xv: 194). But he goes on immediately to say that the Sovereign's actions are done by him "with the consent of all the subjects, that is to say, Uniformly" (DC 15: xv: 194). And the same question arises: Why is there this connection between consent and uniformity? It is not present in other areas where the sovereign acts with the subjects' consent in the name of the whole society. Consent is given generally and in advance in the social contract, and once it is given, the sovereign can act freely in all sorts of ways and in all sorts of matters in the name of the whole commonwealth without requiring anything of his subjects except that they refrain from criticizing or repudiating what he has done.

Another way of putting this is to ask why should Hobbes's theory of sovereign action suddenly become *participatory* at this point. Hobbes's theory does not usually require that subjects actually participate in the actions done in the name of the commonwealth by the sovereign. True, there are one or two actions of the commonwealth that cannot be done without the subjects' participation: The physical defense of the Commonwealth is the most obvious example. [45] But in most other matters, they can be "authors, of everything their representative saith or doth in their name" (L 16: 114) by attribution rather than by active involvement. I suppose that in public ceremonies participation may be required of one or two citizens as thurifers or whatever, but generally passive acquiescence seems sufficient. I think that this line of argument, if followed through, offers the best chance of answering the conscientious objection—though of course it may not answer it in a way that secures the political outcome Hobbes was driving at.

What about the point made earlier about the incompatibility of private diversity and public worship—the claim that "those actions that are done differently, by different men, cannot be said to be a Publique Worship" (L 31: 252–53)?[46] What about the claim that "where many sorts of Worship be allowed, proceeding from the different Religions of Private men . . . it cannot be said there is any Publique Worship, nor that the Commonwealth is of any

Religion at all" (L 31: 253)? Well, now these claims are revealed as question-begging. If public worship is inherently participatory, then these claims are important. But if, like most actions done in the name of the public, they are not inherently participatory, then the claims have no basis. All that needs to be ensured is that it is clear when the sovereign is worshipping in the name of the whole community, and that can be ensured in all sorts of ways that do not involve any requirement that the subjects worship in unison with him.

It is true that, in Hobbes's view, subjects have a natural law obligation "not only to worship God in secret, but also, and especially, in public, and in the sight of men: For without that, that which in honour is most acceptable, the procuring others to honour Him is lost" (L 31: 252). But we must not let an equivocation on the word "public" distract us here. Worship can be "public" in the sense of "visible to all," or it can be "public" in the sense of done in the name of the commonwealth. There is no inherent difficulty in separating the two provided that the visible worship done by the sovereign as high priest for the commonwealth is distinguished by certain clear marks and ceremonies form the equally visible but private worship done by citizens or groups of citizens acting on their own account.

IX

Our interest in this collection is toleration and I think that for us the Hobbesian idea of "publique worship" is unacceptable. We who are opposed to religious establishment need to think what it is about public worship that we find objectionable. Hobbes's argument is an elaborate one, and there are a number of points where we might want to resist its force.

First, we might deny the existence of God, from which it will follow that there are no obligations to worship Him, let alone engage in public worship. But then it is difficult to argue for non-establishment as against believers, and it has generally been thought desirable in the liberal tradition to be able to do so.

Secondly, if we grant the existence of God, we might regard worship as non-obligatory, as a choice that is made by a given person concerning the extent to which he wishes to ingratiate himself to the Almighty. If worship is presented as discretionary, then it will be a matter of prudential decision whether a whole society thinks it necessary or desirable to undertake worship in its own name.

Thirdly, if we think there is an obligation to worship God, we may think it incumbent only on natural persons. This can be because the grounds of the obligation to worship might apply only to natural persons. Or it can be because worship itself might be something that makes sense only for natural persons. For Hobbes, the ground of worship is the danger of not appeasing God by acknowledgment of His power. The danger consists in the neglect of a condition for possible aid as well as in undue provocation to the Almighty. As we have seen, this reason for worship applies to artificial as well as natural persons, because those too can be endangered by God's response to worship (or the lack of it). Moreover, constructing a social entity—a leviathan, a "*mortall God*" (L 17: 120)—does seem unduly provocative if it is not accompanied by an acknowledgment of that entity's low status in comparison with God. (The fall of the Tower of Babel springs to mind). It is possible, however, that Hobbes misconceives the nature of worship. Maybe worship is not just a gesture of self-abasement but a more intensely personal relation between God and the worshipper, something which makes sense only at the level of individual humans.

Fourthly, even if worship is required of the commonwealth, Hobbes may be wrong about what public worship necessitates. In order for a society to be perceived as God-fearing and for its social and political organization not to be convicted of hubris, maybe it is enough that there be a whole array of forms of individual worship and social worship in that society. It may not be necessary or even desirable for this array to be capped off, so to speak, by one unitary form of communal worship organized by the sovereign. (The United States has long been regarded as an intensely religious and God-fearing country on exactly this ground, even though it has set its face against any sort of public religious ceremonies organized by the state.) We have seen that Hobbes is not entitled to resist this on general conventionalist grounds. Not all the social conventions that introduce meaning into our lives and actions need to be orchestrated by a sovereign. Language is a fine example of a social convention which Hobbes acknowledges is not necessarily a politically established convention; it need not even be politically underwritten.

Fifthly, as we saw in the previous section, even if worship explicitly in the name of the commonwealth is required, there is no reason why that should have to engage the actions of private citizens. We could have a form of public worship, conducted purely by officials or by a sovereign acting as the society's high priest. And that might be enough to fulfill the obligation specifically incumbent on the commonwealth, without implicating the beliefs and practices of individual citizens.

I doubt that these five responses will be seen as sufficient by most of Hobbes's readers. There is something just irreducibly weird and offensive about his doctrine of public worship. But I hope I have been able in this chapter to rescue it from its undue neglect and indicate how it fits into contemporary discussions of faith, state practice, and toleration.

NOTES

1. For a fine account, see Alan Ryan, "Hobbes, Toleration, and the Inner Life," in David Miller and Larry Siedentop (editors), *The Nature of Political Theory* (Oxford: Clarendon Press, 1983), 197. See also Richard Tuck, "Hobbes and Locke on toleration," in Mary Dietz (editor), *Thomas Hobbes and Political Theory* (Lawrence: University Press of Kansas, 1990), 153.

2. References of this form—L 00: 000—are to Thomas Hobbes, *Leviathan,* edited by Richard Tuck (Cambridge: Cambridge University Press, 1991), by chapter and page number. Emphasis is in the original, except where otherwise stated.

3. See also L 32: 256 and L 40: 323. For Locke's version of this, see John Locke, *A Letter Concerning Toleration,* edited by James H. Tully (Indianapolis: Hackett Publishing, 1983), 27: "[T]rue and saving Religion consists in the inward perswasion of the Mind, without which nothing can be acceptable to God. And such is the nature of the Understanding, that it cannot be compell'd to the belief of anything by outward force."

4. Locke, *Letter,* op. cit., 49.

5. See, e.g., John Locke, *A Second Letter Concerning Toleration,* in *The Works of John Locke* (London: Thomas Tegg and others, 1823), Vol. VI, at 84. See also the discussion in Jeremy Waldron, *God, Locke, and Equality:*

Christian Foundations in John Locke's Political Thought (Cambridge: Cambridge University Press, 2002), 210–11.

6. Locke, *Letter,* op. cit., 52.

7. The only discussions I have found that touch on it—and they are mostly quite brief—are the following: Michael Oakeshott, *Hobbes on Civil Association* (Indianapolis: Liberty Fund, 1975), at 50 and 56; Ryan, op. cit., at 205–8; S. A. Lloyd, *Ideals as Interests in Hobbes's Leviathan* (Cambridge: Cambridge University Press, 1992), at 115–19; A. P. Martinich, *The Two Gods of Leviathan: Thomas Hobbes on Religion and Politics* (Cambridge: Cambridge University Press, 1992), at 299–303; and Richard Tuck, "The Civil Religion of Thomas Hobbes," in Nicholas Phillipson and Quentin Skinner (editors), *Political Discourse in Early Modern Britain* (Cambridge: Cambridge University Press, 1992), 122–24.

8. For the equation of "Hobbist" and "atheist," see Samuel L. Mintz, *The Hunting of Leviathan: Seventeenth Century Reactions to the Materialism and Moral Philosophy of Thomas Hobbes* (Bristol: Thoemmes Press, 1996), 50–51 and 56–62.

9. Whether Hobbes gives a strictly moral, as opposed to a prudential account, of our obligation to worship God is another matter: for helpful discussion, see Thomas Nagel, "Hobbes's Concept of Obligation," *Philosophical Review,* 68 (1959), 78–79.

10. See, e.g., Ronald Beiner, "Machiavelli, Hobbes, and Rousseau on Civil Religion," *Review of Politics,* 55 (1993), 617.

11. For the claim that this is true of all Hobbes's arguments about religion in *Leviathan,* see Paul D. Cooke, *Hobbes and Christianity: Reassessing the Bible in Leviathan* (Lanham, Md.: Rowman and Littlefield, 1996), 206 ff.

12. Hobbes seems to think that the religions of ancient Greece and Rome are just "part of their policy" and he distinguished the religion of ancient Israel and the Christian religion from them in this regard (L 12: 83).

13. So I disagree with Ryan's assertion, op. cit., 207, that Hobbes "makes uniform public worship a political good and not a religious issue."

14. L 16: 111. See Nagel, op. cit., but see also Howard Warrender, *The Political Philosophy of Hobbes* (Oxford: Clarendon Press, 1957), 212.

15. Thomas Hobbes, The *Elements of Law Natural and Politic,* ch. 8, sect. 6, in Thomas Hobbes, *Human Nature and De Corpore Politico,* edited by J. G. A. Gaskin (Oxford: Oxford University Press, 1994), 49.

16. Thomas Hobbes, *De Cive: The English Version,* edited by Howard Warrender (Oxford: Clarendon Press, 1983), ch. 15, § 9, 188. In the remainder of this chapter, references of this form—DC 00: 00: 000—are to *De Cive* (in this edition), by chapter number, section number, and page.

17. Ryan, op. cit., 209, offers a useful analogy: "[W]hen we shout 'may the king live for ever' at his coronation, we know that he can do no such thing, but the wish is neither insincere nor absurd."

18. This phrase is from a Hobbes manuscript dated 1643 cited by Tuck, "The Civil Religion of Thomas Hobbes," op. cit., at 123.

19. For these aspects of speech act theory, see J. L. Austin, *How to Do Things with Words* (Cambridge: Harvard University Press 1975), 98–132. ("Prostrative," by the way, is my term, not Hobbes's or Austin's.)

20. Some of these might be obvious to reason; others might require close reasoning, which means that ordinary people will have to "rely on those they believe to be wiser than themselves" (L 12: 78).

21. Hobbes also includes words whose evaluative meaning may be equivocal or controversial: these are words which "signify honour, but with some, and scorne with others, or else neither; such as in *Attributes,* are those words which according to the diversity of opinions, are diversly referred to vertues or vices, to honest or dishonest things; As that a man slew his enemy, that he fled, that he is a Philosopher, or an Orator, and the like, which with some are has in honour, with others in contempt" (DC 15: xi: 189). (That being a philosopher is an attribute of honor for some and scorn for others is a nice touch!)

22. There are two possible ways of taking the three-sidedness of the relation. One is that an expression of honor by A naturally evokes attitudes shared between A and B: "in approving the honour done by others, he acknowledgeth the power which others acknowledge" (L 10: 64). On the other interpretation A, in honoring B, indicates to C A's awareness of the greatness of B and of A's weakness compared to B, and this B ought to regard as a very significant thing for A to do because it is an abasement of A not just in B's eyes, but in the eyes of C (who is not so manifestly A's superior). Since B knows that C is A's equal and potentially A's enemy, B will regard it as a big deal that A puts on a display of his (A's) weakness in the sight of C.

23. Hobbes, *Elements of Law,* 11:12:

> To honour God internally in the heart, is the same thing with that we ordinarily call honour amongst men: For it is nothing but the acknowledging of his power; and the signs thereof the same with the signs of the honour due to our superiors, . . . : to praise, to magnify, to bless him, to pray to him, to thank him, to give oblations and sacrifice to him, to give attention to his word, to speak to him in prayer with consideration, to come into his presence with humble gesture, and in decent manner, and to adorn his worship with magnificence and cost. And these are natural signs of our honouring him internally.

24. See Ludwig Wittgenstein, *Philosophical Investigations,* 3rd edition, translated by G. E. M. Anscombe (Oxford: Basil Blackwell, 2001), 80 ff. (§§ 269 ff.).

25. John Locke, for instance, has no doubts on this score: "Every man has an Immortal Soul, capable of Eternal Happiness or Misery; whose Happiness depend[s] upon his believing and doing those things in this Life which are necessary to the obtaining of God's Favour, and are prescribed by God to that end" (Locke, *Letter,* op. cit., 47).

26. For Hobbes's comments on these entities, see L 22: 160–63.

27. The commonwealth is sometimes compared by Hobbes not just to an "Artificiall Man" (L Intro: 9), but to a "*Mortall God*" (L: 17: 120), but he is quick to add that it is one "to which we owe under the *Immortal God,* our peace and defence" (L 17: 120).

28. Of course, the natural law's obligation upon a commonwealth is subject to the same condition as its obligation on anyone who is supposed to be bound in his dealings with others: It only applies *in foro interno,* unless and until others also showed their willingness to be bound (L 15: 110) or until some overarching earthly power is set up (L 30: 244). However, in the case of natural law duties to God, no such restriction applies: the obligations are unconditional.

29. Ryan, op. cit., 209.

30. Tom Sorell, *Hobbes* (London: Routledge and Kegan Paul, 1986), 38. For further discussion of the possibility of Wittgenstenian objections to Hobbes's strictly individual account of naming, see ibid., 86.

31. Hobbes, *Elements of Law,* op. cit., pt. 2, ch. 8

32. Genesis 11: 1–9.

33. Maybe the sovereign can add some meanings to our language, but language as such is not dependent on the sovereign's stipulations. In *The Elements of Law,* op. cit., ch. 29, sect. 8, 181, Hobbes suggests that the laws established meanings for all words not already agreed upon, which seems to suggest a supplementary rather than a constitutive role for the sovereign's stipulations. I owe this reference to Tuck, "The Civil Religion of Thomas Hobbes," op. cit., 123.

34. See supra, sect. III.

35. I owe this argument to Alan Ryan: see Ryan, op. cit., 207.

36. As we saw in sect. III, the sight of the multitude is important because Hobbes thinks worship is a matter of using signs and "a sign is not a sign to him that giveth it, but to him to whom it is makes, that is, to the spectator" (L 31: 249).

37. Similarly he says (DC 15: xvii: 196),

> [A]ll ridiculous ceremonies which have been used by any Nations, will bee seen at once in the same City; whence it will fall out, that

> every man will beleeve that all the rest doe offer God an affront; so that it cannot be truly said of any that he worships God; for no man worships God, that is to say, honours him outwardly, but he who doth those things, whereby hee appeares to others for to honour him.

38. Hobbes says that the power of sovereign by social contract is as great as possible, whereby it includes this power a fortiori: "[E]very Subject hath transferr'd as much right as he can on him, or them, who has the supreme authority, but he can have transferred his right of judging the manner how God is to be honoured, and therefore also he hath done it" (DC 15: xvii: 195–96).

39. It is interesting that the public worship argument has very little to do with the enforcement of an orthodoxy concerning creedal matters. (In that sense it seems a very Anglican doctrine). There is some connection with issues of faith. To the extent that the sovereign controls the words that are used in worship, to that extent they control what men believe about God: "The City therefore . . . shall judge what names or appellations are more, what lesse honourable for God, that is to say, what doctrines are to be held and profest concerning the nature of God, and his operations" (DC 15: xvi: 194). However, Alan Ryan has observed that Hobbes, in his insistence that people not approach these matters too philosophically, may actually underestimate

> the extent to which beliefs about the Deity infect attitudes towards conventions. If God delights not in burnt offerings, will He not delight even less in five-part masses. A man who has read the first in Scripture will find it hard to confine himself to saying that he does not know whether God likes music, and that he is prepared to leave the question for God and the sovereign to settle in due course. (Ryan, op. cit., 210)

The upshot of this is that while Hobbes's distinction between private faith and "public conventions about *what counts as* worship" (Ryan, op. cit., 209, original emphasis) may look superficially plausible, it may end up that "the sovereign must either go farther towards securing uniform belief than Hobbes seems to want or less far towards securing any sort of uniformity" so far as worship is concerned (Ryan, op. cit., 210).

40. See the discussion in sect. V, supra.

41. Locke, *Letter,* op. cit.

42. See Martinich, *The Two Gods,* op. cit., 303.

43. Cf. Shusaku Endo, *Silence,* translated by William Johnson (New York: Taplinger, 1979), 170–71.

44. I am drawing here on the analysis of Hobbes's theory of represen-

tation in "Hobbes and the Purely Artificial Person of the State," in Quentin Skinner, *Hobbes and Civil Science,* vol. III of *Visions of Politics* (Cambridge: Cambridge University Press, 2002), 177.

45. See L Rev and Concl: 484: "To the Laws of Nature declared in the 15. Chapter, I will have this added: *That every man is bound by Nature, as much as in him lieth, to protect in Warre, the Authority, by which he is himself protected in time of Peace.*"

46. See supra, sect. VI.

2

SPINOZA ON WHY THE SOVEREIGN CAN COMMAND MEN'S TONGUES BUT NOT THEIR MINDS

MICHAEL A. ROSENTHAL

Introduction

It has become a central principle of liberal societies that institutions or individuals should not try to compel or coerce a person's beliefs. It was not always this way and in many places it still is not. In the seventeenth century, systematic attempts to compel belief by either the government or the church were not rare—either in the name of civil order or revealed truth or both—and it was out of the subsequent conflicts that many of our contemporary liberal justifications for tolerance developed. One of the best known of these early modern justifications is John Locke's *A Letter Concerning Toleration*, written around the time of the Revocation of the Edict of Nantes in 1685 and published four years later.[1] One of Locke's three arguments for tolerance expresses this central principle:

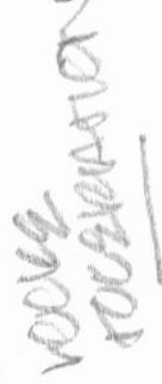

> The care of souls cannot belong to the civil magistrate, because his power consists only in outward force; but true and saving religion consists in the inward persuasion of the mind, without

> which nothing can be acceptable to God. And such is the nature of the understanding that it cannot be compelled to the belief of anything by outward force. (395)

Locke's argument was not particularly original. Fifteen years earlier Baruch Spinoza anonymously published his *Tractatus Theologico-Politicus* (TTP). Its goal, as stated on the title page, was to persuade the magistrate that "the Freedom of Philosophizing not only can be granted without harm to Piety and the Peace of the State, but also cannot be abolished unless Piety and the Peace of the State are also destroyed." It is a fundamental corollary to this view that the sovereign ought to grant a limited freedom of religion as well. Spinoza's argument also rests on the claim that belief cannot be compelled:

> [1] If it were as easy to command men's minds as it is their tongues, every ruler would govern in safety and no rule would be violent. For everyone would live according to the disposition of the rulers, and only in accordance with their decree would people judge what is true or false, good or evil, right or wrong. [2] But as we have noted at the beginning of Chapter 17, it cannot happen that a mind should be absolutely subject to the control of someone else. Indeed, no one can transfer to another person his natural right, *or* faculty of reasoning freely, and of judging concerning anything whatever, nor can he be compelled to do this. [3] This is why rule over minds is considered violent, and why the supreme authority seems to wrong its subjects and to usurp their rights whenever it wants to prescribe to each person what he must embrace as true and what reject as false, and, further, by what opinions each person's mind ought to be moved in its devotion to God. For these things are subject to each person's control, which no one can surrender even if he wishes to. (TTP, xx.1–3; GIII/239)[2]

Some have claimed that Locke was influenced by Spinoza.[3] This claim should not be surprising since Locke wrote his *Letter* while he sojourned in Holland. Also, while Locke's work is better known today in some circles, it has been argued recently that Spinoza's treatise was far more influential in his time and on the development of the Enlightenment and hence the constitution of liberal society.[4] However interesting these historical questions may be, it will not be my business here to propose or assess answers to them. Instead, I want to look at the philosophical grounds of Spinoza's claim that belief cannot be compelled.

In the seventeenth century, not everyone assumed that a tolerant policy would produce a more stable state or that belief could not be compelled. It should be obvious that the two major assumptions here are questionable, at least on empirical grounds, and indeed they were fiercely debated in the sixteenth and seventeenth centuries. First, is it the case that a tolerant regime would be more stable than an intolerant one? As Richard Tuck has pointed out, late in the sixteenth century Justus Lipsius argued for a thoroughly pragmatic position in which tolerance was subservient to political stability.[5] On the one hand, "if repression was politically impossible," a tolerant policy would be justified (26). If, on the other hand, as early modern experience amply seemed to demonstrate, religious debate was about to turn into violent conflict and rebellion, then a sovereign ought to use a heavy hand to quash it. Second, is it really the case that a person convinced of the truth cannot change the mind of another person with the convenient aid of the sword? An answer to this question is crucial because it determines the answer we give to the first. If it is possible to coerce belief successfully, then a sovereign may try to enforce confessional unanimity for the sake of stability.[6] The persecution of heretics and debates over its efficacy has a long history in the church, and this is clearly the background to this early modern debate.[7] Some, following St. Augustine, interpreted the scriptural passage in which Christ asks his disciples to compel those who are sitting outside a feast to enter (Luke 14:23) as a parable that justified the persecution of heretics. Others, such as Spinoza, and later John Locke and Pierre Bayle (who took issue directly with the Augustinian view in his *Commentaire sur les ces paroles de Jésus Christ: "Contrains les d'entrer"*), claimed that it was impossible for a sovereign to compel belief and that the sovereign should tolerate some religious diversity.

An answer to these questions had more than theoretical interest for Spinoza. Just before he published the TTP, his friend

Adriaan Koerbagh had been imprisoned (and later died in prison) because he had dared to publish his own critique of religion, inspired by Spinoza's ideas, in Dutch.[8] And after the publication of the TTP, which provoked widespread indignation and systematic attempts to ban it and prevent its diffusion,[9] Spinoza made every effort to prevent its translation from the Latin to the vernacular.[10] He was obviously afraid that what happened to Koerbagh might happen to him. Although he was cautious in his own actions, nonetheless, the argument in the TTP demonstrates that he wanted to show that such efforts at repression were ultimately doomed to fail.

More recently philosophers have cast a critical eye on all such justifications of toleration. Jeremy Waldron, in an article focused on Locke, but which could equally apply to Spinoza, has argued both that it may indeed be rational to persecute and that, whatever conclusion we reach on this point, such arguments are lacking because they depend upon questionable empirical justifications rather than on solid moral principle.[11] Most recent philosophical discourse on toleration has accepted the essence of this critique and moved away from pragmatic justifications to more principled ones, based on notions of autonomy and respect.

In this chapter, I shall examine Spinoza's attempts to defend the premise that the sovereign cannot compel belief, both in the TTP, where he uses the idea of natural right, and in the *Ethics*, where the argument depends on his attack on free will. I shall raise several objections to these claims, such as the view that knowledge of the truth justifies persecution, and also, most importantly, that without a conception of free will, Spinoza has some difficulty in distinguishing the case in which the sovereign compels someone to change his beliefs from the case in which the sovereign persuades him to do so. I shall argue that Spinoza can distinguish these cases based on his distinction between freedom and constraint, which in turn is based on his conception of human nature. I shall suggest that the reasons why belief cannot be compelled are related to the structure of the argument for toleration itself and I shall make some concluding remarks about the nature of the argument as a whole and its relation to contemporary debates.

The Natural Right Argument

If we look at the beginning of chapter 17 in the *Theological-Political Treatise,* we find that the reason why one mind can never wholly be in the control of another has to do with Spinoza's conception of natural right. In chapter 16, Spinoza notoriously says that "each individual has a supreme right to do everything in its power, *or* that the right of each thing extends as far as its determinate power does" (xvi.4; GIII/189). Unfortunately, in the state of nature, individuals' power is limited and threatened by others. Consequently, they recognize that their power can only be preserved at the cost of giving up some of it to an authority whose function is to provide physical security for its subjects. Thus Spinoza explains the origin of government in terms of a social contract in which individuals in a state of nature transfer their natural right to a single individual or body of individuals and establish a sovereign authority. The definition of right as power also generates some limitations on the power of government. First, the transfer is conditional upon the individual's satisfaction at the result of the transfer. If the individual no longer thinks that the state is able to satisfy his desires (e.g., for peace and security), then he maintains the right to withhold his transfer or give it to someone else. Second, it may not be the case that all individuals in the state of nature will transfer their rights—in other words, there need not be unanimous consent for a sovereign authority to function. A government has the right and power to rule when its power overwhelms (or at least checks) the power of those that oppose it. A democracy is the best, and most stable, form of government, in Spinoza's view, because it involves the greatest number of individuals who have transferred their right and power.

Now at the beginning of chapter 17, he remarks upon another couple of limitations upon the power of the sovereign, which bear directly on the problem of tolerance. However successful the sovereign, it can never demand a complete transfer of right from an individual: "For no one will ever be able to so transfer his power, and hence, his right, to another that he ceases to be a man nor will there ever be any supreme power which can carry out everything it wishes" (xvii.2; GIII/201). In this case, the sovereign wishes the subject to think as it does, but Spinoza seems to insist that this is an impossible demand. On the face of it, this statement seems to be inconsistent with Spinoza's identification of right with power in chapter 16. If the sovereign does have more power than a subject individual, then the identification of power with right would seem to justify the use of that power to compel the subject's mind. However, to understand Spinoza's view it is important to note that "power" has a quite specific meaning. "And because the supreme law of nature is that each thing strives to persevere in its state, as far as it can by its own power, and does this, not on account of anything else, but only of itself, from this it follows that each individual has the supreme right to do this, i.e. (as I have said), to exist and act as it is naturally determined to do" (xvi.4; GIII/189). So this is the essence of Spinoza's position. It is not that a person has a right to do what he wants but could do otherwise. Rather, a person has a right to do what he wants and cannot do anything else. For the sovereign to compel this person to act otherwise would not only be to violate the person's natural right in the juridical sense, but it would also be practically futile. The more a sovereign alienates his subjects through coercive policies, the less support he has from them—i.e., fewer individuals will transfer their right and power to the sovereign—and the less stable the state. The sovereign would seem to have a self-interested reason to be tolerant.[12]

Problems with the Natural Right Argument

The first objection to this view is that it does not explicitly consider the role of truth in the justification of compulsion. If we go back to the source of these debates in St. Augustine's letters, we find that it was knowledge of the truth that justified coercion, that is, distinguished it from another, merely politically justified form of coercion. In a letter to the Donatist Bishop, Vincent, Augustine writes, "There is an unjust persecution, which the ungodly operate against the Church of Christ; and a just persecution which the Churches of Christ make use of towards the ungodly."[13] Unlike some early modern skeptics, like Pierre Bayle, Spinoza did not doubt that it was possible to know the truth in matters of religion.[14] So, would it not be the case that, if the sovereign did know the truth, in this case concerning the salvation of the individual's soul, then he would be justified in using coercive means to compel belief? Spinoza has at least two responses to this question.

First, there is no reason to think that the sovereign, or his priestly advisors, has any privileged access to the truth. This is where it is important to read not just the few chapters in the TTP which deal explicitly with political theory (i.e., chapters xvi–xx) but the whole work. From the very first chapter, Spinoza attacks the common doctrine that revelation is a privileged, supernatural means of acquiring the truth. Certainly, in contrast to "natural knowledge," which is acquired by "the natural light of reason" and "rests on foundations common to all men," prophetic knowledge is unique (i.2; GIII/15). But revelation or prophecy is not supernatural in Spinoza's view at all. It is unique in the sense that it reflects the particular mental constitution and historical circumstances of the prophet. Unlike natural knowledge, which is clear and distinct, prophetic knowledge is imaginative rather than rational in nature and appeals to the passions of its audience in an effort to move them to acts of justice and loving-kindness. "Therefore," Spinoza writes, "those who look in the books of the Prophets for wisdom, and knowledge of natural and spiritual matters, go entirely astray (ii.2; GIII/29).

Spinoza defines the role of the sovereign, and the allied function of traditional religion, in light of this critique of the traditional understanding of revelation. In the third chapter of the TTP, he divides the objects of human desire into three categories: "[i] to understand things through their first causes; [ii] to gain control over the passions, *or* to acquire the habit of virtue; and finally, [iii] to live securely and healthily" (iii.12; GIII/46). While the philosopher is concerned with the first two ends, the prophet and the sovereign authority can only aid us in the pursuit of the third. It is simply not the proper function of either government or public religion to concern itself with any other truths than how to secure the health of the body in this life.

Nonetheless, even if we assume that the sovereign does know the truth regarding the salvation of the soul, then the natural right argument, as we have sketched it above, should provide a reason why this knowledge would not justify persecution. Spinoza insists that any individual, whether human or not, reasonable or not, fool or madman, does what it does with supreme natural right "because it acts as it has been determined according to nature, and cannot do otherwise" (xvi.5; GIII/189). Not surprisingly, most people are led by their desires and passions rather than by reason. As we have seen, the sovereign's concern is to establish his authority through gaining the conditional transfer of natural right from the subjects. Because the sovereign is faced with people who are more likely to be led by their passions than by their reason, he must recognize that some of his actions might adversely affect the desire of at least some of his subjects to transfer their right in support of his regime. Those who are led by their simple but strong desire to survive in a hostile world will not appreciate the sovereign devoting his energy to convincing them or others of otherworldly truths. And those who are ruled by religious passions, and convinced of their own knowledge of the truth, will not appreciate the sovereign's efforts to convert them. So if the sovereign desires to maintain his power, even if he is convinced that he knows the truth, then, according to this argument, he will respect the natural rights of his subjects and refrain from compelling their thoughts.

Of course a juridical or political solution to the problem in terms of natural right is not entirely satisfactory for a few reasons. For one thing, as we shall see later, Spinoza does seem to think that the truth can be persuasive, at least indirectly, and so we are still left with questions about the difference between compelling and persuading someone to think something. For another, the argument depends on the very premise that we called into question above, namely, that the sovereign cannot compel belief. It seems open to the objection that if a powerful sovereign could find a way to compel a person's mind then he would have the right to do. Because the natural rights argument is not foundational in Spinoza's view—that is, it can be reduced to the power each thing has to persevere—its value depends on the underlying claims about human nature. That is why we must turn next to the discussion in the *Ethics* of the will and mind-body relations.

The Will

The crux of the question whether belief can be compelled or not is whether belief is voluntary or not. Interestingly enough, many of those who thought that persecution was effective did not think that force by itself could compel belief. As the historian Mark Goldie states the view, "Certainly force does not convince directly, but it may work indirectly, for its use can be the *occasion* for a reconsideration of views, a salutary means for initiating new spiritual exploration" (347). Writers in this tradition did not have to search far for Scriptural support of this view, pointing, for instance, to the violent circumstances of St. Paul's conversion on the road to Damascus. Thus inspired, Augustine wrote that people who are "first compelled by fear or pain . . . might afterwards be influenced by teaching."[15] His idea is that the will has become enslaved by the obstinate habits of body. You break the body, and the will is now free to voluntarily attach itself to what it had previously rejected.[16]

Although, as we shall discuss below, Spinoza agrees with these writers that force may have an indirect effect on an individual's mind, he utterly rejects their psychology of belief based on the idea of a free will. The origin of his critique is in his metaphysics of a single substance, or God. God is an infinite being whose existence is necessary. God expresses itself in infinite ways, through attributes, which define the essence of substance, and modes of those attributes. All things that follow from God are likewise necessary. Finite things, which Spinoza calls "finite modes," such as human beings, are subject to this necessity in two ways. On the one hand, finite modes are governed by "infinite modes," which, following Curley's interpretation, we can readily understand as the system of natural laws, such as, in the case of bodies, the laws of motion or rest.[17] On the other hand, finite modes are always causally related to other finite modes under their respective attributes in a determinate causal chain. As Spinoza writes in the *Ethics,* "In nature there is nothing contingent, but all things have been determined from the necessity of the divine nature to exist and produce an effect in a certain way" (E1p29).[18]

Spinoza applies this rigorous doctrine of determinism not only to bodies, as the Cartesians had done, but also to the mind. Spinoza adopts a somewhat uncharacteristic tone in the preface to part V of the *Ethics* when he mocks Descartes' theory of the mind-body union, in which the immaterial will attaches itself to the pineal gland, which in turn mysteriously moves the body. Spinoza considers both minds and bodies not as substances, but as finite modes, which are distinguished by their attributes, thought, and extension. As finite modes, they are causally determined by other modes (finite and infinite) of the same attribute. "The modes of each attribute have God for their cause only insofar as he is considered under the attribute of which they are modes, and not insofar as he is considered under any other attribute" (E2p6). Because they do not share the same attribute, minds and bodies do not causally interact. As Jonathan Bennett puts it, there is no "trans-attribute causality." Rather, they are parallel, expressing one thing (i.e., a finite mode of substance) in two different ways (i.e., through the attributes of thought and extension). In this logical, though counter-intuitive, way, Spinoza hopes to avoid the occult hypotheses, such as the pineal gland, which are necessary to explain interaction in the Cartesian system, and provide a sound basis for a scientific study of the mind and its various affections.

Obviously there is no place in this system for a Cartesian, radically free, will, that is, a will independent of causal necessity. The mind is just a finite mode expressed under the attribute of thought. Since it is not a substance, the mind is metaphysically nothing over and above a collection of ideas, which bear a systematic relation to one another, and act in a determinate manner. Because each idea is a finite mode, it must also be part of a determinate causal chain. It is caused by some other idea and will in turn cause others. All ideas, then, are active in the sense that produces mental effects in a determinate causal chain. Unlike the Cartesian theory of mind, in which our intellect produces ideas to which the separate power of the will can either assent or not, Spinoza argues that "the will and the intellect are one and the same" (E2p49c). Hence, as Wallace Matson has argued, there is no meaningful distinction between ideas and beliefs in Spinoza's system.[19] Each idea contains its own intrinsic affirmation (E2p49) and does not require a discrete mental power to transform it into a belief. What we mistakenly describe as our "free will" is just the awareness of ourselves acting—that is, in this case, an idea producing some other idea—without knowledge of the causes of the event. As he writes, "So experience itself, no less clearly than reason, teaches that men believe themselves free because they are conscious of their own actions, and ignorant of the causes by which they are determined" (E3p2s; GII/143).

Spinoza dismisses the concept of a free will as a chimera, but he does not do away with the language of volition. What we describe as our will is nothing other than the idea we associate with our action as a complex mental entity, the mind, as it acts to produce some other idea. When we explain this idea solely in reference to other ideas, under the attribute of thought, we call it a "decision." When we consider the action in relation to other modes of body, under the attribute of extension, we call it a "determination" (E3p2s; GII/144). In neither case are we free of a determinate casual chain. Yet in both cases we describe these actions as more or less ours. It may not have been my free will which caused me to come to Seattle, and it may not have been possible that I would be elsewhere at this moment, but it was my body and my mind that were salient among the causal agents that brought me to this place in the causal chain, and thus I can be held responsible for my actions. Most importantly, for our purposes, my belief that I am currently in Seattle, even if I am responsible for the belief, cannot be otherwise. Or, to take one of Spinoza's examples, I may imagine that the sun "is about 200 feet away from me," but even if I knew this to be false, I may still believe it (E2p35s). It will remain "present" until some other idea eventually displaces it (E2p17s). It may be possible to change that belief, but only through an indirect route, and not through the immediate intervention of a will outside of the causal chain. As he writes:

> [H]uman affairs, of course, would be conducted far more happily if it were equally in man's power to be silent and to speak. But experience teaches all too plainly that men have nothing less in their power than their tongue, and can do nothing less than moderate their appetites (E3p2s; GII/143).

If I am incapable of changing my belief in any direct way, then it must be the case that some outside agent, such as the sovereign, would also be incapable of it.

Freedom and Necessity

Spinoza's version of the classical compatibilist theory of human freedom soon came under attack. Although Spinoza was not explicit about the denial of free will in the TTP, his readers immediately understood this as an implication of what he did say. As soon as the TTP was published, it was banned for its heterodox views, central of which was Spinoza's apparent denial of free will, the power to do otherwise. Even Spinoza's more intimate correspondents harbored doubts concerning this position, or at least wanted to hear more on the subject. Henry Oldenburg reminded Spinoza that "the reason why I advised against the publication of the doctrine of the fatalistic necessity of all things is my fear lest the practise of virtue may thereby be impeded, and rewards and punishments be made of little account."[20] Spinoza's response was to deny that his systematic determinism was the same as fatalism and to argue that necessity was compatible with freedom and contrary to constraint (or compulsion). He writes to another correspondent, Hugo Boxel, "Thus you fail, I think, to make any distinction between constraint [*coactio*] or force [*vis*], and necessity. That a man wills to live, to love, etc., does not proceed from constraint, but is nevertheless necessary."[21]

A thing is free, according to Spinoza, when it acts in accordance with its nature. As he writes in the *Ethics*: "That thing is called free which exists from the necessity of its nature alone, and is determined to act by itself alone" (E1d7). Strictly speaking only God fits this definition perfectly, while finite things can only approach its criteria relatively. As we saw above, unlike God who is a substance, infinite, independent, and subject to no other causal necessity than its own, human beings are finite modes, dependent and subject to the causal action of other finite things. Whereas God is always free, human beings are only free to the extent that they are able to act without interference from things external to their nature. A tentative definition of constraint, then, might be the extent and manner in which a finite mode's actions are limited by the actions of other modes external to it. Some support for this view might be gleaned from Spinoza's use of these terms to distinguish between "adequate" and "inadequate" (i.e., confused) ideas. The mind only knows its body inadequately "so long as it is determined externally, from fortuitous encounters with things, to regard this or that, and not so long as it is determined internally, from the fact that it regards a number of things at once, to understand their agreements, differences, and oppositions"

(E2p29s). Spinoza distinguishes ideas in terms of their causal origin and this in turn becomes the basis of the distinctions between action and passion in part 3 of the *Ethics* and freedom and bondage in part 4.

Nonetheless, terms like "internal" and "external" are difficult to define in the complex system of finite modes. Each finite mode is originally produced by something external to it and constantly requires the input of the external world to survive. We eat to restore our bodies, perceive the world around us, and desire those things that we lack. These ideas have an external source but they have been literally or figuratively incorporated, that is, internalized, into ourselves and our experience of the world. The question is "external to what?" In the case of something simple, like a rock, the physical boundaries are easy to discern. However, if our bodies and minds are permeable to a degree, then what defines our individual nature or activity is not a spatial metaphor but a causal relation. When it comes to bodies, Spinoza says that a collection of simple bodies becomes a complex individual when they "communicate their motions to each other in a certain fixed manner [ratio]" (A2 definition after E2p13s). Although he does not provide a parallel definition of what defines an individual mind (except to say that the mind is the idea of such a body), we can readily conceive of a certain relation among ideas, a relation that is defined by certain cognitive and emotional structures as well as patterns of association. When these structures are able to persist, that is, when they act causally in accordance with their nature, then the individual is free. When something interferes with this causal activity, then the individual is constrained.

Of course there will be many degrees of constraint and of relative freedom. This is because our natures are composites of essential and accidental qualities; that is, those qualities without which we would no longer exist and those without which we would continue to exist. And even among those qualities which are accidental we may over time prioritize some as more important than others. So we would have our first, or essential, nature and then our second nature, which is acquired through experience. Since Spinoza thinks that it is acting in accordance with our nature that makes us free, we could come to understand our freedom as a matter of degree to which we are able to act in accordance with our essential and acquired natures and the different aspects of each. The sovereign may be able to constrain some aspects of our nature but not all of them, at least not without killing us. And it would also be the case that a sovereign that only respected our essential natures would be only respecting part of our nature. A sovereign should also take into account the ways that our acquired ideas (including beliefs and desires) become part of an individual's nature. A sovereign that constrained the expression of these acquired aspects of our nature, aspects which we strive to preserve, would also be impinging on our natural rights to some degree. So the richer the idea of human nature that underlies the idea of a natural right, the more nuanced the account of freedom we have.[22]

This account should help make sense of Spinoza's claim that a person can never willingly transfer all his natural right to the sovereign and that the sovereign's attempt to control a person's beliefs is therefore impossible. As Spinoza writes in the *Ethics*, to act against one's nature, not to strive to persist, would be contrary to our very essence (E3p7). Because no one can act to destroy themselves, such a complete transfer of right would be equivalent to self-destruction, which, according to Spinoza, is impossible (E3p6). At a minimum, any attempt to compel belief, that is, change a person's mind through an external cause, would infringe on that person's freedom through affecting the person's *conatus*, or striving to live in accordance with his essence. It is also possible to see how such an attempt might go even farther and impinge on a person's very ability to preserve himself. Any case of torture would have the effect of disrupting the *conatus*, both physically and mentally, to the extent that the person's body and mind would no longer maintain the unity among its parts required to call that person a distinct individual.[23]

Compulsion and Persuasion

Those who justified coercion of belief in name of the truth did not neatly distinguish compulsion from persuasion. If, as we saw above, they justified themselves in the name of the truth, and if, as we just discussed, they believed that they were not directly changing people's minds but rather giving them an occasion to reconsider, then compulsion could be seen as a necessary, if not sufficient, condition of persuasion. True, the sovereign authority did not always have the pedagogical skills of the clergy, yet with proper preparation they could turn a torture session into learning opportunity. Augustine himself, who earlier in his career did not think such means were justified, was subsequently converted in favor of what he called the theory of "good constraint" by the many "decisive examples" in which heretics came to see the light. In his letters, he quotes testimonies from these experiences to support his claim: "And others again [said]: 'We did not realize that the truth lay there, and did not want to learn it; but fear made us look twice and we recognized it. We thank God for having penetrated our negligence with the sting of fear.' "[24] The combination of fear with other means was part of a broader cultural policy. Mark Goldie notes in his discussion of seventeenth century arguments for intolerance, which were heavily influenced by Augustine's views, that in almost all cases it was recognized that "if coercion is to be a pastoral tool, it is vital that force be married with edification and argument" (350). This involved writing, sermonizing, face-to-face disputation, and other means.

It may seem that, once Spinoza has eliminated the concept of a free will, and established that the effort to compel belief is useless, the sovereign's influence over the minds of his subjects would be drastically limited. Nonetheless, it turns out that early modern theorists of the state had learned something from their theological opponents. Immediately after presenting the natural rights argument in chapter xvii of the TTP, Spinoza goes on to point out just how powerful the state is in these matters. The long passage is worth quoting in full:

> Nevertheless, to understand rightly how far the right and power of the state extend, we must note that its power is not limited to what it can compel men to do from fear, but extends to absolutely everything which it can bring men to do in compliance with its commands. It is obedience which makes the subject, not the reason for the obedience. [6] For whatever reason a man resolves to carry out the commands of the supreme power, whether because he fears a penalty, or because he hopes for something from it, or because he loves his Country, or because he has been

> prompted by any other affect whatever, he still forms his resolution according to his own judgment, notwithstanding that he acts in accordance with the command of the supreme power. [7] Therefore, we must not infer simply from the fact that a man does something by his own judgment, that he does it in virtue of his own right, and not the right of the political authority. For since he always acts in accordance with his own judgment and decision, both when he is secured by love and when he is compelled by fear, to avoid some evil, there would be no political authority and no right over subjects, if political authority did not necessarily extend to everything with respect to which it can bring men to resolve to yield to it. And consequently, whatever a subject does which is in accordance with the commands of the supreme power, whether he has been secured by love, or compelled by fear, or (as is, indeed, more frequent) by hope and fear together, whether he acts from reverence (which is a passion composed of fear and wonder) or is led by any reason whatever, he acts in virtue of the right of the political authority, not his own right (xvii.5–7; GIII/201–2).

It may seem as if Spinoza, at the beginning of this passage, distinguishes between the narrow case of compulsion by fear and the broader means by which a sovereign can gain acquiescence to his policies. Certainly he thinks that in comparison to other means of control fear does not work as well.[25] It tends to control tongues better than minds. However, in section 6 of the quote, he clearly includes this case with the other techniques to induce a belief: it is an action of the sovereign on the mind of the subject, which produces an effect (fear), which in turn causes the subject to act obediently. In every case the action of the sovereign is mediated by the judgment of the subject. Even in the case of the threat of direct physical pain, the subject must be thinking something like, "if I don't obey I may be subject to further pain and therefore I should not resist." This fear might cause the subject to revise some of those other beliefs—such as those that are the ostensible reason for the persecution and accompanying fear—in order to prevent future harm. Even if fear does not work as well as some other method, such as a required course of study, to achieve this change of thought, its mechanism does not seem conceptually distinct from that of other techniques. If so, then it is hard to see how Spinoza can distinguish between compulsion and persuasion.[26]

In an important respect, then, once Spinoza has identified natural right with power, once he has eliminated the free will, which can in principle resist the imposition of external causes, and once he has recognized that the sovereign may have powerful techniques at his disposal to induce belief indirectly, then he seems to have undercut his original argument or at least narrowed its scope to such an extent that it will not serve as a very robust justification for a tolerant policy. The question remains how Spinoza can use the distinction between freedom and constraint as the ground of the distinction between persuasion and compulsion.

Spinoza understands that what we perceive as contrary to our nature depends both on the fixed structures of our nature and on our individual constitution and experience. He writes, "It would be pointless to command a subject to hate someone who had joined the subject to himself by a benefit, or love someone who had harmed him, or not to be offended by insults, or not to desire to be freed from fear, and a great many other things of this kind, which necessarily follow from the laws of human nature" (xvii.2; GIII/201). We are persuaded by something when it aids our striving, which we understand in terms of our particular experience and goals. The persuasive idea fits relatively seamlessly into our mental and physical patterns. We are constrained when the idea does not. There is not always a hard and fast distinction between these two and we can imagine cases in which what appeared to be in our best interest later turned out not to be. Violence may accompany compulsion, and it may be easier as a consequence to mark an effect as coercive when it does, but it need not always do so.

What makes us difficult to constrain is not only our striving to persist in our natures, a fact about ourselves that we share with all individual things, including rocks, but precisely our complex and composite nature. This interpretation helps us make sense of the passage in which Spinoza says that "it must be granted that each person reserves many things to himself, that he is his own master in many things, which depend on no one's decision but his own" (xvii.4; GIII/201). Obviously Spinoza cannot be referring to a will that miraculously preserves our causal independence. Rather it is our unique constitution and the causal activity that follows from it which cannot be totally coerced unless we are simply killed. The sovereign needs to take the particular experiences of his subjects into account along with a general features of human nature. (And even then there will be much of us that escapes him.) The better the sovereign is able to do so, the more he knows us, the less his commands seem like an act of compulsion and the more they seem like an act of persuasion.

I would suggest, then, that the reason why the mind cannot be compelled is similar in structure to the argument in which it serves as a premise, the political argument for tolerance. Just as the state cannot be stable unless there is a certain degree of agreement among its constituent parts, so too the mind must maintain a certain fixed relationship among its parts. This agreement is the foundation of a single sovereign authority in a state and the foundation of personal identity in the mind. Just as the government cannot coerce its citizens without risking instability, it cannot coerce an individual mind without risking the destruction of that mind. Because those individual minds are just the entities that ultimately provide support for the state, the sovereign has an interest to cultivate their well-being rather than disrupt them, which would either destroy them or provoke their anger and possible rebellion. If the sovereign thinks of the mind of each of its subjects as a composite entity, whose components form a complex whole, then it ought not to force any of its elements to act contrary to their nature or in such a way as it would damage its relation to other parts. To do so risks destabilizing the very individual unities whose support he depends upon.

Because a sovereign power would need to use more complex and subtle means to exert control over its subjects, we would need to develop more subtle tools to distinguish between compulsion and persuasion in order to discover if the sovereign's action constitutes a violation of the individual's rights. Here we might add to Spinoza's account, using his own concepts, and establish the criteria of a rough test by which we could determine the degree of compulsion or persuasion. First of all, there would be a test of the *means* used to effect some change in the subject. Did the sovereign use violent means or some more subtle techniques? Even among non-violent means we might distinguish between rational and imaginative attempts to convince, such as appealing to the economic consequences of a policy, on the one hand, and its place within some national myth, on the other. Second, we ought to look at the *emotions* involved, both in the sovereign's attitude toward the subject and the subject's response. Was the sovereign moved to change the subject's mind through fear or through a more virtuous concern for the subject's well-being? Did the subject react by feeling fear or did it produce some sense of well-being or joy? Was the fear short lived or the joy long-lasting? Finally, we would need to examine the ideas themselves for their *truth value*. Do they bear up under rational scrutiny? Are they ideas whose truth cannot be determined in this world? Spinoza certainly believed that there were correlations between the different criteria. For instance, true ideas are achieved through geometric reasoning and produce an enduring joy in the subject. Violence, or the threat of it, produced fear and would be less likely to be rational in its effects. But this need not always be true. Sometimes we are fearful of the truth or made glad by false ideas. None of these alone would be a clear indicator of the degree of compulsion or persuasion involved but together we might be able have a rough gauge or even a blueprint for the empirical testing of the matter.[27]

Conclusion

If we are looking for a defense of toleration in light of a conception of natural right based on an idea of moral autonomy, then we will be frustrated with Spinoza. As such liberals might suspect, on closer examination, Spinoza's defense of toleration is weaker, and more liable to exceptions than it first seemed. Skeptics, who consider that the truth of a belief is irrelevant to the state, and that the sincerity of beliefs justifies their tolerance, would also be disappointed. While Spinoza acknowledges that individuals are all different and that our ideals of human nature are merely useful fictions, he does think that some ideas are truer than others and when we act on the basis of those ideas, whether in the political realm under the guidance of the sovereign, or in the personal realm, we are more likely to flourish.[28] On the other hand, those who would justify the persecution of heterodox beliefs might find his criticisms difficult to refute. Spinoza is a self-declared realist about both the function of the state and about human nature. He thinks that stability is the precondition of a state's freedom, and he grants the state appropriate powers over its citizens. He recognizes that individuals can be subject to enormous political pressure and are malleable. Yet he claims that self-interest and human complexity are enough to thwart the most scheming tyrants.

Spinoza does base his distinction between freedom and constraint on the distinction between internal and external causes and this may strike some as a conception of autonomy. However, Spinoza does not accept the metaphysics of free will that undergird at least some Kantian defenses of autonomy.[29] In any case, this limited idea of autonomy will probably not satisfy those who are seeking an irreducibly normative justification of toleration. While Spinoza may use the idea of natural rights as a functional equivalent of autonomy, he does not make this basic. As we have seen, an individual's natural right is in Spinoza's view ultimately the expression of his striving to persevere, i.e., the *conatus,* and so it is a claim about human nature that grounds his theory of rights. It is more appropriate to place Spinoza in the context of a virtue theory of value, in which the flourishing of a person's nature is the source of value, and our scientific inquiry into that nature and the conditions of its flourishing is an essential part of the philosophical enterprise of ethics. If we accept that as the framework for analyzing Spinoza's claim that belief cannot be compelled, then the normative ground of the argument for toleration will be stronger than its critics would have it.

Although Spinoza's argument has some important points in common with Locke's, it certainly has much wider application, and not simply in the sense that Spinoza extended toleration to Catholics while Locke apparently did not. Locke argued not only that the sovereign could not compel belief but also that the sovereign was no better to qualified to know the ultimate truths of religion than the ordinary man. Spinoza also makes this point, as we have seen. Locke's argument might work well in the case of religion, but it might fail if we extend it to other matters, of which arguably the sovereign could have better knowledge than his subjects. In contrast, Spinoza's argument gives a reason why the sovereign must be tolerant of the beliefs of its citizens about any number of things, precisely because he has shown how the beliefs are part of the striving (or actions) of those citizens and that the sovereign must take them into account if he is to be an effective ruler. This is where the set of distinctions made above comes into play. The sovereign need not remain neutral and does not refrain from trying to convince the public of some view or policy. Whether the sovereign is justified in endorsing some view and trying to convince the public of it will depend both on an analysis of its possible consequences for the public good, and also, more importantly for our purposes here, the means used to convince the public of it. However, the sovereign, and by extension anyone trying to change another's beliefs, must respect the natural rights of his subjects and interlocutors, which means that he must take into account the essential and acquired nature of the person and groups of persons, including a range of beliefs, desires, and dispositions to act. Tolerance is not merely a constraint on government but part of the art of governing itself. In this way, Spinoza's argument has more relevance to contemporary debates over toleration in which the issues go far beyond matters of religion.[30]

NOTES

1. John Locke, "A Letter Concerning Toleration," in *John Locke: Political Writings,* ed. David Wootton (New York: Mentor Books, 1993), 390–435.

2. Spinoza, *Theological-Political Treatise,* trans. E. Curley (manuscript). References to this work will be to chapter (roman numeral), and section number of this translation, followed by the relevant volume and page number of the *Spinoza Opera,* ed. C. Gebhardt (Heidelberg: Carl Winter Universitaetsbuchhandlung, 1972).

3. See John Christian Laursen, "Arming the State and Reining in the Magistrate," in *Difference and Dissent: Theories of Toleration in Medieval and Early Modern Europe,* eds. Cary J. Nederman and John Christian Laursen (Lanham: Rowan and Littlefield, 1996), 194.

4. J. I. Israel, *The Radical Enlightenment: Philosophy and the Making of Modernity 1650–1750* (Oxford: Oxford University Press, 2002).

5. Richard Tuck, "Scepticism and Toleration in the Seventeenth Cen-

tury," in *Justifying Toleration: Conceptual and Historical Perspectives,* ed. Susan Mendus (Cambridge: Cambridge University Press, 1988), 21–36.

6. Here it is important to make a further distinction. One might claim that belief can be compelled but that the sovereign ought not to do so, whether on pragmatic grounds (such as the attempt might produce more unrest than it is worth), or on theological grounds (such as only voluntary beliefs are valid for salvation). Spinoza is clearly making a stronger claim than that: "it *cannot happen* that a mind should be absolutely subject to the control of someone else" (my emphasis. xx.1–2; GIII/239).

7. Two historical studies I shall draw upon are: Joseph Lecler, *Toleration and the Reformation,* trans. T. L. Westow (New York: Association Press, 1960); and Mark Goldie, "Religious Intolerance in Restoration England," in *From Persecution to Toleration: The Glorious Revolution and Religion in England,* eds. O. P. Grell, J. I. Israel, and N. Tyacke (Oxford: Clarendon Press, 1991), 331–68.

8. See Steven Nadler, *Spinoza: A Life* (Cambridge: Cambridge University Press, 1999), 170–71.

9. Immediately after its publication in 1670 the TTP was seized from bookshops in many towns and suppressed. Two years after the overthrow of the Republican regime it was banned in 1674. See Jonathan I. Israel, *The Dutch Republic: Its Rise, Greatness, and Fall, 1477–1806* (Oxford: Oxford University Press, 1995), 920–21.

10. See Letter 44 to Jarig Jelles: "I . . . beg you most earnestly please to look into this, and, if possible, to stop the printing" in *The Letters,* trans. Samuel Shirley (Indianapolis: Hackett Publishing, 1995), 243.

11. See Jeremy Waldron, "Locke: Toleration and the Rationality of Persecution," in *John Locke: A Letter Concerning Toleration in Focus,* ed. John Horton and Susan Mendus (London: Routledge, 1991), 91–124.

12. For a more detailed discussion of this argument, see my article "Spinoza's Republican Argument for Toleration," *The Journal of Political Philosophy,* volume 11 (3), September 2003, 320–35.

13. From Epistle 93, quoted in Lecler, volume 1, 57.

14. This does not mean for Bayle that there is no truth of the matter, but rather that all we humans have is our good conscience. As Thomas M. Lennon puts it, "integrity in the search for truth, rather than the truth itself, is the basis of Bayle's moral theory" (*Reading Bayle* [Toronto: University of Toronto Press, 1999], 100).

15. Quoted in Goldie, 347.

16. See Augustine's Letter 93 to the Donatist Bishop Vincent, quoted in Lecler, volume 1, 56.

17. See E. M. Curley, *Spinoza's Metaphysics: An Essay in Interpretation* (Cambridge: Harvard University Press, 1969), chapter 2.

18. Spinoza, *Ethics,* in *The Collected Works of Spinoza,* volume 1, ed. and trans. Edwin Curley (Princeton: Princeton University Press, 1985). References to this work are in the style adopted by the *Cambridge Companion to Spinoza,* with part, proposition/definition/axiom, number, etc. (see xii–xiii).

19. Consistent with this idea we find that in the TTP we do not find Spinoza using the word beliefs in this context at all, but rather thoughts [*cognitio*]. Interestingly enough, in chapter xiv of the TTP, when he discusses the dogmas of universal faith [*fidei universalis dogmata*], those things in which we traditionally believe, he interprets them as ideas that are kinds of action, not theoretical propositions at all.

20. Letter 77, *The Letters,* 345.

21. Letter 56, *The Letters,* 276–77.

22. There is the further problem for this account, as noted by Isaiah Berlin in his famous essay "Two Concepts of Liberty" (in *Four Essays on Liberty* [Oxford: Oxford University Press, 1984], 118–72) that the sovereign may feel justified in coercion through claiming knowledge of the subject's essence. In Spinoza's case this worry is mitigated by the formal insistence on the natural right of the subject and the practical significance of what I call accidental or second nature in the constitution of the subject. Moreover, as we shall see below, this account helps us understand how a sovereign, who endeavors to understand something about the essential and accidental natures of its subjects, will become a more effective ruler.

23. Modern accounts of torture emphasize just this point, i.e., that the goal of torture is to destroy, first the individual's solidarity with others, and then second, the person's very sense of self. See Elaine Scarry, *The Body in Pain: The Making and Unmaking of the World* (Oxford: Oxford University Press, 1985).

24. See Lecler, 56–57.

25. As he writes, "It follows that the ruler who has the greatest authority is the one who reigns in the hearts of his subjects. If the person who was most feared had the greatest authority, then surely the subjects of Tyrants would have it, for they are most feared by their tyrants" (xvii.8; GIII/202).

26. The question is further complicated by the fact that in at least one place in the TTP Spinoza uses the verb *cogere* (to compel, constrain) in both a philosophical and legal context: "Nor is it credible that . . . Moses would have taught them anything other than a way of living—and that not as a Philosopher, so that after some time they might be constrained to live well [*ut coacti essent bene vivere*] from freedom of mind, but as a Leg-

islator, so that they would be constrained [*coacti*] by the command of the Law to live well" (ii.46; GIII/41).

27. As a corollary of this point we might introduce a typology of means of persuasion. There is rational persuasion, when adequate ideas are used along with the active affect of joy; semi-rational persuasion, when there is a combination of adequate and inadequate ideas plus active and passive affects; irrational persuasion, when inadequate ideas and passive affects alone are used. The precise content of these categories, especially the mixed categories with the imagination, would be historically contingent. So it might, for example, appear rational to have some belief in God as a prerequisite to public discourse in one domain but not in another. It would depend on the set of background beliefs that people contingently hold. This flexibility is precisely what some liberal views lack and explains their failure in a cross-cultural context.

28. On this point see my article "Tolerance as a Virtue in Spinoza's *Ethics*," in *Journal of the History of Philosophy*, volume 39 (4), October 2001, 535–57, especially section 4.

29. It should be noted that there are some interesting parallels in Spinoza with those who eschew Kant's complicated attempts to justify freedom metaphysically and instead rely upon his two-standpoint theory and the pragmatic position of the moral agent. In the TTP, Spinoza writes, "That universal consideration concerning fate and the connection of causes cannot help us to form and order our thoughts concerning particular things. Moreover, we are completely ignorant of the very order and connection of things, i.e., of how things are really ordered and connected. So for practical purposes it is better, indeed necessary, to consider things as possible" (iv.4; GIII/57).

30. An earlier version of this paper was presented to the Department of Philosophy at the University of Washington. I would also like to thank Janelle S. Taylor for her helpful comments.

3

PIERRE BAYLE'S REFLEXIVE THEORY OF TOLERATION

RAINER FORST

> My design is to make a Commentary of a new genre, built on principles more general and more infallible than everything that the study of languages, criticism, or commonplace could afford me.[1]

Pierre Bayle is generally seen as one of the most important theorists of toleration in the classical period of the late seventeenth century, but his work stands in the shadow of his contemporaries John Locke and Baruch de Spinoza. His argument is mostly regarded as a radical—and somewhat exaggerated—plea for the liberty of conscience.[2] A proper appreciation of Bayle's contribution to the discourse of toleration, however, shows that his approach stands out by adding a reflexive dimension to the question of the justification of toleration not to be found in either Locke or Spinoza. Bayle clearly saw that any argument for a general duty of mutual toleration had to rest on normative grounds accessible to and valid for believers of quite different faiths (or of no faith) as well as on a conception of faith that leads to religious self-restraint without implying skepticism (to mention the second important interpretation of his thought that is misleading).[3] This approach, in a reconstructed form, is an essential reference point for any contemporary attempt to justify toleration (and its limits). At least, this is what I want to argue.[4]

To fully understand Bayle, however, we need to go back historically to the most important source for arguments for as well against toleration in the Christian tradition, to Augustine. In addition, a brief look at the debate between Locke and his critic Jonas

Proast will serve as a contrast in order to see how far Bayle's conception avoids the problems of a classic defense of the freedom of conscience. But to start with, a few words about the concept of toleration.

Toleration: Concept and Conceptions

The general concept of toleration can be explained by the three components of *objection, acceptance,* and *rejection.*[5] First, a tolerated belief or practice has to be judged as false or bad in order to be a candidate for toleration; second, apart from these reasons for objection there have to be reasons why it would still be wrong not to tolerate these false or bad beliefs or practices, i.e., reasons of acceptance. Such reasons do not eliminate the reasons of objection; rather, they trump them in a given context. And third, there have to be reasons for rejection which mark the limits of toleration. These limits lie where reasons of acceptance run out, so to speak. All three of those reasons can be of one and the same kind —religious, for example—yet they can also be of different kinds (moral, religious, or pragmatic, to mention a few possibilities).

Obviously, this definition is very general, and the problems begin once these components are fleshed out: what can or should be tolerated, for what reasons, and where are the limits of toleration? Toleration as such is what I call a *normatively dependent concept,* one that is in need of other, independent normative resources in order to gain a certain content and substance—and in order to be something good at all. Hence the most important point about a theory of the justification of toleration is how the three components are provided with content. And it is here, as we will see, that Bayle has something special to offer: he suggests a way to understand the components of acceptance and rejection that uses the very logic of justification built into the question of toleration without reducing the component of objection in a skeptical fashion.

Historically and systematically speaking, a number of different conceptions of toleration have developed (which can be combined with different justifications for toleration). The first one I call the *permission conception.* According to it, toleration is a relation between an authority or a majority and a dissenting, "different" minority (or various minorities). Toleration means that the authority gives qualified permission to the minority to live according to their beliefs on the condition that the minority accepts the dominant position of the authority or majority. As long as their being different remains within limits, that is, is a "private" matter, and as long as the groups do not claim equal public and political status, they can be tolerated on primarily pragmatic grounds—because this form of toleration is the least costly of all possible alternatives and does not disturb civil peace and order as the dominant party defines it. The permission conception is a classic one that we find in many historical instances of a politics of toleration (such as the Edict of Nantes in 1598) and that—to a considerable extent—still informs our understanding of the term. It is what led Goethe to call toleration an "insult."[6]

The second conception, the *coexistence conception*, is similar to the first one in regarding toleration as the best means to end or avoid conflict and to pursue one's own goals. What is different, however, is the constellation between the subjects and the objects of toleration. For now the situation is not one of an authority or majority in relation to a minority, but one of groups, roughly equal in power, who see that for the sake of social peace toleration is the best of all possible alternatives. They prefer peaceful coexistence to conflict and agree to a certain modus vivendi.

In contrast to this, the third conception of toleration—the *respect conception*—is one in which the tolerating parties recognize each other as equal citizens of a state in which members of all groups—majority or minorities—should have equal legal and political status. Even though in their ethical beliefs about the good and true way of life and in their cultural practices they differ remarkably and hold incompatible views, they respect each other as equals in the sense that their common framework of social life should—as far as fundamental questions of the recognition of rights and liberties and the distribution of resources are concerned—be guided by norms that all parties can equally accept and that do not favor one specific "ethical community," so to speak.

In debates on toleration, one finds alongside the conceptions discussed thus far a fourth one, which I call the *esteem conception*. This implies an even fuller, more demanding notion of mutual recognition between citizens, for according to this conception being tolerant does not just mean respecting members of other cultural life-forms or religions as moral and political equals, it also means having some kind of (partial) ethical esteem for these life-forms as valuable social options.

Bayle's thinking about toleration, as we will see, moves between the first and the third conception; in fact, it represents a combination of the two, arguing for social toleration of respect and for political toleration according to the permission conception. But before this can be discussed, the main reference points for Bayle need to be identified—in the first place, Augustine.

Augustine and the Dialectics of Christian Toleration

Bayle's most important treatise on toleration, the *Commentaire philosophique sur ces paroles de Jésus-Christ "Contrain-les d'entrer"* (1685) —written in the year in which Louis XIV revoked the Edict of Nantes and in which Bayle's brother died in a French prison at the hands of the "convertists" while Bayle himself had fled to the Huguenot community in Rotterdam[7]—is an attempt to systematically refute the reasons that could be given for the exercise of religious force. And while there are many contemporaries whom he attacks in these pages—Bishop Bossuet on the one hand, but also fellow Huguenot radicals such as (his former friend and later enemy)[8] Pierre Jurieu—it is Augustine's defense of the duty of intolerance which Bayle sees as the greatest challenge. And rightly so, as we shall see, for, being aware of Augustine's arguments, Bayle already knew of the weaknesses of an argument for the freedom of conscience that Locke only saw when confronted with Proast's critique.

In his major works, Augustine presents a number of important, paradigmatic arguments for toleration, building upon the works of Tertullian and Cyprian, especially.[9] First, he proposes toleration motivated by Christian neighborly *love*. Aware of one's own weak and imperfect human nature as well as of that of others, one is called upon to be patient and tolerant with respect to others' mistakes and sins. Toleration is both a sign of charity and love as well as of inner strength and faith in the face of hardship and evil, following the example of Jesus. Toleration out of love hence also includes those who are your enemies and who fight against the true church.[10]

Second, Augustine uses the argument of the *two kingdoms* in a particular way. On earth, the kingdom of God and that of the world are intertwined, and it is not up to men, with their finite powers of judgment, to disentangle them and to find who is following the right path and who is to be punished for his sins. The biblical parable of the wheat and the weeds (Matthew 13, 24ff.) serves to illustrate this point: Jesus admonishes his followers not to pull out the weeds (inserted by the devil) before due time, for the danger of destroying parts of the wheat was too great. The time of the harvest is not the time of humans, the final judgment not theirs but that of God—and there will be "weeping there, and grinding of teeth."[11] Worldly toleration thus gains its strength from faith in divine justice.

Third, toleration is seen as a means to preserve Christian and church *unity*. The good of the unity of Christians in God is so important that it commands toleration of heretics and the attempt to convince them of the truth with patience and softness, so as to avoid open conflict and possible schism. Those who tolerate such evil are to be praised "because they bear for the sake of unity what they hate for the sake of justice, to prevent the name of Christ from being blasphemed by vile schism."[12]

Fourth, and finally, the argument for the *freedom of conscience* that is not to be and also cannot be forced into a certain belief is of special importance. Only personal faith based on true and authentic inner conviction is pleasing to God; he is insulted by hypocritical or indoctrinated believers. More than that, the workings of conscience are such that it cannot be forced to believe something without true conviction: *credere non potest nisi volens.*[13] Again, it is important to see that it is the very respect for God that carries the normative thrust of the argument: subjective conscience is not something to be respected for its own sake or for the sake of some kind of "autonomy"; rather, it is respect for God which demands the freedom of conscience, even of those who are in error.

In the course of the enduring and bitter violent conflicts with the schismatic sect of the so-called Donatists during Augustine's time as Bishop of Hippo in Northern Africa, however, his views changed and he developed a counter-theory to his own arguments, one which turned the *same* reasons for toleration into reasons for the *duty of intolerance*. First, consider reasons of *love*. Christian love of one's neighbor (or enemy) cannot imply, Augustine argues, standing by and watching him ruin himself, befallen by a deadly sickness:

> If anyone were to see an enemy, delirious with dangerous fever, running headlong, would he not be returning evil for evil if he let him go, rather than if he took means to have him picked up and restrained? Yet he would seem to the man himself most hateful and most hostile when he had proved himself most helpful and most considerate. But, when he recovered his health, his thanks would be lavish in proportion to his former feeling of injury at not being let alone.[14]

Augustine goes on to cite examples of former Donatists, reconverted to the true church, thanking him for being saved, even if that had required the use of force, and he concludes: "Love mingled with severity is better than deceit with indulgence."[15] Tolerance out of love turns into its opposite if it does not heed the call to save the soul of someone in deadly error, and hence intolerance, combined with the use of fear,[16] can be the sign of true and selfless love.

In accordance with this, Augustine develops the doctrine of "benevolent force," which says that "the point to be considered is not whether anyone is being forced to do something, but what sort of thing he is being forced to do, whether it is good or bad."[17] This implies a twofold reconsideration of the argument of the *two kingdoms*. First, it must be possible to disentangle the threads of the good and the bad on earth, and second, it becomes a task of secular justice, i.e., of the state (in the service of the church), to strengthen the truth and punish those who are sinfully wrong. By rejecting the true church, Augustine writes to the Donatists, they show that "you yourselves are the tares and, what is worse, you have cut yourselves off from the good seed before the time."[18] Schism and heresy are seen as crimes that fall within the realm of secular justice, not just because they lead to civil unrest and violence but also because they are crimes comparable to that of poisoning others.[19] And since secular power derives from God, it must pursue the path of truth and of the unity of the church.

The argument of the preservation of *unity* through toleration also falls into a similar dialectics. If the schismatic "madness" becomes too strong, then the use of force may be the only means to stop it. It is here that Augustine refers to the (in)famous biblical parable of "compel them to come in" (Luke 14, 16ff.)—the story of the master of the house who asks his servants to force those who were invited and still do not want to participate in the prepared supper to come in. Augustine thus asks the Donatists: "Do you think that no one should be forced to do right, when you read that the master of the house said to his servants: 'Whomever you find, compel them to come in' (. . .)."[20] This argument was to become a constant reference point in the discourse of justifying religious force, and it is what Bayle directly addresses in the title of his *Commentaire philosophique*.

Finally, Augustine rethinks the argument for the *freedom of conscience* in that context. Most important is that he does not retract the idea that true faith must rest on one's own insight and inner conviction; yet he now argues that *terror* can be useful in bringing about such an insight into the truth. Conscience thus *can* be and also *may* be the object of force, if properly justified and exercised.

> Not that anyone can be good against his will, but, by fear of enduring what he does not want, he either gives up the hatred that stands in his way, or he is compelled to recognize the truth he did not know. So, through fear, he repudiates the false doctrine that he formerly defended, or he seeks the truth which he did not know, and he willingly holds now what he formerly denied. It would perhaps be useless to say this in any number of words if it were not shown by so many examples.[21]

He goes on to cite a number of examples of successful reconversions to affirm that his earlier position against the use of force to influence conscience has changed "by reason of proved facts."[22] In Augustine's eyes, these facts empirically falsify the argument that conscience cannot be influenced by force, though it is still true that beliefs cannot be directly "implanted" from without. But fear is a major power in freeing men from false beliefs and in opening their eyes to the truth, embracing it "from within" if properly guided. Hence there is no independent argument for the freedom of conscience, neither empirically nor normatively speaking; there is no "freedom to err" as there is no freedom to kill one's soul.[23]

From his profound knowledge of St. Augustine and the many further medieval as well as modern interpretations of this form of Christian perfectionism (which regarded the care for the soul of the other as the most important Christian duty—a duty owed to God in the first place and not to men), Bayle was aware of the challenge this doctrine posed, both on a normative as well as on an epistemological level. Locke, however, was not; at least not before he encountered Proast's critique.

Locke, Proast, and Authentic Faith

Locke's *Letter Concerning Toleration,* written at the same time as Bayle's *Commentaire* in Dutch exile[24] and also influenced by the revocation of the Edict of Nantes as well as by the inauguration of a Catholic king in England, may not be the most original, but is surely the most influential of the classic texts on toleration.[25] The main arguments he presented had been known and used before, yet Locke gave them a paradigmatic and powerful form, grounded in a view of human beings as God's "property" and thus having certain inalienable rights of liberty, political as well as religious, that cannot be handed over to a human authority.

Locke's first *Letter* is a complex text which contains a number of different considerations to make the case for toleration by the state as well as by citizens and institutions, especially churches. The central idea is that it is in the superior interest of a human being to take care of his immortal soul so as to achieve salvation; this is the "highest Obligation" a human being has towards himself as a being created by God (hence ultimately it is a duty owed to God).[26] According to Locke's Protestant conception of this duty, no other human being or institution has any authority regarding the relation between an individual and God: each one stands alone before God, on the basis of his own conviction and conscience.

In a further step, Locke distinguishes this "highest" interest in salvation from "civil" interests which the state has to take care of, such as the protection of life, liberty and possessions. Explaining this essential distinction, Locke gives a number of reasons. First, an individual *cannot* hand over spiritual authority to a human institution "because it appears not that God has ever given any such Authority to one Man over another."[27] This is an authority reserved for God, and even if men wanted to, they could not entrust it to other men, for only God can bring about true belief. Conscience is free, in a sense, because it is not free: it belongs to God (as had been taught by Luther).[28]

Second, again, human beings *cannot* leave the care for their soul to another, yet now not for a religious, but for an epistemological reason: "For no Man can, if he would, conform his Faith to the Dictates of another. All the Life and Power of true Religion consists in the inward and full perswasion of the mind; and Faith is not Faith without believing."[29] Human power simply is void when it comes to producing inner belief and authentic faith; the mind is an autonomous entity.

Third, an individual *must not* leave the determination of his or her faith to another, for that would be a sin to God, "Contempt of his Divine Majesty."[30] In matters of faith, the individual is not fully autonomous, for he or she has to seek authentic belief.

Furthermore, it would be very *unwise* to leave matters of salvation to others, for they have no superior knowledge of the true path towards salvation, and they might have other interests in guiding one on a path as they see fit, thus possibly leading one astray. The point about the limits of human knowledge concerning truth is important here, though it is not a skeptical one. For it does not doubt the legitimacy of belief in one's church being the true one, nor does it doubt that there is one true way to salvation[31]—it only doubts that this is anything but a matter of individual or collective belief: "For every Church is orthodox to it self; to others, Erroneous or Heretical."[32]

There are a number of other considerations for toleration besides these most important ones that Locke mentions, such as Christian charity and striving for unity, the chance that truth will manifest itself on its own, without guidance, and reflections on the proper means for civil peace.

Still, the question remains which of the above mentioned major reason is the most important one, and it is a question that

Locke himself poses in the *Letter*, at three points. In the first passage important in this respect, Locke grants for the sake of the argument that human power could in fact change the minds of men, and stresses the epistemological truth-relativizing argument for toleration:

> The care of the Salvation of Mens Souls cannot belong to the Magistrate; because, though the rigour of Laws and the force of Penalties were capable to convince and change Mens minds, yet would not that help at all to the Salvation of their Souls. For there being but one Truth, one way to Heaven; what Hopes is there that more Men would be led into it, if they had no Rule but the Religion of the Court.[33]

In a second passage, things are exactly reversed. Even if the epistemological restraint argument were not valid, he says there, the true church still would have no legitimate secular power to force conscience:

> If it could be manifest which of these two dissenting Churches were in the right, there would not accrue thereby unto the Orthodox any Right of destroying the other. For Churches have neither any Jurisdiction in worldly matters, nor are Fire and Sword any proper Instruments wherewith to convince mens minds of Errour, and inform them of the Truth.[34]

A third passage, then, has to bring clarity. Here, Locke finally stresses his main reason for toleration:

> But after all, the principal Consideration, and which absolutely determines this Controversie, is this. Although the Magistrates Opinion in Religion be sound, and the way that he appoints be truly Evangelical, yet if I be not thoroughly perswaded thereof in my own mind, there will be no safety for me in following it. No way whatsoever that I shall walk in, against the Dictates of my Conscience, will ever bring me to the Mansions of the Blessed. . . . Faith only, and inward Sincerity, are the things that procure acceptance with God.[35]

Toleration thus is a duty out of respect for the only kind of belief or faith that makes one worthy in the eyes of God, namely sincere and authentic belief, and such faith *cannot* and *therefore must not* be compelled by external force.[36] Conscience is autonomous in seeking the truth when it comes to human authority, yet guided by God and heteronomous when it comes to following the truth. Only sincere beliefs arrived at by one's own lights can be pleasing to God; hypocrisy is a grave sin. Hence Locke's main argument for toleration turns out to be very close to the one that already figured most prominently in Augustine: *Credere non potest nisi volens.* And since this is so, one can also anticipate the counterarguments against it, and it did not take long until they were presented forcefully (though without any explicit reference to Augustine).

In 1690, the Anglican priest Jonas Proast published his *The Argument of the Letter Concerning Toleration Briefly Consider'd and Answer'd,* the central counterargument of which clearly locates Locke's main point and its main weakness. Proast does not deny that sincere faith cannot be produced by external force:

> I readily grant that Reason and Arguments are the only proper Means, whereby to induce the mind to assent to any Truth, which is not evident by its own Light: and that Force is very improper to be used to that end instead of Reason and Arguments.[37]

But then he argues that force—Augustine would have said "terror"—can still be very efficient *indirectly* for the purpose of bringing human beings to the truth, namely as a liberating, eye-opening force:

> But notwithstanding this, if Force be used, not in stead of Reason and Arguments, i.e. not to convince by its own proper Efficacy (which it cannot do), but onely to bring men to consider those Reasons and Arguments which are proper and sufficient to convince them, but which, without being forced, they would not consider: who can deny, but that *indirectly* and *at a distance,* it does some service toward the bringing men to embrace that Truth, which otherwise, either through Carelesness and Negligence they would never acquaint themselves with, or through

> Prejudice they would reject and condemn unheard, under the notion of Errour?[38]

Since human beings tend to be careless and full of prejudices when it comes to religious beliefs, Proast argues that it is the true duty of a Christian to lay "Thorns and Briars" in their wrong ways so as to force them to turn around and to make "a wiser and more rational Choice."[39] According to Proast, the method of using the right kind of force for the right reasons has been used many times with good success, and hence if there are no other means to break men loose from their false ideas and beliefs, then this is what needs to be done. It is thus obvious, he concludes, that "outward Force is neither *useless* nor *needless* for the bringing Men to do, what the saving of their Souls may require of them."[40] Furthermore, this kind of care for the soul is the task of government, according to Proast, for what kind of human interest could be more important than that of being brought to the true faith?

Locke's response to Proast, his *Second Letter Concerning Toleration* (1690), shows two things. First, the weakness of his "principal consideration" for toleration, as pointed out by Proast, becomes obvious, yet, second, Locke has alternative arguments at his disposal to challenge Proast—alternatives that bring him close to the position Bayle had argued for.[41] He admits that external force can "do some service indirectly and by accident,"[42] yet he doubts that this can be achieved generally by certain politics, and he also points out that the distinction between "indirect" and "direct" force is very hard to make. Furthermore, he argues that as a consequence of Proast's view there will be a general persecution of all religious dissenters, for it will not be possible to sort out those who are "careless" in their religious faith from others who are sincere.

Still, he sees that his main original argument that true belief cannot be brought about by external force and thus that such force is useless (and therefore wrong, given the demand for sincere belief) cannot carry the weight he thought it could. For there may be many forms of "indirect" force and "education" that can change the minds of human beings so that they give up old and acquire new convictions "from the inside"; and these new beliefs formed under such conditions may be as "sincere" and "authentic" as others. The censorship of "false" teachings is just one example of such "indirect" forms of influence: it "liberates" the public from bad influences without exercising direct "productive" pressure or indoctrination.

As a consequence, Locke revises his argument in two directions, building upon his first *Letter.* First, the epistemological restraint-imperative is brought to the fore, and second, a normative argument is presented that implies that any use of force, especially in the political realm, is in need of mutual and general justification. Taken together, these two arguments mean that in a religious dispute, no side has good reasons to declare its own convictions the only "truth" and impose it on others by legal or political means. Accordingly, Locke directly attacks Proast's "lurking presupposition, that the national religion now in England, backed by the public authority of the law, is the only true religion."[43] And he asks him to put forward a mutually justifiable argument "without supposing all along your church in the right, and your religion the true; which can no more be allowed to you in this case, whatever your church or religion be, than it can to a papist or a Lutheran, a presbyterian or an anabaptist; nay, no more to you, than it can be allowed to a Jew or a Mahometan."[44] For each church claims to be the true church, Locke says, and simply to give the dominant one the power to exercise force would be to legitimize many forms of persecution, in many countries, often to the detriment of Christians. Thus Locke's theory takes a *reflexive* turn, no longer relying on a particular notion of conscience or salvation but on the principle of justification: every form of exercising political force is in need of mutual justification, and in a stand-off between two or more religious parties, such justification does not exist, because for the finite human mind no proof as to the true faith can be attained. The principle of justification at work here is a basic principle of mutual respect, and its application to the case of religion rests on an epistemological claim about the special nature of religious truth claims.[45]

In the ensuing controversy, which I will not go into here, Proast and Locke focused on exactly that point, which Proast quickly identified as the main challenge, trying to force Locke to be on the defensive for appearing as an apostate.[46] In response, Locke affirms that deep and firm *belief* in the true religion is one thing, while *knowing* it to be true quite another—"faith it is still, and not knowledge; persuasion, and not certainty."[47] On the basis of that argument he claims that "every man has a right to toleration"[48]—and that there is a general duty of toleration. As we will see, by that he has moved towards the position Bayle had defended some years earlier, in a superior form.

By overcoming the traditional argument for the liberty of conscience, this Baylean position not only avoided Augustinian or Proastian counterarguments. It also avoided a number of further pitfalls, such as

- that the idea of tolerating "sincere and authentic" beliefs might imply that only such beliefs ought to be tolerated, and that arbitrary criteria could be used to determine sincerity and authenticity, narrowing the realm of the tolerable;[49] and
- that the idea of the "unfree free conscience" is exclusive of persons who either have no such religious conscience, such as atheists, or who are willing to bind their conscience to an innerworldly authority, such as Catholics.

In his discussion of the limits of toleration, Locke indeed argues against tolerating these two groups, yet for reasons that he defines as political rather than religious. As was quite common given the background of conflicts with Rome (and Catholic nations such as Spain), Locke sees no grounds for tolerating a church that assumes the power of being able to excommunicate a king or that claims political and religious authority over its members, possibly making them subject to "another Prince."[50] That expresses a general prejudice against Catholics as possible traitors: they can claim no liberty of conscience, for their conscience turns them into disloyal subjects. In the text, however, Locke chooses to refer to the "Mufti of Constantinople" rather than to the Pope to make that point.

As far as atheists are concerned, Locke also makes a sweeping general claim as to why they are not to be tolerated:

> Those are not at all to be tolerated who deny the Being of a God. Promises, Covenants, and Oaths, which are the Bonds of Humane Society, can have no hold upon an Atheist. The taking away of God, tho but even in thought, dissolves all. Besides also, those that by their Atheism undermine and destroy all Religion, can have no pretence of Religion whereupon to challenge the Privilege of a Toleration.[51]

The fear that Locke expresses here—we can call it "Locke's fear," though we find it in many authors before as well as after Locke, even in a number of Enlightenment thinkers such as Montesquieu, Voltaire, and Rousseau—implies that, without a religious idea of a divine force of justice (and punishment), human beings will not accept the authority of the precepts of morality as binding imperatives. There is no morality on earth without the love and fear of God. Hence persons who do not share that fear are to be feared themselves: they cannot be trusted as fellow citizens, for they will break the law and moral norms as soon as they see fit and profitable.

We see here one side of the restrictions that a Christian founding of morality implies, while with Augustine we already saw another. Locke restricts the community of those who can be trustworthy *moral subjects* to those who share the right kind of faith in divine justice, whereas Augustine held a certain qualified view of *moral objects*: the object of Christian moral concern and care was not the "person" as an individual that was to be morally respected; rather, it was the soul of a human being that commanded respect and special care—even if that meant exercising force upon the person. In both ways, morality is *grounded* in as well as *limited* by religious belief—ultimately, it is the respect for God that grounds as well as limits moral respect and concern. Thus even if Locke strives to overcome the Augustinian conception of moral concern by stressing the individuality of faith and salvation, he also restricts morality due to its Christian foundations. An atheist cannot act morally out of the proper motives, and thus he or she cannot be treated morally in the proper sense, for one cannot fully trust him or her.

If we pull these various threads of argument together, we find that a reflexive case for a *universal duty of toleration* has to

- rest on moral foundations not committed to (and limited by) a particular faith that is reasonably disputed among followers of different religious doctrines; for only then can this duty apply to every person as a moral agent, and every person be seen as someone to be equally respected;
- be combined with an epistemological argument about the special character of religious truth claims that have to be possible as well as limited to the realm of faith; and
- provide an argument concerning the limits of toleration that is not one-sided but that can be generally justified.

These components, taken together, provide the best justification for the respect conception of toleration (see section 1 above), while the argument for the liberty of conscience does not. For apart from its internal problems, that argument is easily compatible with the hierarchical permission conception of toleration. From that vantage point, finally, we can assess the originality and power of Bayle's contribution to the discourse of toleration. It proceeds in three steps, connected to three of his main works.

The Society of Atheists

In December of 1680, the appearance of a comet was seen by many as a sign and message from God, mostly interpreted as a presage of misfortune. For Bayle, strongly influenced by Descartes and Malebranche, it was nothing but a phenomenon of nature, as he explained in his *Lettres sur la Comète* in 1682 (one year later expanded as *Pensées diverses sur la Comète*).[52] What makes this text one of the most remarkable in the history of political philosophy, however, is a long passage in which Bayle treats the question of atheism. In it, he not only puts forth the thesis that idolatry, superstition, and fanaticism are evils worse than atheism, he also explains that it is not the fear of God that makes people act morally, and that a society of atheists would be viable and possibly more peaceful than one based on a religion prone to conflict and violence—and while in the beginning of the passage it is pagan religions that are thus criticized, in the course of Bayle's discussion it is Christianity that is increasingly the object of critique. This is the opposite of what I called "Locke's fear" above, and because it seemed so outrageous at the time, it has been called "Bayle's paradox."[53]

The reason, Bayle argues, why atheism is generally seen as the greatest crime and cause of civil disorder is "a false prejudice concerning the lights of the conscience."[54] The general idea that belief in divine providence and the fear of divine justice motivate persons to act morally has been proven to be false according to Bayle, and he cites a number of examples such as the Christian crusades or the St. Bartholomew's Eve Massacre—which, he adds, would not have been possible in an atheist monarchy.[55] Experience shows that human beings generally do not act according to the principles of "natural equity," common to all reasonable persons, but on the basis of desires, passions, and habits. Many of these are negative, though some do make human beings follow the precepts of morality, if only externally, the most powerful of which are the fear of punishment by law or fear of the loss of social recognition. And this holds true generally, for "Jew and Mohammedan, Turk and Moor, Christian and Infidel, Indian and Tartar."[56] In this context, Bayle formulates the argument for the society of atheists, comparing it to the many crimes committed by religious people:

> It follows manifestly from this that the inclination to act badly is not found in a soul destitute of the knowledge of God any more than in a soul that knows God; and that a soul destitute of the knowledge of God is no freer of the brake that represses the malignity of the heart than is a soul that has this knowledge. It follows from this in addition that the inclination to act badly comes from the ground of man's nature and that it is strengthened by the passions. . . . Finally, it follows from this that the inclination to pity, to sobriety, to good-natured conduct, and so forth, does not stem from the fact that one knows there to be a God . . . but from a certain disposition of the temperament, fortified by education, by personal interest, by the desire to be praised, by the instinct of reason, or by similar motives that are met with in an atheist as well as in other men.[57]

Bayle not only believes in the similarity of negative and positive passions and desires that make human beings act against or in accordance with morality, whether they believe in God or not, he also believes—in a proto-Kantian fashion[58]—that they possess an independent faculty of reason which allows them to tell right from wrong; and he furthermore states that acting morally in the proper sense would be to act out of such an insight into what is right. Examples of ancient philosophers like Epicurus and Seneca "make me believe that reason without the knowledge of God can sometimes persuade a man that there are decent things which it is fine and laudable to do, not on the account of the utility of doing so, but because this is in conformity with reason." And he goes on to affirm that even though God does not reveal himself "fully" to an atheist, "he does not fail to act upon the latter's mind and to preserve for him that reason and intelligence by means of which all men understand the truth of the first principles of metaphysics and morals."[59]

The argument for the autonomy of reason, theoretical and practical, with regard to first principles will be essential for his justification of toleration, developed in his *Commentaire philosophique.* For only if there is a common basis of reasonable argument and insight, both in the sphere of truth claims and of moral claims, can there be a shared ground for justifying and limiting toleration —beyond the various doctrines in conflict with each other. He thereby follows a development in the discourse of toleration prepared by writers such as the humanist Sebastian Castellio: on the basis of a new understanding of the moral person that would challenge the traditional Christian view, they argued for the respect of human beings apart from what they believed in.[60] Hence, against Calvinist justifications for intolerance and persecution Castellio affirmed that "to kill a man does not mean to defend a doctrine but to kill a man."[61] Bayle is the first to fully draw out the consequence of this: both with respect to human beings as objects of respect and as subjects of morality, there has to be an independent insight into the demands of morality common to all human beings. This insight is what those who argue for the general duty of mutual toleration appeal to. Thus, while Locke tried to change the traditional language of caring for and saving the soul for the purpose of toleration, Bayle thought that there had to be a moral language apart from that idiom which made clear why persecuting people could never be justified with an appeal to God or salvation.

Justifying Toleration

Bayle's *Commentaire* is the most thorough and radical attempt to refute possible arguments for religious force and persecution, many of which are based on interpretations of the parable of the *compelle intrare* that Augustine presented (which is why the saying figures prominently in the title).[62] Written at the height of the persecution of his fellow Huguenots in France, Bayle's text is a fervent accusation of "papist" persecution, yet speaking in the voice of an (invented) Englishman, Bayle also takes sides against Calvinist radicals such as Jurieu, arguing for what he considers to be a higher-order justification for toleration. He considers it "childish" to determine the moral rightness of actions on the basis of particular—and irreconcilable—beliefs about belonging to the "true church," regarding the others to be in grave error: "Will anyone ever make them understand what everyone sees clearly, that nothing is more ridiculous than reasoning by always assuming the thing in question?"[63]

Hence the treatise begins where the *Pensées diverses* left off, i.e., with the argument for an autonomous morality. God gave human beings the "natural light" of "universal reason which enlightens all spirits and which is never lacking to those who attentively consult it."[64] While this light conveys the principles of logic and metaphysics as well as of morality, there is a difference between the two realms relevant for the question of religion, for "if it's possible to have certain limitations with respect to speculative truths, I don't believe there ought to be any with regard to those practical and general principles which concern morals."[65] Universal moral precepts thus form a kind of "natural religion," and any interpretation of the gospel that would violate these precepts—such as the "convertist" interpretation of the *compelle intrare*—is therefore false. When it comes to issues of metaphysical speculation, biblical interpretation must of course proceed on the basis of reason, yet there is room for deep disagreement, while in the sphere of the practical there is no such leeway. Yet since passions and prejudice obscure the ideas of "natural equity," Bayle thinks a certain mode of moral reflection is necessary, which he describes in an almost Kantian (if not to say Rawlsian) way:

> I would like whoever aims at knowing distinctly this natural light with respect to morality to raise himself above his own private interest or the custom of his country, and to ask himself in general: "Is such a practice just in itself? If it were a question of introducing it in a country where it would not be in use and where he would be free to take it up or not, would one see, upon examining it impartially that it is reasonable enough to merit being adopted?" I believe this abstraction might effectually dissipate a great many clouds which sometimes come between our understanding and that primitive universal ray of light which emanates from God to show the general principles of equity to all mankind.[66]

This *lumiere primitive et universelle* enlightens every human being capable of such moral reflection and is not bound to a particular belief in God, or even to any belief in God (though to understand it metaphysically one needs to be aware of its divine source).

In the following discussion, Bayle connects this "natural light" of reason with the "private lights"[67] of religious conscience and belief, and argues that one must follow the latter when it comes to the question of true faith and salvation, for God does not want any hypocritical believers, and acting against one's own conscience is sinful. Furthermore, "violence . . . is incapable of convincing the mind and of imprinting in the heart the fear and the love of God."[68] And while at this point he comes very close to Locke's main argument for toleration, he knows from studying Augustine that there is an effective counterargument against this: "The only possible thing to be held against me is this: they do not claim to use violence as a direct and immediate means of establishing religion, but as a mediate and indirect means."[69] He proceeds to attempt to refute this "ingenious illusion and specious chicanery," taking it as seriously as Locke had to when he was confronted with Proast's critique.

Two things then need to be established: first, an independent duty of justifiying one's actions that concern others in a morally relevant way with reciprocally acceptable reasons; and second, a questioning of absolute truth claims that could serve as trumps in such a justificatory exchange. For otherwise, the "convertists" could argue that the way they treated the Huguenots was justified, since "only evils done to the faithful can be properly called persecution. Those exercised on heretics are only acts of kindness, equity, justice, and right reason. Be it so. Let us agree then that a thing which would be unjust if not done in favor of the true religion, becomes just by being done for the true religion."[70] This, according to Bayle, is "the most abominable doctrine that has ever been imagined," for "there would be no kind of crime which would not become an act of religion by this maxim."[71] But to establish that very meaning of "crime," Bayle has to take recourse to universal norms of the "natural light" of practical reason, and also he needs an account of why one's belief that one speaks for the right church may not be a sufficient reason to exercise force, even if indirectly. For only then one sees clearly, he argues, that any literal interpretation of Luke 14:23 turns a vice into a virtue and gives every church that deems itself the true church the right to persecute. In a number of chapters, Bayle spells out what this would have meant in various historical contexts (where, for example, the Christians were the minority) and what kind of perversion followed from the general and reciprocal use of such an interpretation.[72] Hence without an independent language of morality, there is no such language at all, and Bayle shows this by way of a *reductio ad absurdum*:[73]

> If one would say, "it is very true, Jesus Christ has commanded His Disciples to persecute, but that is none of your business, you who are heretics. Executing this commandment belongs only to us who are the true Church," they would answer that they are agreed on the principle but not in the application, that they alone have the right to persecute since truth is on their side. . . . One never sees the end of such a dispute, so that like waiting for the final sentence in a trial, one is not able to pronounce anything upon these violences; . . . The suffering party would only make itself fret by reviewing its controversies one by one and would never be able to have the pleasure of saying, "I'm unjustly treated," except by assuming it is in the right and saying, I am the true church. . . . When one reflects on all this impartially, one is reduced necessarily to this rare principle, I have truth on my side,

therefore, my violences are good works. So and so errs: therefore his violences are criminal.[74]

Bayle is careful *not* to suggest a skeptical conclusion with respect to religious truth claims. Even though the epistemological side of the argument is not fully spelled out in the *Commentaire,* but only later in the *Dictionnaire* (which I will come back to), it is clear enough that his is a view of what we can call the *finitude of reason,* meaning that the epistemic capacities of finite human beings are sufficient to come to a firm and well-considered view of religious matters—but that they are not sufficient to establish this view as the only true one on the basis of objective reasons. Religious views are held on the grounds of trust and faith, not of proof, since in these matters especially "evidence is a relative quality."[75] Due to differences of habit, education, or experience, different persons may judge the same things differently,[76] without thereby violating the bounds of reason. Anyone who is aware of these (one could almost say with Rawls) "burdens of reason"[77] knows that "difference in opinions seems to be man's inherent infelicity, as long as his understanding is so limited and his heart so inordinate."[78] This is an essential component of understanding that those with whom one differs can rightfully be seen to be wrong—but not necessarily unreasonable, especially in matters of religion.

Understanding Bayle, however, not only means seeing how his normative-epistemological grounding of toleration is different from and superior to a classic argument for the freedom of conscience, answering its main weaknesses; it also means recognizing the dynamic and the tensions within Bayle's thinking between these different justifications for toleration. For the close link he established between the moral "natural light" and the "private light" of conscience (mentioned above)[79] leads him into a serious problem at one important point in his argument. In chapter 8 of the second part of the *Commentaire,* Bayle takes up the idea of "erroneous conscience" that had traditionally played an important role in the discourse of toleration, especially in Abelard—meaning that a sincere person who is convinced that he or she follows the right path does not sin, even though he or she is in error. Bayle affirms that, rather, acting against one's conscience is a sin, and he concludes that an erroneous conscience, firmly believing that it is following God, "should procure all the same prerogatives, favors, and assistances for error as an orthodox conscience can procure for truth."[80] Furthermore, he states that "the first and most indispensable of all our obligations, is that of never acting against the promptings of conscience."[81] Thus, however, the conclusion follows that if someone believes that a law of God demands of him to "employ fire and sword to establish" truth, then he is obliged to act accordingly.[82] This creates the paradox of what we can call the "conscientious persecutor," and Bayle quickly realizes—as did his critics[83]—that this paradox could prove fatal for his theory: "My design is to show that persecution is an abominable thing, and yet everyone who believes himself obliged by conscience to persecute would, by my doctrine be required to persecute and would be sinning if he did not."[84]

Bayle is aware that the only way to affirm that persecution out of reasons of conscience is as much a "crime" as any persecution,[85] and to show the absurd results of a generalization of the maxim to follow your conscience wherever it leads you so "that everything which would be permitted to truth against error becomes likewise permitted to error against truth,"[86] is to return to his normative argument for an independent morality of mutual respect and justification combined with the argument for epistemological restraint. To follow these principles and insights of reason—or "natural light"—must be seen as the most important obligation and have priority over other beliefs—a priority made possible for believers by affirming the precepts of morality as a form of "natural religion."[87] And thus Bayle affirms at the end of the book, first, the unconditionality of morality and the principle of reciprocity, accessible to every reasonable human being: "In this regard, namely, in respect to the knowledge of our duties to moral standards, revealed light is so clear that few people can mistake it, when in good faith they are seeking out what it is."[88] And second, he states clearly his doctrine of the nature of faith:

> Now it is impossible, in our present state, to know infallibly that the truth which to us appears as such (I speak here of the particular truths of religion and not of the properties of numbers nor the first principles of metaphysics or geometrical demonstra-

tions) is absolutely and really the truth, because all that we can do is to be fully convinced that we possess the perfect truth, that we are not mistaken, but that it is others who are deceived.[89]

Still, it is only in his *magnum opus,* the *Dictionnaire historique et critique* (1696), that Bayle provides a comprehensive discussion of the relation of faith and knowledge. The *Dictionnaire,* an attempt to write a critical history of philosophy, politics, and science (which became the model for the great *Encyclopédie* of Diderot and d'Alembert), had a very unusual structure—mainly articles on persons with a complex system of footnotes commenting on their work as well their private lives—and pursued a great many topics. One of the main points of Bayle's discussions was the relation of faith and reason, or of theology and philosophy, trying to establish the proper realm for each of these, so that neither would be subsumed under the other—thus avoiding religious dogmatism as well as deism or skepticism. The complexity of this attempt has led to a number of very different interpretations of his thought—as being the thought of an independent libertine,[90] basically an atheist,[91] or devout Calvinist.[92] Ludwig Feuerbach's assessment of Bayle's thought still captures these ambivalences nicely when he first calls him the "dialectical guerilla chief of all anti-dogmatic polemics," only later to criticize his defense of the possibility of faith as the "act of self-negation" of a "spiritual flagellant."[93]

The line Bayle draws between reason and faith does not imply that faith is irrational, so that skeptical or fideist conclusions would follow;[94] rather, he argues that faith provides answers to questions that reason can accept but not answer on the basis of its primarily critical, negative power. Faith is thus "above reason"—*dessus de la raison*[95]—but not against reason, as Bayle explains in the important second of the "clarifications" which became necessary after the critiques the dictionary received, especially with respect to its alleged latent atheism, skepticism, Manicheism, etc. For Bayle, reason is necessary to destroy superstition and false claims to objectivity, but there are many issues of a speculative nature where its finitude forces it to see its limits—making room for faith, which, however, rests on reasons that are allowed for but that can be neither verified nor falsified by reason. Hence faith also finds its proper place, believing its doctrines to be true but not beyond "reasonable disagreement," to use Rawls' term.[96] Reasonable faith knows that it is *faith*; hence it does not compete with reason on reason's terrain—and vice versa. There is room for religious controversy, but not for religious fanaticism using a reference to "true faith" as a legitimation for questioning theoretical and practical reason. In some matters, Bayle argues against skepticism, reason has to recognize its "frailty" and trust a "better guide, which is faith."[97] Faith is based on trust and a kind of moral certainty, and its reasonableness consists to an important extent in the awareness of that. The negative arguments of the Manicheans, Bayle argues, are hard to refute philosophically; and yet it is a permissible and advisable act of faith to believe in the biblical story about the occurrence of evil in the world.[98] Metaphysical questions like that supersede the powers of reason, and this is where the proper realm of faith begins.[99] Hence "a true Christian, well versed in the characteristics of supernatural truths and firm on the principles that are peculiar to the Gospel, will only laugh at the subtleties of the philosophers, and especially those of the Pyrrhonists. Faith will place him above the regions where the tempests of disputation reign."[100] This provides a refined explanation of the epistemic coexistence of faith and reason within and at the same time above reason, saying that those who are scandalized by philosophical skepticism are no good believers, and that those who do not see the proper realm for religion do not understand the limits of reason. Both sides who have witnessed "the mighty contests between reason and faith"[101] have to make their peace with each other, seeing the mistake of trying to colonize the other. This argument completes the epistemological component of Bayle's justification of toleration.

The Limits of Toleration and the Question of Government

What does this conception of toleration imply with respect to the limits of toleration? Again, there are remarkable differences but also parallels when one compares Bayle to Locke. Against the *demi-tolérans* of his time, Bayle argues for a *tolérance générale* that includes "Jews and Turks" as well as "pagans" and the unitarian

"Socinians," for there "can be no solid reason for tolerating any one sect which does not equally hold for every other."[102] The main reason for limiting the realm of toleration, then, is toleration itself, for "a religion which forces conscience has no right to be tolerated."[103] Hence "papists" who are willing to exercise such force and who, beyond that, "endanger the public peace" by questioning the authority of the sovereign, should not be tolerated. Bayle importantly adds that this is meant to restrict the power of the Church of Rome, and that it does not imply leaving persons of Catholic faith "to the least insult, disturbing them in the enjoyment of their estates, or the private practice of their religion," comparing this to the harsh persecution of Protestants in France.[104]

When it comes to the question of the toleration of atheists, the *Philosophical Commentary* makes a concession that we do not find in either the *Pensées diverses* or the *Dictionnaire.* As a defense against the accusation that he opens the door for atheism to spread, he first argues that it is in the power of the sovereign to restrict their liberties if (and only if) they present a danger to the "fundamental laws of the state," which might be possible given their doubts about the existence of "Divine Justice."[105] And, second, he adds that an atheist cannot avoid this by appealing to the "asylum of conscience," since he renounces any bond to a higher authority. Still, atheists are to be treated justly and ought to be tolerated as long as they do not disturb the civil order. The passage remains ambivalent and is open for a rather wide as well as a strict interpretation of what that means. In any case, it is safe to say that it does not draw out the radical consequences that his main arguments for toleration imply and which he pointed out so forcefully in his other writings, clearly arguing for the moral capacities of atheists—which might even be superior to those of Christians since their acting morally is not done for a higher reward.[106]

Hence, similar to Locke, Bayle also argues for drawing the limits of toleration on *political* and not religious grounds, yet his position is more nuanced with respect to the toleration of Catholics and atheists. Still, no text such as the *Commentaire* wards off its context and political purpose (which was, after all, a condemnation of Catholic convertism). But at this point, an important difference with Locke needs to be stressed which is important for the question of how best to justify a respect conception of toleration. While Bayle's reflexive arguments for toleration—normatively and epistemologically—are superior to a classic argument for the liberty of conscience, and while they provide a strong rationale for the respect conception of toleration, Locke's theory has one major advantage when it comes to the question of connecting reciprocal toleration on the social level with toleration on the level of the state.[107] If one combined—as Locke himself did not—his justification of toleration as developed in the debate with Proast with his argument, especially in the *Second Treatise of Government,* for a democratic constitution and exercise of government, one could develop a democratic conception of toleration where the duty of justifying the use of force is seen not just as a social-moral duty, as in Bayle, but as a political duty and *democratic practice* of self-government. Then, the theory of toleration would take yet another reflexive turn: justifying the proper realm of toleration and its limits would become the issue of a democratic form of argumentation and critique, institutionally and procedurally protected, including those who are in danger of being marginalized or seen as "intolerable" by conventional standards.[108]

Bayle, however, even though he provides the necessary theory of justification for such a combination of toleration on the social and the political level, did draw a sharp line between these two realms. When it came to the question of securing stable political conditions for the kind of universal social toleration he argued for, he believed—in the tradition of the French *politiques*—that an independent and enlightened sovereign such as Henri IV would be much more suited for that task than a framework of a political struggle for democratic power that would eventually only lead to further conflict and strife. In this respect, Bayle remained closer to Hobbes than to Locke or the Calvinist monarchomachs of his day.[109]

Still, despite this gap between toleration on the social level and the structure of political government, Bayle's theory of toleration provides a milestone in the historical discourse of toleration. For no one saw more clearly than he did that the traditional arguments for toleration did not lead one out of the vicious circle of intolerance or of partial justifications for tolerance that (at least in part) reproduced the major points of difference between the conflicting views. His main reflexive move was to use the very principle of justification *itself* as the ground for a justification of toleration—since the question of toleration ultimately—and undeniably—is the question of the justification of the exercise of force or of the legitimacy of general norms valid and binding for all: a question of *justice*.[110] If it were possible to interpret that principle as a moral principle of mutual respect and of the duty of reciprocal justification, and if it could be combined with a non-dogmatic as well as non-skeptical epistemological argument for the difference between knowledge and faith, then a higher-order ground for toleration could be established. For then the three components of toleration (see section 1 above) would allow for the *objection* component to be constituted by, say, a particular religious doctrine, while the *acceptance* component would be provided by the normative-epistemological argument for the duty of justification and of self-restraint in the face of "reasonable" disagreement. Finally, the *rejection* component would be determined such that only beliefs and practices that violated the principle of justification would appear as intolerable—a judgment always in need of appropriate reciprocal justification.

Methodologically, such a reflexive theory of toleration does what Rawls suggests for his political conception of justice: it "applies the principle of toleration to philosophy itself."[111] Following Bayle, however, the substantive presuppositions and implications of such a conception of toleration (and of justice) are stronger than Rawls would (at least explicitly)[112] allow for: while the normative component of a Baylean case for toleration implies a certain Kantian conception of practical reason, the epistemological component implies a particular conception of theoretical reason—forms of reason that are to be reconstructed philosophically on a level that lies beyond the struggles between religious doctrines, for example. Otherwise, a reflexive theory of toleration that argues for a general duty of toleration—implying that certain forms of intolerance are morally *wrong* as well as *unreasonable*—would not be possible. As long as we are confident that judgments such as the one that "convertism" is wrong and that a conceptual confusion of science and religion is a mistake, we are working under the assumption that there are reasons for such judgments that can in principle be shared by every reasonable person. Bayle firmly believed that human beings are creatures that share such capacities of reason, even though they are often clouded, for a number of reasons. Maybe we are approaching a historical situation where his conviction and arguments that there is such a common basis of justification and of mutual toleration is as provocative as it was in his time.[113]

NOTES

1. Pierre Bayle, *Philosophical Commentary,* ed. and tr. A. Godman Tannenbaum (New York: Peter Lang, 1987), 27.

2. See for example Sean O'Cathasaigh, "Bayle and Locke on Toleration," in *De l'Humanisme aux Lumières, Bayle et le protestantisme,* ed. M. Magdelaine et al. (Paris and Oxford: Universitas and Voltaire Foundation, 1996) as well as Perez Zagorin, *How the Idea of Religious Toleration Came to the West* (Princeton: Princeton University Press, 2003), 283–88.

3. That Bayle was a skeptic is argued, among others, by Popkin, "Pierre Bayle's Place in Seventeenth Century Scepticism," in *Pierre Bayle: Le philosophe de Rotterdam,* ed. P. Dibon (Paris: Vrin, 1959), 1–19.

4. For a more comprehensive argument that reconstructs the discourse of toleration since the Stoics and early Christianity up to the present, showing the importance of Bayle, see my *Toleranz im Konflikt: Geschichte, Gehalt und Gegenwart eines umstrittenen Begriffs* (Frankfurt/Main: Suhrkamp, 2003).

5. With respect to the first two components I follow Preston King, *Toleration* (New York: St. Martin's Press, 1976), ch. 1. Glen Newey, *Virtue, Reason and Toleration* (Edinburgh: Edinburgh University Press, 1999), ch. 1, also distinguishes between three kinds of reasons in his structural analysis of toleration (which, however, differs from mine in the way these reasons are interpreted). For a more extensive discussion, see my "Toleration, Justice and Reason," in *The Culture of Toleration in Diverse Societies,* ed. Catriona McKinnon and Dario Castiglione (Manchester: Manchester University Press, 2003), 71–85.

6. "Tolerance should be a temporary attitude only: it must lead to recognition. To tolerate means to insult." Johann Wolfgang Goethe, "Maximen und Reflexionen," *Werke* 6 (Frankfurt am Main: Insel, 1981), 507. Trans. R. F.

7. For an informative account of Bayle's life and work see Elisabeth Labrousse, *Bayle,* tr. D. Potts (Oxford: Oxford University Press, 1983).

8. See Elisabeth Labrousse, "The Political Ideas of the Huguenot Dias-

pora (Bayle and Jurieu)," in *Church, State and Society under the Bourbon Kings of France,* ed. R. M. Golden (Lawrence: University of Kansas Press, 1982), 222–83.

9. On this, see my *Toleranz im Konflikt,* §§ 4 and 5.

10. See esp. St. Augustine, *The City of God,* tr. H. Bettenson (Harmondsworth: Penguin, 1984), ch. XVIII, section 51.

11. See ibid., XX, 5.

12. St. Augustine, *Letters,* Vol. I, tr. Sister W. Parsons (New York: Fathers of the Church Inc., 1951), # 43, 201.

13. St. Augustine, *In Joannis Evangelium,* 26, 2, in *Patrologiae cursus completus,* ed. P. G. Migne, Vol. 35 (Turnhout: Brepols, 1981), 1607.

14. St. Augustine, *Letters,* Vol. II, tr. Sister W. Parsons (New York: Fathers of the Church Inc., 1953), # 93, 58.

15. Ibid., 60.

16. Ibid., 57.

17. Ibid., 72.

18. St. Augustine, *Letters,* Vol. I, # 76, 370 (tr. altered).

19. St. Augustine, *Contra Epistolam Parmeniani,* in *Patrologiae cursus completus,* ed. P. G. Migne, Vol. 43 (Turnhout: Brepols, no date), I, X, 16, 45.

20. St. Augustine, *Letters,* #93, 60f.

21. Ibid., 72.

22. Ibid., 73.

23. Augustine, *Letters,* Vol. II, #105, 203.

24. Locke and Bayle had met in Rotterdam in 1686 and kept contact after that with further occasional meetings, both praising each other's works. Locke owned some of Bayle's works (and had sent him the *Epistola*), including the *Commentaire,* yet since his first *Letter* was written shortly before the *Commentaire* appeared, no direct influence can be supposed, at least with respect to that first *Letter Concerning Toleration.* See Raymond Klibansky's "Introduction" to John Locke, *Epistola de Tolerantia/ A Letter on Toleration,* ed. Klibansky, tr. J. W. Gough (Oxford: Clarendon Press, 1968), xxxiif., and O'Cathasaigh, "Bayle and Locke on Toleration," 683.

25. For a comprehensive discussion of Locke's views on toleration, including his writings before and after the first letter, see my *Toleranz im Konflikt,* § 17.

26. John Locke, *A Letter Concerning Toleration,* ed. J. Tully (Indianapolis: Hackett, 1983), 47.

27. Ibid., 26.

28. William Walwyn, *A Helpe to the Right Understanding of a Discourse Concerning Independency* (1644/45), in *The Writings of William Walwyn,* ed. J. R. McMichel and B. Taft (Athens: The University of Georgia Press,

1989), 136f., formulates this—in the English discourse on religious toleration quite prominent—argument in the following way:

> That which a man may not voluntarily binde himself to doe, or to forbear to doe, without sinne: that he cannot entrust or refer unto the ordering of any other: whatsoever (be it Parliament, Generall Councels, or Nationall Assemblies): but all things concerning the worship and service of God, and of that nature; that a man cannot without wilfull sin, either binde himselfe to doe any thing therein contrary to his understanding and conscience: not to forbeare to doe that which his understanding and conscience bindes him to performe: therefore no man can refer matters of Religion to any others regulation. And what cannot be given, cannot be received: and then as a particular man cannot be robbed of that which he never had; so neither can a Parliament, or any other just Authority be violated in, or deprived of a power which cannot be entrusted unto them.

29. Locke, *A Letter,* 26.

30. Ibid., 27.

31. "There is only one of these which is the true way to Eternal Happiness. But in this great variety of ways that men follow, it is still doubted which is the right one." Ibid., 36.

32. Ibid., 32.

33. Ibid., 27.

34. Ibid., 32.

35. Ibid., 38.

36. That human power is insufficient to change the mind is also the central thesis of Spinoza's theory of toleration, see Baruch de Spinoza, *Theological-Political Treatise,* tr. S. Shirley, Gebhardt edition (Indianapolis: Hackett, 2001), ch. 20. It also plays on important role in Hobbes' *Leviathan,* limiting its power; see Thomas Hobbes, *Leviathan,* ed. C. B. Macpherson (Harmondsworth: Penguin, 1985), esp. chs. 26, 29, 32.

37. Jonas Proast, *The Argument of the Letter Concerning Toleration, Briefly Consider'd and Answer'd,* reprint of the edition of 1690 (New York and London: Garland, 1984), 4.

38. Ibid., 4f. For a convincing critique of Locke on the basis of Proastian considerations, see esp. Jeremy Waldron, "Locke, Toleration, and the Rationality of Persecution," in *Liberal Rights. Collected Papers 1981–1991* (Cambridge University Press, 1993), ch. 4. Where I disagree with Waldron, however, is with his claim that Locke did not find a plausible counterargument to Proast. For that, however, he had to change his position

and move towards the epistemological-normative argument that we find in Bayle, as we will see.

39. Proast, *Argument,* 10, 11.

40. Ibid., 12.

41. At that time, Locke knew of the *Commentaire* (a copy of which he owned), so an influence is possible, but also a matter of further research. See note 24 above.

42. Locke, *A Second Letter Concerning Toleration,* in *The Works of John Locke* VI (Aalen: Scientia, 1963), 77.

43. Ibid., 65.

44. Ibid., 111.

45. In the literature on the debate between Locke and Proast, Peter Nicholson, "John Locke's Later Letters on Toleration," in *A Letter Concerning Toleration in Focus,* ed. J. Horton and S. Mendus (London: Routledge, 1991), 163–87, highlights the epistemological component, while Richard Vernon, *The Career of Toleration: John Locke, Jonas Proast, and After* (Montreal: McGill-Queen's University Press, 1997), stresses the normative one. Yet the argument implies a combination of the two.

46. "But as to my *supposing* that the *National Religion now in* England, *back'd by the Publick Authority of the Law,* is the *onely true Religion*; if you own, with our Author, that there is but *one* true Religion, I cannot see how you your self can avoid *supposing* the same. For you own your self to the Church of *England*; and consequently you own the *National Religion now in* England, to be the true Religion; . . ." Proast, A *Third Letter Concerning Toleration,* 11.

47. Locke, *A Third Letter for Toleration,* in *Works* VI, 144.

48. Ibid., 212.

49. On the other hand, the limits of toleration would be very wide if all kinds of beliefs were to be tolerated as expressions of conscience; at one point, Bayle will encounter an important difficulty with such a view himself.

50. Locke, *A Letter Concerning Toleration,* 50.

51. Ibid., 51. For a contemporary discussion and elaboration of that point, accepting its challenge for a modern understanding of morality, see Jeremy Waldron, *God, Locke, and Equality* (Cambridge: Cambridge University Press, 2002), esp. ch. 8.

52. In *Oeuvres diverses* III, La Haye 1712, reprint Hildesheim: Georg Olms, 1966. Translated into English by Robert C. Bartlett as Pierre Bayle, *Various Thoughts on the Occasion of a Comet* (Albany: State University of New York Press, 2000).

53. See Montesquieu, *The Spirit of the Laws,* tr. and ed. by A. M. Cohler

et al. (Cambridge: Cambridge University Press, 1989), book 24, ch. 2, 460.

54. Bayle, *Various Thoughts,* 165.

55. Ibid., 193f.

56. Ibid., 169.

57. Ibid., 180.

58. Bayle's belief in the autonomy of practical reason is stressed, for example, in Ludwig Feuerbach's interpretation of his thought, see Feuerbach, *Pierre Bayle,* in Gesammelte Werke 4, ed. W. Schuffenhauer (Berlin: Akademie Verlag, 1967), 103.

59. Bayle, *Various Thoughts,* 222.

60. With respect to a separation of morality from faith Hugo Grotius is also an important figure in that genealogy, and with respect to the toleration of atheists Dirck Volckertszoon Coornhert is to be mentioned, especially his *Proces van' Ketter-dooden* (1590), a critique of Lipsius. See my *Toleranz im Konflikt,* 212–22.

61. Sebastian Castellio, *Contra libellum Calvini* (1554), quoted in Hans Guggisberg, *Sebastian Castellio 1515–1563* (Göttingen: Vandenhoeck u. Ruprecht, 1997), 121 (tr. R. F.).

62. The full title reads: *Philosophical Commentary on these Words of Jesus Christ, Compel Them to Come in, Where it is Proven by Several Demonstrative Reasons that There is Nothing more Abominable than to Make Conversions by Force, and Where Are Refuted all the Convertists Sophisms for Constraint and the Apology that Saint Augustine Made for Persecutions.* French in *Ouevres Diverses,* II, Hildesheim: Georg Olms, 1965. I cite from the modern English translation by Amie Godman Tannenbaum, which contains the first two parts of the book, originally published in 1686, see note 1 above. An older translation that also contains the third part (published in 1687), a detailed refutation of Augustine, and the supplement (1688), an elaboration on a number of arguments, was edited by John Kilkullen and Chandran Kukathas: Pierre Bayle, *A Philosophical Commentary on These Words of the Gospel, Luke 14:23, "Compel Them to Come In, That My House May Be Full"* (Indianapolis: Liberty Fund, 2005).

63. Bayle, *Philosophical Commentary,* 13f.

64. Ibid., 31.

65. Ibid., 30. A similar argument can be found in Castellio: "But to judge of doctrine is not so simple as to judge of conduct. In the matter of conduct, if you ask a Jew, Turk, Christian, or anyone else, what he thinks of a brigand or a traitor, all will reply with one accord that brigands and traitors are evil and should be put to death. . . . This knowledge is engraved and written in the hearts of all men from the foundation of the world. . . . Now let us take up religion and we shall find that it is not so ev-

ident and manifest." Sebastian Castellio, *Concerning Heretics, Whether They Are to be Persecuted* (1554), tr. R. H. Bainton (New York: Columbia University Press, 1935), 131.

66. Bayle, *Philosophical Commentary,* 30.

67. Ibid., 33.

68. Ibid., 36.

69. Ibid., 37.

70. Ibid., 46.

71. Ibid., 47.

72. The importance of the principle of reciprocity in Bayle is stressed by John Kilkullen, *Sincerity and Truth: Essays on Arnauld, Bayle, and Toleration* (Oxford: Oxford University Press, 1988), essay 3.

73. This is how he describes his method in the supplement to the *Commentaire,* ch. 21.

74. Bayle, *Philosophical Commentary,* 84f.

75. Ibid., 93.

76. The perspectivism of Montaigne's *Essais* seems to have had an influence on Bayle in this regard, though without Montaigne's skeptical conclusions. See also Craig B. Brush, *Montaigne and Bayle* (the Hague: Nijhoff, 1966).

77. See John Rawls, *Political Liberalism* (New York: Columbia University Press, 1993), 54ff., where he uses the term "burdens of judgment," explaining why disagreement between persons can be a result of using reason, not of being unreasonable. In earlier texts he had used the (more appropriate) term "burdens of reason." See esp. "The Domain of the Political and Overlapping Consensus," *New York Law Review* 64 (1989), 233–55.

78. Bayle, *Philosophical Commentary,* 141.

79. On that point, see Gianluca Mori, "Pierre Bayle, the Rights of the Conscience, the 'Remedy' of Toleration," *Ratio Juris* 10 (1997), 45–60.

80. Bayle, *Philosophical Commentary,* 155.

81. Ibid., 156.

82. Ibid.

83. On Bayle's controversy with Jurieu on that issue see Thomas M. Lennon, *Reading Bayle* (Toronto: University of Toronto Press, 1999), ch. 4.

84. Bayle, *Philosophical Commentary,* 166. That this does indeed destroy Bayle's case for toleration is argued for by Walter Rex, *Essays on Pierre Bayle and Religious Controversy* (The Hague: Nijhoff, 1965), 181–85.

85. Bayle, *Commentary,* 167.

86. Ibid., 159.

87. Ibid., 31.

88. Ibid., 183.

89. Ibid., 181.

90. David Wootton, "Pierre Bayle, Libertine?," in *Studies in Seventeenth-Century European Philosophy,* ed. M. A. Stewart (Oxford: Clarendon Press, 1997), 197–226.

91. Gianluca Mori, *Bayle philosophe* (Paris: Honoré Champion, 1999).

92. Labrousse, *Bayle*; Nicola Stricker, *Die maskierte Theologie von Pierre Bayle* (Berlin: de Gruyter, 2003).

93. Feuerbach, *Pierre Bayle,* 3, 160, 163.

94. This is the view presented by Popkin, "Pierre Bayle's Place in Seventeenth Century Scepticism"; Brush, *Montaigne and Bayle,* 300, calls Bayle a "semi-fideist," which is more adequate. I would, at the risk of speaking paradoxically, call him a "rationalist fideist."

95. Pierre Bayle, *Historical and Critical Dictionary.* Selections, tr. R. Popkin (Indianapolis: Hackett, 1991), 410.

96. The most important philosophical text where this relation between reason and faith—and the reasonableness and unavoidability of disagreement—was elaborated (for the first time) is Jean Bodin's *Colloquium heptaplomeres,* translated (by M. Leathers Daniels Kuntz) as *Colloquium of the Seven about Secrets of the Sublime* (Princeton: Princeton University Press, 1975). For an interpretation to this effect, see my *Toleranz im Konflikt,* § 12.

97. Bayle, *Historical and Critical Dictionary,* article "Pyrrho," 204.

98. See especially the article "Manicheans," ibid., 144ff.

99.

> It is obvious that reason can never attain to what is above itself. Now if it could furnish answers to the objections that are opposed to the doctrine of the Trinity and that of the hypostatic union, it would rise to the height of these two mysteries; . . . It would then do that which is beyond its strength. It would rise above its own limits, which is a downright contradiction. It must therefore be said that it cannot furnish at all answers to its own objections, and thus the objections remain victorious as long as one does not have recourse to the authority of God and the necessity of subjecting one's understanding to the obedience of the faith.

Ibid., Second Clarification, 411.

100. Ibid., Third Clarification, 429.

101. Ibid., 435.

102. Bayle, *Philosophical Commentary,* 145.

103. Ibid., 147.

104. Ibid., 129.

105. Ibid., 167.

106. See, for example, the articles on Epicurus, Pyrrho, and Spinoza in the *Dictionnaire,* and especially the "First Clarification" of Bayle's *Dictionary,* 401, where he writes in his typical way of seemingly accepting a conventional point only to question it at the same time:

> Please notice carefully that in speaking of the good morals of some atheists, I have not attributed any real virtues to them. Their sobriety, their chastity, their probity, their contempt for riches, their zeal for the public good, their inclination to be helpful to their neighbor were not the effect of the love of God and tended neither to honor nor to glorify him. They themselves were the source and end of all this.

107. Sally Jenkinson, "Two Concepts of Tolerance: Or Why Bayle Is Not Locke," *The Journal of Political Philosophy,* 4:4 (1996), 302–21, rightly stresses the first difference (though without using the terms of "permission" or "respect" in her distinction between an "early-modern" and a "modern liberal" theory of toleration), but she overlooks the second.

108. I develop such a theory of reflexive democratic toleration, though not on Lockean grounds, in the second part of my *Toleranz im Konflikt.*

109. See especially his articles on Hobbes and de l'Hopital in the *Dictionnaire,* both in Pierre Bayle, *Political Writings,* ed. S. L. Jenkinson (Cambridge: Cambridge University Press, 2000), 79–117.

110. See my "Toleration, Justice and Reason," in *The Culture of Toleration in Diverse Societies,* ed. C. McKinnon and D. Castiglione (Manchester: Manchester University Press, 2003), 71–85.

111. Rawls, *Political Liberalism,* 10, 154.

112. I present a critical reading of Rawls' theory along such lines in my *Contexts of Justice: Political Philosophy beyond Liberalism and Communitarianism,* tr. J. M. M. Farrell (Berkeley and Los Angeles: University of California Press, 2002), esp. ch. 4.2; see also my "Die Rechtfertigung der Gerechtigkeit. Rawls' Politischer Liberalismus und Habermas' Diskurstheorie in der Diskussion," in *Das Recht der Republik,* ed. H. Brunkhorst and P. Niesen (Frankfurt/Main: Suhrkamp, 1999), 105–68. Finally, see *Toleranz im Konflikt,* § 32.

113. I thank Benjamin Grazzini for helpful editorial advice.

4

LOCKE'S MAIN ARGUMENT FOR TOLERATION

ALEX TUCKNESS

It is often argued that Locke's main argument for toleration is the claim that true belief, beliefs that are both correct and sincerely held, cannot be brought about through coercion (I will call this the "true belief argument"). Locke himself encouraged such an interpretation when he wrote,

> But after all, the principal consideration, and which absolutely determines this controversy, is this: although the magistrate's opinion in religion be sound, and the way he appoints be truly evangelical, yet if I be not thoroughly persuaded thereof in my own mind, there will be no safety for me in following it. . . . In vain, therefore, do princes compel subjects to come into their church-communion, under pretense of saving their souls. (28)[1]

This argument has been subjected to serious criticisms both in Locke's day and in our own. In this chapter, I claim that what I will call Locke's "universalization argument" has a better claim to be thought of as Locke's main argument than the "true belief" argument and that the universalization argument has a very different logical structure, one that does not depend on what is instrumentally rational for a particular citizen or magistrate. The universalization argument asks whether a given principle would be desirable if it were universally interpreted and applied by fallible and often biased human beings.

The claim that the universalization argument, rather than the true belief argument and its variants, is Locke's "main argument" immediately raises the question of what makes an argument "main." There is a variety of different things one might mean by such a claim. First, one might mean that the argument is the most *famous* or influential one. I will concede at the outset that Locke is more famous for the true belief argument and that as a result it has been more influential. The universalization argument is most clearly developed in Locke's rarely read *Third Letter on Toleration.* The prevalence of the true belief argument in the secondary literature is further proof of its fame. That other authors in this volume who discuss Locke in this volume refer to this argument as his main one illustrates this point.[2]

Although one can use the argument's fame as evidence that the true belief argument is the main argument, there are other, and better, criteria by which the universalization argument has the stronger claim. In general, one might say that X has a stronger claim than Y to be considered an author's main argument if it is: 1) more *prevalent* in that the argument is used more often; 2) more *foundational* in that more of the author's other arguments depend on it; 3) more *characteristic* in that it is consistent with and not contradicted by other arguments by the same author;[3] or 4) more *persuasive* in that it provides a stronger argument for the author's conclusion. Given the ambiguity of the phrase "main argument," there will be many cases where it is better to forgo the use of it and simply specify that one argument is more prevalent while another is more persuasive, and so on. In the case at hand, however, the universalization argument has a stronger claim to be Locke's main argument according to every criterion except fame. In such cases, charity toward the author should lead us to conclude that the fame of the better known true belief argument is undeserved.

In Section 1, I look at the criticisms of the true belief argument by Proast and Waldron. The cogency of these criticisms undermines the claim that the true belief argument should be thought of as Locke's main argument because it is his most persuasive. In Section 2, I defend the claim that the universalization argument is more prevalent in Locke's later writings on toleration. In Section 3, I briefly argue that the universalization argument is also more foundational in that many of Locke's later arguments for toleration depend on it. In Section 4, I argue that the universalization argument is more characteristic because Locke's later writings contradict the true belief argument and because the universalization argument is consistent with Locke's other writings. Section 5 returns to the question of which argument is more persuasive, noting the strengths of Locke's argument and rebutting some objections to it. In Section 6, I briefly compare the universalization argument to some other interpretations of Locke's argument for toleration.

The Traditional Critique of the True Belief Argument

Almost as soon as Locke's *Letter Concerning Toleration* was published in English, the true belief argument was attacked. In 1690, Jonas Proast, Locke's most famous and prolific critic on the subject of toleration, argued that most of Locke's other arguments begged the question. When Locke claimed that magistrates could not use force in matters of religion because no such authority had been given to them, Proast replied that Locke was assuming what was in dispute. He argued that at the end of the day, Locke's argument hinged on the success of the true belief argument, the claim that force could not aid achieving salvation. Proast argued that while force might not directly change beliefs, it might do so "indirectly, and at a distance."[4] Force might be used to compel people to attend sermons that would convince them to accept the true religion. Force might also be used to protect people from seductive heresies. In other words, one can admit that people will not directly change their beliefs about God in response to force while still thinking that force can be useful in bringing people to the true religion. Proast was not endorsing all methods of persecution, only those that seemed to further the spread of orthodox Christianity. Thus he joined Locke in condemning excessive penalties, since these were often counterproductive. But, in contrast to Locke, he thought that moderate penalties could be of substantial use in causing people to consider arguments that might convince them to join the true religion by offsetting the sinful tendencies that draw men away from the true religion.[5]

Proast granted that, under his scheme, there would be some who would conform nominally but not be saved. But force need not be able, of itself alone, to bring about salvation. Force does not have to guarantee salvation, only increase the number of those who experience it.[6] Put another way, if there are several factors necessary but not sufficient for salvation and force can help some but not all of them, it is still instrumentally rational to use it. That force cannot do everything does not mean we should not use it for what it can accomplish.

Jeremy Waldron recast Proast's best objection for modern readers.[7] Although the two disagree in that Proast thinks Locke's toleration goes too far while Waldron thinks it does not go far enough, they agree in the reasons they give for why Locke's argument cannot meet its objective. In "Locke and the Rationality of Persecution," Waldron sets aside arguments that appeal specifically to Christian revelation and argues that functional arguments beg the question.[8] The main argument left to Locke is one of instrumental rationality: it is irrational for magistrates to use force to bring people to the religion since force cannot alter belief. Waldron notes that this argument would be exceedingly attractive if it worked because it requires so few controversial assumptions. Waldron, like Proast, finds the argument to be a failure. Even if our beliefs are a matter of judgment and not will, and even if force works by acting on the will, at most this rules out one reason for persecution rather than persecution itself. Waldron agrees with Proast that coercion can affect what sorts of arguments we hear and so it may indirectly affect beliefs.[9]

There is a second parallel between Waldron and Proast that is worth calling attention to. Locke occasionally makes reference in the original *Letter Concerning Toleration* to persecution by magistrates whose religion is not true, often invoking other countries where the religion is different from the state religion in England. Both Proast's tracts and Waldron's article find this argument irrelevant. Proast thinks that treating the actions of magistrates whose religion is false as on a par with those whose religion is true reveals skepticism about the true religion. In his first response to Locke, Proast took it as obvious that anyone who sought truth properly would come to the true religion.[10] In his second response to Locke, he was even more adamant in accusing Locke of being a religious skeptic.[11]

Proast argued that discussions of persecution by rulers in other countries were beside the point since there was no reason to think those countries would change their policies based on what policy England adopted. It was the policy for England, and England alone, that was in dispute. Since both he and Locke agreed that the Church of England possessed true religion, worries about false religion were irrelevant.[12] Since Proast agreed with Locke that magistrates who used force to bring men to a false religion were guilty of a terrible sin, Proast thought that Locke was wrong in thinking Proast's principles authorized false magistrates to use force in any way. The magistrate's fallibility is only an argument against authorizing him to enforce his own religion, whatever it happens to be, not against authorizing him to enforce the true religion.[13] Proast also clarified that it is only where the true religion has been presented to people adequately that they can justly be punished for not accepting it.[14]

Waldron agrees with Proast's main point here as well. Responding to Locke's argument about magistrates whose religions are false using force, Waldron writes:

> Notice that this is a good argument only against the following rather silly principle: (P1) that the magistrate may enforce *his own* religion or whatever religion *he thinks* correct. It is not a good argument against the somewhat more sensible proposition (P2) that a magistrate may enforce the religion, whatever it may be, which is *in fact* objectively correct.[15]

Waldron, like Proast, thinks it is far from obvious why someone else misapplying a principle is an argument for why I should not apply that principle correctly if I have good reason for thinking that I can apply it correctly.

Locke thus appears to be left only with his argument that persecution is not instrumentally rational, an argument that fails to adequately defend toleration. Waldron notes that despite the amount of ink Locke spilled in his later letters on toleration, he was never able to salvage this argument from these devastating criticisms.[16] Waldron is, I think, right about that. But I argue below that Locke did not really try to. Instead of showing that persecution is instrumentally irrational from the perspective of any given magistrate, he instead worked to bolster the argument about the application of Proast's principle by magistrates whose beliefs are incorrect. Waldron and Proast were justified in thinking that that argument, as presented in the original Letter, was incomplete. In the *Second* and *Third Letters* Locke advanced one far more powerful.

The Universalization Argument Is More Prevalent

What is striking about the general shift in argument that begins in Locke's *Second Letter* and becomes even more pronounced in the *Third* is that Locke did not try to defend the claim that it was categorically impossible for coercion to affect belief. Instead, his *Second Letter* contained a number of arguments that shifted the frame from one of individual rationality to what we might call "legislative rationality," a perspective that asks what principles it would be rational to legislate for fallible human beings. While the true belief argument is essentially abandoned in Locke's later writings on toleration, the universalization argument is used constantly, as will be shown below. Equally important is how many of the arguments in Locke's later writings on toleration depend on the universalization argument for their persuasiveness. This section thus argues that the universalization argument has a stronger claim to being thought of as Locke's main argument than the true belief argument.

Early on in the *Second Letter,* Locke emphasized a point made in the original *Letter,* that to pose the question in terms of what it is rational to do in England is to pose it wrongly (64). This implies that it is not simply a question of individual instrumental rationality. Locke also emphasizes the issue of authority. It is not enough to show that using force is beneficial in a particular case; one has to show that the one using force has authority to do so (67–69, 80). This authority might come from God through revelation or natural law, or it might come from consent. Locke then asked, "What if God, foreseeing this force would be in the hands of men as passionate, humoursome, as liable to prejudice and error as the rest of their brethren, did not think it a proper means to bring men into the right way?" (84) This short passage combines a belief that authorization is necessary (in this case, from God) and that God might withhold authorization because God foresees the way fallible human beings would apply the principle. It is this thought that Locke develops at length in the *Third Letter.*

Although most of Proast's second response to Locke expounds the same arguments as the first at greater length, there was one new argument that proved a turning point in the debate. Locke had pressed Proast to answer the question of the source of the magistrate's authority to use force in matters of religion. In his second response, Proast granted that there was no specific text in the New Testament that justified the use of force to bring people to the true religion, but argued that this was unnecessary since the magistrate already had the power to do so by virtue of the law of nature.[17] In conceding this point, he opened the way for Locke to make the debate about the actual content of natural law.

The first substantive argument Locke makes in the *Third Letter* (143–48) is not the argument that true belief cannot be forced, but rather that natural law directives are given to all magistrates and that to implement these directives, magistrates must act on their own judgment about what true religion is. Though one can have a high degree of assurance about one's faith and very good reasons for it, it is still faith and not a deductive certainty like a geometric proof. Given those assumptions, a directive to use force to promote the true religion would encourage those who believe false religions to use force on behalf of those religions. Locke then discusses the question of authorization and again notes that the law of nature must apply to all equally (149–50). A few pages later, he again appeals to the harm that would be done if Proast's principle were universalized (163) and notes that the implication is that people in other countries have been left without adequate means for obtaining salvation.

This argument is different from Locke's true belief argument in that it does not emphasize rationality from the standpoint of a single individual. It shows neither why it is ineffective to persecute from the standpoint of a single magistrate nor why it is irrational to consent to government coercion in the area of religion from the standpoint of a given individual. Locke's point is about reciprocal rationality, not individual rationality, in that he considers what principles it would be rational to want all people to hold. Putting it this way will for many readers bring to mind the later approach of Kant who insisted that maxims be ones that we could will for all people. Locke's version differs from Kant's formulation in that Locke focuses on reciprocity in the contexts of limited knowledge and fallible, biased decision makers rather than the idealized decision makers in a kingdom of ends.[18] These themes continue to appear throughout Chapter One.[19]

In Chapter Two of the *Third Letter*, Locke gives one of the most complete statements of the universalization argument. He begins the chapter by quoting Proast's statement that the authorization of the magistrates in matters of religion comes from the law of nature whereby he is commanded to use his power for the good of the people. Proast thinks that since true religion is for the good of the people, that is all the authorization needed (202–3). Locke responds that any command by the law of nature will need to be interpreted and applied by each magistrate (205). Locke then uses an analogy to parents and children to show that people must act on their own judgment about truth: even parents who believe false religions have a right, as parents, to educate their children in what they believe is the truth. This natural law obligation of parents is parallel to that of magistrates. God gives all magistrates the same powers even though they will not use their powers equally well.

As one would expect, Locke goes on to argue that parental and political relationships are quite different. The ends of political society must be grounded either in the consent of the people or the law of nature. Locke emphasizes the latter in the following passage which deserves to be quoted at length:

> . . . you have recourse to the general law of nature; and what is that? The law of reason, whereby every one is commissioned to do good. And the propagating the true religion for the salvation of men's souls being doing good, you say, the civil sovereigns are commissioned and required by that law to use their force for those ends. But since by this law all civil sovereigns are commissioned and obliged alike to use their coactive power for the

> propagating of the true religion, and the salvation of souls; and it is not possible for them to execute such a commission, or obey that law, but by using force to bring men to that religion which they judge the true; by which use of force much more harm than good would be done towards the propagating the true religion in the world, as I have showed elsewhere: therefore no such commission, whose execution would do more harm than good, more hinder than promote the end for which it is supposed given, can be a commission from God by the law of nature. (Locke 1963, 6:213)

Locke goes on to emphasize that commonwealths can act only so far as they have a commission and that there would be a net harm if Proast's principle were generally applied by fallible agents; only a few would benefit (214–15).[20]

Despite its prevalence, those who have written extensively on Locke's later writings on toleration have failed to see the universalization argument's central role in Locke's argument for toleration.[21] The frequency with which Locke used this argument in his later writings is important evidence for its centrality. It reappears in all ten chapters of the *Third Letter.* In Chapter Three, he argues that our concern for idolatry must be from God's perspective and God sees the whole world, not just England (235–36). Locke also quotes a long, unanswered stretch of his *Second Letter* in which he again appeals to the universalization argument (258). As the theme of Chapter Three is "who will be punished," it is fitting that Locke concludes by noting that since magistrates everywhere will have to judge for themselves, it is those who do not conform to the national religion (which may or may not be true) who will be punished. In Chapter Four, Locke's main argument is to show that Proast has no independent standard for what constitutes "moderate" punishment; as part of the argument Locke insists we must consider Proast's vague principle as interpreted and applied by all magistrates (281). In Chapter Five, Locke considers the duration of Proast's proposed punishments. Locke emphasizes that magistrates, unlike God, simply cannot know when a person has given an issue due consideration. Locke connects this with the universalization argument when he argues that God does not, through natural law, make magistrates his agents of wrath towards those not of the Christian faith because fallible magistrates lack the knowledge to do this properly (299–300).

In Chapter Six, Locke's main purpose is to show that, in the end, all of the purposes that Proast gives for punishing, notably punishing men to make them consider, in the end reduce to punishing men for being of a different religion. In doing so, Locke forces Proast to consider instances where magistrates in other countries would apply this principle (309). In Chapter Seven, Locke clarifies that he is not convinced that all religions are equally true, only that people tend to be equally convinced that their own religion is true and that other churches have as much of a right to enforce their understanding of true religion as those in England do (333). This argument is most intelligible as a shortened version of his natural law argument. If natural law directives must always be carried out by fallible agents, then it is irrelevant that we have good reasons for thinking others are wrong in their interpretation. A good legislator will still take foreseeable errant interpretations into account when framing the law. In Chapter Eight, Locke argues that Proast gives the magistrates no guidance on how to find the true religion and even reassures them that good can come of it even if they are wrong. This argument, he concludes, "will serve any magistrate to use any degree of force against any that dissent from his national religion" (369).

Chapters Nine and Ten use the argument repeatedly. In Chapter Nine, Locke emphasizes that there are twenty times more magistrates who believe false religions than true ones (378) and that Proast's principle would more harm than benefit true religion (380). If the power is given to any magistrates, it is given to all (382). Locke insists on drawing a distinction between the reasons we have for thinking we are right and the privilege of using force because we are right (420). Locke argues that there is no way for magistrates to punish men for believing a false religion without first judging, fallibly, which one is true (427).

In Chapter 10, Locke admits that by the "light of nature" as well as revelation magistrates have the authority to promote morals (468, cf 416). Locke contrasts a principle stating that magistrates should promote morals, which he thinks is beneficial even making allowances for human fallibility, with a principle stating that magistrates should promote the true religion, a principle

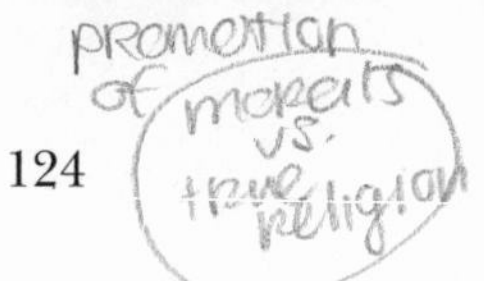

which would not be beneficial. Locke repeats the argument from page 213, reprinted above, arguing that God, as a rational legislator, would not instruct human beings to follow a principle that would undermine its purpose when fallible human beings interpret it (495). God, Locke insists, knows the natural tendency of human beings to punish too much in the area of religion (498).[22] This argument reappears several more times.[23]

While the *Second Letter* and *Third Letter* carry most of the weight in this argument, Locke's first and last letters on toleration offer some additional support. Locke's *Fourth Letter* should be given less weight given the fact that Locke left it uncompleted and unpublished, yet it is noteworthy that the universalization argument again plays a prominent role. In fact, Locke was in the process of making that very argument at the point the manuscript breaks off. There is thus a sense in which it represents Locke's "last words" on the subject of toleration. In the original *Letter*, Locke repeatedly stressed that the religion of every magistrate was orthodox to himself and his references to how the principle would play out in Constantinople and elsewhere indicate that he is assuming that principles must be tested against universal application. He also shows a significant awareness of human fallibility.[24] In sum, the universalization argument far surpasses the true belief in terms of the pervasiveness with which it is used.

The Universalization Argument Is More Foundational

The preceding pages also show that the universalization argument is more foundational in that Locke uses it in conjunction with almost every major argument in the *Third Letter*. Pervasiveness alone is not a convincing argument given the repetitive way in which Locke wrote the *Third Letter*; there are other arguments that are mentioned repeatedly as well. For example, Locke repeatedly argues in the *Third Letter* that Proast will never be able to correctly match punishments with those who need to be punished. He argues that given the imperfect knowledge of those who must apply the principle, any punishment intended to make people consider will be overbroad and any punishment intended to make people conform will likely produce only outward conformity. At some points, he goes so far as to question whether Proast is really arguing in good faith since he thinks Proast knows that "punishing to consider" is really shorthand for "punishing dissenters."

Because of Locke's repetitive writing in the *Third Letter,* it is important that the universalization argument is not only more pervasive, it is also more foundational. While it is certainly true that Locke uses a variety of arguments, these arguments are presented in a context that assumes all principles must be judged by imagining their generalized application by fallible people. This gives us reason to take the universalization argument as the centerpiece of Locke's argument. While it would overstate matters to say that all his other arguments are logically dependent on it, the arguments all become more persuasive if the universalization perspective is assumed. In the case of Locke's argument about Proast's punishment falling on the wrong people, notice the similarities to the universalization argument. Locke is asking how a practical principle would be interpreted and applied by fallible beings with limited knowledge. In the preceding chapter-by-chapter account, we saw how at almost every turn Locke used the universalization argument to strengthen the other arguments he was making. The argument is therefore not one that is repeated often but disconnected from the rest of the argument, but one that plays a foundational role.

The Universalization Argument Is More Characteristic

The point can be pushed even further. In addition to the claim that Locke in his later writings used the universalization argument far more often and that most of his other arguments are connected to it, we can add the claim that the universalization argument is also more characteristically Lockean. It is more characteristic of Locke in two senses. First, Locke made arguments flatly inconsistent with the true belief argument in his later writings (giving support to the claim that he not only abandoned the argument but actually repudiated it). Second, it is more characteristic in that it creates a tighter link between Locke's writings on toleration and Locke's natural law arguments so prevalent in the *Two Treatises.*

With respect to the first claim, consider the following passage from the *Second Letter*. Speaking of the dangers of force being used in countries where the magistrate's religion is false, Locke wrote:

> the greatest part of mankind, being not able to discern betwixt truth and falsehood, that depend upon long and many proofs, and remote consequences; nor having ability to discover the false grounds, and resist the captious and fallacious arguments of learned men versed in controversies; are so much more exposed, by the force which is used to make them hearken to the information and instruction of men appointed to it by the magistrate, or those of his religion, to be led into falsehood and error, than they are likely this way to be brought to embrace the truth that must save them; by how much the national religions of the world are, beyond comparison, more of them false or erroneous, than such as have God for their author, and truth for their standard. (78)

Instead of arguing that persecution in other countries is harmless because belief cannot be changed by coercion, Locke now grants that some people's beliefs are likely to be changed if they are forced to listen to arguments from men far more skilled in controversy and rhetoric than they are, even if those beliefs are false. Locke goes on to tell a story showing that even those who are very learned can be seduced by false arguments (78–79).

Locke made this argument again in the *Third Letter*. He argued that many people might be led to embrace a state religion because "arguments, set on with force, have a strange efficacy upon human frailty; and he must be well assured of his own strength, who can peremptorily affirm, he is sure to have stood what above a million people have sunk under . . ." (400). Rather than claiming that government persecution is incapable of causing people to believe a new religion, Locke here admits it is. As in the *Second*

Letter, Locke argues that it is precisely because persecution often is effective that it would be so disastrous if Proast's principle were the one all magistrates, including those who believe in false religions, acted upon (399). Locke makes essentially the same point a few pages later when he argues that the unlearned are susceptible to pressure from the national church and that Proast's principle would therefore be disastrous for Anglicans if acted on by the

King of France (407–8). These passages provide even stronger evidence that Locke abandoned the true belief argument.

There is a second reason to see the universalization argument as more characteristic of Locke, namely that it relies on arguments more similar to Locke's argument in the *Two Treatises*. One of the more puzzling features of the original *Letter* is that there is only one reference to the law of nature, and that reference is only a passing one that carries no real weight in the argument (43). Similarly, Locke never uses the phrases "natural law" or "law of nature" in the *Second Letter*. Though this does not prove that natural law reasoning was absent in these works, since it is sometimes implicit, it is nonetheless surprising given the central role that the doctrine explicitly plays in the *Two Treatises*.

In the *Third Letter*, there is a drastic change. The phrase "law of nature" appears 39 times (interestingly, the same number of times the phrase is used in the *Two Treatises*). In the shorter and uncompleted *Fourth Letter*, Locke uses the phrase six more times. In both the *Third* and *Fourth* letters, Locke devotes a number of paragraphs to spelling out the role of natural law in the argument for toleration. Not only that, but the arguments presented above indicate that these natural law passages end up carrying a disproportionate amount of weight in the argument. If we take the universalization argument as Locke's main argument, then the dialogue with Proast prompted Locke to spell out what had been implicit before, the connection of the universalization argument with Locke's theory of natural law.

The universalization argument also provides an interesting link to the use of natural law argumentation in the *First Treatise*, Locke's critique of Robert Filmer's claim that God instituted monarchy with the creation of Adam and that Adam's sovereignty automatically passed down to his eldest son according to the standard rules of succession. Locke noted that Filmer's principle of succession could not be accurately applied by human beings since the knowledge of who Adam's true heir was has been lost. Unless Filmer could show from either natural law or God's special revelation who the true heir was, adopting Filmer's principle would "unsettle and bring all into question."[25] Locke then argued that Filmer's law of succession was not a mere positive law, but "the law of God and Nature" since it was prior to any laws a particular king might hand down.[26] Locke concluded that "Divine Institution makes no such ridiculous assignment: nor can God be supposed to make a Sacred Law, that one person should have a Right to something, and yet not give Rules to mark out, and know that Person by . . ."[27] Locke was thus using this same structure of argument in his early writings on patriarchal government that he used in his last writings on toleration: a law of nature that would lead to disastrous results when fallible human beings try to apply it cannot be a law that God has actually legislated.[28]

The Universalization Argument Is More Persuasive

For many readers, the reasons to study the history of political thought are not purely historical. It may be the case that an argument that is not an author's main argument will appear to later generations to be his or her strongest. There is thus a legitimate (albeit anachronistic) sense in which an argument's contemporary plausibility is relevant to whether it should be thought of as the author's main argument. Section one has already presented what are widely taken to be serious, even fatal, flaws in the true belief argument. Coercion *is* sometimes indirectly effective in changing people's beliefs. The universalization argument is more robust in that it can acknowledge this fact and still generate reasons for toleration.

One worry readers may have is that Locke's later argument was indeed a better argument for confronting Proast, but only because Proast shared the same theistic natural law framework as Locke. For readers who reject that premise, Locke's argument would be no more persuasive than his Christian arguments that appeal specifically to Jesus and the Bible. However, those who are committed to the principle of reciprocity, to a respect for the moral agency of others, to a requirement that moral principles be stated in ways that are general (as opposed to arbitrarily narrow), and to a requirement that these principles should be publicly known can also adopt Locke's framework. If we start with these assumptions, then any appeal to moral principle must be to a moral principle that applies to both parties in the dispute, should be known by both parties, and that both parties are able to interpret and apply as moral agents.[29] One need not believe in natural law, though one of course may, to believe that moral principles that authorize coercion should be principles that we would want other fallible people, exercising their capacity as moral agents, to interpret and adopt as well.

The principles used to justify coercion often involve words and phrases such as "true religion" that different people would apply in different ways. Locke asks us to account for that when deciding whether a moral principle does indeed authorize coercion. In some cases we may decide that a rational legislator would be willing to authorize coercion on the basis of principles that contain contested terms because the alternatives would be even worse. It would be impractical to insist that we can only act on moral principles whose proper interpretation could not possibly be disputed. Nonetheless, there will be cases, as in Locke's argument about using force to promote the true religion, where the degree of disagreement combined with the effects of coercion makes toleration the correct policy.

It is also important to remember that real world debates about toleration often do involve at least one side that claims that a universally binding moral principle justifies the proposed measures. Locke's argument is appealing in these situations because it does not require skepticism about the existence of universal moral norms, only recognition of human fallibility and the fact that human beings are moral agents. Because Locke's argument shares more premises with those who appeal to universal moral values than would, for example, Rawlsian political liberalism, it may be more likely to be accepted.

Not only is Locke's style of argument one that could be used even by those who disagree with some of his premises, it is also importantly different from other, better known, approaches. Locke is similar to Kant in that both ask us to imagine the universalization of our maxims, but differs from him in that Locke asks us to imagine our principles universalized in the non-ideal world rather than in a kingdom of ends. We are to imagine real actors with their fallibility and bias interpreting the principles we propose. Locke's argument does involve instrumental rationality of a sort, since it essentially asks whether the proposed rule would further the goals of the one enacting it when interpreted and applied by others. The argument does not establish the substantive ends that are to be pursued, but only blocks certain principles.

Nonetheless, there is an important difference between a perspective that asks whether a given principle promotes the interests of a single individual or justice as defined by a single individual and a perspective that asks whether a given principle could be willed as a general principle to be followed by others who, as independent moral agents, might interpret it differently. Unlike simple individual instrumental rationality, Locke's approach takes both the moral agency of others and the need for universal principles seriously. While meeting Locke's standard of legislative rationality is not sufficient to show that a principle should be accepted, if Locke has successfully shown us a necessary condition for the use of force, it is an important argument.

Although Locke's argument is different from Kant's, the similarities between them call to mind a common objection to universalization approaches, namely that they do not give enough guidance about how the maxim or principle is to be specified. Thus one might object that "coercively promote the true religion" is universalizable while "coercively promote your own religion" is not even if we grant that Locke's claim that universalization is relative to the goals of the agent in question. Here a defense of Locke's argument involves unpacking the significance of the assumptions on which the legislative point of view rests. Because of the commitment to equality, none of us is entitled to exercise coercive power over others simply through our own will; we must appeal to some moral principle that stands over both us and the person with whom we interact. The principle of moral agency requires us to recognize the equal right of the person to interpret the principle and act as a moral agent. When we add to this the constraints of human fallibility and instrumental rationality then we see that it is requisite when adopting principles to account for how various moral agents will interpret them. Thus "coercively promote the true religion," given Locke's assumptions, is essentially equivalent to "coercively promote the religion you think is true" when considering whether the principle can pass the universalization test.

A slightly different version of the "how to specify the principle" problem occurs if we imagine the principle being specified as

"Coercively promote Calvinism." Here the person might claim that such a principle could be universalized and that it would be subject to fewer errant interpretations. While Calvinism is interpreted differently by different people, the range of interpretation is much smaller than with the phrase "true religion." Here we can say on Locke's behalf that with any principle that is intended to provide a justification for coercion, it is always legitimate to ask the person why a given term is morally relevant. In this case, why Calvinism? If the answer relies fundamentally on the fact that Calvinism is true, then we are entitled to reformulate the principle accordingly. If the answer is that Calvinism better promotes productive capitalist behavior than any other religion, then the principle can be reformulated as "promote the religion that best promotes capitalist behavior" and we can proceed to ask why capitalist behavior is morally relevant. In other words, principles that plausibly give coherent political justifications will at bottom rely on shared moral terms that are generally subject to varying interpretations once the implicit values are made explicit.

Locke's position is also interestingly different from utilitarian approaches in that he is not asking us to calculate the likelihood that our adopting a principle will cause others to adopt the same principle. It is not a sophisticated version of act-consequentialism. Instead, it asks us to select principles based on what their effects would be if, hypothetically and even counterfactually, the principle were widely adopted. Thus when Proast argued that it was only the religious policies of England that were in dispute, Locke could reply that if the power claimed was one that came from natural law, one had to consider its universal application. Even if Proast could show that religious persecution in England would not influence behavior elsewhere in the least, that would be beside the point because the situated position of a magistrate in England is not, for Locke, the correct standpoint from which to evaluate the action. Locke thus gives a non-utilitarian reason why we should think in terms of general moral rules applied by fallible agents. While the above considerations are only a brief account of the potential persuasiveness of Locke's universalization argument, given the severe problems of the true belief argument the universalization argument is the more persuasive.

Other Interpretations of Locke

To this point, I have focused on the most well-known interpretation of Locke's true belief argument and shown that this argument was not the one that Locke emphasized in his later writings on toleration. There are, however, other interpretations of Locke's *Letter* that claim to avoid the fatal weaknesses of the true belief argument. Paul Bou-Habib attempts to save Locke's argument by emphasizing sincere inquiry rather than belief. In emphasizing sincerity, Bou-Habib claims that it is crucial that our beliefs spring from the right kind of motives.[30] He rightly points out that Locke is deeply concerned with whether people have a desire to seek the truth in good faith. If God's real desire is that we have the intention of sincerely seeking the truth about God, acquiring true beliefs because of external coercion does us no good. As Bou-Habib explicitly admits, this argument shares the same logical structure as the genuine (or true) belief argument. It shows persecutors that persecution is irrational because it cannot bring about the desired goal. Susan Mendus similarly argues that, while coercion may indirectly generate genuine beliefs in some cases, it does not always do so. She notes that not every sincere utterance reflects a genuine belief, as in the case of someone who is brainwashed.[31] She produces a variety of considerations that show that altering a person's genuine beliefs is more difficult than Waldron suggests because beliefs that are sufficiently manipulated will no longer count as genuine and because of the intensity with which religious beliefs are held.

Both of these arguments are vulnerable to the Proast/Waldron objection. Even if we grant that sincere inquiry into the truth about God is a necessary condition and that force cannot directly bring it about, force may be able to indirectly bring it about. Imagine someone who has been passionately seeking the truth about God for decades but whose initial interest in religion began with an act of persecution. Persecution might get an ambivalent person to begin inquiring into the truth of religious things, an inquiry that the person would eventually pursue for its own sake. This is particularly important since Locke thought that salvation also required another component, belief that Jesus is the Messiah.

Since persecution might indirectly lead more people to be correct on the content dimension, it might be rational to use it even if it could not increase the number of sincere inquirers. One might object that the presence of coercion makes it less likely that people will sincerely seek after truth and that if this effect is strong enough fewer people are likely to be saved. The problem with this response is that it likely leads to an impossibly high bar for what counts as "sincere" inquiry. The causal stories about how each of us comes to acquire any particular belief are likely to be very complex and involve exposures to countless "irrelevant" pressures. This is also the essence of the reply to Mendus. Not every case of pressure counts as brainwashing. Mendus herself admits that all of us, to some extent, acquire our beliefs in environments where we are selectively exposed to information and pressures, and thus it is quite plausible that coercive techniques might be able to bring about beliefs that would still count as genuine.

There is a second, and very different, line of response to these approaches which simply notes that, for all their creativity, they are not the lines of argument that Locke himself emphasized in his later writings. While it is true that in a number of passages Locke indicates a concern for whether people sincerely seek the truth about religion and that he had some concerns about whether coercion would really get more people to search after it, Locke did not present this line of argument as the saving interpretation of the true belief argument.

A different way of saving Locke's argument shifts the focus from what is rational for magistrates to what is rational for citizens. These arguments emphasize Locke's theory of consent and claim that it is not rational for a citizen to consent to government use of force in matters of religion. Thus David Wootton claims that the true belief argument is only one of Locke's arguments and that his consent-based arguments are stronger.[32] He thinks that I, as a rational person, would not consent to allow someone to use force to get me to change my religion because it is unlikely, though not impossible, that I would change my beliefs in response to the persecution and I would not want to risk facing persecution. Thus, even if persecution may occasionally work, it does not work often enough to make it rational for a person to consent to it. A related argument is that the government may be wrong, thus making it even more irrational for an individual to consent to give the government that power.[33]

Richard Vernon's argument that we would not consent to be forced to be right has a similar structure. He claims that we would not consent to allow persons to use force in matters of religion unless there was some sign that was both infallible and always convincing for identifying which people have superior religious knowledge. Again, this is really a claim about what would be instrumentally rational for an individual seeking to maximize his temporal and eternal well-being. Vernon also makes a related argument. He claims that we would not consent to coercion in matters of religion because we want to hold our beliefs for the right reasons. Vernon draws an analogy to a magic pill that causes its consumer to sincerely believe certain propositions. Vernon argues that we would not take such a pill because we would want to believe these propositions for the right reasons.[34] We would want to know that the balance of arguments really favors them.

Although space permits only a brief discussion, these consent-based arguments do hold up better than the true belief argument as an account of what Locke continued to think on the subject of toleration. Consent is certainly a prevalent, foundational, and characteristic concept in Locke's thought and Locke continued to hold a version of the consent argument even in the *Third Letter.* There Locke argued a given power cannot be a legitimate power of government if it would have been irrational for individuals in the state of nature to consent to give the government that power. In the state of nature the need was for force to protect individuals from the attacks of one another. Being forced by someone stronger to worship a different God, Locke argued, is precisely the sort of injury that people in the state of nature wanted to avoid, so they would not give that authority to the government (212). Locke makes this argument as part of a dilemma: if authorization is by consent, the people would not have given consent and if by natural law, natural law does not contain a command to use force in matters of religion.

While Locke did continue to hold a consent-based argument, it was not the position that he emphasized in the *Third Letter*; indeed, the argument appears rarely. It is possible that Locke emphasized it less because he saw that it shared something of the same weakness as the true belief argument insofar as it was presented as an argument about what is instrumentally rational for individual citizens. The citizen asks, "Would it advance my interests to grant the government this authority?" and then calculates the probability of the government being right, the probability of it influencing his beliefs, and the payoffs associated with outcomes ranging from being fined for clinging to one's true religious beliefs by an errant magistrate to avoiding the eternal fires of hell because the magistrate's policies prevented one from being led astray by seductive heresies. If the magistrate is even slightly more likely to be right about which religion is the true one, and if prudent use of state power can slightly increase the chances that citizens will accept it, then Proast could make a strong case for utilizing force. Since the eternal consequences of believing a false religion are potentially infinite, risking a little persecution while on earth might be a perfectly rational choice. If the magistrate had the best religious advisors around or if one thought for Condorcet-type reasons that the majority was more likely to be right,[35] consent to government action to promote true religion might be perfectly rational. Thus, even if we grant that the government has only those powers that it would be rational for citizens to grant them in the state of nature, given certain assumptions about probabilities and payoffs, consent to religious coercion might turn out to be perfectly rational.

Conclusion

The argument for which Locke is best known on the subject of toleration, the argument that persecution is irrational because coercion cannot bring about true belief in the persecutor's religion and because true belief, belief that is both correct and sincerely held, is necessary for salvation, is not his main argument for toleration. In his later writings, he essentially abandoned it and even contradicted it. The true belief argument had serious flaws, flaws that were pointed out almost immediately. In its place, Locke emphasized and significantly developed a different argument based on universalization. Locke's earlier argument that the magistrate might be wrong in matters of religion became more persuasive when he explicitly connected it with the premise that principles that authorize coercion must be universalizable in a world populated by fallible moral agents. It was this argument that Locke repeatedly came back to in his later writings on toleration, and it is this argument that shows the continuities between the theory of natural law in the *Two Treatises* and the theory of natural law in Locke's writings on toleration. This argument was more prevalent, foundational, characteristic, and persuasive than the true belief argument and thus has a strong claim to being preferred to other interpretations of Locke's theory of toleration.

NOTES

1. All parenthetical references refer to Volume 6 of the *Works of John Locke,* 10 vols. (London: Thomas Tegg, 1823; repr. Germany: Scienta Verlag Aalen, 1963).

2. See the chapters by Forst and Smith, this volume.

3. In some cases we might find it necessary to distinguish different periods of time. A thinker might emphasize and defend argument X for 30 years and then abandon it for a contradictory argument Y. In such a case we would likely talk about X as being characteristic of the thinker's "early" period and Y as characteristic of the later period.

4. Jonas Proast, *The Letter Concerning Toleration Briefly Considered and Answer'd* (Oxford, 1690), 3–6.

5. Ibid., 10–13.

6. Jonas Proast, *A Third Letter Concerning Toleration* (Oxford, 1691), 22.

7. Jeremy Waldron, "Locke, Toleration, and the Rationality of Persecution" in *John Locke: A Letter Concerning Toleration in Focus,* eds. John Horton and Susan Mendus (London: Routledge, 1991).

8. Waldron does discuss the Christian aspect of Locke's thought specifically in *God, Locke, and Equality: The Christian Foundations of Locke's Political Thought* (Cambridge: Cambridge University Press, 2002), 208–11.

9. Waldron, "Locke, Toleration, and the Rationality of Persecution," 115–18.

10. Proast, *The Letter Concerning Toleration Briefly Considered and Answer'd,* 7.

11. Proast, *A Third Letter Concerning Toleration,* 12, 47.

12. Ibid., 9–11.

13. Ibid., 15.

14. Ibid., 20–21.

15. Jeremy Waldron, "Locke, Toleration, and the Rationality of Persecution," 108.

16. Ibid., 118–19.

17.

> Tis true indeed, the Author and Finisher of our Faith has given the Magistrate no new power, or Commission: nor was there any need that he should, (if he himself had any temporal power to give:) For he found him [the magistrate] already, even by the Law of Nature, the minister of God to the People for good, and bearing the Sword not in vain, i.e. invested with Coactive Power, and obliged to use it for all the good purposes it might serve, and for which it should be found needful; even for the restraining of false and corrupt religion.

Jonas Proast, *A Third Letter Concerning Toleration,* 31.

18. Though not all may agree with this characterization of Kant, it is useful for illustrative purposes.

19. See pages 166–68 where Locke examines questions of authorization from God's perspective and pages 173–75 where Locke emphasizes that fallible magistrates will have to implement coercive instructions. Locke notes on page 179 that if Proast's argument is sound, it is not only magistrates of the true religion that will have this power, but "all magistrates will have this power alike."

20. Locke returns to many of the previous themes in the remainder of the chapter. He again talks about the fact that we lack the epistemic resources to correctly apply a law designed to punish people for not considering properly which religion is true at pages 225–27.

21. In general, these writers have failed to see the connection of the argument to natural law. Vernon instead rests the argument on Locke's contractualism. See Vernon, *The Career of Toleration: John Locke, Jonas Proast, and After* (Montreal and Kingston: McGill-Queen's University Press, 1997), 23–24, 32–33, 150. Nicholson treats the argument above as if it were two separate arguments, one about universalizability (175) and one claiming that "the law of nature only commissions the magistrate to do good" (176). Nicholson describes the law of nature argument as question begging because he fails to see its connection to the universalization argument. See Peter Nicholson, "John Locke's Later Letters on Toleration" in *John Locke: A Letter Concerning Toleration in Focus,* eds. John Horton and Susan Mendus (London: Routledge, 1991).

22. Locke goes on to show why magistrates may be more likely to err in matters of religion than in other areas. In temporal matters, legislators

must pass general laws and suffer the consequences with everyone else if the laws are misguided. Since false religion may not have negative repercussions until the distant future, no similar feedback loop occurs. I discuss this argument in more detail in *Locke and the Legislative Point of View,* 72–73.

23. Locke criticizes Proast for presuming to legislate for England while not realizing the implications of his argument elsewhere (510–14, 530, 535–36). When Locke concludes the work as a whole on pages 540–46, the first point Locke reiterates is his claim about natural law.

24. See Tuckness, "Rethinking the Intolerant Locke" *American Journal of Political Science* 46 (2002): 294–95.

25. John Locke, *Two Treatises of Government,* ed. Peter Laslett (Cambridge: Cambridge University Press, 1990), 1.124.

26. Ibid., 1.126.

27. Ibid., 1.127.

28. I am grateful to Jeremy Waldron for suggesting this argument.

29. See *Locke and the Legislative Point of View,* chap. 2.

30. Paul Bou-Habib, "Locke and the Rationality of Persecution" *Political Studies* 51 (2003): 611–26.

31. Susan Mendus, "Locke: Toleration, Morality, and Rationality" in *John Locke: A Letter Concerning Toleration in Focus,* eds. John Horton and Susan Mendus (London: Routledge, 1991), 153.

32. David Wootton, *Introduction to John Locke's Political Writings* (London: Penguin Books, 1993), 99–104.

33. Wootton also mentions the sincerity argument discussed above in John Locke's *Political Writings* on 102–3 as well as the unfairness of punishing only some of those who have not considered and punishing others who have already considered deeply on pages 104–5. While both of these arguments, as Wootton casts them, are still in terms of individual rationality, it should be noted that the latter argument is one that Locke continued to press vigorously in his later writings.

34. Vernon, *The Career of Toleration,* 22–23.

35. If the religion to be promoted were selected by majority vote and the average person had a greater than 50% chance of being right about which religion is true, and a large number of people were voting, then a rational person might think authorizing force was a good bet.

5

THE MODE AND LIMITS OF JOHN STUART MILL'S TOLERATION

GLYN MORGAN

Toleration occupies a conceptual space somewhere between approbation and prohibition. We do not, in other words, tolerate that which we have reason either to approve or to prohibit. Within the territory marked out between approbation and prohibition, tolerators can adopt a range of different stances towards the tolerated, including mere indifference, silent acquiescence, and judgmental disapproval.[1] A political theory of toleration ought to prescribe the appropriate stance or, what I intend to call, *the mode of toleration*. A political theory of toleration ought also to identify *the limits of toleration*. Where, in other words, ought we to mark the boundaries between the approved, the tolerated, and the prohibited? A complete political theory of toleration will include an account of both the mode and the limits of toleration.

Since its publication in 1859, Mill's essay *On Liberty* has been a target of conservatives, who believe that Mill tolerates too much that ought to be prohibited.[2] Mill famously refuses to prohibit anything that does not directly threaten the vital interests of other individuals. Neither sexual immorality nor religious heresy —the twin irritants of conservative moralists, then and now—warrants, so Mill believes, prohibition. Some contemporary self-styled liberals have joined conservatives in criticizing Mill's principles for permitting too much.[3] But more commonly liberals now tend to criticize Mill's essay for being insufficiently "respectful"—a distinctively modern form of approbation—of traditional, religious, and communal ways of life.[4] Mill would merely tolerate these ways of life, when they actually deserve, so Mill's critics maintain, a fuller measure of societal approval or respect.

Mill's recent critics trace the roots of his alleged failings of respect to two different sources. For so-called "political liberals," Mill goes wrong in his attachment to a comprehensive conception of the good—a substantive form of human flourishing, in other words—that not all "reasonable persons" can accept. Mill, from this perspective, fails to deliver an "adequate solution to the political problem of reasonable disagreement about the good life."[5] For "radical pluralists," Mill's liberalism suffers from its reliance upon a theory of progress that not only purports to distinguish more and less advanced societies, but refuses to recognize either the intrinsic value of less advanced societies or—more troubling still—their right to self-government.[6] It would be wrong to exaggerate the similarities between political liberals and radical pluralists, but on one key point they agree: "Mill's text simply is no good as the footing for a liberalism comfortable with human plurality."[7]

On the face of it, criticisms of Mill for his hostility to pluralism seem implausible. Mill's essay famously celebrates diversity and laments the increasing tendency to conformity in the society of his day. Mill, to be sure, does prefer individuality to bovine conformism; and he does believe that some societies are more advanced than others. But it is not obvious why these two commitments (to a conception of the good and to a conception of progress) necessarily render the argument of Mill's essay "narrow," "intolerant," "racist," or "ethnocentric."[8] A central task of this essay is to identify the role that these two commitments play in Mill's political theory and his account of toleration in particular. This task is complicated by the fact that Mill's political theory forms a part of a more general sociological theory, the central feature of which is the process of socialization or, what Mill terms, the formation of character. Much of Mill's argument concerning the mode and limits of toleration turns, as we shall see, on a set of claims concerning the interconnections of security, liberty, progress, and character-formation. The first part of this paper identifies the core features of Mill's sociological theory. The second part identifies Mill's conception of liberty, a conception that also fixes the limits of toleration. The third part shows how Mill justifies this conception of liberty with reference to our vital interest in security. The fourth part elaborates Mill's understanding of the mode of toleration. And the fifth part responds to political liberal and radical pluralist criticisms of the alleged "intolerance" of Mill's liberalism.

I: Mill's Sociological Theory

Although Mill presents his essay *On Liberty* as if it were a self-contained argument, it quickly emerges that his position presupposes a more general sociological theory that he does not fully defend in this text. This sociological theory informs all of Mill's political writings, even when it goes unmentioned. The quickest way into this sociological theory is through a number of the essays that he published in the *London and Westminster Review* during the 1830s and further elaborated both in the *Principles of Political Economy* and in Book VI of the *System of Logic.*

Mill himself acknowledges in these early writings the limits of any moral and political theory that ignores sociology (by which he means the study of social change and social cohesion). In his highly critical assessment of Bentham, Mill levels two general charges at Bentham's reformist project: one, Bentham fails to recognize that social and political institutions cannot be prescribed for a society as such, but only for a particular society at a specific stage of social and political development; and two, Bentham neglects the educative role of national culture.[9] "A philosophy of laws and institutions not founded on a philosophy of national character is," so Mill complains, "an absurdity."[10] It is worth unpacking these two criticisms, for they take us to the core of the more sociologically sophisticated political theory that Mill wishes to put in place of Benthamite utilitarianism.

For Mill, societies are culturally and historically distinctive. Societies, in short, have a distinctive national character. Mill conceptualizes this "national character" along two different dimensions: one, organic-cultural; and the other, historic-developmental. Both dimensions are, from the perspective of contemporary sociological theory, controversial. Let's begin with the organic-cultural dimension.

For Mill, a society cannot be understood merely as a conglomeration of self-interested individuals who share a common set of institutions. Mill maintains that "habitual sentiments and feelings, . . . general modes of thinking and acting" are constitutive components of society and shape the character of the individual members of that society.[11] Granted this view of society, Mill has little sympathy with those "philosophical speculators" (from "Plato to Bentham"), who believe that society can become "whatever the men who compose it choose to make it."[12] Each individual society, so Mill argues, has its own distinctive character, which is to say its own distinctive opinions, feelings, and habits. Political institutions and practical policy suggestions must fit the particular character of a society; what is suitable for one society may not be suitable for another. It is the task of "political ethology"—the science of character formation—to identify the causes that determine "the type of character belonging to a people or to an age."[13] While Mill concedes that our knowledge of "political ethology" remains rudimentary, he identifies certain features of society that we can take for granted.

First, he thinks that there is such a thing as "a state of society" defined by that society's material factors (i.e., state of economic development), political factors, (i.e., laws and forms of government) and ideal factors (i.e., beliefs, feelings, and general moral culture). These "factors" (my term not Mill's) coexist in a state of "consensus" (Mill's term not mine), such that they mutually determine the development of each other. Second, Mill thinks that there exist identifiable "uniformities of coexistence" between these material, political, and ideal factors. And third, he thinks that the proximate cause of every state of society is the state of society preceding it. The first and second of these propositions reveal the extent to which Mill—despite his later celebration of "individuality" in the essay *On Liberty*—embraces in his sociological theory a thoroughgoing form of social holism.[14] The third of these propositions make it clear that a philosophy of social science presupposes a philosophy of history. As Mill puts this third point:

> The fundamental problem, therefore, of the social sciences is to find the laws according to which any state of society produces the state of society which succeeds it and takes its place. This opens the great and vexed question of the progressiveness of man and society; an idea involved in every just conception of social phenomena as the subject of a science.[15]

Let's turn now to the idea that societies can be measured along an historical-developmental continuum, which itself is a presupposition of the view that societies can be described as more or less progressive or improved. Mill maintains, as we have seen, that each society has a distinctive character (or state of society), the chief determinant of which is the state of society that preceded it. At its most trivial level, this point amounts to little more than the observation that each society is shaped by its history. At a more controversial level, this point includes a claim about the relative importance of ideational factors—or changes in the state of knowledge—in determining social change.[16] At the most controversial level, however, Mill contends that changes in the state of knowledge follow an identifiable order of progression. This point is worth quoting in full:

> There is a sort of necessity established . . . by the general laws of human nature; by the constitution of the human mind. Certain truths cannot be discovered, or inventions made, unless certain others have been made first; certain social improvements, from the nature of the ease, can only follow, and not precede, others. The order of human progress, therefore, may to a certain extent have definite laws assigned to it.[17]

Granted that when societies develop, they do so following an identifiable order of progression, it becomes possible to identify societies as more or less advanced along a developmental path of progress. This is not to say, however, that there is anything inevitable in movement along this path of progress. Mill recognizes that societies can, if they are not fortunate, stagnate or even regress. Nonetheless, he hopes that the scientific study of society—sociology, in other words—will help identify what "artificial means may be used . . . to accelerate the natural progress [of society] insofar as it is beneficial."[18] Given the importance that Mill attaches to the role of ideas in motivating social change, intellectuals—and more generally, a culture of intellectual vitality—is the most important of these "artificial means." Mill, in short, looks to intellectuals to stimulate change in the character or culture of their society. He faults Bentham for focusing on laws and institutions, when cultural change is a more effective means of reform.

Notwithstanding Mill's criticisms of the sociological deficiencies of Benthamite utilitarianism, Mill still remains something of a Benthamite in his account of the ultimate ends of societal improvement. Mill recognizes that any definition of ultimate ends falls outside the scope of science and belongs to an account of, what he terms, "the Art of Life."[19] For Mill, the ultimate end of human development—and thus the gauge of genuine societal improvement—is happiness. Mill's notion of happiness is, however, complex. Typically, moral and political theorists think that happiness and perfection represent two contrasting options so far as the ultimate ends of human and societal aspiration are concerned.[20] Mill, however, muddies this distinction by interpreting happiness not, in its conventional sense, as a subjective state of mind, nor, in the modern economists' sense, as the satisfaction of preferences, but as the property of a particular type of character. For a sense of just how Mill muddies the conception of happiness, consider this passage towards the end of Book VI of his *System of Logic*:

> the general principle to which all practice ought to conform . . . is the conduciveness to the happiness of mankind. [T]he cultivation of an ideal nobleness of will and conduct, should be to individual human beings an end, to which the specific pursuit either of their own happiness or of that of others (except so far as included in that idea) should, in any case of conflict, give way. But I hold that the very question, what constitutes this elevation of character, is itself to be decided by a reference to happiness as the standard. The character itself should be, to the individual, a paramount end, simply because the existence of this ideal nobleness of character, or of a near approach to it, in any abundance, would go further than all things else towards making human life

> happy; both in the comparatively humble sense, of pleasure and freedom from pain, and in the higher meaning, of rendering life, not what it now is almost universally, puerile and insignificant—but such as human beings with highly developed faculties can care to have.[21]

This passage is revealing not only for its repudiation of happiness as a strictly "want-regarding" consideration, but also for its emphasis upon the development of a particular type of character.[22] Mill's scientific study of society does nothing to suggest that the trajectory of social change will prove propitious to this type of character. Indeed, Mill fears that the rise of the new middle classes will see the triumph of the "puerile and insignificant" at the expense of this type of character.[23] Nor does Mill make it clear why the happiness of this type of character, which he allows is the exception, has any authority with respect to the (subjective) happiness of the more numerous less developed characters that populate society. To pursue this problem further, we need to turn to some of Mill's later writings, especially his essay *On Liberty*.

II: Mill's Conception of Liberty

To grasp Mill's account of the limits of toleration, we need to understand Mill's conception of liberty. This task is more difficult than it initially appears, because it is not clear whether one, two, or multiple different *conceptions of liberty* inform the argument of *On Liberty*. Nor is it clear whether Mill provides one, two, or multiple different *justifications for liberty*. It is clear, however, that Isaiah Berlin's famous distinction between "negative liberty" (i.e., freedom from coercion) and "positive liberty" (i.e., freedom to do something valuable) is not very useful in understanding Mill's position.[24] Nonetheless, Berlin's discussion of *On Liberty* provides a good place to start, not least because his criticisms of Mill's argument have been taken up and amplified by contemporary radical pluralists.

For Berlin, Mill is "the most celebrated" defender of negative liberty. In support of this interpretation, Berlin cites Mill's bold assertion that "the only freedom which deserves the name is that of pursuing our own good in our own way."[25] Yet Berlin also recognizes that Mill's essay contains a number of arguments that recommend a particular life a free person ought to lead. Here Mill appears to endorse a particular type of character development (or "individuality") and to denigrate a life led in accordance with custom. The puzzle for Berlin (as for any interpreter of Mill's liberalism) is to reconcile Mill's defense of negative freedom with his more specific advocacy of "individuality."

Berlin's own solution to this interpretative puzzle involves a rather uncharitable reading of *On Liberty*. Mill, so Berlin argues, "confuses two distinct notions."[26] The first notion is that of freedom from unwanted interference by others (i.e., negative liberty); and the second notion is that of a certain type of character-development—"critical, imaginative, independent, non-conforming to the point of eccentricity" (i.e., individuality).[27] For Berlin, Mill's failure to distinguish these two different conceptions is compounded by his effort to employ the second in justification of the first. In Berlin's interpretation, Mill's argument rests on the claim that individuality "can be bred only in conditions of freedom."[28] Against this view, Berlin contends—arguing here along the lines of Mill's conservative adversary James Fitzjames Stephens—that

> the evidence of history shows . . . that integrity, love of truth, and fiery individualism grow at least as often in severely disciplined communities, for example the puritan Calvinists of Scotland or New England, or under military discipline, as in more tolerant or indifferent societies; and if this is so, Mill's argument for liberty as a necessary condition for the growth of human genius falls to the ground.[29]

Berlin's criticism appears, on the face of it, to be devastating. If true, it would provide confirming evidence that Mill is a muddled thinker, who defends his liberalism with a ragbag of ideas that do not belong together. Berlin's position is not, however, altogether persuasive, either in its interpretation of Mill's argument or in the suggestion that individuality can develop "at least as often" in authoritarian communities as in tolerant liberal societies. In order to rescue Mill from Berlin's misjudged criticisms, it is necessary, first, to identify the specific conception of liberty that Mill defends; and second, to rescue Mill from the charge that this conception of liberty lacks a convincing justification.

Mill introduces his conception of liberty in the context of a broader genealogical discussion of organized power. At the current "stage of progress," Mill informs us, "protection . . . against the tyranny of the magistrate is not enough, there needs protection against the tyranny of the prevailing feeling and opinion."[30] We need, in short "a different and more fundamental treatment of liberty" that fixes the legitimate limits of the power over the individual of both state and society.[31] Central to Mill's own treatment of liberty is his strong presumption in favor of free thought and action. All forms of coercion—whether involving legal penalties or societal control—require a justification. Mill defends a particular principle of justification—"one simple principle," as he rather misleadingly puts it—according to which "the only purpose for which power can be rightly exercised over any member of a civilized community . . . is to prevent harm to others."[32] Although this justificatory principle is now commonly referred to as Mill's "harm principle," it is important to recognize that "harm" is merely one of a number of different terms that Mill employs to express the same point. Thus he tells us at various points in the text that coercion can be justified solely for the "self-protection" (of society); "for the security of others"; when actions "produce evil to someone else"; when actions "concern the interest of other people"; when actions are "hurtful to others"; when an individual "make[s] himself a nuisance to other people"; and when an individual "molest[s] others in what concerns them."[33] Yet, regardless of which words Mill uses to express the point, the task remains that of identifying precisely where the boundaries lie between protected freedom and legitimate coercion, because these boundaries mark the limits of toleration.

Mill himself clearly believes that his own principle of justified coercion yields a determinate sphere of individual liberty (a specific "doctrine" of liberty, as he sometimes terms it). Included within this sphere are a number of specific liberties, including "liberty of conscience, in the most comprehensive sense, liberty of thought and feeling . . . liberty of tastes and pursuits, of framing the plan of life to suit our own character; [and] . . . freedom to unite."[34] Yet, to some of his critics (including Berlin), Mill's principle of justified coercion is simply too vague, no matter what words ("harm," "security," "hurt," "self-protection," "producing evil," "making oneself a nuisance to others") are plugged into the principle. This problem is further compounded by the vagueness of another concept Mill introduces: that of a "self-regarding" sphere of action or conduct.

Mill employs the term "self-regarding" in both a descriptive and a moral sense. The double usage of the term gives rise to confusion. In its descriptive sense, self-regarding action has no social dimension and does not affect others. Thus, when I cut my toenails in the solitude of my windowless study, I act in this (descriptively) self-regarding way. Yet, if I were to take off my socks and cut my toenails in a packed lecture hall, I would not be acting in a self-regarding but in a social way. My actions in the lecture hall affect others, even if only in a trivial way. Rather than employing the term "self-regarding" solely in this descriptive sense, however, Mill also employs the term in a moral (or evaluative) sense. He notices, for instance, that descriptively self-regarding actions can sometimes affect others in a non-trivial way. Take, for instance, the person who drinks at home to excess and cannot look after his children or turn up for jury duty. Such a person cannot, so Mill thinks, be described as acting in a self-regarding way. As he puts this point:

> When a person disables himself, by conduct purely self-regarding from performance of some definite duty incumbent on him to the public, he is guilty of a social offence. Whenever, in short, there is definite damage, either to an individual or to the public, the case is taken out of the province of liberty, and placed in that of morality or law.[35]

The idea here is that when actions damage others, it ceases to be (evaluatively) self-regarding even while it remains (descriptively) self-regarding. Mill recognizes cases where actions *deservedly* lose their "self-regarding" status—as in the case of the drunken jury member—and cases where actions *undeservedly* lose their self-regarding status. Mill is primarily concerned with this latter situation. He wants to warn us of the tendency of public authorities to regulate actions or conduct that is *deservedly* self-regarding. Consider here, for example, a Muslim community that seeks to prohibit a dissenting minority from eating pork. For Mill, this type of prohibition is not "a legitimate exercise of the moral authority of public opinion." Why? Because "with the personal tastes and self-regarding concerns of individuals, the public has no business to interfere."[36] In other words, the eating of pork is a *deservedly* self-regarding issue, no matter how repugnant to the wider community.

Having clarified the different meanings of the term "self-regarding," it must be conceded that the term itself does not help us to decide which actions or forms of conduct deserve to be treated as self-regarding and which deserve to be regulated by law or public morality. In order to settle this issue, we need to focus attention on the different ways that one person's actions can affect others. Without going into the full details of Mill's argument here, we can summarize these ways as follows:

i. Actions that affect merely the agent;
ii. Actions that affect others in a trivial way;
iii. Actions that affect others negatively, but (a) consensually; or (b) justifiably;
iv. Actions that unjustifiably and non-consensually harm the vital or essential interests of others.

Insofar as we are concerned here with Mill's conception of liberty, actions (iv) are the most important. Mill would prohibit only those actions that "harm" (or "hurt," or "damage" etc.) the vital or essential interests of others. Actions that merely affect the agent (i), affect others trivially (ii), with their consent (iii a), or with justification (iii b) do not warrant prohibition. Viewed in this light, Mill's principle of justified coercion—and thus his account of the limits of toleration—depends upon a conception of vital interests. Unfortunately, Mill's own text is less helpful here than it ought to be. Mill recognizes the existence of a certain class of essential or vital interests—which he also sometimes refers to as "rights"—but he does not provide us with a clear account of these interests.[37] True, he informs us that his argument appeals to "utility . . . grounded in the permanent interests of man as a progressive being."[38] But this does little to resolve the problem of identifying these interests.

Berlin himself resolves this ambiguity by interpreting Mill's "progressive being" in terms of the account of "individuality" that Mill provides in Chapter III of *On Liberty*. In this chapter, Mill sings the praises of a particular character type that displays, in the face of increasing pressures to conformity and leveling, a form of originality, spontaneity, and self-fashioning. Mill fears that this type of character, already a rarity, will become rarer still in the modern world. The suggestion (by Berlin and others) that "individuality" provides the justification for Mill's more general conception of liberty—which involves pursuing "our own good in our own way" and allows coercion only to prevent harm to (the vital or essential) interests of others—is, however, deeply problematic: it begs the question why this character-type has any normative authority in a society where (by Mill's own admission) it is rare and unpopular.[39] Unless, we can offer some resolution of this problem, it will be difficult to resist the "traditionalist" interpretation of Mill's political theory as confused and contradictory.[40]

III: Security and Civilization

Granted that Mill's conception of liberty can only be inadequately defended in terms of "individuality," it is important to locate an alternative stronger justification for liberty. The solution lies, I think, partly in Mill's account of security—which he labels our most "vital interest"—and partly in his theory of character-formation. The drawback with this interpretation is that it concedes that Mill's essay *On Liberty* does not contain within itself a fully adequate defense of Mill's "doctrine" of liberty.

Mill informs us in *On Liberty* that compulsion is "justifiable only for the security of others."[41] *On Liberty* itself, however, has very little to say either about "security" or its opposite, "insecurity." Elsewhere in Mill's writings, however, he has a lot more to say about security. Indeed, we must look to Mill's essay on "Utilitarianism" for a clear statement that security is "the most vital of all interests." Mill here goes on to explain why: "security no human being can possibly do without; on it we depend for all our immunity from evil." In the absence of security, we would have no ability to look forward with any degree of confidence to the future. "Nothing but the gratification of the instant could be of any worth to us."[42]

Security also figures prominently in Mill's account of progress and in his understanding of civilization.[43] As Mill makes clear in these writings, security involves not merely immediate, short-term physical safety, but durable long-term protection of personhood and property. Absent this protection, individuals would merely have momentary access to their goods; they would never achieve psychological tranquility. Furthermore, individuals in insecure societies would be unable to save and plan for the future. Mill sees security (understood in this expansive way) as both a precondition and a defining feature of a civilized society. "One of the acknowledged effects [of social progress]," he reports, "is an increase of general security. Destruction by wars and spoliation by private or public violence, are less and less to be apprehended."[44] When Mill refers here to the progress achieved by civilized societies, he has in mind not only the level of security provided by such societies, but also the distribution of the benefit of security to all members of society on roughly equal terms. While in premodern (or "backward") societies, some achieved security at the expense of others. A civilized society provides security to all of its members, which in turn allows for greater cooperation and greater economic productivity.

While it is sometimes said that "security" is the core value of the modern liberal tradition, it is not clear that Mill can rely wholly upon this value to justify his doctrine of liberty.[45] First, security might seem to justify the imposition of a wide measure of liberty-limiting measures. Indeed, security seems to fit more securely into the absolutist tradition than the modern liberal tradition. Second—and more specifically relevant to Mill's argument—Mill professes to appeal to "the permanent interests of man as a progressive being." Security, in contrast, would appear to be an interest of man as such rather than man as a progressive being; it certainly seems to lack the developmental dimension suggested by the term "progressive." These two difficulties are, however, more apparent than real. Security, as Mill understands it, is a sufficiently complex interest to allow the state to protect us from something other than mere physical violence. Indeed, here it is important to recognize that Mill allows the state to punish people who fail to perform various essential duties to society. This more expansive conception of security—which would allow the state to prohibit various types of private "spoliation" of our property—coexists with a refusal to allow state coercion to prevent more indirect threats to security. Mill, for instance, dismisses the arguments of the prohibitionist, who claims that alcohol consumption "destroys my primary right of security."[46] In addition to Mill's complex understanding of the threats to which our security is and is not vulnerable, Mill's security-based argument coexists with a character-based argument that provides an additional set of reasons for limiting the scope of state coercion.

The formation of character is a theme that connects Mill's political theory to his earlier sociological theory. For Mill, our character is everything. Yet, notwithstanding its importance, Mill does not think that the coercive apparatus of the state can play a role in its formation or improvement. Much like Tocqueville, Mill fears that under any absolute forms of power—whether exercised by a government, a factory owner, or male head of household—we develop a dependent type of character. For Mill, the formation of character must proceed *passively*, by way of the influences of our background national culture, and *interactively*, by way of our dealings with each other in a free and open society. Intellectuals can and ought to play a role in the formation of a national character by holding themselves up as models of excellence. The state, in contrast, is largely an obstacle to this bottom-up and interactive form of character formation. This belief gives Mill further reason to think that the state ought to coerce as little as possible—and never, for instance, for paternalist or perfectionist reasons. The Millian state accordingly sets the limits of toleration at a very permissive level. The same point is not true, however, when it comes to organized public opinion, which—as we will see in the next section—Mill expects to play a more intrusive role in the formation of character.

Notwithstanding Mill's reliance upon a character-based argument in his justification of liberty, argument must be kept separate from Mill's own celebration of "individuality." Admittedly, Mill's *On Liberty* is less than clear on this point. Nonetheless, it is important to recall that "individuality" is, merely, as Mill puts it in the title of Chapter II, "*one* of the elements of well-being" (emphasis added). Elsewhere in Mill's writings—especially in his early reviews of Grote's and Tocqueville's books, and his own later works *Considerations of Representative Government* and *Subjection of Women*—Mill offers a much more rounded account of the type of character that, under ideal circumstances, can emerge in a civilized society. Here he has less to say about "originality," "spontaneity," and "eccentricity"—core characteristics of "individuality"—than about independence (the capacity for self-governance), public-spiritedness, and civic-mindedness. These characteristics are considerably less heroic, more democratic—and thus more widely shareable—than those that define individuality. Mill's worry is that even these characteristics, which together define, what might be termed, a free and independent character, will be eroded by one or the other of two regressive developments present in civilized societies. One is the encroachment of the state on social life; the other is the rise of a new conformist middle class. Thus, if overweening state power represents one potential threat to a free society, society itself, in the form of a conformist public opinion, represents another.

If we accept Mill's account of a civilized society, then his doctrine of liberty stands in an instrumental relationship to the vital interest of security. While liberty, as Mill understands it, is essentially "negative" (in Berlin's sense of the term), Mill nonetheless believes that only in a free society (and, more to the point, *never* under a paternalist or perfectionist state) will people acquire the capacities for self-government and sociability that offer a more reliable long-term guarantee of their freedom. In this respect, negative liberty (freedom to do what you want) is the route to a form of positive liberty (freedom to be self-governing), which itself offers the best protection for negative liberty. The state (at least in any of its coercive dimensions) can do nothing, however, to ensure that people take this route and use their negative liberty to develop their self-governing capacities. A limited state focused solely on security interests thus remains a necessary condition of a free and equal society of self-governing individuals.

We are now in a position to explain how Mill's security-based justification for liberty fits into his account of the limits and mode of toleration. Simply stated, the limits of toleration correspond to the boundaries set by the doctrine of liberty. We must tolerate all acts that do not unjustifiably prejudice the security interests of others. In practice, the limits of Mill's toleration would accord closely with what we have come to expect in a modern liberal democratic society. In some areas, Mill would be more tolerant. He would, for instance, regulate rather than prohibit prostitution, gambling, and even the sale of poisons. These examples suggest that Mill would require an act to be an immediate, direct, and a very serious threat to security before it would warrant prohibition. In other areas, however, Mill would be less tolerant than most liberal democratic societies. Mill is, for instance, quite willing to prosecute parents for failures to safeguard the welfare of their children. Presumably, he thinks that children have security interests that impose specific parental duties, the nonperformance of which the state must deter.

While Mill's account of *what* we ought to tolerate (i.e., the limits of toleration) occupies a central and uncontroversial position in the liberal political tradition, this is not the case with his account of *how* we ought to tolerate (i.e., the mode of toleration). Mill's account of the mode of toleration is especially important, because it is here that Mill wrestles with some of the tensions present in his own account of the formation of human character. Mill, as we have seen, believes that a civilized society can form and sustain independent, sociable characters. This belief plays a crucial role in Mill's justification for a minimal security-based liberalism. Yet Mill also recognizes that a civilized society can generate conformist characters that, when organized into an impersonal public opinion, jeopardize not only the formation of independent sociable characters but liberty itself. Mill presents us here with two different stories—one positive or progressive, one negative or regressive—about the process of character-formation in a civilized society. The problem for Mill is that insofar as the regressive process predominates, then his own argument for a minimal security-based liberalism loses much of its force. Indeed, this negative process not only makes Mill's arguments vulnerable to conservatives who reject the enfranchisement of the working classes; it also makes Mill's arguments vulnerable to those who favor a more state-centric, rights-based liberalism. For these state-centric, rights-based liberals—of whom Ronald Dworkin is perhaps the leading contemporary example—the state (and, more especially, judges and the law courts) must assume a much more expansive role in the regulation of our social affairs if we are to safeguard our personal liberties.[47] Mill can resist this state-centric approach, only because he believes that the progressive process of character-formation requires a minimal and non-interventionist state. Furthermore, he thinks that the progressive process of character-formation can still—notwithstanding a rising tide of conformity—be rescued. Mill's account of the mode of toleration can be understood as a key contribution to this rescue operation.

IV: The Mode of Toleration

Chapter IV of *On Liberty*—a chapter not usually read as addressing the topic of toleration at all—might be read as an extended discussion of the mode of toleration.[48] To understand this aspect of Mill's theory, it is important to recall the distinctions drawn above in Section II between:

i. Actions that affect merely the agent;
ii. Actions that affect others in a trivial way;
iii. Actions that affect others negatively, but (a) consensually; or (b) justifiably;
iv. Actions that unjustifiably and non-consensually harm the vital interests of others.

In the case of (iv), Mill's principle permits legal penalties, because such acts violate the vital interests (or "rights") of others. Mill goes to pains, however, to distinguish these acts from actions (ii) and (iii) that have a negative impact upon others, but "without going the length of violating any of their constituted rights."[49] Mill includes under (ii) various types of anti-social behavior and the character flaws that give rise to such behavior. Yet merely because Mill's principles call for the *toleration* of such behavior does not mean that such behavior ought to be ignored or accepted. For Mill, the mode of toleration is consistent with—and sometimes demands—judgmental disapproval.[50] Indeed, Mill is at pains to emphasize that his doctrine of liberty is not one of "selfish indifference."[51] As Mill elaborates this point:

> Though doing no wrong to any one, a person may so act as to compel us to judge him . . . as a fool, or as a being of an inferior order: and since this judgment and feeling are a fact which he would prefer to avoid, it is doing him a service to warn him of it beforehand as of any other disagreeable consequence to which he exposes himself.[52]

Mill laments the customary distaste for this sort of judgmentalism. "It would be well, indeed," he writes, "if this good office were much more freely rendered than the common notions of politeness at present permit." On Mill's account, we must judge others and put these judgments into practice, even by pointedly shunning the judged person's company if necessary, and advising others to do the same. In this way, a judged person might "suffer very severe penalties at the hands of others, for faults which directly concern only himself." The character flaws that merit this treatment include "rashness, obstinacy, self-conceit . . . [and the pursuit of] animal pleasures at the expense of feeling and intellect."[53]

While judgmental disapproval is the right response to self-regarding character flaws, Mill's principles call for a more organized form of "moral reprobation and, in grave cases, of moral retribution and punishment," when a person's anti-social behavior actually injures the interests of others. Mill has in mind here actions that range from "encroachment on [our rights]" to "selfish abstinence from defending [us] against injury." More controversially, Mill also calls for some form of organized moral disapprobation of the character-traits that give rise to this type of anti-social behavior. The character traits that warrant this more punitive response include: "Cruelty of disposition; malice and ill nature; . . . envy; dissimulation and insincerity; irascibility on insufficient cause, and resentment disproportioned to the provocation, the love of domineering over others."[54] Unlike the purely self-regarding character flaws ("rashness, obstinacy, self-conceit," and so forth), these character-traits are signs of "a bad and odious moral character" and are taken out of the self-regarding sphere.

Mill does not think that such traits call for legal punishment, but they do call for us to "make . . . life uncomfortable" for such a person.[55] In this respect, Mill appears to recognize a distinction (at least in these passages of Chapter IV if not elsewhere in the text) between actions that merely prejudice our interests and actions that harm our vital interest in security. While the latter class of actions (e.g., physical violence and robbery) calls for legal punishment, the former class calls for organized moral reprobation.

Mill's focus on the formation of character in Chapter IV of *On Liberty* goes some way to qualifying his reputation as a paradigmatic liberal. Mill is certainly no enemy of the right type of social control.[56] Indeed, Mill's discussion in Chapter IV shows that his own preferred mode of toleration requires us to assume responsibility for each other's character formation. In this respect, Mill's mode of toleration is very different from those who envisage toleration as merely a means of securing civil order between otherwise antagonistic groups. For Mill, toleration is an educative mechanism that must be used wisely if free societies are to build the right type of characters. Viewed in this light, Mill's mode of toleration can be understood as a contribution to, what was termed above, the progressive process of character formation in a civilized society.

It is important to recognize that the contribution of this mode of toleration to the formation of a progressive character rests upon a number of empirical claims concerning the connection between security, liberty, progress, and character-formation. Mill's political theory is far more empirical than much of contemporary political theory, which often justifies liberty on the basis of an essentialist conception of individual well-being. Mill, in contrast, situates his justification of liberty in the empirical world. There are both advantages and disadvantages of proceeding in this empirical fashion. The most obvious disadvantage is that Mill's empirical claims concerning the process of character formation might prove false. Perhaps people will use their freedom to develop pernicious lifestyles and base characters from which they will derive little genuine happiness; perhaps they will use their freedom to oppress each other.

For many contemporary liberals, Mill's liberalism is too contingent and insufficiently universal to be acceptable. For Mill, the circumstances under which liberty leads to a positive form of character formation are bounded by a theory of progress. Only in a modern "civilized" society can we expect liberty to yield such positive consequences. In non-civilized, pre-modern societies, a more substantial form of state control may prove necessary. Few contemporary liberals are comfortable with this non-universalistic form of liberalism. Nor are they comfortable with Mill's reliance upon a process of character-formation as the ultimate guarantee for security and liberty. Most contemporary liberals would prefer to rely instead on the state and the courts, not only to protect a more extensive set of individual rights, but to act as guiding lights in this process of character formation. Mill, in contrast, seems to think that a progressive process of character formation goes awry when the state assumes too much influence. Mill takes this anti-paternalist position to surprising lengths, even to the point of opposing a state monopoly on education. While he is not opposed to guiding lights, these lights, he believes, are best provided by intellectuals in and through their role as shapers of public debate. Mill appears to think that both the progressive process of character formation and, more generally, the cause of progressive liberalism will benefit from the clash of ideas, opinions, and judgments. This belief is a consequence of the line of thought he develops in Chapter II of *On Liberty* concerning the outcome of clashing ideas. Mill is famously optimistic about the likely outcome of the free exchange of ideas. Truth will, he thinks, prevail; liberal values will be proven right; and Gresham's Law—at least in the realm of ideas—broken. Mill's account of toleration, both its limits and its mode, plays a key role in allowing this exchange of ideas to take place.

V: Mill's Alleged Intolerance

In recent years, Mill's liberalism has come in for criticism less because of its empirical uncertainties, than because of its alleged intolerance. This failing is widely believed to stem from his commitment to a controversial conception of the good and to a theory of progress. By way of conclusion, I want to show that neither the political liberal nor the radical pluralist criticisms of Mill's alleged intolerance is warranted. Many of these recent criticisms of Mill's liberalism reiterate Isaiah Berlin's contention that Mill's argument for liberty is confused and unconvincing.[57] Berlin, as I have argued above, misreads Mill by suggesting that Mill seeks to justify his doctrine of liberty on the basis of a conception of "individuality." For Mill, individuality is certainly important, but it does not enter directly into the justification of the doctrine of liberty. Mill justifies this doctrine of liberty in two steps. The first step involves an account of the individual's vital or essential interests. The second step involves an account of character-formation in a modern civilized society. Mill's justification for liberty turns crucially on the claim that a progressive character—by which he means a self-governing, sociable, and civically engaged character—can emerge and prosper in a free society. Mill worries that the development of this type of character will be thwarted by the spirit of conformity and leveling that has accompanied the emergence of a new Victorian middle class. His celebration of individuality might be read as an effort to resist this spirit of conformity. Mill is fully aware that only a few will live such a life to the full. But he hopes that these few will be able to stem the tide of conformity.

Berlin's further contention that "integrity, love of truth, and fiery individualism grow at least as often in severely disciplined communities" also seems to miss the point of Mill's own justification for the doctrine of liberty. Mill has no doubt that excellent individuals—Pericles, Socrates, Marcus Aurelius are among those he mentions—have emerged in earlier non-liberal societies. The recognition of this fact does not, however, entail (as Berlin claims) that Mill's argument for liberty then "falls to the ground."[58] Mill's argument for liberty turns on the claim that our vital interest in security requires the emergence of a progressive character not merely in a few individuals but on a societal scale. To appreciate the nature of this claim, it is important to read Mill's argument in the light of his sociological theory. Mill is a social holist. He thinks that the formation of character proceeds on the basis of a "consensus" of social factors. For this reason, we cannot generally expect the character of individuals in a society to depart too far from the broader national or societal culture. For Mill, "severely disciplined communities" (as Berlin calls them) will be unable to produce *in general* (the odd individual aside) anything other than one-sided stunted characters. No less importantly, Mill is a theorist of progress. He sees modern civilized societies in terms of a trajectory of societal development. Both the precondition and the great achievement of such societies is their attainment of a high level of security for all their members on roughly equal terms. Consider here, for instance, the following passage from the *Subjection of Women*:

> As society was constituted until the last few generations, inequality was its very basis; association grounded on equal rights scarcely existed; to be equals was to be enemies; two persons could hardly cooperate in anything; or meet in any amicable relation, without the law's appointing that one of them should be the superior of the other. Mankind have outgrown this state, and all things now tend to substitute, as the general principle of human relations, a just equality, instead of the dominion of the strongest.[59]

For Mill, a modern civilized society can achieve a high level of security for all its members, because the members of such a society can as equals cooperate together much more effectively than the members of any hierarchical society. Mill's historical sociology is not without its faults. But at this broad level of abstraction, Mill's sociological claims seem more robust than Berlin's. Mill can allow that strong independent characters have existed in disciplined non-liberal societies. But all he needs for his argument to succeed is to show that only a modern, civilized society can possess a national culture capable of mass producing characters who think of themselves as both independent and as equals. Berlin does nothing to show that Mill is wrong on this point.

Versions of Berlin's criticisms of Mill's political theory show up in more recent criticisms of the alleged intolerance of Mill's liberalism. For so-called political liberals, Mill's liberalism is flawed in its reliance upon "a comprehensive conception of the good." "Individuality" is a perfectionist ideal—so this objection goes—that not all citizens can be reasonably required to share. Political liberals recognize that a liberal political theory presupposes some conception of the person, but they dismiss Mill's liberalism as too thick and controversial.[60] The force of the political liberal critique hinges, much like Berlin's, on the claim that Mill's liberalism depends upon (i.e., is justified by) the account of "individuality" in

Chapter II of *On Liberty*. This reading of Mill's *On Liberty* is not, however, persuasive. The more plausible reading justifies the doctrine of liberty merely on the basis of our vital interests in security coupled with a sociological theory concerning the formation of a progressive character. Mill's sociological theory might be falsified on empirical grounds. Mill's progressive character might itself be criticized as embodying a set of undesirable traits (although independence, sociability, civic mindedness are not obviously undesirable). But these traits no more define a comprehensive conception of the good than does the conception of the person that informs the writings of contemporary political liberals.

Mill's liberalism faces an altogether more serious challenge from contemporary radical pluralists, who believe that Mill's liberalism is unjustifiably hostile to traditional cultures in general and cultural minorities in particular. Adding force to this criticism is Mill's personal advocacy of a form of Western imperialism.[61] Without wishing to defend here Mill's imperialism, the question remains whether his imperialism infects and invalidates all aspects of his liberalism. Radical pluralists believe that it does. Mill's liberalism, so they maintain, presupposes a theory of progress that refuses to recognize the value of any society that does not fit Mill's "ethnocentric" and possibly "racist" notion of "civilization." This radical pluralist criticism draws additional force, because it focuses on a dimension of Mill's political theory that (as fully acknowledged here) is absolutely central: namely, his theory of progress.

The most powerful version of the radical pluralist challenge to Mill's liberalism can be found in some of John Gray's recent writings. For Gray, there is no basis to the claim that modern liberal societies have a privileged claim to protecting their members against "generic evils" such as physical insecurity. "Who can doubt," Gray asks "that human beings flourished under the feudal institutions of medieval Christendom? Or under the monarchical government of Elizabethan England?"[62] If Gray is correct here in the suggestion that a wide range of non-liberal regimes can satisfy our need for security and other basic goods, then Mill's justification for liberty would be in trouble. But Gray's claims about medieval Christendom and Elizabethan England are no more plausible than Berlin's claims about pre-modern "disciplined societies."

The point missed by many radical pluralists is that modern liberal societies—call them "civilized" societies, if you wish—are superior to non-liberal societies in two different ways. First, modern liberal societies are wealthier than nearly all pre-existing historical societies. It is simply impossible for a society to eradicate the full range of insecurities that we face, including malnutrition and grinding poverty, unless that society has access to the benefits of a modern dynamic economy, which in turn depends upon knowledge-intensive production processes. Mill was absolutely correct when he noted that the state of knowledge is the principal determinant of social change. A society that lacks access to a knowledge-creating educative process will itself be unable to provide its citizens with a full measure of security. Second, modern liberal societies remain committed to meeting the basic needs of all their citizens on a roughly equal basis. Whereas feudal and early modern European regimes provided *some* people with security, the modern liberal state is premised on the idea that *all* citizens have an equal claim to be secure. Clearly, no one can doubt that *some* people flourished under the political systems of medieval Christendom. But the same might be said of almost any regime, including Saddam Hussein's Iraq, Duvalier's Haiti, and apartheid-era South Africa. The achievement of modern liberal societies is to protect all citizens on roughly equal terms against the major avoidable insecurities of life.

Mill's political theory is quite open in acknowledging the centrality of security and equality. He believes that these values are protected by "civilized societies," and as such are morally superior to "backward" societies where these values go ignored. If Mill wants to say that "civilized societies" (so defined) are more advanced, improved, further along the path of progress, then it is difficult to disagree. Perhaps a radical pluralist might argue that security and equality are themselves merely "Western" values, the appeal to which is "ethnocentric" and perhaps "racist." But Gray himself does not go this far. He recognizes the existence of "generic evils" grounded in the constancies of human nature. To abandon a commitment to any form of common basic values or interests is to adopt a form of radical pluralism that is indistinguishable from a pure form of cultural relativism or a valueless nihilism. Neither of these more extreme positions has a particular objection to Millian liberalism that does not apply to any universalist moral or political theory, even the minimalist version embraced by Gray and other radical pluralists.

The second part of the radical pluralist challenge to Mill's liberalism focuses on the situation of cultural minorities within allegedly modern "civilized" societies. It is certainly not difficult to convict Mill of cultural arrogance and insensitivity. His comments on, for instance, the Welsh are most spectacularly ill-informed.[63] But the more serious allegation of radical pluralists is that Mill's liberalism is itself unjustifiably hostile to traditional and minority ways of life. On the face of it, this criticism seems ludicrous, especially once it is recognized that Mill's doctrine of liberty does not depend upon his account of individuality but merely on a broader account of an independent and sociable character. For Mill, the state can prohibit only those actions that affect in a significant and direct way the security interests of others. This is to set the limits of toleration at a very permissive level. There is very little that a Millian state would do to prohibit those who so choose from enjoying and preserving their traditional or minority way of life. True, Mill does not see any intrinsic value to these ways of life. But the charge of unjustified intolerance draws its force not from Mill's personal opinions, but from some perceived failing in the Millian state.

Despite its permissiveness, there is nonetheless a point at which the Millian state will come into conflict with traditional ways of life. This point arises, when the traditional culture seeks to enforce liberty-limiting constraints on their own members or those of the wider society. Mill discusses such cases in Chapter IV of *On Liberty,* when he takes up such issues as the demand of Muslims that the eating of pork be legally prohibited. Here Mill reiterates his claim that security interests alone can justify coercion. Clearly, this response will not satisfy those who believe that their way of life must be propped up by the coercive apparatus of the state. Nor will it satisfy those who believe that a life led in the tracks of a traditional culture matters more than security itself. But these belief systems would set the limits of toleration at a much less permissive level than in the Millian state. Some radical pluralists are quite open in their advocacy of moving beyond the language and practice of toleration. They envisage a state where every group has its "respect" protected by the state and where all statements of group disrespect go legally punished. These radical pluralists envisage a much less "tolerant" regime than anything Mill has in mind. There is certainly no reason to accept charges of "intolerance" coming from them.

NOTES

1. For excellent recent discussions of the conceptual grammar of toleration, see Rainer Forst, *Toleranz* (Frankfurt: Suhrkamp, 2003); Catrionna McKinnon, *Toleration: A Critical Introduction* (London: Routledge, 2006); and Glen Newey, *Virtue, Reason, and Toleration* (Edinburgh: Edinburgh University Press, 2000).

2. For a compendium of such criticisms, see James Fitzjames Stephens, *Liberty, Equality, and Fraternity* (Cambridge: Cambridge University Press, 1967 [1873]), esp. Chapter One.

3. Consider, for instance, recent criticisms of Mill's liberalism for permitting pornography, racial and religious hate speech, and policies of cultural assimilation. For a discussion of some of these criticisms, see Glyn Morgan, "Mill's Liberalism, Security, and Group Defamation," in *Free Speech in Hard Times,* ed. Glen Newey (Cambridge: Cambridge Scholars Press, 2007).

4. Consider here, for example, the complaint that Mill was "dogmatically secularist, hence less tolerant than is ordinarily allowed." Ira Katznelson, *Liberalism's Crooked Circle* (Princeton: Princeton University Press, 2005), 143.

5. Charles Larmore, *The Morals of Modernity* (Cambridge: Cambridge University Press, 1996), 131; for Rawls' critique of Mill's "comprehensive" liberalism, see John Rawls, *Political Liberalism* (New York: Columbia University Press, 1993), 37, 78.

6. See here, for instance, John Gray, *Enlightenment's Wake* (London: Routledge, 1995), Chapters 8 and 9; and Bhikhu Parekh, "Superior People: The Narrowness of Liberalism from Mill to Rawls," *Times Literary Supplement,* 25 February 1994, 12.

7. Katznelson, *Liberalism's Crooked Circle,* 143; compare also Bhikhu Parekh, *Cultural Diversity and Political Theory* (Cambridge, MA: Harvard University Press, 2000), 40–46.

8. Katznelson, *Liberalism's Crooked Circle* , 138–41.

9. John Stuart Mill, "Bentham," in *Collected Works of John Stuart Mill,* ed. John M. Robson (Toronto: University of Toronto Press, 1963–1991) [hereafter CW], 8, 75–116.

10. "Bentham," CW, 8, 99.

11. *System of Logic,* CW, 8, 891

12. Ibid., 876

13. Ibid., 905

14. For a discussion of this aspect of Mill's thought, see Karl Popper, *The Poverty of Historicism* (London: Routledge, 2002 [1957]).

15. *System of Logic,* CW, 8, 912.

16. Ibid., 927.

17. Ibid., 938.

18. Ibid., 929.

19. Ibid., 949.

20. Thus to Henry Sidgwick "we may perhaps say that *prima facie* the only two ends which have a strongly and widely supported claim to be regarded as rational ultimate ends are the two just mentioned, Happiness and Perfection or Excellence of human nature—meaning here by 'Excellence' not primarily superiority to others, but a partial realization of, or approximation to, an ideal type of human Perfection." *The Method of Ethics* (New York: Dover, 1966 [Seventh edition, 1907]), 9.

21. *System of Logic,* CW, 8, 952.

22. Mill, to borrow Brian Barry's distinction, thereby transforms happiness from "a want-regarding" consideration (which "takes as given the wants people happen to have") into an "ideal-regarding" consideration (which, in Mill's case, involves discounting some wants and treating others, such as those of a more educated character, as more valuable). Brian Barry, *Political Argument* (London: Routledge and Kegan Paul, 1965), 41–42.

23. This was a theme of Mill's early essay "Civilization," CW, 18, 117–48.

24. Isaiah Berlin, "Two Concepts of Liberty," *Four Essays on Liberty* (New York: Oxford University Press, 1969), 118–72.

25. Berlin, "Two Concepts of Liberty," 127. The quoted passage comes from *On Liberty,* CW, 18, 226.

26. Berlin, "Two Concepts of Liberty," 128.

27. Ibid.

28. Ibid.

29. Ibid.

30. *On Liberty,* CW, 18, 217; 18, 220.

31. Ibid., 217.

32. Ibid., 223.

33. See, respectively, *On Liberty,* CW, 18, 223; CW, 18, 224; CW, 18, 225; CW, 18, 224 and CW, 18, 285; CW, 18, 224; CW, 18, 260; CW, 18, 260.

34. *On Liberty,* CW, 18, 225.

35. Ibid., 282.

36. Ibid., 285.

37. For Mill's descriptions of certain interests as "rights," see *On Liberty,* CW 18, 276; compare here also "Utilitarianism," CW 10, 250–51. For sustained efforts to make sense of Mill's account of interests and rights, see especially John C. Rees, *John Stuart Mill's On Liberty,* ed. G. L. Williams (Oxford: Clarendon Press, 1985); and David Lyons, *Rights, Welfare and Mill's Moral Theory* (Oxford: Oxford University Press, 1994).

38. *On Liberty,* CW, 18, 224.

39. For a penetrating discussion of this problem, see G. W. Smith, "J. S. Mill on Freedom," in *Conceptions of Liberty in Political Philosophy,* eds. Zbigniew Pelczynski and John Gray (New York: St. Martin's Press, 1984), 182–216.

40. See John Gray, "John Stuart Mill: Traditionalist and Revisionist Interpretations," *Literature of Liberty* 2 (1979), available online at http://olldownload.libertyfund.org/EBooks/Editor%20-%20Lit%20Lib_0353.06.pdf.

41. *On Liberty,* CW, 18, 224.

42. Mill, "Utilitarianism," CW 10, 250–51.

43. See here, especially, Mill's discussion of security as a presupposition of economic development, *Principles of Political Economy,* CW, 4, Book III, Chapter 17, Section 5.

44. *Principles of Political Economy,* CW, 4, 737.

45. Thus for Stephen Holmes, "security was the *idée maîtresse* of the liberal tradition." *The Anatomy of Antiliberalism* (Cambridge, MA: Harvard University Press, 1996), 236.

46. *On Liberty,* CW, 18, 288.

47. See, for instance, Ronald Dworkin, *Taking Rights Seriously* (Cambridge, MA: Harvard University Press, 1978), and for an extended critique, see Jeremy Waldron, *Law and Disagreement* (Oxford: Clarendon Press, 2001).

48. For useful discussions of this chapter, see Hamburger, *John Stuart Mill on Liberty and Control*; and Jonathan Riley, *Mill on Liberty* (London, Routledge, 1998), 91–107.

49. *On Liberty,* CW, 18, 276.

50. Compare here Michael Sandel who juxtaposes a communitarian conception of "judgemental toleration" to the conception of "liberal toleration" defended by Rawls and other political liberals. Paradoxically, Mill—who Sandel does not mention in this article—is a paradigmatic

"judgemental" tolerator. See Michael J. Sandel, "Judgemental Toleration," in *Natural Law, Liberalism, and Morality*, ed. Robert P. George (Oxford: Oxford University Press, 2002), 107–12.

51. *On Liberty*, CW, 18, 277.

52. Ibid., 278.

53. All quotations in this paragraph are from Ibid., 278.

54. Ibid., 279.

55. Ibid., 279.

56. For an extended discussion of this dimension of Mill's thought, see Hamburger, *John Stuart Mill on Liberty and Control.*

57. See here, for instance, the criticisms of Mill's work—and the endorsement of Berlin's critique—in the new postscript to John Gray, *Mill On Liberty: A Defense*, 130–58.

58. Berlin, "Two Concepts of Liberty," 128.

59. "Subjection of Women," CW, 21, 400.

60. For an account of the conception of the person that informs Rawls's political liberalism, see *Political Liberalism*, 29–34, 81–85.

61. For critical discussions of Mill's imperialism, see Uday Mehta, *Liberalism and Empire* (Chicago: University of Chicago Press, 1999), and Jennifer Pitts, *A Turn to Empire* (Princeton: Princeton University Press, 2005).

62. John Gray, *Postliberalism* (New York: Routledge, 1993), 246. For a discussion of Gray's critique of progress and liberalism, see Glyn Morgan, "Gray's Elegy for Progress," *Critical Review of Social and Political Philosophy*, 9 (2006), 227–41.

63. *Considerations on Representative Government*, CW, 19, 549.

PART II

TOLERATION AND VIRTUE

6

IS TOLERATION A POLITICAL VIRTUE?

DAVID HEYD

Historical or Theoretical Approach

"Is toleration a political virtue?" The question sounds rhetorical. Toleration is usually considered the fundamental, even constitutive virtue of liberalism, and its characteristic playground is the political. What can it be other than a political virtue? In this chapter, I will attempt to answer this allegedly rhetorical question in the negative and to argue that toleration is neither political nor a virtue, at least in the strict sense that I will try to elaborate. This statement certainly sounds odd, especially to political scientists and legal theorists. But then, provocative statements are often made by philosophers only to be later tempered and qualified, which is exactly what I will try to do after arguing for a non-political and non-aretaic concept of toleration.

As everybody familiar with the vast literature on toleration knows, the major obstacle in the philosophical analysis of the concept is characterizing what it is *not*. Two methodological approaches for such a characterization suggest themselves: the broad view, which tries to do justice to the large variety of contexts and linguistic uses with which the concept is and has been associated, and the narrow view, which delineates the contours of the concept in the light of its theoretically distinguishing features. The first method is historical or sociological in nature, whereas the second is philosophical or normative. The historical view is liberal enough to include under the title of toleration political and social phenomena that were either not called by that name in the past or are no longer treated as cases of toleration. The philosophical view is more restrictive, filtering out those phenomena that do not satisfy certain theoretical conditions even if they are in many respects similar to toleration.[1]

In effect, neither of these two methods should be followed in a pure and exclusive way. To put it in Kantian terms, an historical study of toleration with no theoretical guidance is blind; a philosophical-normative analysis of the concept with no regard to its actual evolution is vacuous. A purely historical survey would risk the pitfalls of anachronism and the incommensurability of the phenomena investigated. Abstract theoretical analysis of the idea of toleration that ignores the way the idea has operated in political rhetoric runs the risk of becoming irrelevant, since toleration is not a theoretical concept in the strict scientific sense. So although my approach to the question will be basically philosophical, I shall start with a few comments on the way the historical evolution of the idea of toleration transformed it in ways that are compatible, or even supportive of the normative analysis proposed in the rest of the paper. But I admit that my argument is only partly corroborated by the ordinary language of toleration, and that it is just one conceptualization of a highly heterogeneous idea that cannot by its nature be given a historically adequate account that will also be theoretically coherent. From the point of view of legal theory or political science, my "distilled" concept of toleration will certainly appear artificial and abstract. But I believe that a normative theory of toleration must start with concepts whose contours are theoretically well-defined even at the expense of doing justice to all our intuitions.

The argument of this paper is threefold: toleration is a moral rather than a political concept; toleration is not a virtue in the narrow sense but rather an attitude or a mode of judgment; and toleration is not obligatory but supererogatory. These three claims are interrelated and interdependent.

A Sketchy Genealogy

Unlike the concepts of the good or the just, toleration has a relatively short history and one that is mostly confined to one civilization. Being a "thick" concept, it is much more dependent on particular normative and cultural circumstances than its universal moral cognates. Although the political arrangements within the Roman empire and the New Testament parable of the wheat and the tares (Matthew 13) are often cited as origins of political and religious toleration, the *concept* itself appears only in the early modern period, and even then, in the beginning, not under the title "toleration." The two contexts in which the modern idea of toleration gradually emerged were religion and royal grace. In light of the question raised in this paper, it should be emphasized that neither of these is "political" in the strict sense of the concept.

Take the religious context first. For Erasmus of Rotterdam, a typical example of the early thinkers on toleration, the highest goal is *pax* or *concordia*, that is to say the preservation of the harmonious unity of the Church, even at the cost of relinquishing some traditional Christian practices and declaring them "things indifferent" (*adiaphora*). The "tolerant" acceptance of unorthodox beliefs and practices is not based on the recognition of differences but on the distinction between what is religiously essential and what is merely doctrinal, between the inward effort to save Christian unity and the outward indifference to other religions.[2] Toleration consists of both "sufferance" and "comprehension," that is to say, the patience with nonconformist religious views is ultimately justified by typically inclusive reasons concerning the integrity of the religious community.[3] Erasmus' ideal of accommodation is religious and its justification pragmatic.

The second source of the idea of toleration is grace. From medieval times, the king or the ruler enjoyed the privilege of showing leniency towards communities or individuals under his jurisdiction. When shown to individuals, this "tolerant" attitude is closely associated with mercy, but with regard to groups, primarily religious communities, its effect is similar to our notion of toleration. The existence and some practices of Jews were "put up with" by Christian or Muslim rulers in their respective jurisdictions as a matter of sheer benevolence or pragmatic accommodation.[4]

A common feature of these two origins of the modern idea of toleration, which is of particular theoretical value for the conception advocated in this paper, is *caritas*. Charity or grace is the fundamental motive behind religious toleration as it is conceived by humanist Christians like Erasmus as well as by the merciful ruler. The endurance of differences or deviations from orthodoxy is not grounded in respect for the other, let alone for his rights, but in either love or a sense of power. Toleration, whether shown to Christian sects or to non-Christian religious minorities in a Christian polity, is primarily understood in terms of *indulgence*. Normatively speaking, this indulgence is supererogatory, modeled on the religious ideal of *imitatio Christi,* that is the adoption of Jesus' charitable attitude. Like other supererogatory acts, this idea of toleration is not based on principle, but rather on benevolence; not on justice, but on a higher moral standard.

Both religious toleration and grace-based tolerance of minorities are decidedly of much political significance, but they are not political in their ultimate justification. However, in the course of the sixteenth century there was a growing awareness, for example among the so-called *politiques* in France, that tolerant practices should be adopted for purely political purposes, primarily co-existence and the maintenance of the unity of the state (rather than that of the Church). In the course of the seventeenth century, this typically political understanding of toleration gradually gained a theoretical guise as well as a linguistic title. Toleration became a principle grounded in a specific view of the state and its partial separation from religion and in the emerging concept of individual citizens having inalienable rights as individuals (against each other and against the state). In John Locke's *Letter,* toleration is no longer conceived as either a purely religious ideal for the preservation of the unity of the Christian community or a personal favor granted by the sovereign. It has now become a duty of the *state* towards its citizens, a state whose function is strictly separated from the function of the church.[5] Toleration became political in the strict sense by being transformed into a universal principle, applied to (almost) all citizens of a polity and exercised not as a matter of personal favor but as a duty, not as a personal discretion of the power of the ruler but as a constitutional principle of the law.

Religious tolerance and royal grace do not amount to political principles in the sense that the *authority* of the church or the king to decide matters of religious practices and beliefs was not challenged. But from Locke to Mill the authority of the state is systematically restricted to public matters and subordinated to universally applied laws. In that respect, toleration becomes political in essence, losing its supererogatory and paternalistic dimension. The public-private divide, which has been the major ground for liberal toleration from Locke to Rawls, is not just a religious, pragmatic, or epistemological distinction, but a principled definition of the realm and scope of the political. Thus, for Pierre Bayle, a tolerant political regime is only the second best option, to be gradually replaced by a completely neutral state that is totally indifferent to religious differences in society.

With the establishment of modern liberal democracy, Bayle's vision became a reality. The successful career of the idea of toleration paradoxically led to its own decline, or at least made it superfluous in its traditional political form. In the second half of the twentieth century religious, ethnic, and sexual minorities have become more and more impatient with the status of being tolerated. In a multicultural society, the demand for recognition supersedes that of toleration. The state is expected to be neutral rather than restrained in its treatment of conflicts of value or religion. Pluralistic conceptions of value call for acceptance rather than toleration, which is often considered patronizing and condescending. As Bernard Williams pointed out, toleration may prove to have been an "interim value," a political necessity along the path from a persecuting to a fully pluralistic society.[6] Indeed, toleration had a crucial role in restraining the forces of persecution and intolerance and the gradual creation of a culture of either indifference or respect with regard to unorthodox beliefs and practices. But then, equality before the law and respect for the rights of individuals and minority groups tend to make toleration politically redundant. This does not mean that toleration has lost its meaning in contemporary liberal society. But, as I shall argue in the rest of this chapter, it means that the core of the concept should now be captured in more moral and personal terms, that is to say as applying to the realm of interpersonal and intercommunal relations rather than to the state, the law, or the constitutional structure of society.

This is a very rough skeletal survey of the genealogy of the idea of toleration; it is by no means intended to be understood as a history of the concept. It aims only to uncover a certain dialectical nature implied in the historical unfolding of the idea. A concept, which in its inception was typically religious, gradually transformed into a political one. When it lost its political role, it became (again) a personal or intercommunal value. To put it alternatively, toleration, originally conceived as a "negative" necessity, became in a second stage one of the "positive" values of the liberal state. Finally, it might turn out to be redundant in a truly pluralistic society. What started as an idea of grace or charity developed into a principle of political duty, only to become again a matter of charitable attitude that is supererogatory. In seventeenth-century England, toleration was a way to deal with *intra*religious strife; in Mill's nineteenth-century England, toleration lost its religious acuteness and was relegated to secular differences; in present-day England, toleration has regained a religious role but now applies primarily to the *inter*religious relationship between the majority and the religious minorities in society. This dialectic evolution of toleration does not bring us back full circle to the early modern period, but it does unravel certain tensions inherent in the very concept of toleration. We shall turn now to an analysis of the concept itself, which will be normative rather than historical, although informed by the genealogical account.

Toleration: Moral—Not Political

The idea of toleration evolved side by side with modern notions of rights, respect for individuals, separation of state and church, state neutrality, value pluralism, and skepticism. It was also instrumental in their entrenchment in the political culture of constitutional democracy. But once these ideas have become firmly established, the role and scope of toleration itself became hard to define. Thus, the analytical literature on toleration consists of a long list of what distinguishes toleration from: compromise, peace or co-existence, indifference, skepticism, recognition, acceptance, indulgence, open-mindedness, patience, endurance, condonation, charity, respect, pluralism, and more. Consequently, it is by no means easy to articulate what is left as a distinctive feature of toleration.[7]

This difficulty has led philosophers, like Williams, Walzer, Rawls, and Gray, to argue that toleration must be understood as a political practice rather than a moral virtue. I would like to argue for the opposite position, namely that the only way to mark the distinctive character of toleration is by regarding it as *non*-political. Bernard Williams contends that toleration cannot be a moral virtue since its motives are obscure and varied; it is rather a practice motivated by skepticism or the aspiration to peace than by a systematically moral attitude such as respect for autonomy. This contingent nature of toleration is exactly what makes it for Williams a transitory value, important in our time, but not necessarily beyond it.[8] Michael Walzer states that his interest in toleration lies in its political dimension since any other view would not be able to do justice to the rich history of the concept.[9] Toleration characterizes "regimes" and institutionalized social arrangements of coexistence. John Rawls also insists on the specifically political nature of toleration, which belongs strictly to the sphere of "public reason" rather than to a moral (comprehensive) doctrine. Toleration describes the way in which different but "reasonable" moral conceptions are mutually accepted within the framework of a just political society.[10] John Gray takes a further step by claiming that toleration is not a principled political arrangement but rather a modus vivendi between people and groups who are not necessarily tolerant themselves, that is to say, a concept which applies to coexistence in non-liberal societies that lack an "overlapping consensus."[11]

As I see it, the main problem with the political account of toleration is that for both analytical and normative reasons we do not *want* nowadays to ground liberal democracy on the idea of toleration. The main business of the liberal state is to respect and protect the *rights* of both individuals and groups, to establish justice and equality between its citizens, to secure the rule of law. The state is an embodiment of an impersonal constitutional structure which derives its validity from universalizable principles. In that respect it is neutral, at least with regards to its citizens, even if not with regards to values or moral doctrines. Unlike a medieval sovereign, the state is an impersonal institution which cannot be described as "suffering" in having to reconcile itself with beliefs and practices to which "it" does not subscribe. Hence, it cannot be said to overcome or endure its wish to undermine or interfere with them. In other words, the state cannot be engaged in toleration. The law either permits or prohibits certain practices and activities. The prohibited act cannot be tolerated by the law and the permitted practice cannot be said to be endured as a matter of charity or restraint.

Thus, for example, the issue of Muslim female students wearing headscarves in French state schools is not really a matter of toleration but a question of the correct interpretation of constitutional principles and of the idea of the separation of state and religion.[12] As we shall see, only the way in which this religious practice is viewed by non-Muslim French citizens (rather than the state) may involve toleration. Or, to take another example, Will Kymlicka criticizes Rawls for his model of toleration as applied to individuals' freedom of conscience, arguing that such a freedom has become a "fundamental human right." He suggests an alternative analysis of tolerance, which applies to minority groups or communities.[13] But once we go beyond his example of the Ottoman Millet system (which, being patronizing and pragmatic, could be described as "tolerant" in the traditional sense) and discuss present-day dilemmas of the treatment of minorities, then Kymlicka's own critique points to the irrelevance of toleration. The legal status of minorities and their authority over their individual members is a matter of rights rather than of toleration by the state, of justice towards collective entities which struggle to maintain their identity. A final illustration of my point may be found in the value of freedom of expression. An individual might be appreciated for her toleration of repugnant or offensive speech by another individual. But the state must respect freedom of expression as a fundamental right. This right may be justified in terms of skepticism, personal autonomy, communicative reason, etc., but not as a matter of indulgence or endurance. If a particular expression goes beyond the permissible limits, then the state must interfere with it rather than tolerate it.

State neutrality and the protection of rights does not, therefore, leave room for state tolerance. But can a perfectionist view of liberalism allow for a strictly political analysis of toleration? According to Joseph Raz, the state is not neutral between values; it promotes only those ways of life that advance personal autonomy. But then, Raz himself believes that the state should not tolerate those practices that undermine autonomy. The object of state toleration is thus restricted to the (competitive) plurality of "good" options, those which although incompatible with each other cultivate personal autonomy.[14] However, within that restricted domain of worthwhile alternatives, the state must remain neutral, at least in the sense that it should not prohibit any of these alternatives. It may promote this or that practice (for all kinds of reasons which have to do with democratic choice), but this does not mean that it can be described as "tolerant" towards those ways of life that are not at the top of its priorities. The analysis of toleration suggested here does not necessarily rely on a neutralist conception of the state. It is indeed true[15] that modern liberal states are not neutral in the traditional "night-watch" sense and that they pursue substantive social goals and values. But the active promotion of communal identity, for instance, or the commitment to policies of affirmative action cannot, in my view, be considered as "tolerant" to the beneficiaries of these aims. They should rather be conceived as political duties of the state, or maybe even as the rights of those beneficiaries. Thus, within the framework of pluralism, toleration is an attitude of individuals (or groups) towards each other, exercised in their attempt to achieve their competing goals, rather than a norm of state action or a constitutional principle.

For the same reasons, toleration is not an attitude that can be shown by any state *organ* or institution. The court operates on the basis of the law and has no values of its own which can be overcome or restrained. On the one hand, it is the duty of judges to *ignore* their personal moral views rather than to manifest toleration of other, incompatible views. On the other hand, the court should not tolerate violations of the law, even if the judge personally feels she could tolerate the offensive act. The same applies to political authorities, officials, and institutions. Even the police acting leniently against law breakers should be better described as restrained rather than tolerant, since, as we shall see, the reasons and motives for its indulgent enforcement of the law are different from those typical of toleration. The courts or the police do not do us, individual citizens, any favor by letting us freely criticize the government or express controversial views that sound obnoxious to others. Public officials should definitely exercise discretion in carrying out their public duty; they may even be expected to show equity, i.e., go beyond the strict letter of the law; but this does not mean that by that they display a tolerance to the citizens.

For John Rawls, toleration is a constitutive virtue of political liberalism. Toleration characterizes the way we view comprehensive moral doctrines that are different from ours but are nevertheless recognized as "reasonable." This crucial property of reasonableness is for Rawls derived from the idea of public reason which allows for an irreducible plurality of moral and religious values. Public reason in Rawls' eyes operates on the political level of justice.[16] Thus, toleration, as I understand it in Rawls, should better be seen as a *bridge* between the moral and the political. It belongs to neither: from the moral perspective, a rival moral view or practice cannot and should not be tolerated; from the political perspective, it ought to be fully accepted as reasonable and legitimate, rather than just tolerated. Toleration is the willingness to suspend the comprehensive moral point of view in favor of the narrowly political. But the reason for this suspension is of a practical nature, namely the achievement of social stability and peaceful coexistence in a deeply divided society.

So, although for Rawls toleration is constitutive of political liberalism, the ultimate reason to adopt toleration as a value is pragmatic. Kant, from whom the idea of public reason is derived, offers a more principled basis for toleration. The public use of reason is the condition for the operation of reason, its progress and perfection. In his famous essay "What Is Enlightenment?" the term "toleration" is mentioned only once and in a negative tone, describing it as "presumptuous" or patronizing. According to Kant, it is the *duty* of the prince (rather than an act of tolerance) to allow his subjects to freely exercise their own reason in matters of conscience.[17] Thus the term "toleration" carries for Kant a pejorative meaning, associated with its traditional identification as grace. But, in her seminal article on Kant and toleration Onora O'Neill discusses the way Kant uses the *concept* of toleration, rather than the word. Toleration is justified not in terms of respect for the autonomy of the individual but as a constitutive condition of the free use of reason. It is a value that applies in the public domain rather than in the private (as has been the case in the long tradition of liberalism).[18]

Is this a "political" concept of toleration? It is, in the sense that it amounts to the duty of the prince to allow the free communication of ideas among rational persons in society so as to promote the process of enlightenment. Toleration here means the abstention of the political authority from censorship and intervention in the critical dialogue concerning religious issues and other matters of conscience. However, toleration is not a distinctly political virtue for Kant in the sense that the political is exactly the realm of the *private* use of reason, i.e., what he refers to as the rationality of the exercise of authority. In that sphere, Kant insists that citizens owe absolute obedience. Their freedom of thought and communicative action does not extend to practice and behavior. Toleration, therefore, applies strangely enough only to the "republic of letters," only to communication within the "community of scholars." From our contemporary point of view this is a very limited concept of toleration. Furthermore, the political abstention from censorship amounts at most to a *negative* concept of toleration, and Kant is therefore justified in treating it as the ruler's duty. The positive value of toleration as the intrinsic condition of reason as such (as it is manifested in the community of scholars) is for its part typically *non*-political. It relates to the virtues of critical dialogue rather than to the way state authorities control our lives. In that deep sense of the condition of public reason, toleration is not a political virtue but a universal imperative. It seems that Kant was right in denigrating toleration in the literal sense of patronizing and presumptuous charity shown by the prince to his citizens. Toleration in this negative sense will become more and more superfluous the closer the private use of reason approaches to its public and universal use.

This does not mean that there is no political dimension in toleration, either in Kant or in general. An enlightened prince as well as a modern liberal state can and should promote the value of interpersonal toleration in society. The government has the power to inculcate standards of toleration by education, the support of institutions in which reason is freely exercised, and even to use its authority and capacity to enforce practices that advance communication and narrow the gap between the public and the private use of reason. But this political concept of toleration is, in contradistinction to O'Neill's argument, instrumental precisely in the sense that once this gap is overcome, namely in the Kingdom of Ends, no room will be left to toleration, indeed not even to politics as the private use of reason.

It must therefore be emphasized that although I have tried to argue that toleration is not in its essence a political concept, I do not mean to deny that it has an important role in politics. Although the state cannot be said to be tolerant, either towards its citizens or towards other states, the interrelations between communities, religious or other, within society can be characterized in terms of tolerance. In that respect, the tolerance of individuals towards each other may often have political significance when the object of toleration is a political issue such as abortion. Or consider the demand of orthodox residents in Jerusalem to block traffic on the Sabbath in their neighborhood. Even if the court or the municipality prohibited such road blocks on the grounds of the freedom of movement on main traffic arteries of the city, individual secular citizens could be expected to show tolerance for the orthodox residents by voluntarily avoiding these roads on the Sabbath. Furthermore, we shall see in the next section that toleration tends to raise the level of solidarity and hence may lead to the strengthening of social cohesion and communal bonding. If justice promotes the values of liberty and equality, toleration upholds fraternity.

Another political aspect of toleration is associated with the implications of a tolerant attitude to third parties. Unlike forgiveness, for example, which has no effect on people other than the forgiver and the forgiven, toleration often has social costs.[19] By tolerating an undesirable practice, I might weaken the ability of others who are or will be offended by it to fight against it. I would then be refraining from intervening in behavior from which others may suffer and who have not expressed any wish that I should so refrain. In that respect, my choice of toleration should be politically sensitive. It may call for a joint decision on the part of many people who stand to lose from the tolerated attitude. In the same way as I cannot forgive someone for an offense done to another person, I should not tolerate a behavior that is harmful primarily to other people.

States or nations, then, can be tolerant only in the derivative sense, namely in consisting of tolerant individuals (or communities of individuals). States can only indirectly promote moral norms that encourage tolerant attitudes in interpersonal relations. Cultures may be described as generous, forgiving or tolerant, but states or institutions as such cannot.[20] The state cannot give generously although it can establish tax deductions for voluntary donations as a way to cultivate personal generosity in society. Although the implementation of rights is different from toleration, the two are closely related. Historically, toleration has led to the creation of a system of human rights (both individual and communal). But respect for rights may also foster a tolerant attitude since both require a capacity to separate between the act and the agent, as we shall shortly see.

This section was concerned with the negative characterization of toleration, attempting to show that it is not political in its essence. It is now time to proceed to a more positive account. Toleration in many cases amounts to refraining from insisting on our rights and to acting indulgently towards others who are wrong. In that sense, it goes beyond the political into the moral.[21]

Toleration as a Supererogatory Attitude

A tempting way to approach toleration as a uniquely moral phenomenon is by describing it as a virtue. There is a sense in which it is difficult to deny that toleration is a virtue. Rawls says that justice is the primary virtue of social institutions. Similarly, one may say that toleration is the virtue of liberal society. This is the sense in which toleration is a good, a desirable trait or property, typical of, or even essential to a liberal constitutional system. This does not mean, however, that toleration is a virtue in the more strict, dispositional sense, traditionally associated with Aristotle. According to my analysis it is not. Although it is a personal attitude (rather than an institutional or political arrangement), it is not a naturally based trait of character. It does not have as its basis an inborn disposition. It is not acquired by habituation and conditioning. It benefits other individuals and society at large rather than the agent. It is hard to see toleration in terms of self-realization or the actualization of a human potential. Toleration never comes naturally to us, since it involves the subject's reconciliation with a moral (or other) wrong or failing. Its absence from traditional lists of "the virtues" is not accidental since it does not belong to a general theory of human nature or to moral psychology.

Aristotle defines virtue as the mean between two naturally given extremes. Toleration cannot be subjected to such an analysis. Historically it falls, indeed, between persecution or intolerance and indifference or full acceptance. But this historical process does not refer to natural human dispositions but rather to religious and ethical norms of changing political cultures. Furthermore, Aristotle views virtue as the *manner* in which an action is performed: the courageous act is that piece of behavior as it is performed by the courageous individual, who has acquired the right disposition in the face of risk and danger. In toleration, it is the motive or the intention of the particular act that defines its value and the tolerant disposition is at most derivative of such particular acts.[22] Once I choose to restrain myself from interfering in your wrong conduct it does not matter *how* I do so. For instance, the ease and smoothness with which the act is performed, which Aristotle believes are essential indicators of a virtuous act, are of no relevance to toleration.

The denial of the status of virtue to the concept of toleration should be qualified in two ways. First, the modern usage of the term "virtue" is wider than the Aristotelian. I mentioned justice as the virtue of social institutions. We may add fairness as the virtue of citizens in a just society, or truthfulness in the world of scientific (or other) communication. Toleration may be viewed in that sense as the virtue of citizens and communities in a multi-cultural or heterogeneous society. Secondly, although toleration is not a virtue in the strict Aristotelian sense of a character trait or a natural disposition, it is closely related to certain psychological dispositions that may enhance or impede it. Patience, indulgence, and temperance are natural propensities that make it much easier for people to show toleration. But they do not constitute it and may often promote indifference or compromise rather than toleration. Alternatively, a religious fundamentalist may be of a very kind and patient character, but for ideological reasons choose intolerance in all matters pertaining to competing religious practices. Thus, toleration is more than restraint or self-control, although these personal capacities are highly instrumental in its exercise.

After having proposed that toleration is neither political, nor a virtue in the strict sense of the terms, I turn now to a more positive analysis of its nature. I suggest that toleration be understood as a *supererogatory attitude*. This view relies on the common distinction in theories of toleration between agent and action, or in Augustinian terms, between "sinner and sin." Despite the close relation between acts and their agents and the way they reflect on each other, philosophers have correctly argued that judgments of acts and judgments of actors can, and sometimes should be separated. Respect for the autonomy of the other or the attitude of forgiveness are two examples (which are pertinent to toleration) of the judgment of individuals that is independent of the judgment of their action. And there are of course judgments of actions or beliefs that are independent of judgments of their subjects, typically in court decisions or in the evaluation of scientific theories. However, if we wish to argue that toleration is a matter of the separation of the impersonal judgment of the act or the belief from the personal judgment of the agent or the subject, we must explain the mechanism through which this separation is made and the moral justification for doing so.

I suggest that toleration requires a shift from the impersonal judgment of actions to the personally based judgment of the agent. This shift is, as I have argued elsewhere, of a "perceptual" nature.[23] It involves a Gestalt switch from one legitimate perspective to the other. The two perspectives are basically valid, yet incompatible in the sense that they cannot be adopted simultaneously (like the famous rabbit/duck image). From the impersonal view point, an action or a belief may look patently wrong, but from the personal it may be treated as understandable, tolerable, or forgivable due to the motive for its performance or the way it was adopted by the subject. The two perspectives are mutually exclusive. Thus, when we engage in moral or legal assessment of a type of action, we intentionally *ignore* the personal circumstances of the agent and the way he was led to act in the way he did. On the other hand, when we tolerate a person's behavior or beliefs, we make ourselves blind to the negative features of the behavior and the wrongness of the beliefs. As in perception, we can switch from one perspective to the other (with varying degrees of effort, having to do with moral training), and the alternative perspective always remains in principle available to us. But the adoption of the one necessarily means the temporary suppression of the other. Structurally, this perspectival shift is analogous to the suspension of disbelief, traditionally associated with the aesthetic experience of a theater spectator: we can *either* see the events on stage as the movement of actors who are making their living, *or* as the dramatic deeds of fictional heroes; but we cannot enjoy the magic of the play while reflecting on the actor's personal life.

The perceptual analysis of toleration explains why toleration is not a virtue. The shift from the impersonal judgment that an act is wrong to the personal tolerant acceptance of the agent *despite* the act is not a matter of a general disposition or a character trait. It is an intentional choice freely made by an individual in a particular case. It is more of a decision than a predisposition. Although the capacity to make the tolerant switch is facilitated by certain dispositions like patience and restraint, its *constitutive* conditions are of a cognitive kind, namely the capacity to abstract action from agent, or a belief from the subject holding it.[24] Consequently, contrary to common wisdom, toleration does not consist of a "non-judgmental" disposition or blindness to the failings and defects of others, but rather of the capacity to alternate from one mode of judgment to another. But this capacity is neither a mere behavioral practice, a habit, nor a psychological feature of the agent. Showing toleration is at its core a deliberate choice based on reasons. The Gestalt switch from judging the action to tolerating the agent is undertaken from a specific motive that must be transparent to the tolerant person.[25] Unlike Aristotelian virtuous action, which is typically performed with ease, as a "second nature," tolerating wrong actions and beliefs has a price and takes an effort. It should thus be emphasized that toleration is an *active* attitude, to be clearly distinguished from passive mind-sets like indifference, acquiescence, condonation, or resignation.[26] The personal dimension of the tolerant attitude means then that both the tolerator and the object of toleration must be persons, which explains the previously discussed claim that the state cannot strictly speaking show toleration. Institutions cannot engage in the sort of perspectival shift of judgment that constitutes toleration. Similarly, despite common usage, practices cannot be the object of toleration, but only the individuals taking part in those practices. We may be confident in our belief that female circumcision is morally wrong, in the sense that we have no reason to accept it as such or to approve of it. But we can nevertheless tolerate the individuals or communities practicing it on the grounds that we can understand, or even respect, the way the practice evolved in their culture and the central role it plays in their overall faith and way of life.

However, this analytical description of the idea of toleration, even if it makes sense phenomenologically speaking, requires a normative complement. If the two perspectives, the act-oriented and the agent-oriented, are equally valid, why and when should one be substituted for the other? What kind of reasons could support the renouncement of condemnation of an objectionable action in favor of a tolerant restraint from interfering in it? The two sets of respective reasons are valid but of a different, even incommensurable kind. One set of reasons has to do with the autonomy of the individual, with respect for her authentic commitment to certain values, and with the personal integrity in which these values are pursued. The other set of reasons concerns the wrongness of the act, the cognitive error in the beliefs underlying it, or the harm caused by the action to others. Thus, it is not the case that for the pro-lifer the reasons for tolerating abortions are simply *stronger* or more weighty than those for persecuting women and doctors who perform them. From this point of view, they cannot be overriding, let alone conclusive. But they do have an appeal that may create a switch in perspectives towards a tolerant acceptance of the agent, rather than the acts.

To see how this can take place, consider the case of forgiveness, which in many interesting respects is analogical to toleration, and precisely in the way a perspectival change is justified.[27] When we are harmed or offended we are fully justified in responding with a hostile attitude. Justice requires that offensive actions be punished and their offender suffer the cold shoulder shown to him by the offended party. But then the offended person *may* adopt the alternative approach, trying to understand the other, hoping to restore the broken friendship, wishing to open a new page. Showing forgiveness does not go against justice, it goes beyond it. Forgiveness is supererogatory, that is a morally valuable attitude, though it is not required as a matter of duty or justice. Forgiving is beyond the call of duty exactly in the substitution of the personalized evaluation of the circumstances of the offense for the impersonal assessment of the offensive act. The attitude of forgiveness is moving just because it is a voluntary, optional renunciation of justified hostility and vindictiveness.

Similarly, the second-order reason for ignoring the force of reasons for interfering with the wrong behavior of others does not create a duty, nor is it called for as a matter of justice. Toleration is a supererogatory option that is morally valuable because it lies beyond the call of duty. I cannot interfere with the way my neighbor decorates his home, since it lies within his protected rights (even if his taste is repugnant). But I may call the police if this neighbor holds a noisy party after midnight. When I nevertheless tolerate the neighbor's behavior, I withhold my judgment, or at least do not act on it, although it is within my rights and interference would be justified. Or, for an example from the sphere of relations between groups or communities in society, consider again the non-observant Israelis who are entitled to drive along a major thoroughfares crossing orthodox neighborhoods during the Sabbath but restrain themselves from doing so. The basis for this considerate approach does not consist of appreciation of the religious norms as such (which the non-observant do not share), but of good will towards the potentially offended orthodox neighbors whose sincere faith might be offended by the act.

The reason for adopting a tolerant attitude is, therefore, typically moral, based on good will, on the good intention of putting the agent before the act.[28] Strangely, we return back full circle to the origins of toleration as grace! But unlike grace, the motive of toleration is conceived here as impelled by a special concern for the tolerated person and personality rather than for the self-image or the sense of power of the tolerating party. Hence, this concept of toleration does not involve any haughty or humiliating attitude and is inclusive rather than exclusive. Although the analysis offered here does not regard toleration as a patronizing attitude, nor does it restrict toleration to royal privilege, it shares with grace the discretionary, supererogatory deontic status. And in that respect it supports the genealogical dialectic of toleration, which started as a personal attitude, went through a political phase, and seems to end up nowadays as a matter of inter-personal or inter-communal relations.

The Political Value of Toleration

Even though toleration is not strictly speaking a virtue and is not essentially political, it is undeniable that it has deep political importance, as is primarily, though not exclusively, manifested in liberal societies. Unlike forgiveness, which is a personal attitude between individuals, toleration is also shown by and towards groups, or rather between individuals *as* members of groups or communities. Unlike forgiveness, toleration can be exercised in an anonymous way, that is, towards unidentified individuals who belong to a particular group. This lends toleration a specifically political value. Contrary to forgiveness, which aims at restoring a broken personal relationship like friendship or love, toleration creates social solidarity, a sense of unity among people belonging to a common world even if they do not know each other personally. Toleration strengthens social bonding and trust, since it demonstrates good will, respect, and understanding towards individuals beyond their behavior and opinions. Forgiveness is *ad hoc* in nature, i.e., shown on a one-time basis, to a particular individual. Toleration, in contrast, is shown either to an individual or to a group of individuals for a whole spectrum of actions of a certain type. Thus, avoiding driving through an orthodox neighborhood on the Sabbath on a one-time basis is not tolerance, nor is the selective or haphazard selection of the particular roads in which the "tolerator" avoids driving. Although toleration is optional, it creates a kind of promise to refrain from interference not only in a present objectionable action but also in behavior of the same kind in the future, either of the same agent or of others belonging to the same group. This gives toleration a political dimension that is absent from forgiveness.[29]

Furthermore, although I have taken pains to distinguish between toleration on the one hand and the respect for rights, peace, and co-existence on the other, it must be stressed that toleration is highly instrumental in promoting these specifically political values. For, after all, respect of another person's rights requires exactly the same capacity to separate the actor from her action and respect her freedom to engage in action that is deemed objectionable. It is true that this separation is *obligatory* in the case of rights, while it is supererogatory in the case of toleration; but the two are nevertheless mutually reinforcing. Social solidarity advances political stability and enhances the conditions of the communal co-existence that is of crucial importance in multi-cultural and pluralist societies. Forgiveness, even if it does not render interpersonal duties and obligations superfluous, tends to reduce the level of appeal to these norms in regulating personal relations. Similarly, toleration cannot be expected to serve as a substitute for legal norms and a system of enforceable rights, but it does ease political tensions and decrease the level of litigation in society.

Toleration is particularly called for in heterogeneous societies. The social cohesion of a tribal society, for example, is based on the large extent to which values and beliefs are shared by individual members. But, in pluralistic societies, this cohesion can be achieved only by appealing to other sources. Pragmatic considerations may lead to unity based on compromise. A principled conception separating agent from action establishes toleration. Although it is true that we show tolerance to begin with only to people to whom we feel close in *some* way, the tolerant attitude reinforces the sense of fraternity. In the absence of a substantive shared system of values in pluralist societies, this feature of toleration adds an important value. It also explains why historically speaking, although a tolerant attitude to other individuals has always been a value, the specifically political ideal of toleration was articulated only in early modern Europe, with the rise of religious pluralism and inter-religious strife within previously homogeneous societies.

So again, even if, as I have suggested, a tolerant society is not a society whose laws or institutions are tolerant, it is a society whose individual members and groups adopt a certain measure of supererogatory restraint in not insisting on their full rights. Toleration is not a political matter in the sense that it does not belong to the realm of constitutional arrangements, the rule of law, or the institutional relations of power and authority. But it may have a great political value since, as the old Talmudic saying reminds us, "Jerusalem was only destroyed because judgments were given strictly upon biblical law and did not go beyond the requirements of the law."[30]

NOTES

1. Michael Walzer and Joseph Raz are typical contemporary proponents of these two respective approaches to the study of toleration. Michael Walzer, *On Toleration* (New Haven: Yale University Press, 1997), and Joseph Raz, "Autonomy, Toleration and the Harm Principle," in Susan Mendus, ed., *Justifying Toleration* (Cambridge: Cambridge University Press, 1988), 155–75. As the reader will immediately realize, both commentators to this chapter take the typically broad view of toleration: Kathryn Abrams for empirical reasons relating to the way the concept is used in current discourse; Andrew Sabl for epistemic (and maybe normative) reasons associated with the legitimacy of the diversity of concepts of toleration.

2. Mario Turchetti, "Religious Concord and Political Tolerance in Sixteenth and Seventeenth-Century France," *Sixteenth Century Journal* 22 (1991): 15–25.

3. Gary Remer, *Humanism and the Rhetoric of Toleration* (University Park: The State of Pennsylvania University Press, 1996), 43–54.

4. For the idea of tolerance as grace, see Yirmiyahu Yovel, "Tolerance as Grace and as Rightful Recognition," *Social Research* 65 (1998): 897–919, particularly the opening section.

5. Admittedly, Locke appeals also to religious arguments about the un-Christian nature of persecution, but it seems that he makes these as an *ad hominem* challenge to the proponents of intolerance rather than as independent positive support for the principle of toleration. See particularly Jeremy Waldron, "Locke: Toleration and the Rationality of Persecution," Susan Mendus, ed., *Justifying Toleration* (Cambridge: Cambridge University Press, 1988), 62–63.

6. Bernard Williams, "Toleration: An Impossible Virtue?" in David Heyd, ed., *Toleration: An Elusive Virtue* (Princeton: Princeton University Press, 1996), 26.

7. Kathryn Abrams, for example, associates toleration with the virtues of curiosity, open-mindedness, and humility. Even if these virtues may

prove to be conducive in some contexts to the development of a tolerant attitude, they are by no means constitutive or essential to it. Actually, toleration is typically the attitude of a person who is strongly committed to and confident in the values she holds.

8. Bernard Williams, "Toleration, A Political or Moral Virtue?" *Diogenes* 44 (1996): 36.

9. Walzer, *On Toleration,* chap. 1, and particularly note 3.

10. John Rawls, *Political Liberalism* (New York, Columbia University Press, 1993), 59, 194–95.

11. John Gray, *The Two Faces of Liberalism* (New York: The New Press, 2000), chap. 1.

12. Similarly, unlike Andrew Sabl, I do not consider the restraint from demanding Jews in the U.S. Army to uncover their heads indoors as a case of toleration. It is an issue of the balancing military codes with religious practices which must have an either-or answer: does a Jewish soldier maintain the *right* to wear a yarmulke while in active military service?

13. Will Kymlicka, "Two Models of Pluralism and Tolerance," in David Heyd, ed., *Toleration: An Elusive Virtue,* 81–105.

14. It should be noted that for Raz toleration is a matter of interpersonal relations rather than of the political regulation of the acts of the state towards its citizens. On that point I follow his non-political approach to toleration although my analysis of the concept is different. See, "Autonomy, Toleration and the Harm Principle," 162–65.

15. As argued by Kathryn Abrams and Andrew Sabl in their comments to this article.

16. *Political Liberalism,* 62.

17. Immanuel Kant, "What Is Enlightenment?" in H. Reiss, ed., *Political Writings* (Cambridge: Cambridge University Press, 1996), 58–59.

18. Onora O'Neill, "The Public Use of Reason," Onora O'Neill, ed., *Constructions of Reason* (Cambridge: Cambridge University Press, 1989), 28–50.

19. I owe this reflection to Thomas Pogge.

20. As in the case of toleration, we metaphorically refer to certain states as generous in having a developed system of social benefits. But high unemployment payments or long maternity leaves are expressions of a conception of just distribution and social priorities rather than of a giving disposition or largesse.

21. I will put aside other non-political forms of toleration, such as religious, epistemological, cultural, and aesthetic toleration, all of which, I believe, are derived from the moral core of the concept.

22. See Glen Newey, "Tolerance as Virtue," John Horton and Susan

Mendus, eds., *Toleration, Identity and Difference* (London: Macmillan, 1999), 54. Although I do not consider toleration as a virtue, I agree with Newey's thesis that a tolerant act cannot be fully reduced to a description of the tolerant agent.

23. David Heyd, "Introduction," *Toleration: An Elusive Virtue,* 10–17.

24. These cognitive capacities are lacking or only partly developed in children. Hence their tendency to *ad hominen* arguments on the one hand and intolerance on the other. For a more elaborate presentation of the educational problems in inculcating tolerance in young people, see my "Education to Toleration: Some Obstacles and Their Resolution," in Catharine MacKinnon and Dario Castiglione, eds., *The Culture of Toleration in Diverse Societies* (Manchester: Manchester University Press, 2003), 196–207.

25. Iain Hampsher-Monk, "Toleration and the Moral Will," in John Horton and Susan Mendus, eds., *Toleration, Identity and Difference* (London: Macmillan, 1999), 17–37. For a similar view see also Robert P. Churchill, "On the Difference between Moral and Non-moral Conceptions of Toleration: The Case for Toleration as an Individual Virtue," in Mehdi Amin Razavi and David Ambuel, eds., *Philosophy, Religion, and the Question of Intolerance* (Albany: State University of New York Press, 1997), 189–211. Churchill characterizes toleration as "voluntary forbearance on the basis of reasons," but stops short of categorizing it as supererogatory. A closer approach to toleration as supererogation ("the deliberate suspension of moral entitlement" can be found in Peter Johnson, "As Long as He Needs Me? Toleration and Moral Character," in John Horton and Peter Nicholson, eds., *Toleration: Philosophy and Practice* (Averbury: Aldershot, 1992), 146–64.

26. I take issue with MacKinnon's view that toleration can be manifest in people who simply "mind their own business," since this is an attitude that is too close to indifference. Tolerating another person, according to the analysis advocated here, means an active effort to understand the action to which one objects in terms of the agent's motives, views, and circumstances. This involves what MacKinnon calls "engagement," although she clearly distinguishes it from toleration. Catharine MacKinnon, "Toleration and the Character of Pluralism," in *The Culture of Toleration in Diverse Societies,* 58–59. In this active aspect of the tolerant attitude my analysis lies closer to what Kathryn Abrams calls "engaged toleration" (which she presents as an alternative to my view). For in order to respect and "accept" the agent, tolerator has to understand not only her values and beliefs as such but the way they have been formed and the manner in which they cohere with other values and beliefs of that particular individual.

27. See Hagit Benbaji and David Heyd, "The Charitable Perspective: Forgiveness and Toleration as Supererogatory," *Canadian Journal of Philosophy* 31 (2001): 567–86.

28. For a good presentation of the view of toleration as a moral, rather than political, virtue, see Anna E. Galeotti, "Toleration as a Moral Virtue," *Res Publica* (2001): 273–92. However, Galeotti does not agree with the perceptual model outlined here. She believes that the moral conception of toleration is too abstract to support toleration as a social practice. The approach of this article is to leave the regulation of social behavior in the context of race and gender to legal norms and a system of political rights and promote tolerant attitudes only through educational means.

29. Forgiveness and promise are held by Hannah Arendt to be two conditions of action: forgiveness overcomes the irreversibility of the past, whereas promises overcome the unpredictability of the future. Toleration, according to my description, could be understood as a promise of forgiveness: by tolerating your present behavior I announce that I will also refrain from interfering in it in the future. In this Arendtian sense toleration is definitely of a political nature. Hannah Arendt, *The Human Condition* (Chicago: The University of Chicago Press, 1958), secs. 33–34.

30. Babylonian Talmud, *Tractate Baba Mezia,* 30b.

7

FORBEARANT AND ENGAGED TOLERATION: A COMMENT ON DAVID HEYD

KATHRYN ABRAMS

I. Introduction

I will begin with a confession: on first reading, Professor Heyd's chapter left me largely perplexed. It was easy to admire the clarity and analytic precision of his conception, but more difficult to know how to engage it. Part of the issue was the stringency of his predominantly philosophical or normative approach to defining toleration: it had the puzzling effect of evacuating toleration of many of the characteristics I was most inclined to associate with it. The treatment of politically marginalized sexual, racial, or ethnic minorities—which has, to my mind, the potential to raise paradigmatic issues of toleration—was presumptively excluded, on the ground that there was no basis for legitimate moral objection to such groups, so the restraint of such objection did not constitute tolerance. Complicating this problem was the abstraction of Professor Heyd's formulation. His affirmative account, of a cognitive shift from an act-focused to an agent-focused analysis, was only infrequently embellished by examples of acts and actors to which his version of toleration would apply.[1]

The resulting perplexity sent me into the recent literature on toleration, where I made an interesting discovery: the sense of impasse, or difficulty of engagement, that I experienced with Professor Heyd's paper seemed often to afflict contrasting groups of theorists writing on the subject of toleration. Often it seems that they are writing on completely different concepts: some emphasize the paradoxical or transitional character of toleration—a foregone expression of moral condemnation that is increasingly squeezed between moral demands for intervention and political demands for acceptance—while others see toleration as implicated in the various, ongoing ways that contemporary cultures negotiate the politicization of difference.[2]

In this essay, I will propose a kind of analytic bridge between these different approaches to toleration, by distinguishing two concepts: "forbearant toleration," of which Professor Heyd's understanding is a paradigmatic example, and "engaged toleration," which I will describe as its successor in an extended or diffused political realm in which equality, rather than autonomy, is the human characteristic to which the tolerant pay tribute. I will explain why engaged toleration is appropriate to the circumstances and self-understandings of citizens in contemporary, egalitarian democracies, and why focusing on it leads me to different answers to some if not all of the questions Professor Heyd's essay poses. I will argue, however, that engaged toleration shares certain features in common with Professor Heyd's conception: it involves a cognitive shift, and it reflects not simply a pragmatic accommodation but a principled tribute to an essential human characteristic. These observations lead me to share the conclusion that Professor Heyd's conception of toleration is transitional, although perhaps for different reasons than he intended.

II. Forbearant Toleration and the Advent of Modern Democracy

Toleration, as understood by Professor Heyd, is "the attitude of restraint in responding to morally wrong beliefs and practices."[3] It is a paradoxical practice, in that one intentionally restrains oneself from intervening in actions that one finds morally objectionable. It is accomplished through a cognitive shift "from the impersonal judgment of actions to the personally-based judgment of the agent":[4] the tolerator focuses on "the subject or agent behind [the beliefs or actions], the way that the beliefs were formed, the manner in which they cohere together in a system of beliefs or constitute a life plan of an individual."[5] Toleration had its political moment when early modern democracies sought to constitutionalize it as a vehicle for the separation of church and state; but after this brief transition, it returned to its prior domain in "the realm of interpersonal and intercommunal relations."[6] Both the definition of toleration and the nature of the modern state make clear that the former cannot be exercised by the latter:

> The state is an embodiment of an impersonal constitutional structure which derives its validity from universalizable principles. In that respect it is neutral, at least with regards to its citizens, even if not with regards to values or moral doctrines. Unlike a medieval sovereign, the state is an impersonal institution which cannot be described as "suffering" in having to reconcile itself with beliefs and practices to which "it" does not subscribe. Hence, it cannot be said to overcome or endure its wish to undermine or interfere with them. . . . The law either permits or prohibits certain practices and activities. The prohibited act cannot be tolerated by the law and the permitted practice cannot be said to be endured as a matter of charity or restraint.[7]

In Professor Heyd's view, the direct operations of the state define the domain of the political. Its neutrality and its prescription of duty through practices of codification and constitutionalization mean that toleration cannot be practiced by the state, and must, therefore, be a non-political practice.[8] It is the supererogatory act of an individual citizen or group, a contemporary version of grace that pays tribute to the autonomy of the tolerated agent.

As will be clear in the following discussion, my differences with Professor Heyd are importantly definitional. But my differences with Professor Heyd are also methodological. After describing two approaches to defining toleration—the historical (or contextual) and the philosophical or normative—Professor Heyd opts for the latter, offering a few introductory historical comments that are consistent with, or supportive of, his normative understanding.[9] My approach will be roughly the complement of Professor Heyd's: I will offer an analysis that takes its bearings from certain descriptive features of the contemporary context, and is attentive in ways that Professor Heyd acknowledges that his approach is not, to the "ordinary language of toleration."[10] But my effort will also attempt to conceptualize "engaged" toleration in ways that have some normative impetus.

As is perhaps appropriate to this method, I will begin with Professor Heyd at his most historical: at that moment in his brief genealogy of toleration where, he claims, toleration becomes obsolete as a political concept:

> With the establishment of modern liberal democracy, Bayle's vision became a reality. The successful career of the idea of toleration paradoxically led to its own decline, or at least made it superfluous in its traditional political form. In the second half of the twentieth century, ethnic and sexual minorities have become more and more impatient with the status of being tolerated. In a multi-cultural society, the demand for recognition supersedes that of toleration.[11]

In the argument that follows, I will contest Professor Heyd's conclusion that "equality before the law and respect for the rights of individuals and minority groups tend to make toleration politically redundant."[12] This will involve, first, contesting Professor Heyd's definitional notion that the political consists entirely of laws, institutional arrangements, and their justifications. It will consist, second, of challenging his suggestion that the ascent of equality has rendered toleration in the political realm obsolete. One of the most interesting aspects of Professor Heyd's genealogy is the variation and contextuality it reveals in understandings of toleration at different historical moments. These movements reinforce my conclusion that emergence of egalitarian democracy has not rendered toleration superfluous, so much as it has created the need for a new foundation: one that reflects the equality of citizens in the public realm, as opposed to what Professor Heyd might refer to as the autonomy of citizens in the private realm. This new grounding suggests a need for a more engaged, as opposed to a more forebearant, conception of toleration, which I will elaborate in Part III.

A. The Extension, or Diffusion, of the Political

I am largely in agreement with my co-commentator, Professor Sabl, in finding Professor Heyd's statist conception of the political unacceptably narrow. The domain of the "political" consists of more than the formal actions of the state—which is, in any case, not the impersonal monolith evoked by Professor Heyd. The blurring of the public and private, the institutional and individual, in the increasingly diffused realm of the political results not only from the salience of "informal politics" in giving practical meaning to governmental pronouncements, but from the popular mobilizations and institutional changes associated with the rise of equality as a public value.

First, as Professor Sabl observes, "the state" is in fact comprised of human actors who inevitably exercise discretion that is informed by their own conceptions of toleration. The judge who must determine the scope of an asserted right—a matter that is often far more ambiguous than Professor Heyd suggests—often draws on his own intuitive or elaborated understandings of toleration (and other relations among the claimants) in so doing. Moreover, the meaning or import of governmental actions in the lives of affected citizens goes beyond official declarations: it often depends on how those actions are received and made part of the shared fabric of social life by private citizens, who act without any official connection to the organs of government. For example, the extent to which women experience toleration of their decisions to terminate their pregnancies depends not only on formal declarations of the right to abortion, but the ways that these formal declarations are interpreted and acted upon by abortion providers, members of the religious right, and other individuals and groups.[13] The form and extent of toleration manifested by citizens in such informal politics inevitably affects this process of translating or assimilating governmental decisions.

Second, given the dense interconnection between public and private, official and informal, action in the political realm has been apparent in a range of governmental transformations that have accompanied the rise of equality as a public value. If one takes as examples two governmental enactments centrally associated (in popular parlance, if not in Professor Heyd's terms) with the norm of toleration—the constitutional proscription on state action that violates equal protection, and the federal statutory implementation of this guarantee by legislation such as the Civil Rights Act of 1964 and the Voting Rights Act of 1965—it is clear that these provisions did not spring full-blown from the heads of governmental officials. They took shape in response to a range of efforts by private actors, from the legal strategies of the NAACP Legal Defense Fund, to the various forms of non-violent protest by African Americans and their allies—from sit-ins at lunch counters to voter registration drives—that risked or invited intolerant responses by state and private actors in order to mobilize public opinion. The understandings of these actors about what was owed them as citizens, as well as about how to respond tolerantly to intolerant resistance richly infused their strategies and pronouncements.[14] It therefore seems incorrect to exclude from the domain of the political private engagements that resisted state restrictions, mobilized support for new federal guarantees and, significantly, reflected efforts to express and operationalize tolerance.

Moreover, the embrace of equality as a public value has accelerated a series of institutional changes which have further distanced government from the limited, prohibitory role which Professor Heyd's analysis envisions. Since the New Deal and the subsequent rise of the administrative state, government officials have become involved in the regulation of the economy, the provision of services, and the granting and validation of entitlements to opportunities and resources. This bureaucratic or administrative role creates armies of quasi-state-like actors: state contractors, social workers, and other service providers, who further blur the boundaries of the political that Professor Heyd would seek to keep intact. The civil rights legislation enacted in the wake of nationwide mobilization contributed to this pattern. Through constitutional, federal, and state law, entitlements to resources, and to public and private opportunities, have been secured for members of historically and presently disadvantaged groups. The provision of "set-asides" for minority business contractors, the requirement of accommodation under such statutes as the Americans with Disabilities Act, and the entitlement to temporary public assistance under the recent welfare reform statute, are only a few examples. In each of these areas, we find legions of public and quasi-public actors concerned with implementation, whose attitudes toward those differences they encounter have major implications for the meaning of equality in their respective domains. The attitude of the welfare worker toward non-nuclear families, or the educational or employment specialist toward dyslexia or alcoholism, contributes as meaningfully to the elaboration of "equality" as the formal decisions of judges or legislators. In addition, the ongoing social and cultural negotiations over the content of these statutory categories, and the legitimacy of the assistance that follows from them, have been an integral part of the process of giving meaning to formal guarantees that aim to produce equality in this society.

Thus, occasions for the operation of tolerance—even the forbearant tolerance espoused by Professor Heyd—exist within formal institutions of government, among the legions of quasi-public officials who implement the projects of the administrative state, and among the private citizens whose discussions and mobilizations both instigate and give concrete meaning to governmental action. It is in all these senses that toleration is, to my mind, a "political" virtue. Toleration would also appear to be required by the conceptual framework of egalitarian democracies, and necessary to their functioning, which would make it an obligatory rather than a supererogatory practice. But the answer to that question—which I will not fully engage in this comment—may become clearer as I elaborate the conception of tolerance that seems most appropriate to this form of polity.

B. Forbearant Toleration in Egalitarian Democracies

The conditions of contemporary, egalitarian democracies (such as that of the United States) lead me to question not only Professor Heyd's view of the "political," but his conception of toleration itself. The institutional, attitudinal, and cultural changes heralded by the rise of equality as a public value have not made toleration obsolete, so much as they have rendered Professor Heyd's distinctive, forbearant form of toleration insufficient. One way that we can gauge this inadequacy is by considering the dissatisfaction with forbearant toleration on the part of those toward whom it is directed.

In his earlier work, Professor Heyd appears to discount the perspective of the tolerated in assessing the value of his particular account of tolerance. He notes that "people do not like to be tolerated because toleration is only partial acceptance, the acceptance of the right of a person to lead a certain life or entertain certain beliefs; it does not extend to the practices or beliefs themselves."[15] In a more specific reference to the perspectival shift reflected in his particular theory, Professor Heyd adds that:

> the asymmetry between the tolerant and the tolerated on this matter can be explained by the fact that the subject of the beliefs or the agents of the practices in question find it harder to make the perspectival shift because they identify with their beliefs and practices in a much stronger way.[16]

But both the suggestion that the tolerated are inevitably dissatisfied with tolerance, and the implication that this dissatisfaction provides no reason for rejecting a particular understanding of tolerance seem to me to demand closer consideration. Although neither Professor Heyd's genealogy of tolerance, nor his affirmative account stress the relational character or goals of toleration,[17] other accounts of toleration find its justification in the relations it establishes between fellow citizens. T. M. Scanlon, for example, argues that we should value toleration because it "involves a more attractive, appealing relation between opposing groups in society"[18] and because "rejecting it involves a form of alienation from one's fellow citizens."[19] If these positive relations, which arise from some form of valuation of the tolerated, are not achieved, there may be reason to doubt the adequacy of the practice. Moreover, the impatience of the tolerated with the forbearant version of tolerance cannot simply be discounted as a constant. Even Professor Heyd, in discussing the impatience of minorities with toleration, acknowledges this development as a particular feature of egalitarian democracies in the late 20th century.[20] And it is possible to identify more particularized reasons for the growth of such dissatisfaction in contemporary egalitarian democracies.

First, the identification of the individual subject with his beliefs or cultural practices, which Professor Heyd sees as complicating the tolerated subject's appreciation of forbearant tolerance, has intensified dramatically in the contemporary period. This development has been fueled, in general terms, by the advent of "identity politics": in our political culture, the growing salience of group membership to individual identity has led us to view practices and opinions, which we might formerly have said we held or engaged in, as an integral part of who we are.[21] This identification of individual subjects with beliefs or practices distinctive to their group has also been fueled by a legal framework for the vindication of equality that makes one's claim to equal resources or opportunities dependent on one's membership in a protected category or group, or a conceptual analogue to a protected category or group.[22] The partial displacement of reductive versions of identity politics by complex accounts of contingent social formation has not arrested this trend. It has often produced a sense of individual identification with a broader—if more variable and contingent—range of practices and opinions, even as it has complicated or attenuated the notion of autonomy that has served as a second-order justification for restraint.[23] Both this complication of liberal understandings of autonomy, and the increasing difficulty of distinguishing the subject from his beliefs or practices may make forbearant tolerance unsatisfying or incoherent for the tolerator as well as the tolerated.

Beyond the difficulties associated with Professor Heyd's distinctive perceptual shift, the forbearant posture itself may seem gratingly inadequate in egalitarian democracies. Forbearant tolerance secures insulation from interference; but citizens in egalitarian democracies may find non-interference, which speaks to liberty or autonomy, a poor substitute for the recognition that is perceived as being more directly related to equality. This point was made clear in a telling example, involving minority religious practices during that most dominant and public of religious celebrations, the Christmas holiday. In a New Year's installment of Aaron McGruder's Boondocks strip, the main character bemoaned the mainstream treatment of Kwaanza. He sighed: "Another Kwaanza has come. Spurned. Forgotten. Existing just outside the public eye. We all know it's there, but nobody wants to acknowledge it. It's the Essie May Washington of holidays." The analogy to Strom Thurmond's African-American daughter, whom he supported personally and financially, but whom he failed to acknowledge publicly because of her race, is a telling one. Autonomy is one thing, but visibility or public acknowledgment, is another.[24] What is significant about this lament is that it takes place in a context of meticulous non-interference. No government official or private actor has challenged, or proposed to interfere with, the celebration of Kwanzaa. Yet that non-interference is thin gruel for McGruder's character, who synonymizes being "spurned" with "exist[ing] just outside the public eye." For him, equality requires public recognition of, or engagement with, his observances or beliefs. It is useful to consider why.

In his essay, "The Politics of Recognition," Charles Taylor offers a historical explanation. With the collapse of social hierarchies ushered in by political modernity, the "honor" associated with distinctive locations in that hierarchy was replaced in two ways.[25] First, it was replaced by universalist notions of "equal dignity," which have found contemporary expression in the non-discrimination principle, or the protection of political and civil rights. Second, as notions of identity associated with social role or status gave way to notions of individualized identity associated with the ideal of "authenticity," modern culture experienced a turn toward inwardness, subjectivity and particularity. This movement has found its contemporary expression in a "politics of difference," in which claims to equality are satisfied not by universal rights but by public recognition of the particularity or unique identity of an individual or group. The need, and consequently the demand, for recognition as a political tribute to equality arises in part from the insecurity created by the collapse of durable social categories. Taylor explains:

> General recognition was build into the socially derived identity by virtue of the very fact that it was based on social categories that everyone took for granted. Yet inwardly derived, personal, original identity doesn't enjoy this recognition a priori. It has to win it through exchange, and the attempt can fail. . . . This is why the need [for recognition] is now acknowledged publicly for the first time. In premodern times, people didn't speak of "identity" or "recognition"—not because people didn't have . . . identities or depend on recognition, but rather because these were too unproblematic to be thematized as such.[26]

But the demand for public recognition of difference also responds to the homogenizing tendencies of contemporary democracies. "It is precisely [the unique identity of this individual or group] that is being ignored, glossed over, assimilated to a dominant or majority identity. And this assimilation is the cardinal sin against the ideal of authenticity."[27]

This latter point is given a more pragmatic and power-sensitive gloss in a recent essay by Anne Phillips.[28] Phillips suggests that the need for public recognition and acknowledgment of difference arises from an experientially grounded sophistication, particularly among relatively disempowered groups in egalitarian societies, about the varied and subtle forms that inequality may assume. For sexual and religious minorities, Phillips observes, social and political invisibility has often been the price exacted for decriminalization or non-interference:

> The decriminalization of homosexuality, for example, redefined sexual preference as a matter of private variation, but this carried with it an implicit warning the homosexuality should not be too public. Those who happily tolerate their unassuming gay neighbour may still object violently to the high-profile activist who "flaunts" his sexuality in public. . . . The toleration was offered at a price and keeping things private was part of the deal.[29]

This price has been assailed as conspicuous and burdensome, for example in United States' "Don't Ask, Don't Tell" policy toward gays and lesbians in the military. As Phillips concludes: "The dispensation offered to homosexual falls distinctly short of what is taken for granted by the heterosexual majority, and the dispensation offered to cultural and religious minorities strikes many of them as unfair as well."[30] Members of minority groups or cultures have also chafed at the subtle non-neutrality of the "liberal resolution of difference."[31] This approach, Phillips notes:

> [served] as the basis for assimilating a plurality of ethnic groups into a unified citizenship: what Joseph Raz describes as "letting minorities conduct themselves as they wish without being criminalized, so long as they do not interfere with the culture of the majority." . . . The hands-off toleration that relegates difference

> to the private sphere leaves the presumptions of the host culture untouched, and all the adjustment is then one-way. This asymmetry of treatment falls considerably short of equal treatment; the liberal resolution of difference has not been as even handed as it claims.[32]

The dispensation to take part in particular practices at the sufferance (figuratively and literally) of government officials and fellow citizens, which arises from a principled commitment to autonomy, does not fully respond to contemporary aspirations for equality. To fulfill these perceived needs requires a form of toleration that more explicitly acknowledges and engages dissonant or minority opinions, practices, or cultures. It is to this more engaged form of toleration that I now turn.

III. Engaged Toleration

What I will refer to as "engaged toleration" is a practice that helps citizens acknowledge, investigate, and learn from the range of group-based differences, and corresponding inequalities, that are present in many contemporary, pluralist democracies. As such, it is broader in scope than the form of toleration described by Professor Heyd. It applies not only to those opinions, acts, or group practices that the tolerator finds to be immoral, but also those that the tolerator finds to be erroneous, inappropriate, distasteful, or inapproachably "other." Engaged toleration may also apply to acts, opinions, or practices as to which the tolerator is indifferent or has formed no opinion, but substantial segments of society judge to be immoral, inappropriate, or distasteful. Like Professor Heyd's forbearant toleration, engaged toleration also begins with a cognitive shift: the tolerator disengages herself from her own moral or normative frame, and its implied negative judgment of the tolerated. But instead of shifting the focus to the tolerated agent, the tolerator shifts her focus to the moral or normative frame underlying the opinion, act, or practice in question.[33] The goal of engaged tolerance is, first, to understand the opinion or practice on its own terms, and second, to reflect on the implications it may have for the tolerator's own moral, normative, or intuitive frame.

This conception of toleration is not unprecedented in the literature. It has antecedents in the suggestion of John Horton, for example, that toleration implies not only forbearance from acting on one's moral disapproval, but "narrowing the range of what is considered objectionable."[34] Elements of this understanding are also previewed in Jonathan Wolff's distinction between "grudging toleration," which might be described as a pragmatic embrace of forbearance and "accommodative toleration," in which the tolerator seeks to take in the understandings underlying a dissonant practice and reflect on the light they shed on his culture's dominant practices. The equality-respecting elements of this formulation, in particular, are previewed by T. M. Scanlon's view of tolerance. In Scanlon's view, tolerance reflects the judgment that "all members of society are equally entitled to be taken into account in determining what our society is and equally entitled to participate in determining what it will be in the future";[35] moreover it demands that citizens, and governments contemplating interference with group-based actions or practices ask "the question of accommodation": "are there other ways, not damaging to the system of tolerance, in which respect for the threatened group could be demonstrated?"[36]

Professor Heyd has, himself, responded to forms of toleration that seek to enter into the normative frame of the tolerated. In discussing Peter Gardner's approach, which emphasizes "open-mindedness, critical skepticism, the power of deliberation and the willingness to change one's mind,"[37] Professor Heyd observes:

> Gardner's conception of toleration definitely accords with everyday usage of the term. However, it does not capture the most difficult and demanding contexts in which toleration is called for (and considered intrinsically valuable). It tends to blur the boundaries between tolerance, on the one hand, and open-mindedness, critical skepticism and moderate judgment, on the other. It does not do justice to the suffering of the tolerator, the price of restraint and the effort involved in it.[38]

To my mind, this criticism underestimates the moral and intellectual effort required by more active forms of toleration. I will try to spell out my differences with Professor Heyd, on this count, by elaborating two of the virtues most strongly associated with engaged toleration. Whether either of these associated virtues, or indeed toleration itself, constitutes a virtue, in the Aristotelian sense preferred by Professor Heyd,[39] may be subject to dispute.[40] But one must acknowledge that all are attributes of character, capable of being described as means between more extreme forms of human behavior, and supported by conditioning and practice. Moreover, each is an effortful undertaking—a far cry from a simple admonition to proceed gently in relation to difference. By illuminating these associated virtues, which typify and support toleration, I hope to specify with more particularity both the operation of engaged tolerance and its particular challenges.

The first such virtue is curiosity. I first learned about the full meaning of curiosity in a superb essay by Joan Nestle called "The Fem Question."[41] In that essay, she arrestingly described curiosity as "the respect one life pays to another,"[42] and she illustrated how such curiosity might operate in investigating a specific practice: the embrace of butch/fem roles, which are both privately assimilated and publicly performed, by a subset of lesbians in relationship. Nestle observes that such roles are frequently misunderstood, particularly that of the fem who is popularly viewed as comparable to a "straight woman who is not a feminist."[43] These assumptions subject butch/fem lesbians to a range of intolerant behaviors, from street harassment, to police raids on bars that are particularly identified with the group, to uninformed assertions about the meaning of the practice, or the nature of the identities involved. Nestle invites readers to disengage themselves from their preconceptions—that is, their intuitive normative frame—and investigate this practice, with the curiosity that another life deserves. This means understanding the history of the practice; the shifts or alterations in its manifestations over time; the way its roles are understood by participants, in a variety of contexts; and the way that these self-understandings vary from the understandings frequently ascribed to practitioners by those outside the group. Curiosity of this sort involves a genuine eagerness to know about life in all of its permutations, and an intellectual persistence or rigor in identifying and asking the questions that will reveal a given practice in its historical context and in its full complexity. It involves a commitment to investigation, discovery, and self-education that is, at least temporarily, greater than one's commitment to the idea that she already knows what is present in the practice in question.

This last condition points to a second, related, virtue involved in engaged tolerance: the virtue of humility. The way that humility functions in engaged toleration is nicely illustrated by Charles Taylor in his essay "The Politics of Recognition." Taylor takes his bearings from a statement often ascribed to Saul Bellow that "when the Zulus produce a Tolstoy, then we will read him."[44] This perspective may not be intolerant in the sense envisioned by Professor Heyd: Bellow is not proposing to interfere with the artistic production of Zulu authors. But it is intolerant in at least two senses underscored by my discussion of egalitarian democracies. First, because this kind of judgment often informs curricular decisions at major universities, it contributes to the denial of visibility or recognition to the ostensibly non-Tolstoyesque works of Zulu authors. Second, it judges those works unworthy without fully reflecting on the metric that should be applied in assessing them. Taylor focuses on this second difficulty, arguing that Bellow displayed an unacceptable cultural arrogance in assuming that a work of value from the Zulu culture would or could have the characteristics that distinguish Tolstoy, and that those are the characteristics by which any work should be judged. Instead, Taylor argues, readers should pay tribute to the presumptive equality of cultures by assuming that they are capable of producing works of enduring value, and committing themselves to learn enough about works from unfamiliar cultures to determine whether they supply additional criteria that we should utilize in forming our metric of value. This, according to Taylor, involves an openness to a Gadamerian "fusion of horizons,"[45] in which we do not assume the completeness of our own evaluative frame, but inquire into how it might be modified by the introduction of features of another, less familiar frame. Speaking of the attribute(s) required by this effort, Taylor states:

> . . . what the presumption [of equality among cultures] requires of us is not peremptory and inauthentic judgments of equal value, but a willingness to be open to the comparative cultural study of the kind that must displace our horizons in resulting

> fusions. What it requires above all is an admission that we are very far away from that ultimate horizon from which the relative worth of different cultures might be evident.[46]

Although the foregoing examples foreground aesthetic judgments and intuitive or political judgments about sexuality, the humility and curiosity integral to engaged toleration can be applied in contexts involving moral judgment as well. Leslye Obiora's excellent essay on female genital cutting, "Brides and Barricades: Rethinking Polemics and Intransigence in the Campaign Against Female Circumcision"[47] is a case in point. Obiora, an African feminist living and writing in the United States, exhorts Western feminists to both humility and curiosity in the face of these practices: she invites them to investigate such practices as they are understood by dominant African cultures and by the women involved, before formulating a normative approach to addressing them. After a Neslean investigation of history, cultural context, variations in the practice and in the meanings assigned to it, Obiora does not shy from the construction, or reconstruction, of a normative frame. But her proposed framework seeks to produce an integration of, or accommodation among, the priority placed by Western feminists on women's autonomy and bodily integrity, the values placed by some African women on the preservation of their cultural practices and on the ritualization of female identification within those practices, and the norms advanced by NGOs concerning the health risks of some forms of cutting. This reconstructed frame leads Obiora to endorse some limited forms of the practice, conducted under conditions designed to protect the health of the women involved, and to reject the practice in its more extreme and health-threatening manifestations. She proposes that advocacy along these lines be conducted by a coalition of Western feminists newly involved with this practice, and African women already engaged in work on this issue.

Obiora's analytic progression underscores several features of engaged tolerance.[48] First, the investigation of the historical, contextual, and normative basis of a contested practice is aimed not simply at achieving greater understanding of the practice, or at achieving the dialogic ventilation that offers a form of recognition to members of minority groups, although it may achieve both of these objectives. The exploration characteristic of engaged tolerance is also, and perhaps more importantly, aimed at shedding potentially critical or transformative light on the normative frame that produced the initial negative judgment. That process of illumination may or may not succeed in producing a transformation, and may or may not produce the related policy outcomes that members of the tolerated group seek. After such inquiry tolerators may conclude that the unfamiliar norms diverge too sharply to be reconciled in any meaningful way with their own normative framework;[49] this is a conclusion, for example, that even some of the most inquisitive interlocutors have reached concerning the controversy over abortion.[50] Or tolerators may succeed in at least partially modifying their normative frame, yet discover that implementing their reconstructed vision is difficult in practice; those who have sought to integrate works from a variety of cultures into Great Books programs, for example, have sometimes encountered this difficulty.[51] It is also possible that tolerators may pursue the implementation of a modified normative framework in directions that the tolerated did not propose or anticipate.[52] This indeterminacy of substantive outcome is a feature which may distinguish engaged tolerance from its forbearant counterpart. Though proponents of such an account of toleration might differ on this element, I would suggest that what it requires is a thoroughgoing effort to disengage from one's own normative framework, inquire deeply into another's, and strive—where it is required, for example, by practical or policy conflicts—to develop some accommodation or integration between them.[53] In this respect, as well as others,[54] engaged toleration may also be distinguished from full embrace of difference; the failures of integration, practical accommodation, or even thoroughgoing comprehension in investigation, that are always possible may lead members of tolerated groups to feel that they have not received their due. But it is a form of accommodation between one's normative commitments and the dissonant practices[55] that one is likely to encounter in a pluralist society that pays appropriate tribute to the ascendant value of equality. It signals to its objects that they are, as Scanlon suggests, "equally entitled to be taken into account in determining what our society is." It offers sought-after visibility, and casts the light of dialogic contestation, on the practices and identities of a variety of individuals and group members.

IV. Conclusion: Forbearant Tolerance as a Transitional Understanding

In this comment, I have disputed Professor Heyd's claim that toleration is a non-political practice, and challenged the adequacy, in contemporary egalitarian democracies, of his "forbearant" version of toleration. However, I find in his account of tolerance elements integral to the "engaged" account of tolerance that I have attempted to develop here. The notion of tolerance as entailing a perceptual shift, a disengagement or dis-orientation from one's normative frame, is integral to both accounts; and the practice of shifting one's focus from normative condemnation of an act to respect for the autonomy of the agent may, in fact, prepare citizens for the practice of shifting their focus from their own normative frame to that of a less familiar individual or group. Moreover, the "second-order" character of forbearant toleration—the requirement that one redirect one's initial normative response in deference to a second-order value—is a feature that unites both accounts, though Professor Heyd envisions tolerators as responding to the value of autonomy, while I see them as paying tribute to the value of equality. In this sense, Professor Heyd's account of toleration might indeed be described as transitional, if not to a post-tolerant regime of acceptance, then to a form of toleration premised on the equality of citizens.

NOTES

1. I should mention that this issue has been ameliorated to some degree in the latest version of Professor Heyd's chapter. While the draft on which I originally commented included only a handful of examples, most relating to religious minorities and one involving a decision not to summon the police in the face of a noisy party, the latest version also includes a discussion of female circumcision and a more extended consideration

of the practice of avoiding driving in orthodox Jewish neighborhoods during the Sabbath.

2. For examples of anthologies that reflect (predominantly, though not exclusively) these distinct emphases, compare David Heyd, ed., *Toleration: An Elusive Virtue* (Princeton: Princeton University Press, 1996) with Catriona MacKinnon and Dario Castiglione, eds., *The Culture of Toleration in Diverse Societies* (Manchester: Manchester University Press, 2003).

3. This definition comes from David Heyd, "Education to Toleration: Some Philosophical Obstacles and Their Resolution," eds. Catriona MacKinnon and Dario Castiglione, *The Culture of Toleration in Diverse Societies,* 197. In this comment, I will sometimes make use of discussions from Professor Heyd's other recent work on toleration to flesh out the "forbearant" conception, as I understand it to be substantially in accord with the arguments in his chapter in this volume.

4. David Heyd, "Is Toleration a Political Virtue?" 185.

5. David Heyd, "Education for Toleration: Some Philosophical Obstacles and Their Resolution," Catriona MacKinnon and Dario Castiglione, eds., *The Culture of Toleration in Diverse Societies,* 199.

6. "Is Toleration a Political Virtue?" 175.

7. Ibid., 177–78.

8. As Professor Heyd explains, "the issue of Muslim female students wearing headscarves in French state schools is not really a matter of toleration but a question of the correct interpretation of constitutional principles . . . only the way in which this religious practice is viewed by non-Muslim French citizens (rather than the state) may involve toleration." Ibid., 178.

9. Ibid., 175.

10. Ibid., 172.

11. Ibid., 175.

12. Ibid.

13. Furthermore, it may be useful to elaborate a point that seems implicit, if not explicit in Professor Sabl's analysis: to the extent that democratic governments remain "limited"—that is, that they reflect restraint in defining the domain of prohibition—the attitudes and responses described above play a comparatively larger role in defining individuals' freedoms and shaping their expectations. When the federal government, in its effectuation of constitutional rights, declines to intervene in the provision of abortion services, groups such as Operation Rescue enter this hiatus to offer moral objection and "sidewalk counseling." Their action is not the action of the state, but it is central to the experience of women in negotiating their reproductive rights, and central to what most

of us would call *political* contestation over the reproductive choice, and ultimately, the equality of women. This complex and vexing debate does not become political simply when clinics seek to enjoin such actions and the matter winds up in federal court, or a state legislature.

14. The injunction to "love the sinner, hate the sin" that informed many of these tactics has interesting parallels to Professor Heyd's perspectival shift.

15. David Heyd, "Introduction," David Heyd, ed., *Toleration: An Elusive Virtue,* 16.

16. Ibid.

17. Professor Heyd's examples tend to emphasize the pragmatic justifications (as in toleration among the early Christian sects), or normative justifications that involve some quality to be cultivated in the tolerator (caritas, Christlike magnanimity) or, secondarily, some quality to be recognized in the tolerated (autonomy). They do not appear to draw justification from a relation that toleration fosters or recognizes between the tolerator and the tolerated.

18. T. M. Scanlon, *The Difficulty of Tolerance,* David Heyd, ed., *Tolerance: An Elusive Virtue,* 231.

19. Ibid.

20. "Is Toleration a Political Virtue?" 175.

21. An interesting example of this commitment to the confluence of act or practice and subjectivity or identity may be seen in the rise of queer activism. As illustrated, for example by Michael Warner's recent work *The Trouble with Normal,* queer theorists and activists protest the tendency of mainstream advocacy organizations to separate gay and lesbian identity from the sexual practices with which it is commonly associated. See Michael Warner, *The Trouble with Normal* (Durham: Duke University Press, 1999), 41–80.

22. This feature of contemporary egalitarian democracies has been critiqued, perhaps most compellingly by Wendy Brown, who argues that it leads subjects to hold fast even to identities constructed predominantly around an injury or a sense of oneself as injured. See Wendy Brown, *Wounded Attachments in States of Injury* (Princeton: Princeton University Press, 1995), 52–76. My point, however, is not to defend the normative value of such identification, but to concur in its descriptive prevalence.

23. See, e.g., Kathryn Abrams, "From Autonomy to Agency: Feminist Perspectives on Self-Direction," *William and Mary Law Review* 40 (1999): 805–46.

24. Interestingly, this sentiment had been echoed during the same holiday season by my then-seven-year-old daughter. I had overheard her leafing through the holiday editions of several mail order catalogues,

muttering to herself, "No Hanukkah, no menorahs, no Jews." After a while, she shook her head, and said to me—without McGruder's astringent irony but with the same sense of ill treatment—"why don't the Christians like us?"

25. See Charles Taylor, *The Politics of Recognition,* Amy Gutmann, ed., *Multiculturalism and the Politics and Recognition* (Princeton: Princeton University Press, 1992), 25–40.

26. Taylor, *The Politics of Recognition,* 35.

27. Ibid., 38.

28. See Anne Phillips, "The Politicisation of Difference: Does This Make for a More Intolerant Society?" John Horton and Susan Mendus, eds., *Toleration, Identity and Difference* (New York: Palgrave, 1999), 126–45.

29. Ibid., 127.

30. Ibid.

31. Ibid.

32. Ibid., 127–28. George Fletcher also argues that an asymmetry or non-reciprocity to arrangements of tolerance for sexual minorities make acceptance or recognition a more attractive option than forbearant toleration: gays and lesbians, under conditions of tolerance, accept the sexual proclivities of their heterosexual counterparts but are granted only forbearance in return. See George Fletcher, "The Instability of Tolerance," David Heyd, ed., *Toleration: An Elusive Virtue,* 120–21. This assimilative version of equality has been contested, for example, by women in professional workplaces, who perceived that they were admitted under assumptions that left the pre-existing culture—with its androcentric metrics of achievement, and its inflexibility in accommodating parenting responsibilities—unaffected.

33. Whereas Heyd argues that the perspective shift implicit in his form of toleration as analogous to "the suspension of disbelief" (186), I might argue that the perspective shift entailed by engaged toleration can be described as a "suspension of belief"—a distancing of the tolerator from his or her own normative framework, in preparation for entering fully into the normative framework or perspective of another—which would seem to me to be at least as strenuous as shifting from an act-centered to an agent-centered perspective.

In practicing engaged toleration, one does not tolerate others simply out of respect for them as unmarked, autonomous agents. One tolerates and respects them not in a universal, but in a particularized way, as subjects with specific identities or affiliations constituted by group membership, collective acts or shared opinions; and one demonstrates that respect by inquiring into that membership and those acts. See my discussion of curiosity, infra. In the most recent version of his essay, Professor

Heyd has moved slightly in the direction of tolerance as reflecting interest in or respect for particularity, rather than simply for human agency. His discussion of female circumcision (187), reflects an awareness of or interest in the effects of culture on the choices of individuals, and his discussion of the value of avoiding driving in orthodox neighborhoods during the Sabbath reflects awareness of the meaning of such intrusion on the observance of orthodox Jews, an appreciation of the "sincer[ity]" of their faith. However, I would distinguish the limited acknowledgment of the particularized lives of the tolerated that emerges in Professor Heyd's essay from the more thoroughgoing examination one might find, for example, works such as Debra Renee Kaufman's *Rachel's Daughters: Newly-Orthodox Jewish Women* (New Brunswick, NJ: Rutgers University Press, 1991), which examines the embrace of orthodox Judaism by adult women. This exploration is aimed not only at understanding the lives and choices of these women (through an elaborate set of interviews), but at scrutinizing the assumption of many secular women—including, initially, the author—that orthodox women must have little interest in their own equality with men. To my mind, this book typifies the spirit of engaged toleration, as it reflects the author's effort to suspend her own normative commitments in order to enter fully into those of a different group, which leads in turn to her own critical reflection on her initial opinions or assumptions.

34. John Horton, "Toleration as a Virtue," David Heyd, ed., *Toleration: An Elusive Virtue,* 38.

35. T. M. Scanlon, "The Difficulty of Tolerance," David Heyd, ed., *Toleration: An Elusive Virtue,* 229.

36. Ibid., 237. The contention, which underlies my view of engaged tolerance, that minorities or disempowered groups in egalitarian democracies require not simply the autonomy to conduct their lives as they please but the affirmation implicit in visibility and recognition, is also prominent in the work of Anne Phillips which I cited earlier. Interestingly, however, Phillips adheres to a more traditional forbearant notion of toleration, and describes the "politicization of difference" that she endorses as something beyond tolerance. See Anne Phillips, "The Politicisation of Difference," John Horton and Susan Mendus, eds., *Toleration, Identity and Difference,* 126.

37. David Heyd, "Education to Toleration: Some Philosophical Obstacles and Their Resolution," 204.

38. Ibid.

39. "Is Toleration a Political Virtue?" 183.

40. I would argue that engaged toleration meets several of the criteria he sets forth: it can readily be described as an attribute of character; it re-

flects a kind of mean, between rigid insistence on and wanton abandonment of one's own normative perspective; it is supported by practice and habituation—indeed exhorting individuals to such practice is one of the goals of the emerging literature on this form of toleration.

41. Joan Nestle, "The Fem Question," Carole Vance, ed., *Pleasure and Danger: Exploring Female Sexuality,* 2nd Edition (Boston: Routledge, 1992), 232.

42. Ibid., 234.

43. Ibid., 236.

44. Charles Taylor, "The Politics of Recognition," Amy Gutmann, ed., *Multiculturalism and the Politics of Recognition,* 71.

45. Ibid., 67.

46. Ibid., 73.

47. L. Amede Obiora, "Brides and Barricades: Rethinking Polemics and Intransigence in the Campaign Against Female Circumcision," *Case W. L. Rev.* 47 (1997), 275.

48. In this discussion, I have focused, and will focus, exclusively on toleration as it is practiced in engagements among individuals and groups. As I have argued above, I consider such engagement to be importantly political, both when they are undertaken by lay citizens and when they are undertaken by individuals acting in their capacities as governmental or quasi-governmental agents. What this discussion does not consider is what the formal (e.g., legislative or judicial) organs of government might do to implement or foster engaged toleration, although this seems to me a valuable subject for future inquiry.

49. Jonathan Wolff refers to something similar to this outcome ("being prepared to consider accommodation but finding that this is not possible without 'too much' revision") "reasoned intolerance," see Jonathan Wolff, "Social Ethos and the Dynamics of Toleration," Catriona MacKinnon and Dario Castiglione, eds., *The Culture of Toleration in Diverse Societies,* 157. To my mind, this is a misnomer, because, as I note below, I see the practice of engaged toleration as consisting primarily in the process of disengaging from one's own normative frame, inquiring deeply into another's, and attempting some integration or reconciliation. No particular outcome is assured (or perhaps one might say a range of possible outcomes, or not at all, could be treated as definitive by proponent of this view), an understanding which is perhaps distinct from that involved in forbearant tolerance.

50. For an example of such an engaged, tolerant interaction which nonetheless does not lead to a thoroughgoing convergence of views among participants, see Sidney Callahan and Daniel Callahan, eds., *Abortion: Understanding Differences* (New York: Plenum Press, 1984). My

reference to particular examples here is not intended to indicate that the specific practices of engaged toleration that I have proposed have been applied to these cases; my point is to propose that they might be, and to suggest that some features of investigating the normative frame of another may have been undertaken in these cases, with a variety of results.

51. For a thoughtful discussion of this controversy, including practical aspects of the challenge, see Amy Gutmann, "Introduction," Amy Gutmann, ed., *Multiculturalism and the Politics of Recognition,* 13–24.

52. This may be the best way to characterize Obiora's limited endorsement of some practices of female genital cutting. Another example is provided by T. M. Scanlon, who discusses the example of Muslims in Britain, who did not initially support the Ayatollah Khomeini's edict against the *Satanic Verses,* but felt compelled to support it because of what they perceived as more generalized intolerance toward Muslims in Britain. See T. M. Scanlon, "The Difficulty of Tolerance," David Heyd, ed., *Toleration: An Elusive Virtue,* 239 n. 9. An accommodation by the British government which resulted in a rejection of the Ayatollah's edict, but improved treatment of Muslims (e.g., the modification of British blasphemy laws to protect Islam as well as Christianity, which they did not at that time) might reflect this kind of outcome as well.

53. In this choice, I believe that I subscribe to roughly the view expressed by Charles Taylor above, although he does not explicitly identify the practice he describes as a form of toleration.

54. Engaged toleration may also be distinct from acceptance in that some theorists describe acceptance as a "first-order attitude." See George Fletcher, "The Instability of Tolerance," David Heyd, ed., *Toleration: An Elusive Virtue,* 159 (describing respect, which is used interchangeably with acceptance, as a "first-order attitude"). I am puzzled by the suggestion that thoroughgoing acceptance, in a political culture that is infused in many ways with suspicion of difference, could be a "simple, first-order attitude"; but it seems clear to me that engaged toleration, like forbearant toleration is a practice in which "the tolerant decide . . . not to follow their first-order instincts." Ibid.

55. Although I do not share Professor Heyd's inclination to focus on the suffering of the tolerator as a defining characteristic of tolerance—I see the determinative criteria for tolerance in egalitarian regimes as more properly focused on the cognitive or accommodative relation between the normative system of the tolerator and that of the tolerated—I have little doubt that this understanding of tolerance would produce its share of suffering in those attempting it. As Professor Heyd acknowledges, his account of toleration requires the tolerator to shift his focus away from his moral commitments, but it does not require any weakening of cer-

tainty about those commitments. See David Heyd, "Introduction," David Heyd, ed., *Toleration: An Elusive Virtue,* 15. Engaged tolerance—as my discussion of humility, and the work of Charles Taylor suggest—requires precisely that weakening of certainty, as a predicate for the cognitive shift from one normative frame to another, and as a predicate for the effort at normative revision or reconstruction. This weakening of certainty is likely to produce substantial suffering in many of those who attempt it.

8

"VIRTUOUS TO HIMSELF": PLURALISTIC DEMOCRACY AND THE TOLERATION OF TOLERATIONS[1]

ANDREW SABL

David Heyd's careful chapter makes the double claim that toleration, often considered the "fundamental," even "constitutive" virtue of liberal politics, is in fact neither political nor a virtue. Moreover, he claims, toleration is not strictly a duty but supererogatory, "beyond the call of duty." His argument is absolutely valid given how he defines "political," "virtue," and "toleration." My comments will, however, question the utility of all three of Heyd's definitions. This may seem impertinent: one should not simply quarrel over terms. But a chapter so well reasoned leaves no choice: finding no flaw in an argument, one can only contest premises. I shall argue that in this case certain terms are really more productive than others in the sense of being more true to the circumstances that liberal democracies actually face and that make toleration necessary in the first place.

Heyd rightly sees his three claims as interrelated. So are mine. While Heyd defines politics as what pertains to the neutral state, toleration is in fact a political virtue because politics in a pluralistic democracy starts from the premise that the neutral state may not exist and certainly cannot be counted on. Democratic politics needs toleration to guide public decisions both because laws universal in scope admit of discretion in application and because the prospects of sustaining neutrality and other liberal values depend, in a democracy, on the attitudes and virtues of the ordinary citizens who control politicians' jobs. As for virtues, political theory has long (since Machiavelli, Mandeville, and Montesquieu) drawn a distinction between the perfectionist or Aristotelian virtues that help people be good human beings and the more instrumental virtues that helps them be good citizens of their polity.[2] Heyd must be right that toleration is not a virtue if that means a state of character based on trained natural impulses and conducive to an agent's own good. But, as he recognizes, it might be a virtue in a broader sense relating to what a heterogeneous society needs to work well. If this is true, toleration, like the other liberal-democratic virtues (though few others are uncontroversial), means any attitude, emotion, reason, or habit that helps us get along with beliefs, behaviors, or people that we find morally objectionable, stipulating the anti-utopian assumption that no one is likely to become perfectly good or wise. Finally, given a realistic view of how liberal democratic politics works and how citizens must act to keep it working, toleration does start to appear necessary, not supererogatory. Essentially, toleration is what liberal democratic citizens need to get along, not only with the openly intolerant, but also with people—in fact, this is most people—who believe in and live by ideologies of *toleration* that strike "us" as obviously wrong and possibly dangerous.

I. "State" Neutrality and Official Discretion

For Heyd, the triumph of the neutral state has made the virtue of toleration less important than it used to be, in at least three ways. First, a "state," being an "impersonal institution," is not the kind of entity that can display toleration or any other virtue: it lacks feelings, beliefs, and wishes.[3] Second, the officials of states operate by impartial and universal rules that rule out the kind of discretionary decisions in which virtue can be (or "ought to be"?) displayed. The idea, if I understand it, is that state *agents,* the kind of entities that *could* display virtues, *ought* not to if they are acting as they should: "it is the duty of the judge to *ignore* her personal moral views rather than to manifest toleration of other, incompatible views." Heyd would apparently say that, if state officials do act on their attitudes or are governed by their virtues, they are illicitly freelancing and no longer count as state officials. Finally, the triumph of states that enforce neutrality means that the rest of us have less scope for exercising toleration: we refrain from burning witches not because we consider and (virtuously) reject this as a possible course of action, but because the act violates rights that the law protects.[4]

A full response would involve a theory of the state. Standing on one foot: it may be doubted whether such an entity exists, much less whether "the establishment of liberal democracy" has established it and its neutrality for all time. We should note competing traditions here. One tradition of talking about "the state" (and about toleration), drawing inspiration in various materialist and idealist forms from Hobbes, Bodin, some *philosophes,* Kant, and Hegel, stresses the duties of enlightened magistrates, who are to establish and enforce toleration precisely because popular passions on their own will do the opposite. Over time, an increasingly educated public can be trusted with more and more responsibility and authority.[5] Another tradition, more pluralistic, democratic, skeptical towards elites—and therefore quintessentially though not exclusively American—follows instead Montesquieu, Madison, and Tocqueville, and has an affinity with political theory rather than philosophy in focusing on the actual practices of democratic polities rather than the *ethos* that animates their theoretical defenders. This tradition points out that when government officials are selected by the people, toleration as a government policy can only survive if popular attitudes support it, either directly or through complex institutional or social mechanisms. This second tradition tends even to define toleration differently—opposing it not to state partiality but to majority tyranny. And it stresses the need to make toleration consistent with personal liberty and equality of political power rather than redefining (or ignoring) the latter to accord with ideals of neutrality.

Arguments below will draw, as will surprise no one, on the second tradition. But even the first cannot eliminate the need for virtue among governing officials. Actual government officials will always have discretion, and toleration is among the many virtues that will guide that discretion. This is true even of judges, whose decisions may be free of personal or partisan interest but are still far from automatic. But it is even more true, and legitimately so, of legislators—who necessarily represent partial and controversial points of view—and even of executive officials who may be implementing laws that apply universally but who have as politicians stated, or implied, specific positions on what they will do with their inevitable discretion—which evils will be most sought out and what actions will be taken in fighting them.

Moreover, even an *ethos* of neutrality (stipulating for argument that we are governed by one) cannot settle difficult cases. Cases involving religion notoriously show that neutrality as a policy, refusal to actively favor or persecute a moral or religious outlook, does not always mean neutrality in effect. The rule that men and women in the U.S. Air Force must remove their headgear indoors was meant to ensure military uniformity, not to harm Jews—but still meant that observant Jews could not serve.[6] The law forbids Native Americans and whites alike from using peyote, but forces only the former to abandon their religion or face the public disadvantages accruing to felons.[7]

In such cases, the virtue of toleration prompts a decent government to respond to these asymmetric disadvantages by not doing some of the things that might be constitutionally allowable. Toleration is a virtue that guides the governing power in making such accommodations precisely when constitutional neutrality and universality do *not* require this. And, in a democracy, that governing power ultimately rests in all of us. When we vote, organize, or persuade others, we have the choice of punishing officials who accommodate unusual religious and moral practices; and we must hope for the internal and social resources that overcome whatever tendency we may have to do so excessively. Far from making toleration understood as "mercy" or sovereign discretion superfluous, liberal democracy makes it universally necessary.[8] And toleration, like most virtues, involves a mean. Too little toleration and we harm people who are trying to live as best they can by their own lights, in order to vindicate our love of abstraction; too much and we have no laws.[9]

Since collective decisions on such matters are not always politically salient and most people pay politics only occasional attention, this aspect of toleration will be intermittently useful for most citizens, a job requirement only for a few public officers. But toleration on the private scale remains crucial more generally because states cannot do everything. Many discussions of toleration imply, unrealistically, that the government has so much power as to eliminate all opportunities for private intolerance of the coercive variety.[10] On the contrary: no police force can prevent all hate crimes, vandalism, and other acts of overt intolerance, and these acts cause substantial harm and social fear even when punished after the fact. Religious, ethnic, and national prejudice historically and currently lead to strong temptations to violate even quite stringent laws and norms of political behavior, especially those enjoining procedural neutrality and equal treatment. To the extent that those who harbor prejudice restrain themselves from acting on these temptations, they are exercising a virtue whose importance is clear. It would of course be better if nobody had the prejudice to begin with.[11] But this does not make toleration a marginal subject for theoretical reflection. On the contrary, a theory of a prejudice-*free* society is a view towards nowhere.

II. Pluralism and Tolerations

Toleration is commonly defined as "the degree to which we accept things of which we disapprove."[12] This of course describes the practice of toleration, not the virtue. Even when a given act of toleration can be described without great controversy (which is not always), the kind of disapproval a given actor feels, and the motivations she has for not acting on it, can vary. Many combinations are logically possible.[13] But the politically interesting question is which are likely to occur with some frequency and have a political manifestation.

Heyd defends in a highly articulated and subtle version a broad approach to toleration that he has helped make fairly standard among moral philosophers.[14] This *moral-philosophical* view of toleration assumes, as most philosophers do, that "being judgmental with regard to beliefs and practices in the abstract is a desirable attitude."[15] It further holds that some sort of respect for the moral *agents* whose practices we condemn should prompt a switch in perspective that keeps us from putting this judgmentalism into practice (or at least changes the way we would think about doing so—the intended effects on *action* are sometimes ambiguous). On this account, toleration means refraining from doing what we would normally think praiseworthy, namely correcting a wrong. Hence the paradoxical tone, shared with many moral philosophers, of Heyd's conclusion.

Both of the above assumptions can, of course, be challenged. Many people who are not moral philosophers regard judgmentalism about other people's actions and practices as alien at best and impolite at worst; and few have a full-blown Kantian or similar theory of moral agency to ground whatever toleration they may practice. But more interesting than the theoretical possibility is the practical existence of a plurality of foundations for toleration.[16] Besides moral-philosophical toleration, the common grounds for toleration currently in use include at least these:

(1) Libertarian/economistic: beyond a strictly limited list of actions that violate others' concrete rights, most matters of private belief and action are a matter of individual choice, and it is wrong not only to interfere in others' choices but to judge them morally.

(2) Nonviolent: given the horrors of violence and cruelty, almost nothing would justify coercive interference in others' lives, regardless of the wrongness of what they do.

(3) Populist/solidaristic: democratic citizens ought to gain, through personal and egalitarian forms of interaction, an active and friendly appreciation for all the ways of life that a pluralistic society makes possible. One engages with others out of a camaraderie that renders cultural, religious, and ethnic differences irrelevant.[17]

(3a) Rationalist solidarism: we refrain from oppressing others out of "mutual respect" grounded in active engagement with, and reasoned debate about, one another's moral beliefs and judgments.

(4) Freethinking-elitist: fanaticism or "enthusiasm" is simply silly or vulgar, below the dignity of an intelligent, enlightened person.[18]

(5) Religious free-conscience (sectarian Protestant, liberal Catholic, etc.): As no one can be saved against his or her will, religious coercion is useless and perhaps self-defeating. Moral agency is *not* therefore "autonomous": we all retain a duty to pursue religious truth and obey God's command.[19]

(5a) Secular-sectarian, e.g., some versions of feminism and environmental ethics that have nonviolence and/or noncoercion as part of their deeply held, activist, and non-skeptical creeds.

(6) Skeptical: one doubts that one can anyone can have firm reasons for their own convictions or for their disapproval of others.'

(7) Apathetic: one simply does not care much about the big questions that some people are willing to kill or die for.[20]

(8) Latitudinarian: life objectively presents us with big questions to which religions seek answers. Religiosity of an unspecified variety ought to be publicly encouraged to reflect our serious attitude towards them—but those questions are too mysterious for clear answers to be possible, let alone fit grounds for persecution.[21]

(9) Anti-clerical or militant secularist: strong religious beliefs are inherently dangerous and demonstrably false. Fortunately the forces of modernity and enlightenment—helped if necessary by state policies to undermine religion's social power—make religion less common over time, resulting in toleration.[22]

(10) Principled individualist (Humboldt, one side of Mill, on some accounts Montaigne): Toleration, when politically viable, maximizes the human good because it is objectively and everywhere the case that individuals prosper most fully when they are allowed to make their own mistakes and develop in their own way.

(11) Utilitarian (another side of Mill): Error, in thought and action, should generally be tolerated because the social disputes it engenders help us to remember the reasons that ground currently known truths and to make progress towards learning new ones—but it is still error.

(12) Institutionalist: one may for whatever reason care deeply about moral questions and regard others' choices as wrong, but one cares even more deeply about political institutions that establish free speech and dissent.

If this list has some surface plausibility both descriptively (those perspectives are out there) and normatively (they are *prima facie* tolerant rather than actively persecutory), it suggests two conclusions. First, the starting points other people have for thinking about toleration may be very different from what "we" first assume. Given that toleration involves a psychic fight within the agent, even a polity with common political values governing citizen behavior may embody many, very different, kinds of (internal) toleration among citizens. Each will consist in a combination of (1) a folk- or sophisticated belief or judgment that tempts a particular group of people to be intolerant, and (2) the countervailing considerations that stop members of that group from acting on their belief and bring them back to observing tolerant norms.

Toleration is indeed "an elusive virtue."[23] But this is not primarily because religion and other matters of intense moral commitment have become matters of public indifference (this is true in some tolerant polities but not others) nor because liberal states reliably enforce impartial laws that render toleration largely unnecessary (for even if people consistently wanted states to do this, it would not be possible). It is elusive, rather, because virtues—in either the pure or the politically instrumental sense—are always appropriate responses to particular temptations that human beings must habituate themselves out of.[24] And while the virtues Aristotle treats respond to fairly universal human temptations (to eat too much, have sex when one should not, talk excessively, run from danger, and so on), the virtues of toleration respond to temptations that are *not* universal. The temptations involved are relative to a particular subgroup's world-views and mores, and to how these views and mores characteristically clash (or don't) with those of other groups in a given society. The countervailing attitudes, reasons, or moral demands that enable tolerant behavior are similarly multiform. There are many views about which moral violations should or should not be judged and attacked and why;

and there are many dispositions of mind and character that restrain different people from doing so. Each of the latter can be called one among many virtues (or quasi-virtues) of toleration if it keeps a group of people, to some fairly large extent, from acting coercively against behaviors and beliefs that those people condemn but their practitioners value.

Crucially, some of these temptations, and even some of the considerations that lead to toleration, may strike "us," or the practitioners of other toleration ideals in general, as unreasonable or even outrageous. Libertarian noninvolvement offends the matey (or deliberative) populist; elitist freethinking, militant secularism, principled individualism, and moral-philosophical toleration offend sectarians and latitudinarians alike; skeptical and utilitarian toleration offend (for different reasons) the institutionalist, the moral philosopher, the sectarian, and many others; apathy offends almost everyone who takes moral issues seriously. Other combinations also clash; and most of these forms of offense are mutual. Nor is the list of tolerations above close to comprehensive.

Moreover, "offense" here is a shorthand for something much more serious. People who hold each of these perspectives often think that *only* widespread, even near-universal acceptance of that perspective makes common life possible among people who disagree on other things. To reject their perspective is to proclaim oneself indifferent or hostile to the "clearly" necessary basis for social peace and cooperation. In other words, from each of these perspectives, some of the other perspectives—perspectives, again, that *to those who hold them* justify *toleration*—seem so anti-social and prone to cause harm (a useful but infinitely controversial concept)[25] that it is hard to imagine letting them go unmolested. The question of tolerating the intolerant is often badly posed. Self-aware fascist or communist attacks on toleration as such are (now) rare. More often, people whom one group regards as intolerant appear very tolerant to themselves.

Toleration in a pluralistic society is therefore *toleration of tolerations* or meta-toleration. We put up not just with other people's false and potentially dangerous world-views, but with other people's false and potentially dangerous ways of thinking about why they should put up with ours.

III. Circumstances of Meta-Toleration

On the account above, Bayle has never triumphed. As neutrality is not universally (or perhaps even widely) recognized as the governing principle of state action, it cannot reliably ground toleration. There is no unified "modern" or "liberal" ethos, described by Heyd as including "rights, respect for individuals, separation of state and church, state neutrality, value pluralism and skepticism," that "the political culture of constitutional democracy" lives by and through (assuming that a "democratic" culture means one that most people actually recognize).[26]

In stable liberal democracies, religious, and even ethnic conflicts now rarely turn violent on a large scale. Most citizens lack even the impulse to settle their moral differences through direct physical violence, and the state has the legitimate power to suppress them if they do. This is a huge political gain that makes us immeasurably better off. But we should not therefore conclude that fundamental *social* conflicts no longer occur, nor that political order rests on a deep *moral* consensus. After repeated experience of sanguinary state-run or communal persecution of (and by) the intolerant, the reliable human sentiments of fear, conformity, and greed—all much more cunning than reason—have in many countries worn the harshest edges of previously popular worldviews.[27] The motley remnants described above are as a result all tolerant in some sense. Inside our lucky countries, we can count on a minimal, "overlapping consensus" toleration under which only marginal individuals and groups want to settle conflicts of private belief with rifles and racks. But the pursuit of more consensus than this is quixotic.[28] Only massive persecution of ideological diversity could achieve it; and all versions of pro-toleration world-views make this (fortunately) unattractive.

But there must be more to the story. Remember that certain of the above views appear to other perspectives not just strange but *intolerable,* because harmful. Therefore, any coalition of perspectives that commands a steady majority (or, in the less-than-democratic case, whatever other source of authority the state rests on) will be tempted to *legally* persecute—or at least undermine through de facto discrimination compulsory civic education, and so on—the perspectives it sees as dangerous. The temptation to achieve through official policy "the proper" conditions for toleration will often seem overwhelming, even to those who *display* the virtue of toleration in one of its many forms. For this course will seem to those tempted *not* partisan or narrow but on the contrary *moral* and justified and even necessary (and the other adjectives that a given perspective sees as reasons for state action: "liberal and enlightened" as opposed to superstitious and hypocritical; or "patriotic and public-spirited" as opposed to selfish and divisive; or "civilized and Western" as opposed to atheistic and materialist; or "democratic" as opposed to crypto-fascist; or "reasonable" as opposed to passionate, partial, or moblike).

These battles will shift as political and social power does. The postmodern attack on liberalism is wildly overblown, and the claim that some Nietzschean alternative would give everyone more freedom than liberalism does is absurd. But it remains true that the last two centuries provide myriad examples of what now look like official intolerance and unnecessary social strife occurring when one faction that saw itself as the engine of modern progress, freedom, civilization, reason, or enlightenment succeeded another such faction—and tried to establish a modern, just, and civilized society on a firm foundation by rendering the enemies of same permanently powerless.[29] So one reason it is so attractive to posit that toleration relies on a single, stable, unified political culture is that it would seem logically necessary. For if there is more than one such culture, each will try to get rid of the others.

What in fact prevents this outcome is a social accident, though policy can help it along: partisans of various forms of toleration will refrain from persecuting one another if and only if none forms a stable majority and none knows whether its current opponents might be its future allies. This is a Madisonian solution: since people under conditions of free speech will always disagree about toleration, the various factions representing beliefs about toleration—like factions representing religious belief—must be allowed to multiply in the hope that none will become predominant.[30] A virtuous circle is possible, though hardly guaranteed. As long as government intolerance does not lead to actual prohibition—or leads to inconsistent prohibitions against different groups at different times—we can expect world-views to multiply beyond measure, making durable persecutory majorities less and less imaginable over time.

Where this works, it has costs: we shall actually have more toleration in practice than any group would like. Many things will be tolerated that from the perspective of one group or another, possibly our own, look not like proper forms of toleration but like unwise and illogical allowances of wrongs or harms. Nor will those who believe in any particular version of toleration have any guarantee that they will gain over time. They will have no systematic reason to think that either the practices they think outside the legitimate bounds of toleration or the social groupings that lend support for such views will lose popularity over time. In fact, it is likely that most such views, and most such groups, will persist indefinitely.

This is, I think, what the United States has today. Hard-core pornography is tolerated, to the horror of religious conservatives (and some feminists) who in their eyes allow freedom of speech and sexual fantasy but draw the line at the "clear harms" that pornography causes to the family and our whole moral order. Gun ownership is tolerated, to the horror of the nonviolent, the utilitarian, and the moral-philosophical, who believe in personal liberty and are neutral towards the hobby of hunting but draw the line at allowing instruments that "must" be directly responsible for high murder rates. Nobody is satisfied; government policy is both incoherent and mocked; likely social harms tend to fester where other societies would probably attack them (because we refuse to act until every group with an ideology, a lawyer, and a lobbyist has had a chance to plead that it is *not* a harm but their reason for living). But no one can deny that persecution is minimal and liberty flourishes in the absence of clear agreement on what these mean.

This result is not the most attractive one imaginable. The above account entails the triumph of toleration, or meta-toleration, over another ideal, styled either moral progress or civilization. If toleration is an umbrella term for conflicting and partisan views, we can still support political reforms, and need not even renounce the belief that our favored reforms are morally justified. We must renounce, however, the hope that the reforms will ever be *uncontroversial*, that the justifications will ever be universally accepted. Everything that looks like reform to us will look like persecution to someone else.

But we could do worse. In practice, the attempt to settle publicly and authoritatively "the correct interpretation of constitutional principles and of the idea of the separation of state and religion" can unintentionally, as social forces mobilize and take sides, guarantee a bitterly contested rather than a neutral state. The headscarves issue in France (which Heyd describes as involving not toleration but the question of "the correct interpretation") pits an American-style religious-pluralist conception of state neutrality directly against the conception embodied in republican *laïcité*. Because the state rather than society or the individual *is* regarded as authoritative in these matters, issues of religious, ethnic, and national identity become subjects of constant political mobilization. The quest for a universally valid principle of toleration is what rules out the policies that embody the most obvious and commonsensical forms of toleration: either individual choice, with no suggestion that the State either sanctions or opposes that choice,[31] or else regulation by the option of local school authorities, which France practiced for many years (until recently) as politicians blessedly avoided "addressing the problem."

IV. Conclusion

This chapter has suggested alternatives to common philosophical assumptions about toleration: that the state through a policy of neutrality has largely solved the problem of toleration; and that the individual attitude of toleration only makes sense as a combination of moral judgmentalism towards beliefs and moral respect for human agents. Instead, the modern state (or rather, its agents) cannot help judging, and relies on official and citizen toleration to judge well. Many moral attitudes can be called toleration (reflecting a diversity of worldviews and worldly temptations). And the struggle among these several tolerations is just as potentially contentious as—though far less dangerous than—raw and self-conscious intolerance used to be. What contains this struggle is not moral consensus but the multiplying of toleration-based factions such that none has sufficient certainty of its own power to oppress the others.

We liberals are having to tolerate an awful lot, considering how much we know government policies and others' social practices to fall short of moral requirements. When we confront those who, through their (politically influential) selfishness, sexism, racism, and propensity to environmental destruction, make the world morally worse than it should be, why should we have to keep in mind all these political and moral-sociological *caveats,* incapable —as Robert Frost said liberals were—of taking our own side in the argument?

One could respond with a piece of skepticism. Given that meta-ethics is not a deductively demonstrable science, how sure can we be of our moral judgments? But a political point is more likely to persuade.

Debates about toleration often start from the premise that people like us are the ones *doing* the tolerating. We should not assume this. True, reflective, open-minded, egalitarian, non-materialist people like us are being asked to tolerate as fellow citizens —immune to persecution, discrimination, and even compulsory reeducation—fundamentalist, fuel-guzzling, warmongering, anti-feminist, ethnocentric fanatics. But one must remember that hard-working, God-fearing, patriotic citizens with strong family values are also being asked to tolerate us: dangerously relativistic, offensively godless, snobby New Class intellectuals who endanger not just our immortal souls but others' lives (since we clearly lack the moral fiber to fight wars in defense against our enemies). Given the numbers, "we" need toleration more than "they" do—especially in the United States, but to some extent in other countries too.[32] There are also many places where they need toleration more than we do. The proper inference to draw is not cynicism but humility. While both we and they should feel free to take our own sides in argument, we should in doing so remember that others view us, not themselves, as the persecutors. And we should resist the temptation to engineer society so as to eliminate the other side *to* the argument. Toleration's best friend is the fact of factionalism, not the ideal of neutral statism. And barbarism, in moderation, is to be preferred to persecution.

"Every one is Orthodox to himself"[33] is not just a doctrine congenial to liberals but a warning that we liberals should heed ourselves. And the political virtue—or rather virtues—called toleration will seem superfluous or obsolete only if we forget that a democratic "state" can in the long run be tolerant, towards us as well as others, when its citizens are.

NOTES

1. Dedicated to the memory of Judith N. Shklar. I would like to thank for their useful comments Ron Den Otter, William Galston, Chris Laursen, Melissa Williams, and the ASPLP conference participants generally. Very late in the drafting of these comments I came across what seem to be similar views, expressed very differently, in Jeremy Waldron, "Toleration and Reasonableness," in Catriona McKinnon and Dario Castiglione, eds., *The Culture of Toleration in Diverse Societies: Reasonable Tolerance* (Manchester: Manchester Univ. Press, 2003). I have not had time to think through the relation between his argument and mine.

2. Political theorists who claim that toleration is a virtue do so, I think, because they take for granted that "political virtue" means not a full Aristotelian or Stoic virtue, directed at human happiness, but rather any disposition, attitude, or habit instrumentally productive of political goods. For a defense of the distinction see Andrew Sabl, *Ruling Passions: Political Offices and Democratic Ethics* (Princeton: Princeton Univ. Press, 2002), Chapter 2; idem, "Virtue for Pluralists," *Journal of Moral Philosophy,* forthcoming. For claims that it characterizes liberal-democratic political theory both now and historically, see respectively Thomas A. Spragens, Jr., *Civic Liberalism* (Lanham, Md.: Rowman and Littlefield, 1999), 213 *et passim,* and John Parrish, "From Dirty Hands to the Invisible Hand: Paradoxes of Political Ethics," Ph.D. dissertation, Harvard University, 2002. While it is possible to defend toleration for intrinsic rather than instrumental reasons, one does so at the cost of caring more about people's internal dispositions than about their propensity to confer benefits or harms on others. I would also suggest that judgments about which qualities of mind and character are intrinsically attractive are even more controversial in a plural polity than judgments about which actions are justified. A separate question is *which* ends the virtue of toleration is supposed to be instrumental *towards.* This chapter takes for granted that toleration is meant to reduce conflict, coercion, or cruelty—and not, primarily, inequality, which toleration as such does not address one way or the other. I thank William Galston for comments on this last point.

3. David Heyd, "Is Toleration a Political Virtue?" 177.

4. This is a variation on Heyd's theme: his brief example involves the right to decorate one's own home in poor taste. But I assume his account of why we may not attack those we believe to be witches would be similar in form.

5. That Heyd follows this narrative broadly is suggested by the following passage: "An enlightened prince as well as a modern liberal state can and should promote the value of interpersonal toleration in society. The government has the power to inculcate standards of toleration by education, the support of institutions in which reason is freely exercised, and even to use its authority and capacity to enforce practices that advance communication and narrow the gap between the public and the private use of reason."

6. *Goldman v. Weinberger,* 475 U.S. 503 (1986). While the Supreme Court upheld the military regulation described, Congress later reversed the decision through statute: 10 U.S.C. $774.

7. *Employment Division, Department of Human Resources of Oregon, et al., v. Smith et al.,* 494 U.S. 872 (1990). In that case, contrary to common assumptions, the respondents faced no criminal penalties. Rather, the state had denied them unemployment compensation after they were fired by a private drug rehabilitation organization for using peyote. Thus the state could have accommodated their religious practices by giving them unemployment compensation *without* forcing their former employer to hire peyote users.

8. Toleration in the sense of accommodating those who violate neutral laws for conscientious and non-dangerous reasons seems (and has seemed to others whose contributions currently escape my notes) to call for similar intellectual and moral virtues to Aristotle's *equity* or decency: the quintessential virtue of governing officials who must match laws—which necessarily lack full understanding of prospective cases—to particular instances. Aristotle describes equity as "a sort of justice" even though it goes beyond the decider's technical entitlements: the person who practices it is "not an exact stickler for justice in the bad way, but tak[es] less than he might even though he has the law on his side." *Nicomachean Ethics,* trans. Terence Irwin (Indianapolis: Hackett Publishing Company, 1985), 1138a; for the political official's use see *Politics* 1308b27. Though the question of whether equity is supererogatory is anachronistic applied to Aristotle, he does say that it is part of justice. The granting of pardon when circumstances call for it is the *just* thing to do. John Tomasi, *Liberalism Beyond Justice* (Princeton: Princeton Univ. Press, 2001) makes a contemporary case for systematically accommodating non-neutral effects, though without using toleration language.

9. Heyd suggests something similar when he notes that toleration among social subgroups "ease[s] political tensions and decrease[s] the level of litigation in society." But in slighting the dependence of official actions on public judgments, he downplays the extent to which the institutions and practices that he considers political—"constitutional arrangements, the rule of law, or the institutional relations of power and authority"—might depend on a democratized form of equity, perhaps something like the non-official equity that Aristotle calls "pardon" or "consideration" (*Nicomachean Ethics* 1143a20f.).

10. As noted by Randolph Head, "Religious Coexistence and Confessional Conflict in the *Vier Dörfer*: Practices of Toleration in Easter Switzerland, 1525–1615," in John Christian Laursen and Cary Nederman, eds., *Beyond the Persecuting Society: Religious Toleration Before the Enlightenment* (Philadelphia: Univ. of Pennsylvania Press, 1998), 146.

11. As noted, *inter alia,* by Scanlon, "The Difficulty of Tolerance," in David Heyd, ed., *Toleration: An Elusive Virtue* (Princeton: Princeton Univ. Press, 1996 [henceforth *Elusive Virtue*]), 226.

12. Bernard Crick, "Toleration and Tolerance in Theory and Practice," *Government and Opposition* 6, No. 2 (1971): 144.

13. See the summary by Peter Laslett, "Political Theory and Political Scientific Research," *Government and Opposition* 6, No. 2 (1971): 221–22.

14. See David Heyd, "Introduction" to *Elusive Virtue,* 3–17. Versions of this approach appear in Scanlon (op. cit., 226–39) and Albert Weale, "Toleration, Individual Differences, and Respect for Person," in John Horton and Susan Mendus, eds., *Aspects of Toleration: Philosophical Studies* (London and New York: Methuen and Co., 1985), 16–35. Peter Nicholson describes it as "the most promising line of moral argument in favor of an extensive policy of toleration at both the personal and political levels" ("Philosophy and the Practice of Toleration," in John Horton and Peter Nicholson, eds., *Toleration: Philosophy and Practice* [Aldershot, England and Brookfield Vermont: Ashgate, 1992], 5).

15. Heyd, "Introduction," in *Elusive Virtue,* 15. As far as I can tell, Heyd's chapter here is consistent with the same assumption: the state is not supposed to care about religious views, or moral ones so far as they are reasonable, but neither moral philosophers nor individuals generally are discouraged from doing so.

16. Note that not all of the below count as foundations for *tolerance* if one takes that to mean a very specific kind of internal moral disposition. But that begs the question, since I deny that it makes sense to talk about toleration so narrowly (and unpolitically). If a *political* virtue is a state that conduces to a (desirable) kind of political action, the same external ac-

tion may be motivated by a great variety of internal states. The list below provides foundations for several virtues that may all be called toleration or tolerance because they lead people to accept things of which they disapprove. I thank Ron Den Otter for discussion on this.

17. Todd Gitlin describes the "Democratic Americanism" of the Popular Front and New Deal as involving "tolerance in the interest of composing a popular commons—a 'people's America' against 'the interests.' . . . The war against fascism became a war of liberation in [*sic*] behalf of what was distinctly American: the diversity of the *demos* fused into a single, solid phalanx" (*Twilight of Common Dreams* [Henry Holt and Company, 1996]), 57, 60. Cf. Saul Alinsky, *Reveille for Radicals* (New York: Vintage, 1946), chapter 1. Australian political culture—with its ideal of "mateship" and the slogan "a Jack's as good as his master"—expresses this ideal more durably and less breathlessly.

18. Voltaire's *Treatise on Toleration* often expresses this argument, among others.

19. For arguments that the latter sentiment is key to sectarian Protestant arguments for toleration today, see Leif Wenar, "*Political Liberalism*: An Internal Critique," *Ethics* 106, No. 1 (October 1995): 32–62, and for the historical case Joshua Mitchell, "Through a Glass Darkly: Luther, Calvin, and the Limits of Reason," and Alan Houston, "Monopolizing Faith: The Levellers, Rights, and Religious Toleration," both in Alan Levine, ed., *Early Modern Skepticism and the Origins of Toleration* (Lanham, Md.: Lexington Books, 1999), 21–50 and 147–64. On some accounts, Kantianism is a form of sectarianism, though Pelagian rather than Christian. But this seems too pat.

20. This is sometimes glossed, in a more positive vein, as "indifference" (e.g., by Bernard Williams, "Toleration: An Impossible Virtue?" in Heyd, *Toleration,* 20–21; and in other terms by Peter Laslett, "Political Theory and Political Scientific Research," *Government and Opposition* 6, No. 2 [Spring 1971]: 219–20). The difference seems to be one of connotation: apathy means not caring about world-views or social practices that one should care about; indifferentism means not caring when caring would in fact be inappropriate. The distinction's boundaries are naturally subject to debate.

21. Shirley Letwin, "Skepticism and Toleration in Hobbes' Political Thought," in Levine, 174–75, attributes this doctrine to Hobbes, and (somewhat more convincingly) to British Anglicanism up to this day. As she stresses, it cuts directly against many forms of philosophic rationalism and materialism (176).

22. This view is often attributed to Hobbes and Bayle and sometimes

Spinoza. In various post-Spinozan and post-Marxist forms it characterizes much of the European Left as well as the "republican" or "radical" Center. For an account and endorsement, see Jonathan Israel, *Radical Enlightenment: Philosophy and the Making of Modernity 1650–1750* (Oxford: Oxford Univ. Press, 2001); and more neutrally John Christian Laursen, "Baylean Liberalism: Tolerance Requires Nontolerance," in Laursen and Nederman, 197–215. In the United States, Deweyan calls for a "common faith" grounded in democratic and scientific ideals rather than obsolete religious ones are the closest analogue, and again exist in both radical and centrist versions (both dedicated to undermining religious schools). Of course there are also moderate forms of anticlericalism which involve private disdain for religion and no particular political program. But these have few implications for toleration.

23. David Heyd, *Elusive Virtue.*

24. Aristotle, *Ethics,* 1109a.

25. Kirstie McClure, "Difference, Diversity, and the Limits of Toleration," *Political Theory* 18, No. 3 (August 1990): 361–91; also John Horton, "Toleration, Morality, and Harm," in Horton and Mendus, op. cit., 113–35 and esp. 132: "What liberalism represents as the neutral requirement of preventing harm to others will be perceived by those with different conceptions of what is harmful as the enforcement of a morality they do not share."

26. One could, of course, define "the political culture of liberal democracy" as including only those who adopt a certain doctrine of toleration; others, whatever their numbers, will then not count as proper "liberal democrats." Heyd does not make anything like this argument. When some other liberal theorists implicitly or explicitly do make it, they are justifying toleration through an argument that strains the label.

27. This whole argument assumes a skepticism towards rationalist (or crypto-rationalist) claims to the effect that only "valid" ideas, "capable of justification" in a non-relativistic sense, can persist in an open society. It does *not* require substantive relativism, skepticism towards the idea that some arguments are better than others—merely doubt that the metaphysical quality of an argument has much to do with its empirical popularity. I thank Melissa Williams for forcing me to clarify this.

28. "Certainly, it would be an untidy and unsatisfactory state of affairs if we had to construct a fresh line of argument for toleration to match each different orthodoxy that was under consideration." Jeremy Waldron, "Locke: Toleration and the Rationality of Persecution," in Susan Mendus, *Justifying Toleration: Conceptual and Historical Perspectives* (Cambridge: Cambridge Univ. Press, 1988), 63. With apologies, I claim that is the state of

affairs that we face—except that the arguments for toleration need not be constructed "fresh" but exist in rough form embedded within most existing fairly tolerant orthodoxies.

29. See Hans-Ulrich Wehler's account of how Bismarck's politics relied on "negative integration," defining the modern German Empire in terms of the successive groups that had to be persecuted to vindicate it. The *Kulturkampf* against Catholics, the campaign against "republican" or left-wing liberals, various official and unofficial policies against Jews, *and* the anti-socialist laws were pursued in the name of liberalism, modernity, and the state standing over partisan and ideological factions that endangered its unity. And all received the full support of the National Liberal party, the one group that was always part of the persecuting coalition. Hans-Ulrich Wehler, *The German Empire 1871–1918,* trans. Kim Traynor (Leamington Spa, England: Berg Publishers, 1985), 52–118. France's Second Empire and Third Republic displayed some similar dynamics.

30. James Madison, *The Federalist,* No. 10.

31. As suggested by *The Economist,* December 13, 2003, 14—with characteristic contempt for both French statism and the United States' alleged multiculturalism. To be sure, this kind of "live and let live" proposal slights the problem of *private* intolerance, of families or bands of radical Muslim youths forcing girls to wear headscarves on pain of ostracism or sexual violence. I am not qualified to assess accounts of how common such things are. But many defenses of French laicism do not stress such harms in any case.

32. As a rough measure: theism as commonly understood is no doubt an unusual attitude among moral, political, and legal philosophers. But fifty-eight percent of respondents in the United States—and about a third of Germans and Canadians—say that it is necessary to believe in God to be moral. (Pew Global Attitudes Project, "Views of a Changing World," Pew Research Center for the People and the Press, June 2003, 115–16). Much of the toleration literature assumes a context in which "liberal," "secular," "neutralist," "majority," and "state" are synonyms or close cognates: the question is whether "we" will tolerate traditionalist cultural or religious "minorities" (see, e.g., Melissa Williams, "Tolerable Liberalism," in Avigail Eisenberg and Jeff Spinner-Halev, *Minorities within Minorities* (Cambridge: Cambridge Univ. Press, 2005). This might be valid for Canada or Britain, or the United States in the era of *Yoder*—but seems a tricky assumption applied to Israel or the United States today. On these matters there is no ratchet but rather an unpredictable pendulum. Many no doubt thought that Italy had become "safely" secular until the Berlusconi regime's policies on sex education and artificial reproduction in

Italy—which orthodox Catholics of course defend not as persecutory but as humane and tolerant measures that safeguard the preconditions for respecting persons.

33. John Locke, *Letter Concerning Toleration,* first paragraph, trans. William Popple, ed. James H. Tully (Indianapolis: Hackett Publishing Company, 1983), 23.

PART III

LIBERAL TOLERATION

9

TOLERATION AND LIBERAL COMMITMENTS

STEVEN D. SMITH[1]

Toleration is a venerable notion, but it is often disparaged by criticism from either of opposite directions. One kind of criticism (less common today than formerly) objects to toleration for being *too liberal.* Thus, toleration is said to be incoherent and impossible as a logical or psychological matter, or else possible but too permissive and thus undesirable as a normative matter. Given the choice, why should we knowingly put up with error? A different and in modern times more familiar kind of criticism objects to toleration for being *not liberal enough.* The ideal of toleration implies, after all, that there is a preferred or orthodox position which deigns to "tolerate" or put up with dissenting views; and this discriminating and condescending posture may seem offensive to the liberal notion that the state must be "neutral" towards religion or toward conceptions of the good, or that the state must treat persons and their ideas as equal.

My own view is that these criticisms are misguided, and that if our political community aspires to be liberal (or at least to claim the political benefits associated with liberalism) it will necessarily adopt a posture of toleration.[2] The only choice, at this level, is whether we will confess to holding this position or will pretend to operate on some other principle.

In the United States, an appreciation of the centrality of toleration seems especially important at this point in American history. There may be times when we can successfully practice toleration without avowing or defending it, but ours does not seem to be such a time. Looking inward, we perceive an exhausted liberalism striving vainly to contain or conceal a series of "culture wars." Looking outward, we perceive prospects of a "clash of civilizations" which calls upon us to forgo the complacent agnosticism of "neutrality" and to affirm and defend what is central to our way of life. Under these conditions, I will suggest, a renewed exploration of the meaning and grounds of toleration becomes urgent.

My argument will unfold as follows: in Part I, I will offer a brief explanation of what a position of toleration entails. In Parts II and III, respectively, I will attempt to respond to the criticisms noted above—namely, the criticisms objecting that toleration is too liberal or else not liberal enough. In Part IV, I will discuss the timeliness of toleration at this point in our history.

I. The Elements of Toleration

Although the term is used in different ways, for present purposes I offer the following as a stiff but useful statement of the elements of toleration: toleration describes the practice[3] of a position adopted when (a) in a condition of *pluralism* (b) an *agent* (c) adheres to a *base position* or orthodoxy under which (d) competing values and ideas are classified into *three categories*: (i) those within or at least not inconsistent with the orthodoxy, (ii) those that while inconsistent with the base position or orthodoxy are nonetheless within the field of toleration, and (iii) those that are intolerable. Each of these elements needs elaboration.

(a) Pluralism: The possibility of and need for toleration arise only in a situation in which different values or ideas, or perhaps different classes of persons, occupy a common space in potential opposition to each other. The pluralism might be of religious or political views, or of races, or of cultural practices; thus, we sometimes talk of religious toleration, political toleration, racial tolerance, or just plain tolerance. In this essay, my concern is mainly with a condition of pluralism in the core *beliefs,* including religious beliefs, that are often taken to be central to human life. My main concern, in other words, is with toleration as a possible philosophy of or strategy for the kinds of issues we discuss under the heading of the First Amendment to the United States Constitution.

(b) The agent: This condition of pluralism presents a question about how to negotiate or deal with the competition among beliefs. We can refer to the entities that must confront this question as agents. An agent might be an individual person or some institutional entity; in this essay, the agent I am primarily concerned with is an institution—namely, government, or the state.[4] I do not of course mean to deny the importance of tolerance as a virtue of individual persons or as an element of social interaction—points stressed in Professor Morgan's response[5]—but those aspects of tolerance are not the focus of this essay.

(c) The base position: In making judgments about how to deal with or react to competing ideas, an agent will act on the basis of certain beliefs that he or she or it holds and that seem relevant at some level to the conflicts that arise. We can describe this set of beliefs that inform the agent's judgments as a "base position" or an "orthodoxy." However, I emphatically do not mean these terms to suggest that the base position or orthodoxy must be coherent, or permanently fixed, or even fully conscious. Usually the contrary will be true: persons and even more so the governments of large and diverse communities will act in different situations on the basis of beliefs that are in tension with each other and in constant process of reexamination and change, and that are often held only tacitly. My modest point—virtually a truistic one, I hope—is simply that as conflicting ideas present themselves for acceptance and action, an agent will necessarily make judgments, and these judgments will be shaped by beliefs the agent holds.

(d) The three-category scheme: Though every agent will of necessity act from some sort of base position, not every such position can plausibly be described as tolerant. A tolerant position, I have suggested, entails a three-category scheme for classifying ideas (although it is theoretically possible that in a given context the second or third categories, like Hell in gentler theologies, might happen to be empty). Some ideas will be within or at least not inconsistent with the currently prevailing orthodoxy. At least potentially, other ideas will be contrary to the orthodoxy but nonetheless within the field of toleration; if the agent is the government, this means that the government will not attempt to suppress such ideas. And the term "toleration" implies that, at least potentially, still other ideas may be outside of the field of toleration, and hence "intolerable," so that an agent will attempt to defeat or discourage or suppress such ideas.[6]

I hasten to admit that this description makes the categories seem cleaner than they actually are. In the real world, the application of these categories will present a host of questions. It will often be debatable whether a particular idea is or is not consistent with the base position; this uncertainty is inevitable given the fact that the base position itself, as noted above, may be inconsistent and changing and not entirely consciously held. Similarly, the boundaries separating the field of toleration from the domain of the intolerable will often be obscure and contested. Moreover, within the latter domain there will still be ethical and prudential questions about what means are appropriate for discouraging or suppressing intolerable ideas. Should heretics be burned? Or merely denied state subsidies that the proponents of more acceptable ideas receive? And so forth.

Instead of the three-category scheme, it might be more accurate to say that there are degrees of tolerability and intolerability: some ideas receive our fullest endorsement and support (they are highlighted in presidential addresses, perhaps, or are part of the required curriculum in public schools); other ideas receive less support; others are left alone; and still others may be banned—albeit with sanctions of varying degrees of severity. This "sliding scale" model may indeed be more true-to-life. I think the three-category scheme, however simplified, has the advantage of permitting a useful contrast with the positions (also purified) that represent toleration's main competitors.[7]

Thus, what we can call the "illiberal" position in essence discards the middle category—the category of presumptively wrong but nonetheless tolerable ideas. Consequently, in this view an idea will be part of (or at least not inconsistent with) the orthodoxy, or else it will be intolerable. "Agree with us or else." Conversely, what we can call the ultraliberal position attempts to get by with only one category. Or rather it dispenses with categories altogether, vowing to treat every person's beliefs as equal and thus to remain neutral among beliefs and the persons who hold them.[8]

I doubt that this last position is entirely coherent. How can the ultraliberal agent really be neutral toward, say, anti-liberal views, or toward the idea that neutrality among beliefs is shameful or impossible? But then, as I have already noted, a base position need not be fully coherent. So to say that the ultraliberal position is incoherent is not to say that it is impossible for someone to hold that position (or at least to *think* he holds it). And indeed modern experience seems to prove the point: what is, is possible.

Since toleration is not the only possible response to pluralism, we naturally will want some reason for adopting a position of toleration. Why adopt the three-category scheme rather than the two-category or the one- or no-category schemes?

II. Tolerance versus Illiberalism: Why Put Up with Error?

We can consider first the two-category position, or what I have called the "illberal" position, which urges that ideas should be classified as either consistent with the prevailing set of beliefs or else intolerable. Though its public appeal may have declined in recent times, the illiberal position has enjoyed considerable historical support; it also claims some ongoing visible support,[9] as well as more justification (and perhaps more latent or perhaps unwitting support)[10] than we sometimes suppose.

A. The Case for Intolerance

We can divide the arguments for illiberalism and against tolerance into two main kinds (though in actual argumentation these strands are often blended). One kind of argument suggests that the two-category scheme is logically or perhaps psychologically irresistible. If you think that *X* is true, then you will naturally think that not-*X* is false.[11] And how can you treat a false idea with respect? On the contrary, you are in principle committed to resisting, opposing, and defeating false ideas if you have the power to do so. Thus, "persecution for the expression of opinions seems to me perfectly logical," Holmes famously observed. "If you have no doubt of your premises or your power and want a certain result with all your heart you naturally express your wishes in law and sweep away all opposition."[12]

In short, belief in the truth necessarily commits you to oppose falsehood. Let us call this view—the view, that is, that belief in *X* necessarily commits you to suppressing not-*X*—the *entailment argument.* "Error has no rights," as the old slogan had it: belief in truth entails intolerance of falsehood.

A different kind of argument concedes that a posture of tolerance is possible but argues that it is undesirable or unattractive. Toleration means that error and falsehood are allowed to flourish unopposed. But how can beings with commitments to truth adopt this careless and perhaps dangerous stance? Let us call this the *normative argument* against toleration.

B. Resisting Intolerance

The arguments against toleration and for illiberalism have *prima facie* force, I think, but they are not unanswerable.[13] Let us consider the "entailment" argument before discussing the more troublesome normative argument.

1. The entailment argument

Standing alone, the entailment argument seems faulty because it assumes that *disagreement* with an idea automatically entails a desire or perhaps a duty to *suppress* the idea. An equivocation may be at work here. Disagreement with an idea does indeed entail (or simply amounts to) "opposition" to the idea in one sense of the word. If you disagree with idea *X*, you "oppose" *X*—intellectually, at least. But that sort of opposition—mere disagreement—is not normally thought to constitute "intolerance." On the contrary, disagreement is a prerequisite for the possibility of tolerance: it would be odd to say that you "tolerate" an idea that in fact you find wholly unobjectionable.[14]

The sort of opposition that is typically described as "intolerance" is something more aggressive, consisting of overt efforts to condemn or suppress. But intellectual rejection does not necessarily entail, either logically or psychologically, such more aggressive opposition. On the contrary, it is perfectly possible to disagree with an idea and yet, for all sorts of laudable or less than laudable reasons, to refrain from any attempt to eliminate it—perhaps because you respect the freedom of those who hold the (erroneous) idea, or because you just don't care, or even because you are malicious and enjoy seeing others wallow in error.[15]

2. The normative argument

The normative argument, on the other hand, is more formidable. After all, though free speech advocates like Mill sometimes declaim on the benefits of falsehood, it is hard to maintain that a world in which truth is mixed with falsehood is somehow preferable to a world in which truth is triumphant. If people's truth-discerning capacities became too highly developed, would we really feel the need to promote or subsidize views known to be erroneous just to obtain the benefits of error?[16] The point is not merely abstract or academic: if error inhabits the world, and if its proponents are allowed to promote their falsehoods in alluring ways, there is a significant chance that your friends, your children, perhaps you yourself will be induced to embrace falsehood. Who wants that?

Nonetheless, over the centuries, proponents of tolerance have developed a variety of rationales for tolerating divergent ideas. Though the list is hardly exhaustive, I think the leading rationales can be grouped under four main headings. Some of these rationales seem stronger than others, and none makes the case for toleration in any decisive and across-the-board way. Moreover, some rationales are more closely tied to a pure idea of toleration than others are. Still, in various contexts, each of these rationales can provide a persuasive warrant for putting up with beliefs we disagree with.

Indifference: One kind of argument for tolerating ideas with which an agent disagrees suggests that ideas—or at least the particular ideas for which tolerance is advocated—are not really important or threatening anyway. Thus, religious toleration may increase in proportion as religious doctrines become less important to people. So creedal distinctions that once produced inquisitors and martyrs now provoke queries of "Who cares?" and "What difference does it really make?"[17] In a similar vein, Justice Douglas opposed suppression of communist advocacy on the ground that domestic communism (as opposed to international communism) was impotent—a "bogey-man."[18]

The toleration that results from indifference arguably produces a cheap sort of freedom. There is nothing much to admire in an agent who tolerates ideas she disagrees with because, in the end, she really doesn't care enough to suppress them.[19] Nor does this attitude of indifference convey much respect for the persons and beliefs being tolerated; rather, it suggests something closer to contempt. Nonetheless, indifference probably has been among the leading rationales for—or at least causes of—a practice of toleration.

Skepticism: Another leading rationale for toleration is skepticism deployed to temper the agent's own beliefs. Holmes famously employed this rationale. We have already noted how Holmes conceded—or rather he reveled in asserting—that persecution of people with false ideas is perfectly logical.[20] But he then went on to suggest that would-be persecutors should realize, upon mature reflection, that their confidence in their own ideas is misplaced, and they should accordingly leave the determination of truth to the marketplace of ideas.[21] In a similar vein, skepticism about religion or religious beliefs is often said to be a leading cause of the rise of toleration in early modern Europe.[22]

Once again, the accommodation that results from skepticism is arguably an insipid sort of tolerance.[23] If I decline to suppress an opinion that deviates from my own only because, come to think of it, I'm not so sure about my opinion anyway, I will hardly earn much praise. Indeed, a fully successful skeptical strategy arguably does not promote tolerance at all, but rather obviates and negates it; that is because skepticism, by subverting the agent's base position, in effect dissolves the disagreement which is a prerequisite to tolerance.

Conversely, upon reflection it seems that a *partial* skepticism—or at least a lively sense of our own fallibility—does nothing by itself to justify tolerance of ideas with which we disagree. Suppose I have the power to suppress idea *X*, which some people hold but which I think is erroneous and pernicious; but then I reflect that *X* (and the people who believe *X*) might be right, while I might be wrong. This reflection doesn't lead me to conclude that I actually *am* wrong, of course—or if it does I will abandon *X* for myself, so the issue of toleration will go away—but I concede that I *might be* wrong. Without more (and I stress the "without more"), this concession gives me no more reason to permit other people to hold a pernicious idea that I think is *probably* wrong than it gives me to adopt that presumptively pernicious idea for myself. At least from my perspective, the risk of error is the same for them as for me: so if I am willing to take that risk for myself, why should I not take it for them?[24]

In short, I think the efficacy of skepticism as a source of and rationale for tolerance is greatly overrated. Still, it seems undeniable that as a historical matter, and logically or not, skepticism has played a role in persuading people of the value of toleration.

Practical limitations: Probably one of the most effective rationales for tolerating objectionable ideas has been simple practicality. We would suppress the heresy if we could, but we can't. Or it would be too costly—in money, or morale, or whatever.[25] In an ideal world, perhaps, we would eradicate pernicious ideas *X*, *Y*, and *Z*; . . . and we would also have quality education for all children, first-class universal health care, and a private jet for everyone, and . . . But all of these things are costly, so we put up with a second- or third- or fourth-best state of affairs.

Arguments for toleration are often of this character: they point out that efforts to suppress disfavored ideas are likely to be unsuccessful, or even counterproductive. Suppression may make the erroneous ideas seem more enticing, or it may drive those ideas underground where they cannot be effectively opposed or criticized. Or even if suppression were possible, it may be too costly: we just can't afford to expend the resources (including, as the early modern Wars of Religion remind us, the human lives) that would be needed to stamp out some heresy.

Once again, practical rationales do not leave toleration looking like an especially moral or noble stance: the ruler who declares "I *would* crush you but I just can't afford to" does not win our admiration. Nonetheless, it seems likely that such rationales can have considerable practical efficacy. For example, practical considerations surely played a leading role in the change by which nations that for decades had battled to establish the true religion were induced to embrace the alternative of peaceful coexistence among competing sects.

Voluntariness or authenticity rationales: A different and more morally appealing type of rationale derives from the contention that some human goods cannot be realized except by voluntary acceptance, or that they necessarily depend on the quality of personal authenticity. Any number of goods appear to be of this character: love, friendship, and (perhaps most importantly for our purposes) belief or faith. I may desire your friendship, but the very nature of this good entails that I cannot compel you to give it. My smitten eight-year-old son's tragic romantic reflection may serve to make the point. "I wish I could *make* Kelly like me," he said, but then a moment later added despondently, "But I guess if I could, it wouldn't really be *her*; I'd just be friends with myself." Essentially, the same argument has been advanced by proponents of religious freedom from Lactantius to Locke and from Roger Williams to James Madison.

The argument from voluntariness appears to provide a more admirable or principled rationale for toleration than the rationales we have considered earlier. I may believe (perhaps with unshakable confidence) that your religious belief is false: nonetheless, even if I could somehow force you to relinquish the idea, my goal of inducing a genuine true faith would not thereby be realized. So I respect your autonomy: I treat you as a person whose beliefs and choices matter *because they are yours,* even when I think they are mistaken.

It is not surprising that arguments of this kind have played a major role in justifying tolerance and opposing illiberalism. Such arguments are powerful and important, I think, but they are not quite as decisive as we sometimes like to suppose, for two main reasons. First, the argument from voluntariness is not freestanding or self-justifying. It depends upon a base position—and not just any base position, either: rather, it requires a base position that emphasizes goods that depend for their realization upon free, authentic acceptance.[26] Second, even with respect to a base position that emphasizes these sorts of voluntariness-dependent goods, illiberalism has two *prima facie* plausible responses to the voluntariness argument.

First, illiberalism can respond that even if suppressing heresy *X* will do no good for those who already hold that damnable view, a policy of suppression can prevent the spread of error to others, who will as a result maintain the true view voluntarily and authentically. In this vein, proponents of suppression have often compared error to counterfeit money that must be kept out of circulation, or to a contagion that must be kept from spreading. In early modern Europe, the historian Brad Gregory explains, it was thought that "[m]urderers killed bodies, but heretics killed souls." Consequently, "[t]he spreading of heresy was religious reckless endangerment by spiritual serial killers."[27] Not surprisingly, the dominant view was that such killers should be stopped.

Second, even for those who already hold the heresy we might seek to suppress, compelled renunciation might tend to produce, over time, an authentic and ultimately voluntary embrace of truth. If errors are suppressed, potential or erstwhile heretics may consequently be forced into greater exposure to true ideas, and they might thereby come to perceive the superiority of those ideas. Or error might be viewed as a sort of addicting drug: forced to go cold turkey, people might overcome the addiction and come to realize the virtues of embracing truth. Theories of cognitive dissonance may suggest how, in order to avoid the dissonance between (initially compelled) public professions and (initially contrary) inner belief, a person might reshape her belief so as to achieve a more satisfactory harmony. In any of these ways, beliefs (or at least professions) that were initially compelled might come to be sincerely and even freely held.[28]

To these arguments, I think, there is no decisive, once-and-for-all response. In children, we do often proceed on the assumption that involuntary measures can help in the achievement even of goods (good attitudes or character traits, correct ideas) that *ultimately*—the qualifier is crucial—depend on sincere acceptance. In adults, perhaps, we may rightly think these measures less appropriate, or less effective: in some cases they may merely produce resentment and resistance. But then of course the distinction between children and adults, though practically indispensable, is to a large extent conventional and pragmatic and normatively conclusory; it is scarcely a hard-and-fast natural fact, like the difference between copper and iron. It is easy, and not wholly illogical, to regard those who cling to manifest foolishness as "children" in an important sense.

3. A "universal" rationale for tolerance?

The tenuous, provisional nature of the case for toleration suggested above may leave us uneasy. It would be comforting to have some more sweeping, once-and-for-all, knockdown argument for toleration. Not surprisingly, therefore, arguments claiming this character have often been entertained. And though I do not think these more universal arguments hold up well under examination, they probably have been influential in gaining or at least consolidating support for the practice of toleration.

Perhaps the most popular "universal" rationale for tolerance is rooted in the ideal of "reciprocity." Thus, Jürgen Habermas reports that "[i]nitially, the toleration of religious minorities was justified only pragmatically, e.g., for mercantilist reasons; in order to maintain law and order; for legalistic reasons, since spontaneous convictions elude legal constraint; or for epistemological reasons, since the human mind is deemed to be fallible."[29] These rationales, of course, are among those considered above. But Habermas suggests that this "pragmatic" defense of toleration eventually matured into a more Kantian and "universally convincing" position based on the notion of reciprocity. As an illustration, Habermas cites Pierre Bayle's argument that Christians cannot consistently object to the suppression of Christian evangelization in Japan and at the same time forbid Muslim proselytizing in Christian Europe.[30]

Far from being "universally convincing," however, this reciprocity argument would likely seem merely obtuse to those to whom it is supposedly directed. *If* Christianity, Islam, and, say, Shintoism are relevantly similar, then of course reciprocity may indeed suggest that if Christians expect to be permitted to evangelize in territories dominated by Islam or Shinto they ought to allow representatives of those religions to proselytize in Christendom. But that premise—that the religions are relevantly similar—is precisely what is at issue, and what the believers in these faiths deny.[31] In *their* view, one of the religions leads to salvation, while the others may lead to damnation: that is hardly equivalence. So why would reciprocity demand that truth be treated in the same way falsehood is? It is as if a failing student were to argue, on grounds of reciprocity, that if the school gives credit for true answers on a test it must give equal credit for false answers.

To be sure, even the most fervent devotees of the different religions might be able to acknowledge that the religions are similar in the sense that their own followers *believe* them to be true. But that similarity is the dispositive one only if we tacitly assume that *belief*, not actual *truth* (or salvific efficacy), is the relevant factor—an assumption that the believers themselves are likely to find as implausible as the school would find a similar claim made by students who insist that they *believed* their (erroneous) answers were correct (or perhaps still believe this, quite possibly on the basis of epistemic criteria that the school does not accept as valid).

We can put this point in a different way. Toleration, as I have said, is a possible response to pluralism—and most likely, in the modern world, to a deep pluralism that applies not only to what we might call primary belief systems such as religion but also to second order beliefs regarding matters such as the nature of justice, the meaning and scope of democracy, and the proper or best ways of negotiating primary religious, political, and epistemic disagreements. It would be wonderful if we could decree that although people will and should be allowed to disagree with each other at one level (about, say, religion), at some other level (such as where coercion by the state is involved) we will all act only on universally acceptable grounds. A large body of modern political theory can be understood as a powerful (if often ponderous) expression of this pleasant illusion.[32] And if such universally acceptable grounds were available, we might also hope for a "universal" argument for toleration.[33] But to recommend this solution is simply to refuse to acknowledge the depth and reality of the pluralism that gives rise to the possibility of and need for toleration in the first place.

4. The "instability" of tolerance

The burden of the discussion thus far has been that there *are* arguments favoring tolerance, and taken cumulatively they may often be sufficient to justify a practice of toleration. But their force will vary with the circumstances. So the case for toleration cannot simply rest on any one-time articulation of a value such as voluntariness or reciprocity. The case depends, rather, on the ongoing defense of base positions that support liberty or tolerance, and on contextual application of voluntariness considerations, probably in conjunction with other rationales. As Bernard Williams explains,

> the practice of toleration has to be sustained not so much by a pure principle resting on a value of autonomy as by a wider and more mixed range of resources. Those resources include an active skepticism against fanaticism and the pretensions of its advocates; conviction about the manifest evils of toleration's absence; and, quite certainly, power, to provide Hobbesian reminders to the more extreme groups that they will have to settle for coexistence.[34]

It follows, I think, that toleration is not a position that, once attained, is a secure resting place. It is, as George Fletcher says, an unstable position.[35] As such, it is a position that must be constantly defended.

III. Ultraliberalism: The Objection to "Mere" Toleration

By contrast to illiberalism, the ultraliberal position finds toleration unsatisfactory not because it is too permissive, but rather because even while forbearing from coercion or suppression a tolerant agent continues to treat some ideas and values as superior to others that are merely "tolerated": in this way, toleration may seem to violate liberal commitments to equal concern and respect.[36] Michael Walzer describes the objection: "To tolerate someone else is an act of power; to be tolerated is an acceptance of weakness. We should aim at something better than this combination, something beyond toleration, something like mutual respect."[37]

This objection is long-standing. In this vein, Thomas Paine scoffed that "[t]oleration is not the *opposite* of intoleration, but is the *counterfeit* of it. Both are despotisms."[38] And in a similar spirit, the young James Madison managed to defeat George Mason's Virginia proposal to protect "the fullest *Toleration* in the Exercise of Religion," to be replaced by a provision providing that "all men are *equally* entitled to the full and free exercise of religion."[39]

This objection is reinforced by the suggestion that core beliefs are in a sense "constitutive" of who a person is.[40] On this assumption, if the state embraces beliefs held by some citizens but not by others, it may seem to treat those whose views are merely tolerated with less than equal respect. This attitude is easily discernible in, for example, the modern jurisprudences of free speech and freedom of religion that purport to require "neutrality" of the state, at least in limited domains. Thus, viewpoint neutrality has become the centerpiece of modern free speech doctrine.[41] And the principal rationale for the modern "no endorsement" interpretation of the establishment clause asserts that if government says or does things that send messages endorsing or disapproving of a religion, it thereby treats citizens who disagree with that message as "outsiders, not full members of the political community."[42]

Appealing though this ultraliberal position is, it is also self-defeating—at least as a response to pluralism in the realm of *ideas* (including religious ideas). The reasons for this conclusion have been argued for at length elsewhere;[43] here I will only state them summarily. In the first place, "ultraliberalism" is itself a position or set of beliefs; more specifically, it is a position that some people accept and others reject. So if it is impermissible for the state to affirm by word or action some ideas while rejecting or declining to affirm other ideas, it should follow that the state is forbidden to affirm or act upon the ultraliberal position.

Second, any state that would maintain the allegiance and support of its citizens—and not merely their acquiescence—arguably needs to appeal to their beliefs (as in fact our political tradition acknowledges in countless ways: mottos and pledges and pronouncements and rituals of various kinds). But this appeal, if it is to be effective and not merely insipid, will necessarily involve the public affirmation of actual, substantial beliefs—beliefs that, inevitably, some but not all citizens will hold.

Not surprisingly, therefore, the ultraliberal position flourishes only in the realm of theory: it does not correspond to the way governments typically acknowledged to be "liberal" ever have behaved, or behave now—or, we can confidently say, ever will behave. On the contrary, governments constantly and necessarily affirm some beliefs and reject others—in the public school curriculum, in decisions about which programs and art forms and research agendas to subsidize, in official pronouncements of various kinds that routinely issue from governments at all levels, and in the justifications given for every decision that is made and every piece of legislation that is enacted.

Notice that these objections apply only to the ultraliberal ideal of equality as a strategy for addressing pluralism in matters of *belief*; they do not apply to liberalism as a response to other forms of pluralism. There is no incoherence in asserting that a liberal regime will treat *persons* with equal respect.[44] So it is perfectly plausible, for example, to say that a liberal regime must not privilege any race while merely tolerating other races. Conversely, the notion that one or some races are "orthodox" and that other races are merely tolerated does indeed seem contrary to the meaning and spirit of liberal democracy. In this domain, in short, equality rather than tolerance seems the appropriate ideal. It may be that the ultraliberal notion of equality as expressed in the jurisprudences of free speech and freedom of religion gains some of its appeal from its evident rightness in the area of race or, more generally, in describing the liberal attitude toward *persons*.

The difficulty occurs in the transition from an ideal of equal respect for *persons* to an ideal of equal respect for or equal treatment of *beliefs*. Though rhetorically parallel, these ideals are not mutually supporting. On the contrary, they are mutually incompatible: if the state embraces the idea that persons are in some sense of equal moral worth, it thereby necessarily rejects contrary beliefs or ideas—namely, inegalitarian beliefs—and it thereby rejects the notion that beliefs or ideas can be treated with equal respect. That "all men are created equal" is one of the "truths" that "we hold"—and that we hold over against contrary claims that we reject.

In sum, ultraliberalism in the realm of beliefs is a position that could never be maintained. Or even if somehow it could, it would undermine the very liberalism that it seeks to uphold.

IV. The Timeliness of Toleration

If liberalism is to prevail, consequently, it will do so only by adopting a posture of toleration. It does not necessarily follow, however, that a liberal regime must *acknowledge* its commitment to toleration. Ultraliberal equality might serve a diplomatic function; it might provide an attractive rhetoric for concealing or disguising the difficult and potentially divisive choices among competing beliefs that the state will inevitably make. In short, a liberal state might *practice* toleration while *talking* the language of ultraliberalism.

There is no way to say in the abstract, I think, whether this diplomatically deceptive rhetoric is warranted. It might be—in some contexts. But in our own time this prescription begins to look increasingly ineffectual and even perilous.

A. Citizen versus Person?

The difficulties can be traced back to a disturbing paradox at the heart of the ultraliberal position. On the one hand, liberalism strives for a sort of unity between government and "We the people." Indeed, the distinctive feature of liberal democracy, as opposed to other forms of government in which "the rulers" and "the ruled" are more decisively separated, is that democracy is supposed to be government "of the people, by the people, for the people." On the other hand, the ultraliberal or "neutrality" approach to democracy insists on a sharp divide between what we might call the moral mindset of government and that of individual persons. *Persons* are supposed to hold and actively pursue thick "conceptions of the good." They are expected to have beliefs—beliefs that reflect the acceptance of some ideas and the rejection of others.[45] *Government,* by contrast, is supposed to remain neutral or agnostic in these matters.

In sum, government is supposed to be constituted by "the people" but it is also supposed to adopt an approach to the issues of life that is utterly different from the approach that people themselves—or, if you like, *persons*—adopt. The prescribed divide is especially sharp in the area of religion, where ultraliberalism assumes that people (many of them anyway) will embrace and live by religious beliefs but that government is absolutely forbidden to maintain any views whatever on such matters.[46]

It is not so hard to imagine some such division of mindset operating in non-liberal or undemocratic regimes. On the contrary, it seems natural to suppose that if the rulers are one class of persons and the ruled are a different class, these classes might well operate on the basis of significantly different assumptions and values. The problem, once again, is that in a liberal democracy these classes are supposed to converge—the government and the people are supposed to be in some sense the same—but their ways of thinking are nonetheless supposed to diverge drastically (at least according to the ultraliberal prescription). John Smith the Person is supposed to express and act on beliefs about the good, including religious beliefs; but John Smith the Official (or even, by extension, John Smith the Citizen) is expected to refrain from any such expressions or actions.

To be sure, the scope of conflict might be reduced in various ways. We might limit the neutrality constraints, perhaps, to matters involving religion . . . or to *coercive* regulations of speech . . . or perhaps to matters involving "constitutional essentials and matters of basic justice."[47] Or we might imaginatively try to abstract the "government" that is subject to such ultraliberal constraints away from the real people who staff the government as officials and citizens.[48] But these containment measures seem suspect. If the ultraliberal ideal is just and right, after all, why should it be necessary to be continually shrinking its scope of application?[49] And why would a liberal want to abstract government away from the people? Isn't the identification of government with the people —the actual, flesh-and-blood people—supposed to be the essence and glory of democracy? The repeated resort to limiting measures thus suggests that there is something wrong with an ultraliberal ideal that must be repeatedly qualified and contained.

So perhaps the more forthright approach would be to champion the ideal and insist that although the government and the people-as-citizens are indeed the same body, whenever people are acting *as citizens*—that is, when they are constituting and administering the government—they must strive to suspend their normal modes of thinking and to refrain from believing and acting on the basis of religious beliefs and particular conceptions of the good. But this prescription provokes powerful objections. Is it really possible for John Smith so to divide himself between Smith-as-Person and Smith-as-Citizen? And supposing it is possible, is this course healthy? And even if we can answer these questions in the affirmative, haven't we sacrificed the liberal democratic ideal after all? The goal, once again, was to establish a government "of the people, by the people, for the people." It would be natural to assume that this means government "of John Smith et al., by John Smith et al., for John Smith et al." But if democracy imposes such a sharp divide between Smith the Person and Smith the Citizen, then it is doubtful whether a government of "We the Citizens" can accurately be described as a government of "the people" after all: "We the People" for government purposes turns out to be an entity quite independent of me and you.[50]

And in any case, it seems more likely that the prescribed division between person and citizen will not be realistically maintainable.[51] But if the division between person and citizen is breached, then it seems that either the Citizen will come to overwhelm the Person, or else the Person will commandeer the Citizen. Neither outcome seems attractive, as becomes apparent if we consider them in turn.

B. The Impoverished Soul

Consider the first alternative. Suppose that Smith the Citizen, steeped in the anti-judgmental language of neutrality and equality, comes to dominate Smith the Person. Smith accordingly comes to believe (pardon the incoherence) that "there is no such thing as a false idea"[52]—an initially cheering notion which upon reflection seems to imply, sadly, that there is no such thing as a genuinely true idea either. (Much in the same way that the happy thought "Nobody can lose" entails that "Nobody can win.") In this contingency, Smith will slip into a kind of lackluster or ironic agnosticism toward the issues of life: he will lose his grip on his convictions and his capacity to act resolutely to choose among and pursue contested ideas of the good. With luck, his life will be peaceful—or at least untroubled by the struggles of conviction that have sometimes convulsed both communities and individual consciences—but also empty, devoid of larger purpose or meaning.

William Galston expresses the concern: "The greatest threat to children in modern liberal societies is not that they will believe in something too deeply, but that they will believe in nothing very deeply at all."[53] In a similar vein, Larry Alexander argues that the liberal embrace of cosmopolitanism as a good leads to "a way of life [that] is shallow, denatured, bereft of deep commitments."[54] Ronald Beiner argues that modern liberal theory, with its commitment to an agnostic neutrality, has produced a "reluctance to engage with the kind of large and ambitious claims about human nature and the essence of our social situation that alone furnish a critical foothold for bedrock judgments about the global adequacy or deficiency of a given mode of life."[55] Instead, quoting Richard Rorty, he argues that modern liberalism deliberately seeks to produce individuals who are "bland, calculating, petty and unheroic."[56]

This description surely captures one aspect of our contemporary culture—but not all of it. If we look beyond the world of Seinfeld and the complacent consumerism of the stereotypical suburbs, it seems that belief is still very much alive and well—or at least alive—in other quarters. But that phenomenon presents a different sort of problem.

C. Impoverished Discourse

Looking inward: From one perspective, the modern world suffers not so much from an absence of conviction, but rather from an excess of it.[57] On the domestic scene we see a series of "culture wars" pitting people of strong and incompatible views against each other. One widely noted study of this phenomenon is James Davison Hunter's *Culture Wars.*[58] Hunter reports that across a wide variety of seemingly independent political and social issues, Americans tend to coalesce into two broad camps, which he calls "progressive" and "orthodox." The progressive camp is composed partly of "secularists" but also of persons who, though counting themselves religious, place their trust in "personal experience or scientific rationality." By contrast, the "orthodox" camp, reflecting a "biblical theism" that includes "many Catholics, Protestants, and Jews," is defined by "*the commitment on the part of adherents to an external, definable, and transcendent authority.*"[59]

Because their views and assumptions are so different, these cultural camps have difficulty communicating with each other. "Each side of the cultural divide," Hunter observes, "speaks with a different moral vocabulary." Each side operates out of a different mode of debate and persuasion. Each side represents the tendencies of a separate and competing moral galaxy. They are, indeed, "worlds apart."[60]

In another sense, though, the public rhetoric employed by the sides exhibits common and worrisome features—a sort of "symmetry in antipathy," as Hunter puts it.

> Both ends of the cultural axis claim to speak for the majority, both attempt to monopolize the symbols of legitimacy, both identify their opponents with a program of intolerance and totalitarian suppression. Both sides use the language of extremism and thereby sensationalize the threat represented by their adversaries. And finally, each side has exhibited at least a proclivity to indulge the temptation of social bigotry.[61]

Whether this divide can be bridged is uncertain. What seems clear, though, is that the ultraliberal discourse of equality and neutrality, though developed as a strategy for dealing with such cultural conflict, has proven inadequate not only to dissolve the differences but even to comprehend or express them. This failure is hardly surprising; on the contrary, it is in a sense deliberate. How could a discourse intentionally crafted to keep fundamental premises and commitments off the public agenda hope to express deep convictions, and disagreements, on such issues? But the upshot is that ultraliberal discourse becomes ineffectual—a source not of engagement and resolution but of manipulation and suspicion.

One familiar response to this concern suggests that liberalism does not exclude the presentation of religious or "comprehensive doctrines," or of reasons based on such doctrines, in the public sphere: liberalism merely holds that important public decisions should not be *based on* such reasons.[62] This position in effect tells citizens: "You're free to express your deep convictions in public and in political debate—so long as those beliefs don't ultimately make any difference in the public decisions that are made." At the very least, this restriction obviously reduces the incentive to present and discuss such reasons in public discourse. Moreover, insofar as the "so long as the reasons make no difference" restriction is embodied in constitutional doctrine—the establishment clause doctrine, for example—there remains a significant incentive *not* to present such reasons in order to avoid the risk that a decision will be invalidated based on a court's perception that the decision was based on an impermissible reason or purpose.[63]

We can put the point in terms of the Citizen *versus* Person conflict noticed earlier. Suppose that rather than being subjugated by Smith the Citizen, Smith the Person manages to dominate his civic *alter ego,* using the citizen now as a sort of puppet to advance his own views and interests. So Smith will hold and act on his convictions both in private and in the civic sphere. But if the discourse norms of ultraliberalism persist in the civic sphere, then when acting in that context Smith will of necessity learn to hide his true motives and convictions, translating them into the bland discourse of equality and neutrality. And if John Smith acquires these arts of concealment, we can imagine that Mary Adams and Carlos Sanchez and Anita Wang will do the same—and that each of them will come to suspect the others of speaking and behaving in this deceptive way. Their discourse will become unpersuasive and manipulative, and known to be such; and each of these characteristics will reinforce the other. The more manipulative, the less persuasive; the less genuinely persuasive, the more merely manipulative.

The modern judicial discourse of constitutional law is to a significant degree a fulfillment of this dark prophecy. To a large extent, constitutional decisions under the First and Fourteenth Amendments are exercises in the deployment of the vocabulary of equality and neutrality. The same themes are sounded again and again, whether the cases concern nonestablishment or free exercise or free speech or race or gender or sexual orientation. And as critics from all points on the political spectrum point out, these judicial decisions seem increasingly incapable of either conveying or inspiring conviction. Modern Supreme Court opinions, as Dan

Farber observes, are "increasingly arid, formalistic, and lacking in intellectual value": they "almost seem designed to wear the reader into submission as much as actually to persuade."[64] At the same time, the decisions also fail either to express or to conceal the cultural differences that lie behind the Justices' positions. "Kulturkampf" is of course a theme often asserted in dissent by Justice Scalia,[65] and whatever one may think of Scalia's choice of rhetoric or his own favored alternatives, in this respect his assessment often seems more cogent than anything offered in the majority opinions he criticizes.

As a result, what the Court is pleased to call "reasoned judgment" often amounts, as Robert Nagel has persuasively shown, to little more than thinly veiled exercises in name-calling, as the Justices peremptorily dismiss the positions they disfavor as products of "prejudice," "fear," "antipathy," "irrationality," or "a bare . . . desire to harm a politically unpopular group." "[T]o a remarkable extent," Nagel observes, "our courts have become places where the name-calling and exaggeration that mark the lower depths of our political debate are simply given a more acceptable, authoritative form."[66]

Looking outward: If we look outward beyond our boundaries, we perceive a similar phenomenon on a global level. One widely discussed diagnosis puts the situation in terms of a "clash of civilizations," with "civilizations" and "cultures" being treated almost as interchangeable terms.[67] The culture of Western civilization, Samuel Huntington argues, is constituted by features that include rule of law, a Christian and classical heritage, a separation of spiritual and temporal authority, social pluralism, individualism, and government by representation.[68] Against the view that sees these values as a sort of natural or even inevitable destination for the world as a whole, Huntington argues that other civilizations see this particular constellation of values as decadent and, given Western power, threatening. And though Western civilization is easily the most powerful at the moment, its economic and cultural power relative to some other civilizations appears to be in the early phases of decline.[69]

Over the long run, therefore, the continuing viability of the culture distinguished by these values is very much in jeopardy. Huntington stresses in particular the ongoing competition with

Islamic culture—in comparison with which, he asserts, the "twentieth-century conflict between liberal democracy and Marxist-Leninism is only a fleeting and superficial historical phenomenon."[70] Given this conflict, the preservation of Western civilization depends very much, he argues, on our ability to affirm and defend what he calls (perhaps unfortunately, especially given his own emphasis on "civilization" as the important unit) "the American Creed." This Creed includes the values of "liberty, democracy, individualism, equality before the law, constitutionalism, private property," as well as the Christian foundation from which these commitments historically arose.[71]

Whether any such defense will succeed is unforeseeable. One obstacle, however, is a sort of self-imposed paralysis that hinders the affirmation and defense of this Creed. Huntington's comment on that abnegation sounds desperate: "Rejection of the Creed and of Western civilization means the end of the United States as we have known it. . . . Americans cannot avoid the issue: Are we a Western people or are we something else? The futures of the United States and of the West depend upon Americans reaffirming their commitment to Western civilization."[72]

I do not mean to affirm Huntington's overall diagnosis here. Obviously, not only the details but many of the broad outlines of his argument are eminently debatable.[73] For present purposes, though, the important point is the scarcely deniable fact of serious cultural conflict on the global level. The recent Iraq war together with the conflict in Afghanistan, following in the wake of September 11, surely confirm Huntington's claim that history is not foreordained to any happy, smooth convergence on a culture of human rights, representative democracy, and rule of law. Even on the contestable supposition that these commitments enjoy the support of a *domestic* "overlapping consensus,"[74] allowing us to appeal to them for internal purposes without invoking any more fundamental premises or "comprehensive views," they clearly do not enjoy any such consensus on the global level. Hence, the ambition to defend such values in the long run and even to extend them to other communities characterized by other cultures—say, Iraq—probably involves, among other things, an effort to articulate and defend the premises—the Creed, as Huntington puts it—in which such values are grounded.

But once again, the ultraliberal discourse of neutrality and equality subverts and obstructs that effort.[75] Perhaps ironically, this incapacity is perhaps most conspicuous with respect to one of ultraliberalism's core values—that is, equality. The Declaration of Independence asserts, as one of the central truths on which the Republic was founded, that "all men are created equal." In recent decades, equality has become arguably the central value in some of our most justly celebrated political movements (in particular the civil rights movement), in a good deal of political philosophy, and also in much constitutional law, not only under the equal protection clause but in First Amendment jurisprudence as well.[76] In these contexts, "equality" is regarded as a positive and morally dignifying attribute, not merely the more brutish Hobbesian ability to kill each other: hence we talk of "equal worth," "equal dignity," or entitlement to "equal concern and respect."

Yet this assertion of equality or equal worth, ennobling and exhilarating though it may be, is not on its face intuitively compelling, or even plausible. George Fletcher observes that "[n]othing quite like 'all men are created equal' is ever cited in the German jurisprudence of equality or, so far as I know, in any other legal culture of the world."[77] And he adds that "[a]s a descriptive matter, the thesis that 'all men are created equal' is obviously false. People differ in every conceivable respect—size, strength, intelligence, musical talent, beauty."[78]

So then what is the justification for saying that all persons are in some important sense of equal worth? The Declaration of Independence is quite clear in offering a religious foundation for the doctrine of equality: we "are created" equal, and we are equal at least in the sense that we "are *endowed by* [*our*] *Creator*" with rights. Thus, as Fletcher explains, "[b]ehind those *created* equal stands a Creator—the source as well of our basic human rights."[79] More generally, Louis Pojman argues that as a historical matter, the idea of human equality descends from religious rationales. Often the justification takes the form of a claim that all humans are made by, and in the image of, God.[80] The justification is also expressed in the imagery of family: "The language of human dignity and worth implies a great family in which a benevolent and sovereign Father binds together all his children in love and justice."[81] And that rationale can be given more analytical form: Pojman identifies two principal justifications in the religious tradition, which he calls "the Essentialist Argument" and "the Argument from Grace."[82]

But the ideal of ultraliberal neutrality operates to exclude these sorts of justifications from public discourse,[83] thus reviving the question: What *is* the justification (if there is one) for this momentous but counterintuitive claim about equal human worth or dignity? Fletcher observes that "[m]odern philosophical approaches toward equality . . . are strongly committed, . . . but they offer no reason why they are so intensely committed to this value. . . . In the contemporary liberal culture, equality is one of those values that has become so deeply held that it is neither questioned nor justified."[84] In a similar vein, Louis Pojman examines ten leading secular arguments advanced by theorists such as Dworkin, Rawls, Kai Nielsen, Joel Feinberg, Thomas Nagel, and Alan Gewirth; and he finds all of these arguments wanting. Sometimes the arguments turn on demonstrable fallacies or on flagrant and unsupported discursive leaps; more often they do not actually offer any justification for equality at all but instead simply assert or assume it, or else posit that in the absence of any persuasive justification one way or the other we should adopt a "presumption" of equal worth.[85] Jeremy Waldron's recent analysis of Locke's arguments for equality points to a similar conclusion.[86]

Patrick Brennan comments that "[t]he persistent inquirer will find a kind of circularity in the equality-talk, a sort of pseudo-analytic house-of-mirrors that would confirm Michael White in his judgment that equality-talk is destined for triviality, if not downright dishonesty."[87] And triviality, dishonesty, or mere evasion or muteness with respect to our most fundamental political commitments hardly provide a secure basis for enduring political community. Whether the liberal commitment to equality can be supported on more secular or neutral grounds remains a complicated and contested question, of course, but it is at least risky to suppose that we can afford to forgo the kind of rationale, summarily asserted in the Declaration of Independence, that historically provided that justification for that commitment.

In sum, whether we look inward to the domestic "culture wars" or outward to the more global cultural conflicts, the impoverished discourse of ultraliberalism seems powerless not only to acknowledge and engage the fundamental issues but even to defend its own animating commitments.

D. Toleration as Remedy

The preceding discussion has described two sorts of impoverishment that seem to afflict at least parts of contemporary culture: a spiritual impoverishment (or impoverishment of the soul) manifested in an inability to hold and affirm convictions of the kind that arguably are central to what makes human life distinctively meaningful and valuable, and an impoverishment of discourse that renders us incapable of engaging our most fundamental convictions and differences or of defending our most fundamental commitments. My argument has been that this unfortunate condition is a direct result of the commitment to an ultraliberal position that tells us, in essence, that when "We the People" are acting in a public capacity, we are not supposed to affirm our most fundamental beliefs—not overtly, at least.

This position produces a sort of squeamishness about even acknowledging that our liberal commitments are grounded in a (contestable but, hopefully, defensible) base position or orthodoxy. And it in effect seeks to sever the Citizen from the Person. But if a strong ultraliberal divide between Citizen and Person is not maintainable (as seems likely), then it looks as if the result will be either a sort of anemic, least-common-denominator culture lacking in conviction or purpose, or else a deceptive civic culture in which participants disguise their true interests and convictions in a homogenizing public vocabulary that is "neutral" but ineffectual, or else some combination of these.

The principal reason for maintaining this unhappy state of affairs, perhaps, is fear of the alternative. If the only alternative to ultraliberalism is an intolerant illiberalism, that is, then we might prefer to stay with what we have been doing regardless of the dissonances it creates. But the burden of this essay has been, first, that under current conditions there is no warrant for confidence that the ultraliberal position itself is maintainable in the long run but, second, that there is an alternative: toleration. A position of tolerance allows us to affirm forthrightly that we are acting on the basis of beliefs—beliefs, to be sure, that are substantive and non-trivial and, hence, contestable and, usually, contested. Having acknowledged as much, we would then be in a position to consider, openly and deliberately, whether those beliefs are warranted and whether and how they support toleration of other, inconsistent beliefs.

We might worry that a more candid examination will not end up providing convincing reasons for tolerance: it might lead us to the illiberal position. Realistically, though, this does not seem to be a serious risk. Or, rather, it does not seem to be an objection that an ultraliberal can cogently make. That is because whatever reasons the ultraliberal may have for favoring ultraliberal neutrality (even as a pretense) over illiberalism ought to be capable of being elaborated in the form of cogent rationales for tolerance. This suggestion assumes, perhaps, that the ultraliberal's reasons are plausible and admissible ones. But if they are not, then the ultraliberal should not be averse to being persuaded otherwise.

Conclusion

The essential argument is captured in a brief response by Richard John Neuhaus, editor-in-chief of the journal *First Things,* to a recent essay by Bernard Lewis, the noted historian of Islam. Lewis maintains (at least according to Neuhaus) that the possibility of peace and mutual respect among Muslims and Christians depends on the "relativists" in each religion prevailing over the true believers, or "triumphalists." If this is in fact Lewis's view, then it resonates with the "ultraliberal" response to the challenge of pluralism. But Neuhaus argues that Lewis's view misconceives the basis of Christian tolerance. "[T]he reason we do not kill one another over our disagreements about the will of God is that we believe it is against the will of God to kill one another over our disagreements about the will of God. Christians have come to believe that." (Neuhaus admits that the development of Christian tolerance has been slow, complicated, and uneven.) By the same token, "[i]f Islam is to become tolerant and respectful of other religions, it must be as a result of a development that comes from within the truth of Islam, not as a result of relativizing or abandoning that truth." By contrast, the relativizing strategy "plays into the hands of Muslim rigorists who pose as the defenders of the uncompromised and uncompromisible truth."[88]

As a historical matter, both responses—truth-oriented tolerance, and the strategy of indifference and skepticism and "relativism" culminating in what I have called "ultraliberalism"—have surely contributed to the domestication of pluralism. But the burden of this essay has been that in the world as it is now and in the face of current challenges both internal and external, the kind of tolerance that is compatible with (and indeed derived from) the affirmation of truth deserves renewed emphasis.

NOTES

1. Warren Distinguished Professor of Law, University of San Diego. I thank Larry Alexander, Jack Coons, Michael Perry, Andrew Sabl, and Melissa Williams for helpful comments on an earlier draft. I also benefited from the very thoughtful responses by Professors Forst and Morgan.

2. To say that a good and attractive regime will be tolerant is not of course to say (as Professor Morgan seems to understand me to suggest) that every regime that can be classified as "tolerant" will necessarily be good and attractive. See Glyn Morgan, "How Impoverishing Is Liberalism?" in this volume.

3. Different writers talk about toleration as a "practice" or an "attitude" or perhaps a "virtue." These dimensions are difficult to disentangle, but my emphasis in this paper is on the "practice" of toleration (which will, to be sure, both grow out of and manifest itself in certain beliefs or attitudes).

4. Toleration thus presents the familiar question of how an entity such as "the state" or "the government" can be said to have or act on beliefs. However, that is not the question with which I am concerned in this essay.

5. Morgan, this volume, 293–99.

6. As Jürgen Habermas writes: "Each act of toleration must circumscribe a characteristic of what we must accept and thus simultaneously draw a line for what cannot be tolerated. There can be no inclusion without exclusion" in his *Intolerance and Discrimination,* 1 I.CON 2 (2003), 5.

7. In this respect, my use of a three-category scheme for understand-

ing toleration tracks the explanation of Rainer Forst, "Tolerance as a Virtue of Justice," *Philosophical Explorations* 3 (2001), 193–94.

8. See Nomi Maya Stolzenberg, "The Return of the Repressed: Illiberal Groups in a Liberal State," *Journal of Contemporary Legal Issues* 12 (2002), 897–98 (noting that "[a]ccording to the standard view, . . . [t]he liberal state neither favors nor disfavors any particular belief-system; it is neutral.").

9. Perhaps the most conspicuous proponent in recent academic writing has been Stanley Fish. See, e.g., Stanley Fish, "Mission Impossible: Settling the Just Bounds between Church and State," 97 *Columbia Law Review* 2255 (1997) and Stanley Fish, "Why We Can't All Just Get Along," *First Things* 18 (Feb. 1996).

10. For example, it is possible (and critics often charge) that the ultraliberal position easily collapses into a form of intolerance. Cf. Stolzenberg, supra note 8 at 898 ("Generations of critics have argued that, despite—and indeed because of—its commitments to diversity, tolerance, and pluralism, liberalism is intolerant and inhospitable to certain ways of life and beliefs, especially traditional and illiberal ones.").

11. Stanley Fish observes that although "modern theorists try in every way possible to avoid" the fact, it is nonetheless true that "[i]f you believe something you believe it to be true, and perforce, you regard those who believe contrary things to be in error." Fish, "Mission Impossible," supra note 9 at 2256.

12. *Abrams v. United States,* 250 U.S. 616, 630 (1919) (Holmes, J., dissenting).

13. Holmes tersely foreshadowed several of the major answering rationales in his *Abrams* dissent: "To allow opposition by speech seems to indicate that you think the speech impotent, as when a man says that he has squared the circle, or that you do not care whole-heartedly for the result, or that you doubt either your power or your premises." Id.

14. Cf. Forst, supra note 7 at 193 ("[I]t is essential for the concept of toleration that the tolerated beliefs or practices are considered to be objectionable and in an important sense wrong.").

15. For more detailed consideration of the point, see Steven D. Smith, *Getting Over Equality* (New York: New York University Press, 2001), 144–47.

16. James Gordley observes that "[c]ertainly, if there were a shortage of plausible sounding racial bigots, the state wouldn't subsidize bigotry and the development of plausible arguments for it simply to ensure their citizens were exposed to them." James Gordley, "Morality and the Protection of Dissent," *Ave Maria Law Review* 1 (2003), 127, 140.

17. See Alan Wolfe, *The Transformation of American Religion* (New York:

Free Press, 2003), 67–95. No doubt with some exaggeration, Martin Gardner colorfully describes the current culture:

> Today, you will have a hard time discovering what any prominent Christian actually believes. . . . Who cares? It is not so much that the public is irreligious, but that it is lukewarm, indifferent to religious dogmas. . . .
>
> Millions of Catholics and Protestants around the world now attend liberal churches where they listen to music and Laodicean sermons, and (if Protestant) sing tuneless Laodicean hymns. They may even stand and recite the Apostles' Creed out of force of habit and not believe a word of it. . . .
>
> It is a scandal of American Protestantism that no one knows whether Reinhold Niebuhr did or did not believe in the afterlife taught by Jesus. I once tried to find out by writing to his widow, but she replied in a diplomatic letter that she had to let her husband's writings speak for themselves. Alas, nowhere in those writings can one find a clear answer to this question. Either Mrs. Niebuhr herself didn't know, or she wouldn't tell me.

See Martin Gardner, "Introduction," G. K. Chesterton, *The Ball and the Cross* (New York: Dover Publications, 1995), vi–vii.

18. *Dennis v. United States,* 341 U.S. 494, 588 (1951) (Douglas, J., dissenting).

19. In this vein, George Fletcher observes that in "a posture of indifference" there is "no issue of tolerance, properly understood": "Calling my hands-off attitude a matter of tolerance cheapens the virtue." George P. Fletcher, "The Instability of Tolerance," David Heyd, ed., *Toleration: An Elusive Virtue* (Princeton, N.J.: Princeton University Press, 1996), 158.

20. See supra note 12. In a letter to Learned Hand, Holmes made the point more dramatically, asserting a "sacred right to kill the other fellow when he disagrees." The correspondence is recounted in Gerald Gunther, "Learned Hand and the Origins of Modern First Amendment Doctrine: Some Fragments of History," *Stanford Law Review* 27 (1975), 755–56.

21. "But when men have realized that time has upset many fighting faiths, they may come to believe even more than they believe the very foundations of their own conduct that the ultimate good desired is better reached by free trade in ideas." *Abrams,* 250 U.S. at 630.

22. See generally *Early Modern Skepticism and the Origins of Toleration,* Alan Levine, ed. (Lanham, Md.: Lexington Books, 1999).

23. Bernard Williams thus observes that "with indifference and skepticism, . . . the point will be reached at which" apathy prevails, and "tolera-

tion will not be necessary." But Williams concedes that these attitudes can support "toleration as a matter of practice." Bernard Williams, "Toleration: An Impossible Virtue?" *Toleration: An Elusive Virtue,* supra note 19 at 18, 25, 20.

24. For an elaboration of the point, see Steven D. Smith, "Skepticism, Tolerance, and Truth in the Theory of Free Expression," *Southern California Law Review* 60 (1987), 685–89.

25. Cf. Jonathan Harrison, "Utilitarianism and Toleration," 62 *Philosophy* (1987), 425 (presenting as rationale for toleration the claim that "[p]reventing wrong is always expensive, involving paying policemen and detectives and lawyers and prison wardens, and the money may be better spent").

26. Cf. Fletcher, supra note 19 at 162 ("Without these ultimate values, . . . the basis for tolerance collapses."). See also Williams, supra note 23 at 25 (arguing that "it is only a substantive view of goods such as autonomy that could yield the value that is expressed by the practices of toleration").

27. Brad S. Gregory, *Salvation at Stake: Christian Martyrdom in Early Modern Europe* (Cambridge, Mass.: Harvard University Press, 1999), 85–86.

28. Cf. Jeremy Waldron, "Locke: Toleration and the Rationality of Persecution," *John Locke: A Letter Concerning Toleration in Focus* 120, John Horton and Susan Mendus eds. (New York: Routledge, 1991): "Censors, inquisitors and persecutors have usually known exactly what they were doing, and have had a fair idea of what they could hope to achieve. If our only charge against their enterprise [is that it was] hopeless and instrumentally irrational from the start, then we perhaps betray only our ignorance of their methods and objectives, and the irrelevance of our liberalism to their concerns." See also Steven H. Resnicoff, "Professional Ethics and Autonomy," *Law and Religion* 329, 334, Richard O'Dair and Andrew Lewis, eds. (New York: Oxford University Press, 2001) (emphasis added, footnotes omitted):

> In a society governed by Jewish law, rabbinic leaders would use coercion—including physical force if necessary—to induce an individual to perform a commandment requiring a specific action. . . . Jewish law believes that a person is metaphysically affected by his deeds. Fulfillment of a commandment, even if not done for the right reason, leads a person to performing more commandments and, *ultimately, to doing so for the right reason.* . . . Thus, such coercion leads to the coerced individual's ultimate perfection.

29. Habermas, supra note 6 at 4.

30. Id. at 5.

31. Indeed, on the not implausible assumption that these religions teach contradictory doctrines (or even explicitly assert the falsehood of the others), it is hard to see how anyone could view them as relevantly equivalent except perhaps by regarding them all as false, or at least by declining to take the propositional content of their teachings at face value in the way the believers themselves typically do. Very likely the popularity of the reciprocity rationale in recent times reflects some such attitude.

32. See the virtual libraries of work by and about John Rawls.

33. See Forst, supra note 7 at 196–97.

34. Williams, supra note 23 at 26–27.

35. Cf. Fletcher, supra note 19 (explaining "instability" of tolerance).

36. Thus, George Fletcher observes that "we would all prefer to have our religion, our political views, or our sexual orientation respected rather than merely tolerated." Fletcher, id. at 159. In a similar vein, John Horton remarks on "the frequently observed pattern that what begins, when people are faced with intolerance, as a demand for toleration becomes transformed into a demand for more than *mere* toleration." John Horton, "Toleration as a Virtue," *Toleration: An Elusive Virtue,* supra note 19 at 28, 35–36.

37. Michael Walzer, *On Toleration* (New Haven, Conn.: Yale University Press, 1997), 52.

38. Thomas Paine, "The Rights of Man," *Reflections on the Revolution in France and The Rights of Man* (Garden City, N.Y.: Anchor Press/Doubleday, 1973), 267, 324 (emphasis in original).

39. See John T. Noonan, Jr., *The Luster of Our Country: The American Experience of Religious Freedom* (Berkeley: University of California Press, 1998), 69–70.

40. Cf. John Rawls, *Political Liberalism* (New York: Columbia University Press, 1996), 31 ("[Citizens] may regard it as simply unthinkable to view themselves apart from certain religious, philosophical, and moral convictions").

41. See Kent Greenawalt, "Viewpoints from Olympus," *Columbia Law Review* 96 (1996), 698.

42. See, e.g., *Lynch v. Donnelly,* 465 U.S. 668, 687–88 (1984) (O'Connor, J., concurring).

43. For my own attempts to show the errors of ultraliberalism, see, e.g., Steven D. Smith, "*Barnette*'s Big Blunder," *Chicago-Kent Law Review* 78 (2003), 625; Steven D. Smith, "Believing Persons, Personal Believings: The Neglected Center of the First Amendment," *University of Illinois Law Review* (2002), 1233; and Steven D. Smith, "The Restoration of Tolerance," 78 *California Law Review* (1990), 305.

44. Inconsistencies arise, however, under a strong version of the claim

that persons are *constituted by* their beliefs, so that an agent who rejects inegalitarian *beliefs,* for example, would be deemed to be treating *persons who hold those beliefs* with less respect. The claim that persons are constituted by their beliefs, though intuitively appealing on some levels, also seems highly problematic; but this problem lies beyond the scope of this essay.

45. Cf. Larry Alexander, "Illiberalism All the Way Down: Illiberal Groups and Two Conceptions of Liberalism," *Journal of Contemporary Legal Issues* 12 (2002), 625, 626 ("As individuals, we cannot be 'neutral' about what is good and what is true. To live is to make choices—to pick A over B because we prefer A, or value A, or believe A to be right.").

46. Thus, Andrew Koppelman argues that in the midst of raging controversies about the meaning of religious freedom it is nonetheless a secure "axiom" that the "Establishment Clause forbids the state from declaring religious truth." Andrew Koppelman, "Secular Purpose," *Virginia Law Review* 88 (2002), 87, 108. Kent Greenawalt concurs that "[t]he core idea that the government may not make determinations of religious truth is firmly entrenched." Kent Greenawalt, "Five Questions about Religion Judges Are Afraid to Ask," *Obligations of Citizenship and Demands of Faith,* Nancy L. Rosenblum, ed. (Princeton, N.J.: Princeton University Press, 2000), 196, 197. See also Douglas Laycock, "Equal Access and Moments of Silence: The Equal Status of Religious Speech by Private Speakers," *Northwestern University Law Review* 81 (1986), 1, 7. ("In my view, the establishment clause absolutely disables the government from taking a position for or against religion. . . . The government must have no opinion because it is not the government's role to have an opinion.").

47. See Rawls, supra note 40 at 214.

48. Cf. Ronald Dworkin, *Law's Empire* (Cambridge, Mass: Belknap Press, 1986), 172 (arguing that "the community can adopt and express and be faithful or unfaithful to principles of its own, distinct from those of any of its officials or citizens as individuals").

49. Though the domain of obligatory "public reason" in Rawls's theorizing seems to have shrunk over the years as Rawls responded to objections by introducing various qualifications, see, e.g., "The Idea of Public Reason Revisited," reprinted in John Rawls, *The Law of Peoples* (Cambridge, Mass.: Harvard University Press, 1999), 133–35. Rawls also quietly acknowledged that if the notion of public reason is viable and attractive then the progression *ought* to run the other way—toward a *larger* scope of application. See Rawls, *Political Liberalism,* supra note 40 at 215:

> Some will ask: why not say that all questions in regard to which citizens exercise their final and coercive political power over one another are subject to public reason? Why would it ever be admissible

to go outside its range of political values? To answer: my aim is to consider first the strongest case where the political questions concern the most fundamental matters. If we should not honor the limits of public reason here, it would seem we need not honor them anywhere. Should they hold here, we can then proceed to other cases. Still, I grant that it is usually highly desirable to settle political questions by invoking the values of public reason.

50. Cf. Michael J. Perry, "Morality," *Politics and Law* (New York: Oxford University Press, 1988), 181–82:

> One's basic moral/religious convictions are (partly) self-constitutive and are therefore a principal ground—indeed, the principal ground—of political deliberation and choice. To "bracket" such convictions is therefore to bracket—to annihilate—essential aspects of one's very self. To participate in politics and law—in particular, to make law, or break law, or to interpret law—with such convictions bracketed is not to participate as the self one is but as some one—or, rather, some thing—else.

51. Thus, John Tomasi observes that "[p]olitical norms, even gently and indirectly, cannot help but shape the character of people in their own image." Consequently, "[l]iberals have increasingly recognized that liberal institutions unavoidably influence the ethical worldviews of all reasonable citizens." John Tomasi, *Liberalism Beyond Justice* (Princeton, N.J.: Princeton University Press, 2001), 11, 14.

52. *Gertz v. Robert Welch,* 418 U.S. 323, 339 (1974).

53. Quoted in Tomasi, supra note 51 at 14.

54. Alexander, supra note 45 at 631.

55. Ronald Beiner, *Philosophy in a Time of Lost Spirit* (Toronto: University of Toronto Press, 1997), 55.

56. Id. at 12.

57. Contrary to initial appearances, these phenomena—that is, the lack of and the excess of conviction—are not necessarily contradictory; they may even be complementary. See Martin Marty, *The Public Church* (New York: Crossroad, 1981), 134–35:

> Fanaticisms, including twentieth-century totalitarianisms, grow on the soil of those who lack conviction, until the worst, filled with passionate intensity, take them over. People who live in a culture of *anomie,* normlessness, fall victim to the assertions of every kind of norm. Victims of *accedia,* the inability to affirm in the face of spiritual good, are vacuums ready to be filled by the most potent pourers. To leave a spiritual void by touting weak faith or wan commit-

ment in a pluralist society is to invite the overcoming of pluralism by any demagogue who has a convincing manner and promise.

58. James Davison Hunter, *Culture Wars* (New York: Basic Books, 1991).

59. Ibid., 44–45, 71, 44 (emphasis in original). Hunter elaborates:

> Such objective and transcendent authority defines, at least in the abstract, a consistent, unchangeable measure of value, purpose, goodness, and identity, both personal and collective. It tells us what is good, what is true, how we should live, and who we are. It is an authority sufficient for all time.

Id.

60. Id. at 128.

61. Id. at 156.

62. I understand Professor Forst to take this position, see Rainer Forst, "Toleration and Truth," this volume ("That decisions should not be based on reciprocally contested beliefs for which no side can give mutually non-rejectable arguments does not mean that such views would not be allowed in the public realm" [289]); Rawls's "proviso" and "wide view" are to similar effect. Rawls, *Political Liberalism,* supra note 40 at li–lii.

63. See, e.g., *Edwards v. Aguillard,* 482 U.S. 578 (1987) (striking down "Balanced Treatment" statute because of impermissible religious purpose inferred from legislator's statements); *Wallace v. Jaffree,* 472 U.S. 38 (1985) (invalidating "moment of silence" law on similar grounds).

64. Daniel A. Farber, "Missing the 'Play of Intelligence,'" *William and Mary Law Review* 36 (1994), 147, 157. For a collection of similar judgments by scholars from all points of the political and jurisprudential spectrum, see Steven D. Smith, *The Constitution and the Pride of Reason* (New York: Oxford University Press, 1998), 125–26.

65. See, e.g., *Lawrence v. Texas,* 539 U.S., 123 Supreme Court 2472, 2496–97 (2003); *United States v. Virginia,* 518 U.S. 515, 566–67 (1996); *Planned Parenthood v. Casey,* 505 U.S. 833, 979 (1992).

66. Robert F. Nagel, *Judicial Power and American Character* (New York: Oxford University Press, 1994), 126, 128, 129.

67. Samuel P. Huntington, *The Clash of Civilizations* (New York: Touchstone, 1997), 41 ("Civilization and culture both refer to the overall way of life of a people, and a civilization is a culture writ large.").

68. Id. at 69–72.

69. Id. at 81–91, 305–308.

70. Id. at 209.

71. Id. at 305. See also id. at 311 (Western civilization's distinctive "values and institutions . . . include most notably its Christianity, pluralism, individualism, and the rule of law.").

72. Id. at 306–7.

73. For example, although Christianity has surely been historically important in the development of Western civilization, it is arguable that its political significance in promoting the values of rule of law and human rights has derived not so much from its distinctively *Christian* theology as from its capacity to carry, support, and develop a *classical* natural law tradition. See, e.g., John Courtney Murray, S.J., *We Hold These Truths* (New York: Sheed and Ward, 1960). And the recent international politics surrounding the Iraq war may subvert Huntington's depiction of a substantially unified "Western" civilization.

74. A common and plausible objection to Huntington's position observes that non-Western cultures and nations are not monolithic: many persons in such cultures and nations favor "liberal" values such as democracy and human rights. The observation is surely correct. But of course, as discussed, Western cultures and nations are not monolithic either, which is why "liberal" commitments (and especially particular versions of those commitments) are in need of defense for internal purposes.

75. Cf. Alan Levine, "Introduction: The Prehistory of Toleration and Varieties of Skepticism," *Early Modern Skepticism* (Lanham, Md.: Lexington Books, 1999), 4: "Far from attempting to justify liberalism to outsiders or on first principles, Rorty and Rawls prefer not to take up the challenge. Content to harmonize our pre-existing opinions, they do not and cannot address the fundamental challenges that Nietzsche, for example, poses."

76. See generally Ronald Dworkin, *Sovereign Virtue* (Cambridge, Mass.: Harvard University Press, 2000).

77. George Fletcher, "In God's Image: The Religious Imperative of Equality Under Law," *Columbia Law Review* 99 (1999), 1612–13 (citations omitted).

78. George P. Fletcher, *Secret Constitution* (New York: Oxford University Press, 2001), 95.

79. Id. at 102.

80. See also Louis Pojman, "On Equal Human Worth: A Critique of Contemporary Egalitarianism," in *Equality: Selected Readings,* Louis P. Pojman and Robert Westmoreland, eds. (New York: Oxford University Press, 1997), 295 ("The argument implicit in the Judeo-Christian tradition seems to be that God is the ultimate value and that humans derive their value by being created in his image and likeness.").

81. Id. at 295. For a careful argument in the same vein focusing not on equality *per se* but on the equally fundamental idea of human rights, see Michael J. Perry, *The Idea of Human Rights: Four Inquiries* (New York: Oxford University Press, 1998), 11–41.

82. The first argument holds that "God created all humans with an

equal amount of some property P, which constitutes high value." The second argument suggests that "actual value may be different in different people but grace compensates the difference." Pojman, supra note 77 at 295.

83. A dramatic example is the controversial Ninth Circuit decision in *Newdow v. United States Congress,* 292 F.3d 597 (9th Cir. 2002), reversed, *Elk Grove Unified School District v. Newdow,* 542 U.S. 1 (2004), invalidating the phrase "under God" in the Pledge of Allegiance: the phrase "one nation, under God" comes of course from the same speech—the Gettysburg Address—in which Lincoln asserted that "this Nation under God" was "dedicated to the proposition that all men are created equal."

84. Fletcher, *Secret Constitution,* supra note 75 at 95–96.

85. Pojman, supra note 77 at 283–94. Pojman concludes that egalitarian commitments are "simply a leftover from a religious world view now rejected by all of the philosophers discussed in this essay." Id. at 283. Secular egalitarians are free riders, living off an inheritance they view with disdain. And he wonders whether "perhaps we should abandon egalitarianism and devise political philosophies that reflect naturalistic assumptions, theories which are forthright in viewing humans as differentially talented animals who must get on together." Id. at 296.

86. Waldron argues that Locke's commitment to equality was firmly based in religious assumptions, and that modern efforts to support the commitment have not to this point succeeded. See generally Jeremy Waldron, *God, Locke, and Equality* (New York: Cambridge University Press, 2002). Waldron's concluding observations sound faintly ominous:

> [M]aybe the notion of humans as one another's equals will begin to fall apart, under pressure, without the presence of the religious conception that shaped it. . . . Locke believed this general acceptance [of equality] was impossible apart from the principle's foundation in religious teaching. We believe otherwise. Locke, I suspect, would have thought we were taking a risk. And I am afraid it is not entirely clear, given our experience of a world and a century in which politics and public reason have cut loose from these foundations, that his cautions and suspicions were unjustified.

Id. at 243.

87. Patrick McKinley Brennan, "Arguing for Human Equality," *Journal Law and Religious* 18 (2002), 121.

88. "Why Aren't Muslims Like Us?" *First Things* (June/July 2003), 60–61.

10

TOLERATION AND TRUTH: COMMENTS ON STEVEN D. SMITH

RAINER FORST

I.

Toleration is a concept full of paradoxes, normative as well as epistemological. How can it be right to tolerate what is wrong or bad? How can I be convinced that my beliefs are true and yet also believe it to be true that I should tolerate those beliefs which are not true?

There are (at least) three prominent answers to these questions.[1] First, the *skeptical* solution (or rather, evasion of the problem): there is no sufficiently justified belief in the truth or untruth of said beliefs; and among reasonable people in such an epistemological predicament, toleration is the normative conclusion that follows. Second, there is the *dualistic* approach (which comes in various forms): the truth of, say, my religious beliefs is one thing, and the truth of my normative commitments to toleration quite another. Reasons connected to the latter tell me why it is right—or even demanded—to tolerate what is wrong as seen from the first perspective. Finally, there are *monistic* positions: it is one and the same belief system that gives me reasons both to disapprove of certain beliefs or practices and to tolerate them nevertheless.

Such a system of beliefs can be of a religious or "liberal" or some other nature.

In his impressive and challenging chapter, ranging from a conceptual and normative discussion of a number of arguments for (and against) toleration to a cultural-sociological discussion of the present predicament of American liberalism, both internally and externally, Steven D. Smith argues against the first two approaches for a particular, complex version of the third one. He opts for a form of monistic liberalism that is closer to Locke than to Kant or Mill (or contemporary Kantians and Millians), one that generates its inner strength from knowing its particular ethical-religious roots and that can be tolerant because of that rootedness. This can be phrased in terms of another paradox—which for Smith is only apparent—that liberal toleration of religion must itself be justified on the basis of religious beliefs. In my brief comments, I will discuss some of the problems I see with this intriguing view and present some arguments for a certain form of the second, dualistic approach.

II.

I should start by saying that I agree with Smith's critique of the first, skeptical solution. Not only does it try to evade the main problem too easily, but there also is no natural way from skepticism to toleration, for it can also lead to social and religious conservatism, as in Montaigne and Lipsius, or to intolerance towards those skeptical of skepticism. Hence I also believe that we should look for a "kind of tolerance that is compatible with (and indeed derived from) the affirmation of truth" (271). More specifically, I am in agreement with Smith on

(a) the need for a conception of toleration that does not sacrifice the tolerant person's belief in the truth of his or her ethical or religious doctrine but rather presents normative reasons for toleration that a religious believer can accept. This means that

(b) such reasons must not rest on a skeptical epistemology or on a "neutralist" standpoint that—in a self-defeating way—doubts the truth of its own moral stance.

Yet I disagree with Smith's main thesis, which is that

(c) the "orthodoxy" that grounds toleration cannot rest on some "universal" norms—which Smith sees as an illusion—but rather on the self-conscious affirmation of the "liberal" or, more specifically, "American creed" consisting of a firm belief in the truth of sentences like "all men are created equal," knowing that there can be no secular *ersatz* for the religious grounding of such a creed.

My central argument is that this main thesis (c) is a possible, but not the only and not the best conclusion based on premises (a) and (b). Thus my counter-thesis is, to be sure, not that there can be no toleration of religions that is itself based on a particular, Christian moral stance. Rather, my thesis is that this is an insufficient basis for a justifiable form of democratic toleration in a pluralist society, where we need a general argument for the duty of toleration as well as its limits. It seems to me that Smith's position, according to which liberal toleration of religions presupposes a kind of religious liberalism, harbors the danger that this very ground will necessarily limit the possibilities of toleration in a problematic way.

These are large and complex issues, and in these brief comments, I cannot do more than present a few short arguments for my critique and counter-proposal.[2]

III.

As far as Smith's first section on the "Elements of Toleration" is concerned, I want to note two things. First, if we distinguish (as we should) three kinds of reasons characteristic of a judgment of toleration—reasons of *objection* to a certain practice or belief, reasons of *acceptance* that say why the false or wrong beliefs or practices still should be tolerated, and reasons of *rejection,* marking the limits of toleration[3]—Smith's analysis seems to presuppose that all of those reasons have only one source: what he terms the "base position" or "orthodoxy." Yet at this point of conceptual analysis, we should allow for the possibility that there is more than one source for such reasons, i.e., that there could be religious reasons of objection to a belief and yet other, moral reasons for toleration. A dualistic position cannot be ruled out from the start by way of conceptual argument.

Second, it is noteworthy that the agent of toleration Smith focuses on is "the state" (or "government") and that therefore the state itself judges certain views or ideas from a "base position" (244). Hence from the start we find toleration to be an issue not primarily *between citizens* but *between the state and certain individuals or groups the views of which the state judges as being false or wrong* yet—given certain considerations—still within the realm of the tolerable. By definition, the structure is a vertical one, not one of horizontal, reciprocal relations.[4] This leaves open the possibility that the state's "orthodoxy" is a religious one and that its tolerance is reduced to not forcing this orthodoxy on (certain) citizens who have different beliefs, for example because it is believed that forcing the conscience of others is a sin before God—very much the same way as was historically the case in the Edict of Nantes (1598) or the Toleration Act (1689). Hence I doubt that such a scheme already deserves the (admittedly quite vague) name of "liberalism" (as counter-posed to "illiberal" and "ultraliberal" views), for surely the early Augustine already believed in such an argument.[5] If we look for a "liberal" scheme of toleration, we need to say more about the way the distinctions between the three categories of the orthodox, the tolerable and the intolerable are being made.

IV.

This is exactly what we find in Smith's next section on arguments against and for toleration. I agree with his discussion of arguments against the claim that possession of the truth legitimates the use of force on non-believers, and I also think that he rightly highlights the strengths and weaknesses of the arguments that have been given, both epistemological (such as the argument for skepticism) and normative, such as the one about the voluntariness of faith. The later Augustine had refuted this argument long before Jonas Proast did so in his debate with Locke, and much in the same way: it is not true that conscience cannot be brought to the truth by the proper use of force, for even if we cannot produce inner convictions directly by external force, we can liberate men with the help of *terror* (Augustine) from their false beliefs and then instruct them in the right way, so that they can find their own way to the one and only truth (we present them with). Blocking the road of error with "thorns and briars" (Proast)[6] is a way of leading human beings to the path of truth and inner conviction. And more than that, the true believer has a duty to do so, not just for the sake of those who might be infected in the future (*haeresis est infectivum vitium,* as Aquinas said), but also for those who already are infected and could lose their eternal life. Ultimately, of course, these are all duties one owes to God, not primarily to human beings.

At this point, however, I diverge from Smith's position and turn to Pierre Bayle, while Smith dismisses his approach. Since I explain my interpretation of Bayle in my article in this volume, I will be brief here. He presents a reflexive normative argument for toleration combined with an epistemological one. The approach does indeed, as Smith notes, rest on what we can call the principle of reciprocity, or better yet the principle of reciprocal justification, which Bayle takes to be a higher-order principle that cannot be reasonably contested. Now the reason for Smith's rejection of such a theory is that, according to him, Bayle's call for reciprocal restraint in the face of irresolvable religious disagreement rests on a dubious, seemingly skeptical premise: "that the religions are relevantly similar" (254) with respect to the truth. Smith argues (a) that such a skeptical stance does not do justice to what it means to believe in the truth of one's doctrine and (b) that the idea that there could be a mutual willingness among citizens to "act only on universally acceptable grounds" is a "pleasant illusion" (255).

These arguments go to the core of my own views on toleration, and I disagree with both of them. First, Smith rightly points out that Bayle's reciprocity argument does require an epistemological premise, a "relativization" of the truth claim of religions. Yet the argument that Bayle presents is not—contrary to what many think about him—a "skeptical" argument. Rather, it is an argument about the difference between *faith* and *knowledge,* an argument for a distinction between two kinds of truth claims: those that can be finally decided by the means of "natural reason" alone, and those that are allowed for but not clearly decidable by reason, but ultimately by faith. About the latter, there can be and there will be what Rawls calls "reasonable disagreement":[7] disagreement about beliefs that are being held as true for reasons that are *not contrary* to reason but "*beyond* reason" (*dessus de la raison,* as Bayle says)[8] in the sense that among finite reasonable beings there can be no "proof" of that truth. Yet what is important to see is that this is *not skepticism*; you have good reasons to believe your religion to be the right one and superior to the others, just so long as you see it for what it is: religious faith. According to Bayle, those who would give up their faith because of that, i.e., because they cannot prove its truth in a demonstrative way, are not good believers.[9]

As far as Smith's second point with respect to the normative principle of reciprocity is concerned, I would hold with Bayle that the best case for toleration is a combination of the above-mentioned epistemological argument with a normative principle of reciprocal justification: any use of force has to be mutually justifiable, and religious reasons that are disputed among the relevant parties are not good reasons for forcing others to act in a certain way (or believe certain things). Such a principle of justification Bayle sees as a principle of practical "natural" reason, of "natural light" which "enlightens all spirits," whether they belong to a specific faith or not.[10] Here is where I find the normative "truth" I would see as a ground for toleration: the truth of a principle of practical reason in light of which every person has a "right to justification," as I call it, a right to be given adequate reasons for norms to which he or she is supposed to be subject. It is a reflexive truth, for it is presupposed by those who seriously engage in the controversy over the grounds and limits of toleration respecting others as persons worthy of equal respect.

As I see it, there are two reasons for Smith's rejection of such a principle or right. Either it is the combination of that principle with skepticism and the view that skepticism fails in the face of religious beliefs—a combination that does not exist, as I tried to show—or it is the argument that such a principle of reciprocity is not generally acceptable, as a matter of fact, given the higher order "deep pluralism" not just of religious beliefs, but also of conceptions of justice and morality (255). Yet, at this point, Smith's argument seems to shift significantly: So far, the question has been what the superior *normative* argument for toleration is; now the question seems to be which argument, empirically speaking, is generally accepted, or rather actually acceptable in given circumstances, as the argument proceeds. But this change of argument seems to commit a particular kind of naturalistic fallacy, a shift from the sphere of "ought" and "ought not" to the sphere of "is" and "is not" *and back* such that from the assumption of a factual nonexistence of a moral consensus on the principle of reciprocity it is inferred that the principle in dispute has no claim to be morally valid. Yet this is an invalid inference: morality is about the legitimate solution of conflicts and can thus hardly expect to be beyond conflict; general *acceptability* is what morality aims at, but general *acceptance* is not what constitutes it. I have reason to believe that Smith would agree with that, for as I said the main point of his argument is that we must hold onto moral truth—in a counterfactual, objective sense—if toleration is a to have a firm grounding.

Hence the grounding I suggest is a Baylean-Kantian one: an epistemological argument for "reasonable disagreement" that does not sacrifice religious truth claims—in line with point (a) in section II above—and a moral argument for reciprocal justification, i.e., a "freestanding" principle of respect (and, I would add, but cannot argue here, of practical reason). This accords to point (b) in section II above.

V.

Such a justification of toleration does not, I believe, fall into the category of a self-defeating "ultraliberalism," for the basic moral right to justification clearly is a substantive moral principle. And as compared to the conception of toleration that Smith proposes, one that is ultimately based on religious truth, the one I suggest has two major advantages.

The first advantage is that its notion of "equal respect" has a closer connection to the idea of democratic self-government. This avoids the problem alluded to above (section III), that Smith's conception seems to allow for a religious majority, even if democratically formed, to dominate basic political institutions and deny minorities equal standing within them (though tolerating these groups, as long as they accept their inferior status). Toleration would not mean that "the state" or dominant majorities "put up with" minorities without granting them equal status in the law (think of homosexual marriage, religious symbols in the classroom, etc.)—which is not, to be sure, what Smith argues for, but it is a potential danger I see in his conception. Toleration, rather, would mean that in the case of religious disagreement, both sides, majority and minority, see that their reasons are insufficient to be the basis for general legal norms regulating basic social and political institutions. Democracy, I agree, is government "of the people, by the people, for the people" (259), yet that does not mean that majorities have the right to make their religious views the basis of general law, if basic institutions are concerned. Contrary to Smith's critique of an "ultraliberal" notion of democracy, this is what democracy means: rule by mutually justifiable norms.[11] This is a fundamental demand of democratic justice.

Such a notion of democracy encounters two of Smith's important critical arguments, that of the "impoverished soul" and that of "impoverished discourse" in the public realm (261–69). Against the first argument, I believe that it is not an impoverishment but rather an enrichment of the "soul" if a person, in her full identity as person *and* citizen, keeps holding fast to her beliefs and still sees that it would be wrong if all those like her, say, all "Smiths," would impose their religious beliefs on all the others, say, the "Millers," by making those beliefs the basis of general legal norms. Every such "Smith" remains committed to his or her beliefs, yet sharing a belief in *justice* with all others, he or she acts in a tolerant way. One does not have to shed one's identity in order to be tolerant and accept the borders of mutual justification; rather, this is part of one's overall moral identity. There is no schizophrenia involved here. You can, of course, firmly believe that the cross is a symbol of the true faith, yet you can at the same time firmly believe that in a pluralistic society it would be wrong to have it put up in classrooms of public schools by law.[12] Ultimately, then, the dualistic approach I defend has to be able to provide a comprehensive and complex view of a moral person who sees him- or herself within different contexts of justification, knowing what kinds of reasons are good reasons in a given practical context.[13] A dualistic view does not split people's minds; what it does is explain the insight that I may be convinced of the truth of certain values, constituting what it means to live a good and worthy life, and yet know that for reasons of justice and respect I must not impose this view on others who disagree with these values. I know that in order to have the authority to subject them to certain norms, I need moral arguments of a different, a stronger kind. I "owe" them mutually acceptable reasons.

Political discourse in such a society would not be impoverished, either, for such forms of mutual toleration presuppose that one knows the other's point of view and argues against it; tolerating them requires knowing what one dislikes about them. The public forum would in no way be empty. That decisions should not be based on reciprocally contested religious beliefs, for which no side can give mutually non-rejectable arguments, does not mean that such views would not be allowed in the public realm. Rather, it is a matter of political fairness that they are—just as the demand for justified toleration is a matter of fairness.

VI.

The second advantage of my conception of toleration over Smith's approach concerns the issue of moral foundations. From a Baylean-Kantian perspective, the attempt to ground toleration on religious "truths" like "all men are created equal in the image of God" is haunted by problems that lead us back into the historical struggles for toleration—and that require us to look for an alternative normative framework by learning the lessons of that history. Let me mention two important considerations in that respect.

(a) It was a long and painful process in European history to establish the idea of the independent moral worth of a "human being" *without* seeing that being primarily in the light of divine creation. For as long as the latter was the case, human beings had the highest duty to honor their creator and to observe his laws. The religious idea of "human dignity" did not exclude atheists and heretics by accident: they were seen as betraying their own creator and appeared as not morally trustworthy; in an important sense, they were morally illiterate. A secular notion of human dignity is by no means easy to establish philosophically,[14] yet the attempt to do so has good historical and philosophical reasons. For to ground moral respect in a religious framework at the same time means to limit and qualify it. After all, it is the care for the soul that is the main concern for a Christian, and every moral duty first and foremost is a duty owed to God. Any argument for the moral respect of the autonomy of human beings has to be constructed on that basis and cannot be an independent one.

(b) This is not to deny, of course, that there can be an identity between one's "most fundamental beliefs" (269) as a religious believer and as a "liberal," i.e., that the commitment to liberalism can be grounded in a commitment to God. And if that is the case, toleration may be based on beliefs like that of the freedom of conscience or other considerations. Yet, if one's religious beliefs and one's liberal commitments part company in a given conflict, where the former say "X is God's will," while the latter say "X is incompatible with liberal principles," and if these very principles have their *foundation* in religion—what will then take priority? At this point, orthodoxy may turn orthodox and religious liberalism return to religion; and contrary to Smith, who discusses this risk and sees it as not very "serious" (270), I think such conflicts show the problem of religious arguments for toleration: they end where the "fundamentals" are concerned but it seems that the conflicts where they are concerned are precisely the conflicts where we need toleration the most. Toleration is the virtue that is required when one's fundamental beliefs are challenged, at which point we would hope that persons have a "most fundamental" belief that they owe each other mutual respect, apart from what God seems to demand. Otherwise, there is no shared language of justice or of the duty of toleration—or, of the critique of acts of intolerance as morally wrong. With Bayle, I do not believe that it is a vain dream of reason to argue for such a common viewpoint;[15] rather, it is the real lesson that the history of conflicts over freedom and toleration teaches us: that there is a "truth" in the principle of reciprocal justification and the right to be respected equally that lies on a different level than a clash of religious truths. The idea that both the reflexive principle of mutual justification for norms that are to be generally binding (and that claim to be mutually justifiable), on the one hand, and a religious conviction about the nature and will of God, on the other, are "creeds" that lie on the same level of justification and contestation strikes me as a form of "ultraliberal" relativism that is impossible to defend.

VII.

Though I cannot go into it here, this may also be what we have to keep in mind when we are "looking outward" to the conflicts on the global level, to the so-called clash of civilizations. Here I find a position that advocates the affirmation of an "American creed" that is at the same time universalist and culturally "thick" (and local) potentially self-defeating and quite problematic, especially with regard to the question of the "extension" of such values to "other communities characterized by other cultures" (266). Even if it is true that in intercultural conflicts it is important to be aware of one's own values and principles and their limitations, it is also true that solutions to such conflicts call for the construction of a common normative basis that is mutually justifiable. And thus the idea of mutual justification itself should be good starting point.

NOTES

1. Historically and systematically speaking, there are more than these three approaches to toleration, such as those concerned with pragmatic and strategic considerations. For an analysis of the variety of justifications for toleration from early Christianity onwards, see my *Toleranz im Konflikt. Geschichte, Gehalt und Gegenwart eines umstrittenen Begriffs* (Frankfurt/Main: Suhrkamp, 2003), part one.

2. As fully developed in Forst, *Toleranz im Konflikt,* part two. Briefer versions of the main arguments are to be found in my "Toleration, Justice and Reason," in Catriona McKinnon and Dario Castiglione (eds.), *The Culture of Toleration in Diverse Societies* (Manchester: Manchester UP, 2003), 71–85, "Tolerance as a Virtue of Justice," *Philosophical Explorations* 4, 2001, 193–206, and "The Limits of Toleration," *Constellations* 11, 2004, 312–325.

3. For this analysis of toleration, see my "Toleration, Justice and Reason," 71f. See also the analysis of the components of "objection" and "acceptance" by Preston King, *Toleration* (New York: St. Martin's Press, 1976), ch. 1. Glen Newey, *Virtue, Reason and Toleration* (Edinburgh: Edinburgh UP, 1999), ch. 1, also distinguishes between three kinds of reasons in his analysis of the structure of toleration.

4. On this point, see the distinction between a "permission conception" of toleration and a "respect conception" in "Toleration, Justice and Reason," 73–76.

5. I discuss Augustine's arguments against and (later) for religious force in my "Pierre Bayle's Reflexive Theory of Toleration," this volume 78–113.

6. Jonas Proast, *The Argument of the Letter Concerning Toleration,* reprint of the edition of 1690 (New York: Garland, 1984), 10.

7. See John Rawls, *Political Liberalism* (New York: Columbia University Press, 1993), 54–66. Also Charles Larmore, "Pluralism and Reasonable Disagreement," in *The Morals of Modernity* (Cambridge: Cambridge University Press, 1996), ch. 7.

8. Pierre Bayle, *Historical and Critical Dictionary,* Selections, tr. by Richard H. Popkin (Indianapolis: Hackett, 1991), 410.

9. Ibid., 429.

10. Pierre Bayle, *Philosophical Commentary,* tr. Amie Godman Tannenbaum (New York: Lang, 1987), 31.

11. See my "The Rule of Reasons. Three Models of Deliberative Democracy," *Ratio Juris* 14, 2001, 345–78.

12. I refer here to a famous case in Bavaria, more fully discussed in Forst, "A Tolerant Republic?," in: Jan-Werner Müller (ed.), *German Ideologies Since 1945* (New York: Palgrave Macmillan, 2003), 209–20.

13. On this point, see my *Contexts of Justice: Political Philosophy Beyond Liberalism and Communitarianism,* tr. J. M. M. Farrell (Berkeley: University of California Press, 2002), esp. ch. 5.

14. For such an attempt, see my "Moral Autonomy and the Autonomy of Morality: Toward a Theory of Normativity After Kant," *Graduate Faculty Philosophy Journal* 26, 2005, 65–88.

15. For a different view, see Jeremy Waldron, "Toleration and Reasonableness," in McKinnon and Castiglione (eds.), *The Culture of Toleration in Diverse Societies,* op. cit., 13–37.

11

HOW IMPOVERISHING IS LIBERALISM? A COMMENT ON STEVEN D. SMITH

GLYN MORGAN

Professor Steven Smith's splendidly provocative and highly original chapter challenges "political liberals" who counsel us not to take sides—at least in our capacity as citizens—in the conflict between enlightenment and counter-enlightenment values.[1] Smith fears that this "ultraliberal position" (his idiosyncratic term for "political liberalism") exercises a baleful influence both on our private and civic lives. The nub of this argument is contained in the following passage:

> The preceding discussion has described two sorts of impoverishment that seem to afflict at least parts of contemporary culture: a sort of spiritual impoverishment (or *impoverishment of the soul*) manifested in an inability to hold and affirm convictions of the kind that arguably are central to what makes human life distinctively meaningful and valuable, and an *impoverishment of discourse* that renders us incapable of engaging our most fundamental convictions and differences or of defending our most fundamental commitments. My argument has been that this unfortunate condition is *a direct result* of the commitment to an ultraliberal position that tells us, in essence, that when "We the People" are

> acting in a public capacity, we are not supposed to affirm our most fundamental beliefs–not overtly, at least. (emphasis added)[2]

Smith wants to solve these problems of impoverishment by replacing today's ultraliberal polity—a polity that respects equally all reasonable beliefs—with a tolerant polity—a polity that affirms the belief-system of the majority while accommodating others. This solution is considerably more controversial than it initially seems, not least because Smith adopts a very narrow view of what toleration entails.[3] For Smith, a tolerant polity can act on the basis of a set of substantive beliefs—an "orthodoxy"—so long as it allows dissent and does not seek to suppress non-orthodox beliefs. A tolerant polity—in contrast to the ultraliberal polity—is not required to respect equally the (reasonable) beliefs of all individuals and groups. Indeed, a tolerant polity is not required to limit itself to enacting laws or pursuing policies that it can justify on neutral, public, or even secular grounds. Smith's tolerant polity is, in short, a polity that would permit state officials to appeal to and advance a substantive conception of the good. This tolerant polity offers, so Smith argues, a welcome "establishmentarian" alternative to the bogus neutrality of ultra- (or political) liberalism.[4]

While Smith offers toleration as his preferred alternative to "ultraliberalism," toleration, as Smith understands it, has no necessary connection to any liberal or individualist conception of the good. Toleration, as he understands it, presupposes a substantial, "base-line," conception of the good—an "orthodoxy."[5] But the more important—and the more troubling—point to recognize here is that Smith's chapter does not itself specify any *particular* base-line conception of the good. Smith appears to be so eager for an orthodoxy that he is not too troubled about which orthodoxy. True, he defends only those forms of orthodoxy that allow for toleration. Furthermore, the underlying arguments he offers in support of toleration—skepticism, indifference, voluntariness, and so forth—rule out a number of the more oppressive, totalizing orthodoxies. Nonetheless, his position allows for a wider range of "tolerant" orthodoxies than any liberal—whether political liberal or otherwise—could accept.

Although Smith does not develop his argument in this direction, his position could also be read as a defense of a more majoritarian form of democracy. It is important to recognize here, however, that this position would allow majorities to affirm their way of life, while recognizing only a very minimal form of "accommodation" to minorities. All of the following regimes would, I suspect, qualify as "tolerant" if we were to follow Smith's expansive usage of the term: Ireland (1937–94); Northern Ireland (1918–68); and twentieth century Quebec (prior to "the Quiet Revolution" of the 1960s). These regimes were all majoritarian democracies; they all protected a minimal set of rights; and they all permitted certain forms of dissent. But all of these regimes lacked any genuine separation of Church and State—and in some cases, *Ethnos* and State—and those members who shared the dominant orthodoxy derived a wide range of ideal and material benefits that were not available to the dissenting minority. Smith's defense of toleration amounts—whether he intends this to be the case or not—to a defense of this type of regime. His chapter (as I read it) seeks to persuade us that this type of regime has some important advantages over the impoverished "ultraliberal" regime advocated by political liberals.

After being regularly denounced by "pluralists" for their "civic totalism," political liberals will doubtless find Smith's attack on, what might be termed, their "civic nihilism" quite refreshing.[6] It is not my intention here, however, to defend political (or ultra-) liberalism. Indeed, I share some of Smith's misgivings about the use of the courts to block expressions of majority will. Instead, my remarks will focus merely on one core feature of Smith's argument; namely, his claim that political (or ultra) liberalism yields certain civic and personal impoverishments. I want to suggest that the recent history of the United States (the focus of Smith's chapter) suggests that this is not the case.

For Smith, political (or ultra-) liberalism requires the state to treat all people as equals; the ultraliberal state is thus not allowed to privilege one set of beliefs as elements of a substantial public orthodoxy. Political liberalism thereby prevents, so Smith argues, "We the People" from publicly affirming our most fundamental beliefs and commitments. It imposes a disjuncture between "Smith the Citizen" and "Smith the Person." The result is the impoverishment of citizenship and personhood. In a less impoverished "tolerant" democracy, the government of the day would be free to affirm its beliefs and commitments while merely *tolerating* dissenters. Smith illustrates our current ultraliberal plight with contemporary references to the domestic "cultural wars" between "secularists" and "theists" and the international conflict between the West and Islam.

The important point to recognize in this part of Smith's chapter is that his discussion of these problems will only support the defense of his preferred "tolerant polity" if these problems are genuine. They cannot simply be a part of a personal *Kulturkritik.* To be more precise, the dual impoverishments of "discourse" and "soul" must—if they are to do any real work in the argument—satisfy three conditions: (i) they must actually threaten the stability and survival of a liberal society; (ii) they must be plausibly related to "ultraliberalism"; and (iii) they must be remediable by "a tolerant polity." Yet, these "impoverishments" do not, I think, satisfy any of these conditions.

Let me begin first with the threats these "impoverishments" pose to the stability of a liberal society. Here it would be quite possible to allow that the ultraliberal polity does indeed prevent religious enthusiasts from employing the state to preserve, protect, or express their belief systems. But issues of fairness aside, this form of exclusion does not seem to pose any real threat to the social order. Even in the United States—the most religious modern democratic society—there is very little evidence to suggest that those who embrace theistic religion are alienated from their nominally "ultraliberal" polity. Nor is there much evidence that these people are losing their convictions and becoming nihilists. If anything, the United States suffers from an excess of deference to those beliefs designated "religious." This excess of deference shows up in the very idea of offering religious groups "exemptions" from general laws and in the social norm that discourages anyone from criticizing another's religion no matter how preposterous and pernicious. This social norm goes a long way, I suspect, to explaining the current impasse between "secularists" and "theists." But this is to invoke my own personal *Kulturkritik,* which possesses no greater authority than Smith's. The fact remains, however, that unless Smith can provide us with some sociological evidence to suggest that disgruntled religious groups pose a threat to the stability of a liberal society, then it is difficult to worry too much about the forms of exclusion built into ultraliberalism.

Even if we were to grant *arguendo* that religious groups are suffering from the two impoverishments that Smith mentions, it is far from obvious that these have any causal relationship to ultraliberalism. A more plausible explanation for these problems is modernity itself rather than the ultraliberal separation of Church and State. Here it is worth recalling that the impact of the bureaucratic state and the capitalist economy on the world's religions formed the great theme of Max Weber's sociology of religion.[7] Weber, like most of the classical social theorists of the last century, expected theistic religions to dissolve in the corrosive solution of modernity. He was wrong about this; he was especially wrong in the case of the United States. But any account of the fate of religion in the modern world will have to make some effort to disentangle the more general impact of modernity from the more particular impact of ultraliberalism. On the face of it, the ultraliberal polity of the United States seems to coincide with the maintenance rather than the erosion of religious belief. This fact does little to support Smith's case against ultraliberalism.

Finally, even if we were to accept Smith's critique of ultraliberalism, this critique only lends support to his preferred tolerant polity, insofar as that polity offers some remedies for the problems he has identified. Clearly, Smith seems to think that were the United States to become a tolerant polity that allowed the religious majority greater scope to affirm their beliefs, then the United States would be in a better position to respond to today's "serious cultural conflict on the global level."[8] Here Smith reiterates Samuel Huntington's call for the re-affirmation of "the American Creed," a creed that contains a strong religious component. Smith notes, however, that this re-affirmation would first require overcoming the paralysis imposed by the ultraliberal discourse of neutrality and equality.

This suggestion is alarming for a number of reasons. For one thing, it seems to ignore the very pronounced strain of religiosity that already informs US foreign policy—even under the alleged constraints of ultraliberalism. Thus we live in a polity with a President who informs us that his favorite philosopher is Jesus Christ;

an Attorney General who leads his senior officials in the singing of hymns; a leading public evangelist who proclaims that Muslims worship an evil religion; and the defense department's head of intelligence—one General William Boykin—who gives speeches around the country reporting that the American God is bigger than the Muslim God.[9] These events do not fit easily into any description of a United States paralyzed by neutrality and equality.

The idea that we can and ought to expect more of this *doxa* in Smith's tolerant polity is deeply disturbing. It is very difficult to believe that the West's relations with the Islamic World will be helped by a more full-throated, unexpurgated expression of "the American Creed." Unfortunately, it is impossible to inquire further here into the circumstances most propitious for the spread of modernity to the Islamic world. But recent events in Iraq and elsewhere suggest that to the extent that modernity comes wrapped in any particular foreign national flag, the more likely it is to be rejected. In this respect, a suitably reformed European Union is a better vehicle for the transmission of modern liberal values than the United States.[10] For unlike the United States, the EU's version of modernity is thoroughly non-national and de-Christianized. Whereas the United States might follow Smith and choose to reject the ultraliberal language of neutrality and equality, new Europeans fortunately do not have this option.

NOTES

1. For the canonical statement, see John Rawls, *Political Liberalism* (New York: Columbia University Press, 1991). For somewhat different versions of political liberalism, see Joshua Cohen, "A More Democratic Liberalism," *Michigan Law Review* 92 (1994), 1503–46; Ira Katznelson, *Liberalism's Crooked Circle: Letters to Adam Michnik* (Princeton: Princeton University Press, 1996); Charles Larmore, *The Morals of Modernity* (Cambridge: Cambridge University Press, 1996); and Stephen Macedo, *Diversity and Distrust: Civic Education in a Multicultural Democracy* (Cambridge, MA: Harvard University Press, 2000).

2. Steven D. Smith, "Toleration and Liberal Commitments," 269.

3. Smith's position on toleration and his misgivings with "ultra-liberalism" are more fully apparent, when the present essay is read in conjunction with a number of the essays he mentions in his footnotes, including,

especially, Steven D. Smith, "*Barnette's* Big Blunder," 78 *Chicago-Kent Law Review* 625 (2003); Steven D. Smith, "Believing Persons, Personal Believings: The Neglected Center of the First Amendment," *University of Illinois Law Review* 1233 (2002); and Steven D. Smith, "The Restoration of Tolerance," 78 *California Law Review* 305 (1990).

4. Michael W. McConnell, "The New Establishmentarianism," *Chicago Kent Law Review* 75 (2000); for Smith's position on McConnell's critique of "establishmentarianism," see "*Barnette's* Big Blunder," 664–65.

5. Smith contends—wrongly, in my opinion—that ultra- (or political) liberals lack any underlying conception of the good; and therefore, political liberals cannot *tolerate* (in Smith's sense of the term) others. This interpretation is, I think, mistaken even in the case of Rawls, whose thin conception of the good is (a) not that thin, and (b) certainly thick enough to sustain a form of Smithian *toleration.* See here Rawls, *Political Liberalism,* 15–22.

6. For various "pluralist" critiques of political liberalism, see McConnell, "The New Establishmentarians"; William Galston, *Liberal Pluralism* (Cambridge: Cambridge University Press, 2002); Stuart Hampshire, *Innocence and Experience* (Cambridge, MA: Harvard University Press, 1989); and John Gray. *Two Faces of Liberalism* (New York: The New Press, 2000).

7. Max Weber, *Economy and Society* (Berkeley: University of California Press, 1979).

8. Smith, "Toleration and Liberal Commitments," 266.

9. For these details, see Gary Wills, "A Country Ruled by Faith," *New York Review of Books,* November 16, 2006.

10. For more on this contentious point, see Glyn Morgan, *The Idea of a European Superstate: Public Justification and European Integration* (Princeton, NJ: Princeton University Press, 2005).

12

IS THERE LOGICAL SPACE ON THE MORAL MAP FOR TOLERATION? A BRIEF COMMENT ON SMITH, MORGAN, AND FORST

LAWRENCE A. ALEXANDER

To many, the notion of toleration as a morally praiseworthy stance is deeply paradoxical. If an act or practice is morally wrong, should it not be condemned and punished? We never encounter claims that murder, rape, or theft should be tolerated, and rarely do we encounter claims that we should tolerate acts or practices manifesting racism or sexism. Claims for "toleration" are usually directed at acts or practices that the claimant believes are morally insignificant or even morally good. But then, what is there about those acts or practices that requires toleration? That is the so-called "paradox of toleration."[1]

I believe there is space on the map of the moral terrain for toleration, and that the "paradox of toleration" is overstated. Nevertheless, I shall argue that this space is smaller than many "tolerant" liberals believe, and that in order to enlarge this space, some liberals attempt to ascend to a "neutral," above-the-fray position that does not exist.

In what follows I shall draw my map of the moral terrain and locate the spaces for toleration on it. I shall then briefly comment on the arguments of Smith,[2] Morgan,[3] and Forst[4] in terms of locating them on the moral map.

I. The Circumstances of Tolerance and Its Moral Mapping

Demands for tolerance arise when people who interact hold conflicting views of right and wrong and good and bad. I shall call this situation a clash of first-order moral views. When this clash occurs, the call for toleration is addressed to partisans of one of the first-order moral views and, if heeded, results in various possible forms of forbearance—forbearance from punishment of those holding and acting upon the clashing first-order views, forbearance from other forms of tangible publicly imposed penalties, forbearance from public condemnation, and, in some cases perhaps, forbearance from private shunning and discrimination.

Toleration is possible when the values within each of the clashing first-order views lead to what I shall call "non-engagement." What I mean by this is best conveyed through examples. Consider the following clashes of first-order moral viewpoints:

(1) Group B holds a religious belief that dictates the holding of sexual orgies among the faithful—all consenting adults—including group sex, both hetero- and homosexual. Group A finds Group B's practice morally abhorrent and degraded. Nonetheless, Group A, which holds Millian moral beliefs regarding the proper use of state coercion, believes it would be wrong to punish or penalize Group B for its orgies. And Group B in turn believes that it would be wrong to compel participation in its orgies by non-consenting adults and children. Both Group A's and Group B's moral beliefs, therefore, although different, do not result in any legal or social conflict. Although as beliefs they are opposed, they fail to engage each other conflictually in action, a result that follows from the other beliefs the groups hold.[5]

(2) Group A is in control of the state but is super-pacifistic. That is, it believes that it is morally wrong to use coercion of any sort to enforce moral requirements. When

members of Group B, who hold different moral views, do things that Group A regards as morally wrong, Group A forbears from punishing or penalizing them because of Group A's own beliefs about the immorality of coercion. Again, Group A's and Group B's moral beliefs, though opposed as beliefs, do not result in conflict. As I am using the term, they do not "engage."

(3) Group A believes homosexual acts are wrong and should be punished. Group B believes the opposite. Group A is in control of the state and could punish homosexuality. It believes, however, that if it were to do so, there is a good chance either that Group B would rebel, and that property loss, injuries, and deaths would occur, or that Group B would gain enough converts to its views to gain control of the state and impose its views on Group A. Group A believes, therefore, that it is morally prudent to forbear from punishing homosexuality. Put differently, Group A's second-order moral views about what should be done when not all of its first-order moral views can be realized except at great cost or risk dictate that Group A forbear from imposing its particular first-order moral views about homosexuality. This morally prudential forbearance results in a *modus vivendi* in which opposed moral beliefs do not engage conflictually.

In these and similar examples, views that Group A holds to be morally wrong are "tolerated" by Group A because Group A's own moral views dictate a stance of non-engagement.[6] Toleration—avoidance of conflictual engagement—is a position within a partisan moral point of view. *There is no stronger sense of toleration that is possible.* Forbearance due to doubts about one's own moral views is not tolerance. Nor is forbearance due to moral skepticism or beliefs in moral relativism. (In any event, neither skepticism nor relativism entails forbearance.)

When conflicting moral views *do* engage, toleration is not an option. If Group A believes abortion is the murder of an innocent human being, and Group B believes that it is on a par with the killing of microbes and should be within the scope of the right of a woman to control her body, then neither group can tolerate the acts of the others—that is, unless they are like the pacifists in (2) above, or decide that a *modus vivendi* is the best moral strategy, as in (3) above.

As with abortion, so too if Group A believes homosexuality is wrong and merits punishment, while Group B believes homosexuality lies within a general right to choose the forms and objects of intimacy and should be immune from state sanction. And so too if Group A and Group B agree that V is a virtue, but Group A believes there is a moral duty to teach V to all school children, while Group B believes there is a moral duty *not* to teach V to children in the public schools (because of the rights of dissenting parents). And, *a fortiori,* so too if Group A believes that certain religious truths should be propagated by the state, while Group B either rejects the religious truths or rejects that aspect of them that dictates that they be propagated by the state.

Certain views of political morality—particularly the "liberal" political moralities of Mill, Nozick, and Rawls[7]—either because they do not take stands on matters of the Good and religious duties, or because, if they do, they dictate forbearance from direct coercion—potentially leave open large domains of moral non-engagement, which I have claimed toleration must be. I say that those views *potentially* leave open large domains of moral non-engagement, and not that those views *actually* do so, because whether non-engagement is possible depends not only on whether one is a Millian, a Nozickian, and so forth, but also on the views of those whom one opposes. For whether Group A can tolerate Group B, or whether instead their views engage conflictually, is jointly determined by both groups' views. Millians and Nozickians can tolerate religious groups like Group B in (1) above. But that is because Group B does not believe in coercing children or non-consenting adults. Millians cannot tolerate groups that would punish self-regarding conduct. Nozickians cannot tolerate groups that would redistribute property or harm some as a means to aid others. When groups' views conflictually engage, toleration is impossible. Force or conversion are the only alternatives remaining. Converting non-Millians to Mill will surely eliminate engagement. But conversion—leading to the abandonment of the view one opposes—is surely not *toleration* of that view. And to repeat, Millian, Nozickian, and Rawlsian views result in the *potential* for toleration by taking no view on certain moral and religious matters other than that non-engagement by everyone is required vis-à-vis those views; and of necessity they cannot tolerate acts inconsistent with that requirement of non-engagement.

So the call for toleration speaks to someone from within a partisan view, either as a reminder of what is entailed by that view for those who hold it, or as an attempt to convert people to that view. It cannot be a view from nowhere, from above the partisan fray of contending moral and religious views, as liberal views are sometimes wont to characterize themselves. There is no such "neutral" position.[8] If A believes abortion is murder, and B believes it is a right, the argument that A may be right but should nonetheless tolerate B is incoherent. It entails a rejection of A's views, which means that it cannot claim to be "neutral" about those views. Liberal views are not held at some higher epistemic level than the conflicting partisan moral views on whose partisans the liberal urges tolerance. The liberal is just another partisan. That is not to say that the liberal is not correct in terms of what political morality requires. But if the liberal is correct, she is correct at the same epistemic level on which the non-liberal is then necessarily wrong.

Thus, if the non-liberal believes—perhaps because of statements in the Bible coupled with a belief in scriptural inerrancy—that homosexuality is wrong and should be punished, and the Millian, Rawlsian, or Nozickian liberal believes that homosexuality should not be punished, *then the liberal must necessarily believe that the non-liberal has misinterpreted Scripture, or else that Scripture is wrong.* Moreover, the liberal cannot tolerate the non-liberal's punishing homosexuals because the non-liberal's view that homosexuals must be punished engages conflictually the liberal's view to the contrary. If the liberal tolerates homosexuality—because her views do not engage those of homosexuals—then she cannot tolerate the non-liberals who would punish homosexuals. She may try to convert them to her brand of liberalism. But if she fails, she then must oppose them, coercively if necessary.

II. Finding Smith, Morgan, and Forst on the Moral Map

A. Smith

If I were to characterize Steve Smith's rich and provocative essay in terms of the moral map I have described, I would say that Smith's principal claim is that liberalism should understand that it is a partisan first-order moral position, not a "neutral" second-order position above the fray of contending first-order moral positions.[9] Smith endorses liberalism, at least generically, and endorses liberalism's toleration of non-liberal views of the Good, most notably non-liberal religious views.

Smith's focus is on the state and its forbearance from coercion of those with heterodox moral views, not on moral agents more generally.[10] When the state confronts the various moral views persons hold within a pluralistic society, it will find that they fall into three categories.[11] First, there are views that are consistent with the views expressed by the state's policies. These views are within the prevailing orthodoxy. Second, there are views that are inconsistent with the prevailing orthodoxy but are nonetheless tolerable. And third, there are views that the prevailing orthodoxy cannot tolerate.

Smith is quick (and correct) to point out that the lines separating these three domains will be blurry and shifting.[12] Some moral views will be absolutely intolerable. To a (non-pacificistic) liberal, a religious view demanding the killing of infidels or the sacrifice of virgins will be absolutely intolerable. Other views may be tolerable insofar as the criminal law is concerned, but intolerable insofar as whether, say, public school students should receive instruction or training in them. Think of prostitution, for example.[13] Still other views may be deemed immoral (by the orthodoxy the state reflects) but fully tolerable. Thus, a small anti-liberal religious group may be fully tolerated in its teachings that liberalism should give way to theocracy, so long as it abjures coercion of its members and violence against others, and complies with laws controlling the education of its children.

Smith's first and second categories—the orthodox and the tolerable—are, in terms of my moral map, views that do not conflictually engage with the dominant views. An orthodox view does not, of course, conflict with itself. And the tolerable are, by definition, those views that do not engage the orthodox views conflictually. What Smith emphasizes is that there may be degrees of tolerability.[14] Some acts that from the state orthodoxy's perspective are immoral may nonetheless be legal (because they do not engage the orthodoxy's moral views if one includes moral views regarding the limits of the criminal law). They may not get taught or subsidized, and they may not escape official criticism, but they will not be punished.

As I said, Smith's arguments for toleration are largely consistent with my moral mapping. He rejects the ultraliberal "neutral" position above the fray of partisan moral positions as incoherent, as do I.[15] And Smith argues that a fullblooded moral case for toleration cannot be based on moral indifference, moral skepticism, or moral fallibility.[16] He briefly discusses the *modus vivendi* version of toleration but declares it not terribly inspiring.[17] And he points out that arguments for toleration based on the futility of coercing agreement are rather limited. The case for toleration, he concludes, resting as it does principally on practical limitations, is neither powerful nor stable.[18]

Liberalism—necessarily of the partisan type *à la* Mill, Rawls, Nozick, *et al.*, given the impossibility of non-partisan, "neutral" liberalism—is distinguished by its deeming the Right to be prior to the Good and its concomitant elevation of moral autonomy to supremacy among values. Liberals need take no affirmative position on matters that fall within the domain of the Good. They need only reject as false any views of the Good, religious or secular, that would conflict with the priority of the Right. All "reasonable" views of the Good on this account recognize the right of autonomous persons to choose the Bad so long as the Bad is not the Wrong (violative of the right of autonomous persons to choose the Bad, or unjust regarding the distribution of wealth or liberty). So liberalism is tolerant of—does not engage conflictually—all "reasonable" views of the Good, even if those views are wrong. However, it is, and must be, intolerant of "unreasonable" views of the Good.[19]

Smith appears doubtful that liberalism's sharp distinction between the Right and the Good can be maintained.[20] For example, what provides the ultimate ground for the liberal's elevation of autonomy in choosing ("reasonable") conceptions of the Good? Would that not be some conception of the Good itself? If it is just the thin value of freedom to choose, how can it outweigh Truth, Beauty, Dignity, and so forth? And cosmopolitanism as a Good is dependent on the existence noncosmopolitan ways of life from which to be a cosmopolitan sampler.[21] But if autonomy derives its value from a thicker conception of the Good, then the liberal's case for tolerating choosing the Bad is considerably undermined, and the liberal seems driven to accept a more perfectionist liberalism, such as that of Raz,[22] Galston,[23] or Moore.[24] And perfectionist liberalism may engage conflictually with more moral views and thus leave less room for toleration.

B. Morgan

As I read Glyn Morgan's original response to Smith,[25] Morgan is a latter day Millian liberal who is attracted by the rhetoric of ultraliberalism, even if ultraliberalism—the non-partisan, neutral, above-the-fray liberalism—is an impossibility. What is not clear is whether Morgan is a Millian liberal out of first-order moral conviction, or whether instead he holds some less tolerant secular position that, for strategic reasons, is best furthered by adoption of a Millian framework. In other words, toleration that for Mill or Millian liberals like Joel Feinberg[26] might be a matter of moral principle might be for Morgan a matter of the second-best.

There are strong indications that Morgan views Millian liberalism as a second-best, strategic choice. For example, he declares that the second part of his paper "seeks to show that enlightenment liberals would be *tactically wise* to opt for a politically liberal polity rather than the tolerant polity that Smith recommends."[27] This passage, and the part of his paper it refers to, imply that Morgan is an "enlightenment (Millian) liberal" as a matter of moral conviction, and that political liberalism is a strategy to secure enlightenment liberalism.

On the other hand, it is not at all obvious to me what the operative differences are between Millian, enlightenment liberalism and a "politically liberal polity" that Morgan urges enlightenment liberals to endorse as a tactical matter. If there are no differences, then either Morgan's endorsement of Mill is itself tactical, leaving unanswered in service of what first-order moral views is Millian liberalism "tactically wise," or Morgan endorses Millian liberalism as a matter of principle, leaving it unclear in what sense opting for a liberal political polity is "tactically wise."

C. Forst

Rainer Forst acknowledges that the case for toleration "must not rest on a skeptical epistemology or on a 'neutralist' standpoint that—in a self-defeating way—doubts the truth of its own moral stance."[28] But having said that, Forst essentially takes it back. For he relegates the claims of religion to a separate epistemological realm, the realm of "faith," and contrasts religious claims to secular claims, the latter of which fall within the epistemological realm of "reason" and "knowledge."[29] Disputes over religious matters cannot, therefore, be settled by reason, and disputed religious claims are, says Forst, "not good reasons for forcing others to act in a certain way (or believe certain things)."[30] For Forst, "any use of force has to be mutually justifiable"; and religious justifications will fail that test.[31]

Forst not only rejects the "unity of epistemology" that I and others have argued for in the past, a view that would put religious claims on a par with other knowledge claims. He also rejects Smith's contention that religious believers will be forced into schizophrenia by having to accept the Forst principle of mutual justification, which puts religious claims off the table as not based on reason, along with the truth of their own religious beliefs.[32] But it is Forst, not Smith, who is wrong here, at least if religious believers' own religious beliefs do not entail Forst's principle. For if religious believers take their beliefs to be true—which is tautological—they will not perceive the distinction between faith and knowledge that Forst perceives, nor will they take their beliefs to be other than "reasonable." If they have had a vision on the road to Damascus, and the vision instructed them to extirpate certain practices or views, they will surely not be moved by Forst's principle. Of course, they may be deluded; and perhaps Forst can convince them that they are. But that would be a substantive, partisan attack on the truth of certain religious views—an attack that may be justified, but an attack nonetheless.

In the end, both Forst and Morgan may be engaged in an enterprise of conversion—with Forst, conversion to his principle of mutual justification and its denigration of religious "knowledge"; with Morgan, conversion to Millian liberalism. If either succeeds, the realm of potential conflictual engagement will be greatly narrowed because the space of moral agreement will be increased. What follows will not necessarily be toleration, especially in Forst's case, for toleration entails moral disagreements, and the enterprise of moral conversion aims at eliminating moral disagreement.

For me, what is important is that we get clear about just why we should not conflictually engage moral views that we deem erroneous, if it is true that we should not do so. What kind of moral view is self-effacing to that extent, and why is such a view compelling? Moral prudence—the modus vivendi account of toleration—is comprehensible, if uninspiring. Arguments from the self-defeating nature of coercion are less convincing wholesale and equally uninspiring retail. Arguments that go to the moral wrongness of imposing what is morally correct promise a sturdy foundation for toleration, if only those arguments can be shown to be convincing.[33]

as opposed to arguing tolerance's neutrality

NOTES

1. The "paradox of toleration" is oft noted. *See, e.g.,* Alex Tuckness, *Locke and the Legislative Point of View* (Princeton: Princeton University Press, 2002), 17–19; Susan Mendus, *Liberalism and the Limits of Toleration* (London: Macmillan, 1989), 18–19.

2. Steven D. Smith, "Toleration and Liberal Commitments," this volume.

3. Glyn Morgan, "How Impoverishing Is Liberalism?" this volume.

4. Rainer Forst, "Toleration and Truth," this volume.

5. For a recent approach to toleration that is Millian in nature, see Hans Oberdiek, *Tolerance: Between Forbearance and Acceptance* (Lanham: Rowman and Littlefield Publishers, 2001).

6. There is a fourth form of toleration as non-engagement that is identified by Steven Wall. Sometimes Group A tolerates a practice of

Group B that Group A regards as immoral, not out of respect for Group B's rights to autonomous decision making, as in (1) above, and not because of super-pacifistic or strategic reasons, as in (2) and (3), but because the immoral practice is inextricably a part of a broader practice that has moral value. Steven Wall, "The Structure of Perfectionist Toleration," in Steven Wall and George Klosko, eds., *Perfectionism and Neutrality: Essays in Liberal Theory* (Lanham: Rowman and Littlefield Publishers, 2003), 231 et seq.

7. *See* John Stuart Mill, *On Liberty* (New York: F. S. Crofts & Co., 1947); Robert Nozick, *Anarchy, State, and Utopia* (New York: Basic Books, 1974); John Rawls, *Political Liberalism* (New York: Columbia University Press, 1993).

8. *See* Larry Alexander, "Liberalism, Religion, and the Unity of Epistemology," *San Diego Law Review* 30 (1993), 763. For a somewhat Millian view of what should and should not be tolerated, but one with a more conservative cast than most contemporary Millian views, see John Kekes, *The Illusions of Egalitarianism* (Ithaca: Cornell University Press, 2003), 168–86. Kekes recognizes that the toleration he endorses is and must be the product of decidedly partisan views of Right and Wrong, Good and Bad, and the limits of justified coercion; it cannot be the product of some ultra-liberal neutrality. Whatever moral views one holds to be correct, "one cannot treat with equal concern [neutrally] their protectors and violators." Ibid., 186.

9. Smith, "Toleration and Liberal Commitments," 243–80.

10. Ibid., 245.

11. Ibid., 244.

12. Ibid., 246.

13. See Scott A. Anderson, "Prostitution and Sexual Autonomy: Making Sense of the Prohibition of Prostitution," *Ethics* 112 (2002), 748.

14. Smith, "Toleration and Liberal Commitments," 246.

15. The ultraliberal attempt at universal toleration of all positions reminds me of the joke about the two Jewish scholars arguing about a point of religious doctrine. They agree to take their dispute to the rabbi. The rabbi listens to the arguments of the first disputant, at the end of which he declares, "You're right." But the second one then presents his arguments for the contrary position, at the end of which the rabbi declares, "You're right." Perplexed, the first disputant objects: "Rabbi, you said that I was right, and then you said that he was right. But we can't both be right." To which the rabbi replies, "You're right."

16. Smith is less certain about the relation between fallibility and tolerance than he is about the lack of connection between tolerance and either skepticism or indifference. If one believes an act is morally wrong,

but also is aware of the possibility that his moral views on the subject are mistaken, does he not have a reason to tolerate the act? I believe that the answer is complex and turns on the degree of confidence one has in one's views and, as importantly, on what is at stake if one tolerates the act and if one does not tolerate it. Suppose John believes abortion is morally equivalent to murder but realizes that he may be wrong in that judgment. Should he tolerate Mary's abortion, assuming he can coercively prevent it? If he tolerates it, he believes he is, more likely than not, allowing a murder. If he fails to tolerate it, he believes he is risking to some (lesser) extent a serious intrusion on autonomy, bodily integrity, family planning, etc. Awareness of one's moral fallibility might not result in toleration in that case, nor, arguably, should it. In other cases—say, deciding whether to tolerate discrimination by a private club that one believes is morally wrong and not shielded from coercion by any moral right—the stakes are (somewhat) lower and one's sense of moral fallibility may lead to a different result regarding toleration.

17. Smith, "Toleration and Liberal Commitments," 251.

18. Ibid., 256.

19. *See* Jürgen Habermas, "Religious Tolerance—The Pacemaker for Cultural Rights," *Philosophy* 79 (1) (2004), 5.

20. Smith, "Toleration and Liberal Commitments," 260.

21. *See* Larry Alexander, "Illiberalism All the Way Down: Illiberal Groups and Two Conceptions of Liberalism," *The Journal of Contemporary Legal Issues* 12 (2002), 625.

22. Joseph Raz, *The Morality of Freedom* (Oxford: Clarendon Press, 1986), 380–422.

23. William A. Galston, *Liberal Pluralism* (Cambridge: Cambridge University Press, 2002). For a critique of Galston's attempt to derive liberalism from value pluralism, see Robert B. Talisse, "Can Value Pluralists Be Comprehensive Liberals? Galston's Liberal Pluralism," *Contemporary Political Theory* 1 (2004), 1.

24. Michael S. Moore, *Placing Blame* (Oxford: Clarendon Press, 1997), 763–95. *See generally* Larry Alexander, "The Legal Enforcement of Morality," R. G. Frey and Christopher Heath Wellman, eds., *A Companion to Applied Ethics* (Oxford: Blackwell Publishing, 2003), 128–41.

25. Glyn Morgan, "Can Liberals Tolerate Religious Minorities?" Paper presented at the American Society for Political and Legal Philosophy, Atlanta, Georgia, January 2, 2004 (on file with editor).

26. *See, e.g.*, Joel Feinberg, *The Moral Limits of the Criminal Law, vol. I: Harm to Others* (Oxford: Oxford University Press, 1984); Joel Feinberg, *The Moral Limits of the Criminal Law, vol. IV: Harmless Wrongdoing* (Oxford: Oxford University Press, 1988).

27. Morgan, "Can Liberals Tolerate Religious Minorities?" 7–8 (emphasis added).
28. Forst, "Toleration and Truth," 282.
29. Ibid., 285–86.
30. Ibid., 286.
31. Ibid.
32. Ibid., 288.
33. I thank Steve Smith for commenting on drafts of this paper.

PART IV

TOLERATION AND IDENTITY

13

TOLERATION, POLITICS, AND THE ROLE OF MUTUALITY

INGRID CREPPELL

Martin Luther famously declared "Here I stand, I can do no other." In this declaration, we see a pure kind of moral stance—one of immovable identity and purpose. While toleration also stands for something, the essence of its stance is of a different kind, that of interaction. Its value is grounded upon how it enables persons to maintain relationships in a world made up of many persons and groups all standing for something different, and often at odds with one another. In this essay, I shall focus on an aspect of toleration that has been submerged in the extensive discussions about its nature, grounds, and limits: that toleration must include an element of relationship, or a form of mutuality. The relational feature of toleration has not been ignored, but has been conceived in stereotypical ways. Interestingly, the view of the relationship in toleration has undergone a shift over the years. For the most part, and historically, this dimension is criticized as too minimal, as just a form of "putting up with" and condescension.[1] Recently, toleration has come to be appropriated by those who seek to reconceptualize it as a version of multiculturalism, so that it comes closer to meaning full acceptance and embracing of difference.[2] Toleration is a type of relationship but it is not simply either forbearance or openness. It uniquely attempts to balance both an attitude of separation/disapproval and an attitude of acceptance. How is this balancing possible?

In this chapter, I explore the element of mutuality as part of the core meaning of toleration. My argument is that for toleration to come about there must be an initial "will to relationship."[3] This will is defined as an initiating psychological-political stance, creating a condition of opportunity to build an on-going relationship. For the relationship to be one of toleration, this condition must be extended and sustained through institutions and political norms consciously projected to maintain the relationship that acknowledges the presence of conflict and disagreement. Specifically, for toleration to survive, the institutions and ethos of politics itself must be valued for more than strategic purposes. Persons desire to live together on some terms; their will to do so is realized in political rules and loyalty, which exemplify and protect their relationship to one another. In the next section, I give an argument about why we must take the element of relationship into account and the implications this has for studying toleration. In section two, I revisit the early modern period in order to highlight the extent to which a will to relationship was an element in the initial establishment of toleration and forced an ethical dimension to political settlement. Section three considers how three typical contemporary debates can be illuminated by and can help clarify the meaning of mutuality. In the last section, I conclude with a preliminary basis on which to limit differences—what substantive values underlie toleration?

I. The Role of Mutuality

The standard definition of toleration highlights two components as basic to its structure: (a) disapproval of or disagreement with practices, beliefs, or persons and (b) restraint of oneself from imposing one's reaction.[4] According to this conventional view, toleration is the positive act of not interfering with or coercing another despite one's negative response. It is a unilateral act of one person toward another, an act that must be undertaken for the right reasons in order to be considered a value, virtue, or principle. To restrain oneself for purely self-interested purposes (e.g., economic reasons), or because one had no choice (e.g., one's minority status) would not be considered toleration in a moral sense. This basic definition of toleration must be amended by adding a third component to its normative structure. One may disapprove and then restrain oneself but crucially (c) one remains in a relationship with the person or group with whom one is in conflict. We do not call an act toleration if disapproval and restraint are followed by a retraction of contact, or by ignoring or making the other invisible.[5] The restraint is meaningful because the parties continue in the presence of one another in a nontrivial way, acknowledging a relationship of accommodation.

The literature on toleration is most often focused on the possibility and nature of the morality of constraint, and generally ignores this essential feature of the conditions for it—the commonality or mutuality of the ensuing relationship. This gap in the literature results from the conceptual residues of toleration's original use in situations of asymmetrical power. Where a Catholic majority tolerates a Huguenot minority, the ensuing "relationship" may represent progress insofar as there is no longer active persecution, but given our principles of equality this may appear to be a severely unsatisfactory model for contemporary toleration. Two points need to be emphasized in this regard. In the historical section of this chapter, I stress that we can learn a great deal more about the conditions of toleration than the stereotypical picture presents. The virtue of restraint is a great one, but the innovation in the policy of toleration between radically unequal opponents is not reducible to "constraint." The fact is that restraint is motivated because of a preexisting will to relationship which thereby sets the stage for institutions and norms of political mutuality. Second, today we do live in conditions of relative equality. The ideal of toleration does not become superfluous because of this fact; rather, different aspects of its normative force come to the foreground. The conventional liberal solution to conflict—public neutrality—is strained when demands for recognition and interaction ask for more than blindness to difference in the public sphere. Toleration as a form of mutuality is an attempt to address this impasse.

Therefore, we should replace the idea of toleration as a virtue of self-restraint undertaken for moral reasons with an idea of a specific type of political-social relation, the fundamental feature of which is the maintenance of relationship in the midst of the potential for conflict due to disagreement or difference. The ability to hold difference and commonality together simultaneously is a normal human capacity. All people (and the most traditional or dogmatic person must be able to do this) allow slippage or flexibility in applying the norms we carry about in us.[6] But a description of tolerance in this elemental, cognitive sense should lead us to mark out what more is needed for an explicit value or principle of toleration. How are we to find moral terms in addition to cognitive and emotive means to facilitate toleration not within (even) a traditionalist world but between highly distinct world-views and systems of belief? I hope to answer that question here.

The use of the words "relationship" and "mutuality" in toleration can generate a great deal of confusion. First, we say in the simplest descriptive and morally neutral sense that toleration *is* a relationship of some type. For purposes of understanding the language of toleration in the contemporary world, this is a claim with some theoretical significance, and I examine toleration as a political-social relationship, not as an individual duty. Second, relationship or mutuality is *part* of toleration. In this second sense, it is a specific aspect of toleration that describes it as positively linking people together in spite of and because of their differences: there is a will to relationship, which is not yet fully morally specified. This will to relationship is instrumental or causally important in initiating toleration. Finally, mutuality is also a more fully ethically negotiated relationship and ought to be an objective of toleration. A pre-ethical will to maintain a relationship with persons whom we disagree with or disapprove of begins a search for the grounds of that relationship, and may eventually lead to a further aim to sustain a fair and on-going basis of membership in one society. Thus, the will to relationship is a psychological-political predisposition and must become a more explicit norm of mutuality realized in institutional purposes and conceptual innovation.

The importance of an independent role of mutuality is brought out by a reading of Thomas Nagel's well-known article in which he attempts to work out how liberalism might "provide the devout with a reason for tolerance."[7] Nagel seeks to establish a point of view that the devout would be "compelled to" or "must" adopt, by the logic of seeking a *legitimate* ground to proceed in a context of deep disagreement. This "common ground"—a process of reasoning—is an "idea of something which is neither an appeal to my own beliefs nor an appeal to beliefs that we all share."[8] We take up a "higher-order framework of moral reasoning . . . which takes us outside ourselves to a standpoint that is independent of who we are."[9] But there is a basic ambiguity in the source of the compulsion to rise to this framework of reasoning. What would lead the devout—the deeply and wholeheartedly committed—to "look at certain . . . convictions from outside,"[10] to see their truths as "beliefs," one set among many others? Nagel suggests: "I believe that the demand for agreement and its priority in these cases over a direct appeal to the truth, must be grounded in . . . a kind of epistemological restraint: the distinction between what is needed to justify belief and what is needed to justify the employment of political power depends on a higher standard of objectivity." And he elaborates: "We accept a kind of epistemological division between the private and the public domains: in certain contexts I am constrained to consider my beliefs merely as beliefs rather than as truths."[11]

The obvious question arises here: why would that reasoning be a necessary logic *for the devout,* from *within* their point of view? It is a logic for the devout who, living within liberal democratic polities, seek terms of legitimacy on which to base public policies affecting themselves and other citizens. But what of those who would claim, as upholders first and foremost of religious truth: I would prefer and will work to live in a religious community that shares only my beliefs. My primary aims as a person are to realize those devotions to my religious ideals; I don't seek to live in a diverse society based upon secular legitimacy. These devout do not look reasonable insofar as they don't care about the terms of legitimacy grounding public laws. Nagel might reply that it doesn't matter that these devout do not *care* about legitimate bases of coercion—they would be obligated by the fact that they live in a society that must find legitimate grounds for laws, grounds that do not coerce for the wrong types of reasons. But, if this is his reply, then he has failed to give the *devout* a reason for tolerance that would be compelling and not simply abstractly obligatory.

To focus on the intransigent devout does not mean that attempting to convince the deeply religious who do wish to live on legitimate terms is not a compelling aim. Nagel offers reasons for tolerance for this type of devout. This is noteworthy because it suggests a line of reasoning that might be more broadly appealing: the legitimacy of a liberal polity is not based upon the need to remake all citizens into individualists or liberal persons in a deep way.[12] Even though deeply committed to religious truths, one could recognize the need to find a space of reasoning applicable to all persons, oneself included. But a distinction between the "reasonable" devout and the "unreasonable" devout brings out the step preceding efforts to construct legitimacy. One must desire to move to an "impartial" point of view. One is only compelled to see one's truths as mere beliefs because legitimacy matters at least as much. The devout must care about building a common world with persons different from them.

Nagel's concern with the devout brings up another puzzle in the study of toleration that leads to a focus on relational aspects. For much of its conceptual history, toleration has been equated with freedom of conscience, which came to mean "autonomy" in its modern variant. As previously noted, claims for equal respect also developed in conjunction with toleration. Enlightenment values that increase access to rights for disenfranchised groups are consistently linked to the call for toleration. The puzzle is: calls for toleration seem (historically) always to have followed on demands for freedom and equality, yet it is exactly the point that we cannot count on those who oppose the claims for freedom and equality to agree with the logical or moral necessity of such ideas. That is why there is conflict. The historical correlation of freedom and toleration is not matched by logical moral necessity. I suggest that we view the demands for freedom and equality in a different light. They were not originally conceived as reasonable arguments made to convince the other side (from this latter side they don't appear "reasonable" at all—as Locke noted in *A Letter Concerning Toleration*—"every one is Orthodox to himself");[13] rather, they were and are demands by certain oppressed and suppressed groups in a society to become active participants in constructing the terms of relations in that society. Thus, demands for freedom and equality are demands to reconfigure social relations. Toleration has been consistently linked to these demands because its principle is that adjustment between different groups must be made and relationships maintained. In a context of hierarchy and asymmetry, people's rejection of their restricted position means that toleration seeks to find the terms on which the demands of freedom can be acknowledged. In a context of legal equality, people's demands for recognition of difference means that toleration seeks to find terms of mutuality that can accept claims of difference. In both cases, the claims made against the status quo are for the realization of a group's or persons' access to social meaning and well-being, which I discuss in section 4.

It is not absolutely necessary that one accept freedom/autonomy or equality as one's supreme value in order to accept toleration. In general, and historically, this has tended to be the case: these have promoted toleration because they predispose a person to accept diversity first and foremost and not to insist on conformity. But one may come to toleration from another direction —from that of peaceful coexistence—and therefore accept diversity and claims for freedom and equality for the sake of a unified community.[14] Thus, toleration can be arrived at from the direction of seeking diversity or from the direction of seeking coexistence, but in either case it serves as the capacity and will to relationship in the face of diversity. Hence it exemplifies a unique, modern, and *sui generis* value.

Before turning to political history, we ought to consider briefly the question of the source of the will to relationship itself. If the construction of this will does not rest upon moral reasoning, on what is it based? I have been speaking as if the will to relationship is an original moment of encounter but we might think of it more as a metaphorical situation in time. A sudden encounter between diverse groups because of conquest, for example, is by far the exceptional situation. Usually issues *become* politicized and groups or peoples come to see each other in political terms that need working out. When exactly a compulsion or motivation to find a common ground arises is an historical question for a particular regime of coexistence. Groups find themselves confronting one another due to various historical, cultural, economic, and military forces and developments, and needing to determine the political nature of the relationship that will obligate them to common laws and norms.

We actually begin with a compulsion then, often not well articulated, to find a ground to build or, more often, rebuild a joint world. The critical first step is the willingness of persons to go on together, putting themselves on a path of interaction. This raises the difficult (intractable?) question of how we know such a "will" exists. Suppose a minority group simply has no choice but to put up with the situation of coexistence when they would ideally wish to live a separate life. Or a majority group wishes the minority would disappear. Each side may be prevented for practical reasons from being able to pursue their ideal of separate ends. Does their failure to pursue separatism display a will to live together? It seems to me that the fact that there is usually a necessity or involuntary element to living with others does not undermine the description of toleration as inclusive of a will to live together. Our lives are not worthwhile only insofar as we choose the terms we live by, without the interference of heteronomous necessities. Indeed, we are constantly presented with many features of existence we would not have chosen, and yet we can affirm these and find a will to accept them. We might see worth as coming out of the capacity to recognize why we might want to will to live together in the context of difference when we cannot do anything else. Perhaps the question ought to be: on what terms can we create grounds in order to transform necessity into a will to affirm a common life?

This necessity leads people to search for or conceptualize reasons and values they can agree on to govern that world. Their search is the elaboration and thereby transformation of political thinking, to build mutually comprehensible terms. In this interpretation, toleration does not come about because people "resolve their differences" but because they come to rebalance those differences through seeing their commitments and beliefs as broader than they did at the beginning of the encounter. The role of politics is to find a means to acknowledge and incorporate claims, but its ethical role is to make the will to mutuality sustainable in the long run. To argue then that reasons of freedom and equality arise subsequent to a will to relationship is not to render such reasons superfluous. The will to relationship is only made good if grounds can subsequently be found for the terms of relations between people. A preliminary will to relationship is not equal to toleration and depends for its development and stability on the grounding that will guide resolution of conflicts, which inevitably persist in societies needing and aiming for toleration.[15]

II. Extending a Will to Relationship: History and the Intrinsic Importance of Politics

Toleration depends upon an initial will to interaction in the face of differences. This will is certainly not enough to secure toleration and it can fail in two senses. First, we might say that all political relations throughout history have been based on a "will to interaction in the face of differences" and that this has led to domination by the powerful, not an acceptance of differences. Second, in confrontations between groups, the attempt to find grounds for continued interaction could fail because common grounds might not be possible to prevent groups rejecting a settlement. What is crucial therefore is to establish a will to relationship that will not lead to domination and that can be given longevity, in order to prevent groups from continually fragmenting and rejecting a common life. This is only possible through a reinvention of the public, political sphere. My aim in this section is to show how that might come about. Politics must be innovative and transformative, and not simply a calculation of static interest or balance of power if toleration is to be feasible.

We are not condemned to thinking about politics in purely strategic terms, as a mere mechanism to guarantee rights, if we consider the following logic. In every encounter between groups, there will be the more and less powerful. The impulse of the powerful is to dominate the less powerful, yet the latter have a power in that their differences cannot be eradicated *and* the powerful seek to continue in relationship with them.[16] These two conditions force the parties to go up to a level of interaction that both can find comprehensible and sustainable. They must make it mutually comprehensible together even if this does not insure completely equal power. The political terms of the relationship represent their coming to terms. Thus politics here is transformative of both the identifications of the groups—they come to see who they are as tied to the political institutions they build—and of the public morality or ethics—the parties come to use a public set of terms or language enabling them to reason about what is common to them. Toleration isn't possible without making politics transformative in both these senses.

For a relationship between diverse groups to become acceptable and stable, the parties are pushed to build a political realm to which they can all become loyal. The main story I want to present here is of the development of an independent political public sphere in early modern Europe, as a practical and also (gradually) morally justified construct enabling the stability and coherence of toleration. Politics as a normative force is key because we cannot expect groups to converge on toleration in the long run and across broad differences just by persons individually coming to accept reasons of freedom or equal rights. Group identity all too frequently trumps these individual values. Hence individuals must also see themselves as invested participants in a public political realm, in which the meaning of freedom and equality will be worked out. This is why the concept of identity is important: people must accept citizenship as part of who they are for toleration to be possible. Indeed, their particularist identities (religious, ethnic, racial, etc.) come to be part of the political identification that toleration requires.

The emergence of toleration after the Reformation is still a very rich source of knowledge for understanding the normative and practical features of change.[17] In particular, it is worth briefly tracing aspects of the historical story to show how the ontological needs of relationship in a context of diversity gave politics a transformative ethical role for conflicting groups.

The usual answer to the question of the origins of toleration is sheer exhaustion due to incessant religious war.[18] While this may seem obvious, we might remember that the Crusades brought religious conflict but not toleration. The fact of war alone cannot explain a fundamental transformation in ideas about the foundations of social order, which is indeed what the settlement of toleration required. The expediency solution continues, however, to inform much of political theory. In Rawls' much-quoted observation: "the principle of toleration came about as a *modus vivendi* following the Reformation: at first reluctantly, but nevertheless as providing the only workable alternative to endless and destructive civil strife."[19]

Perez Zagorin offers a corrective to this view of the strategic foundations of toleration, arguing that expediency in almost all cases failed to establish lasting regimes of tolerance. He writes that "without an underlying theoretical rationale that was both philosophical and religious . . . and without the gradual acceptance by political and intellectual elites and others of principles and values enabling them to subordinate and set aside religious difference and strive for concord through mutual understanding, religious toleration, and the freedom it implied could not have been attained." He emphasizes the essentially principled, religious nature of the foundations of toleration: "In the battles over religious toleration that were so bitterly and widely waged in the sixteenth and seventeenth centuries, the idea of toleration was itself very largely inspired by religious values and was fundamentally religious in character" and furthermore for the proponents of "a policy of peace and tolerance toward religious differences, their supreme concern was the welfare of religion itself."[20]

This sharp contrast, pervasive in the toleration literature, between principled, religious sources and a "pragmatic," expedient sources of toleration misses a crucial point about toleration's development, that it wove together both aspects of motivation.[21] Consider Zagorin's contention that values and principles (a critique of the notion of heresy is one important theoretical innovation he examines at length) "enable" people "to subordinate and set aside religious difference." Certainly, had there been no language with which to critique persecuting policies of church and state, there would have been no ideological tools to conceive alternatives or by which to mobilize forces against the status quo. Nevertheless, it should be possible to give an explanation of this change that is more attuned to the conditions in which changes in belief become politically and sociologically viable and powerful. Ideas about freedom of religion were not unheard of before this time, hence the question arises: what was it about this particular set of circumstances that led to the proliferation of debate and the push to a new settlement about religion and the political realm?

The centrality of questions of identity and citizenship to conflicts at this time is clearer when we consider the conundrum raised by the disuniting of what had been one united normative community of moral-political order. How did one maintain one's identity as a Christian and as a citizen in these circumstances? In 1560, Michel de L'Hôpital observed: "We . . . see that a Frenchman and an Englishman of the same religion are more friendly towards each other than two citizens of one town, but of different religions, so far does the relationship of religion surpass that of nationality."[22] To us, living in liberal democratic societies, nearly five hundred years later, the passion to defend to the death one's particular religious beliefs and the hysterical fear of religious diversity are hard to fathom. It becomes more comprehensible when we realize the depth of the challenge. The dynamics making this a crucible of change included the fact that political-religious relations were premised on a principled intolerance, that is, the moral authority of the Church and thereby politics rested on an elaborate justification of persecution (begun by Augustine) of beliefs diverging from the Church. What was at stake in the conflicts was not only the functioning of a previously secured framework for identity.

The complex origins of toleration depended on endogenous changes in religious beliefs about conscience, heresy, and the community of believers on earth (along with other internal doctrines); exogenous changes in the accumulation of ideological and concrete power by secular rulers; and finally, changes in conception of the self and allegiance. The capacity of persons to come to identify with one another on political terms served as the linchpin between innovations in beliefs about toleration and the external forces that made adopting these beliefs feasible and attractive. Specifically, the emergence of the state, a public realm, and groups' connection to it proved the crucial resolution. While the appeal of toleration became stronger with both religious and political changes, I focus on the latter, because ultimately, I believe the capacities of the political realm were the driving force, though not in simple strategic terms.

Toleration was initially a top-down initiative: political sovereigns attempted to impose order and peace within their realm by adopting policies of coexistence. However for the state to be able to implement toleration and hope to have it survive as public policy, elites and the people would need to believe the state could protect them. This was not just a question of coercive power but essentially one about faith in the state. The more competing groups took a risk and relinquished power to the state, the more it could protect the diverse groups within it. This iterated process (repeated efforts at coexistence collapsing back into violence and chaos) took decades to achieve a relatively stable regime of tolerance in France, England, and the Netherlands.

The belief that the duty of the magistrate is to enact the dictates of the Church's orders called for a type of implementation of religion in the world. This command does not appear verbatim in the Old or New Testament but served complex political-religious (indeed social-cultural) purposes, one of which was to legitimize the normative authority of the secular ruler. Ironically, this belief also kept politics in a condition of dependency and derivative value. For toleration to come about, people could no longer expect the ruler to compel them and others to live in a uniform way.

Changes in religious ideas such as the deconstruction of the idea of heresy and the elaboration of a notion of individual conscience were certainly integral to dislodging this belief. But even these crucial conceptual developments would not have enabled a ground for a relationship of toleration to develop. No necessary path of action follows inevitably from a complex set of ideas contained in a body of religious beliefs. What may appear a foregone conclusion in hindsight is that particular elements of belief-systems make them susceptible to manipulation for the ambitions of rulers, or for the propagation of a system of power. We can see today the lengthy process of religious reinterpretation undertaken as a political-social-cultural phenomenon in the case of Islam and its articulation of authentic arguments for toleration. Part of this process will require more than hermeneutical retrieval or innovation and will depend on a revaluation of the political realm in Islamic societies. Once we focus on the fact that religious differences were not just ideas but also communities of believers, we see how the solution of toleration in the early modern period required that people and groups be able to rethink their loyalties. For those who had already rejected coercion for the sake of salvation and doctrinal unity (for reasons of its cruelty to the human body—e.g., Montaigne; or for reasons of peace—"irenicism" —e.g., Erasmus or Franck), the mental leap required to think of oneself as accepting this reorientation to the political sphere would not have been as difficult. But most people could not let go of the immediate connection between faith and the belief that this faith must be shared by all members of a community. The process of change was long in the making and required major identity re-orientation.[23]

For decades, an unmixable amalgam persisted—of traditional ideas about faith and implementing God's will on earth, new ideas about faith and God's relation to human life and the individual, and old ideas about the duties of the political magistrate, or of the relative value of the earthly realm. Not until new ideas about the nature and value of the political realm and its connection to human life could be formulated was there any chance for toleration's becoming a stable idea. Perhaps we can say that a humanization of religion had to be matched by a corresponding elevation of politics.

In this process, the political identification of the people with the state or polity might appear initially to have been purely strategic and provisional: as long as the sovereign could protect them, the people would go along with him or her. But this purely strategic view inadequately grasps the nature of the relationship between the people and the conception of the political sovereign emerging during this period. To be moving or persuasive as a source of allegiance, sovereign rulers worked to reinforce the justice-providing features of the state. For example, Jean Bodin, as the theorist of the absolutist state, was also a firm supporter of toleration. He depicted the function and nature of the sovereign as a neutral and depersonalized power, not as a paternalistic oligarch. Hobbes, while he did not support freedom of worship, did support freedom of belief. His depiction of sovereign power can be interpreted as supporting the rule of law. Finally, Locke extended the concept of political power as the realm of secular law accountable to the people. These conceptualizations of political power and the public realm were constructed to create a political-social order that could appeal across deep differences of belief and moral commitment. Thus the aspirations contained in ideas of the "neutrality" or "impartiality" of the state should not be seen as a false universalism, but as built precisely to represent a concrete creation of a common world overarching deep differences. When religious believers relate to this state, in an ideal conception of this process of political identification, they do not approach the state solely as a provisional tool for achieving their own divisive purposes. If everyone were to conceive the state in such manipulative terms, the state could not actually achieve the goal of protection, but would continually be suspect and therefore guaranteed to fragment.

For the survival of a political unity in the face of conflicting groups, there must be a constitutive element of moral universalism in the essence of the state: people must be able to conceive part of who they are through participating in the "impartial" realm of the public sphere. This neutrality is not devoid of identity but constitutive of part of one's identity—it creates political identification—as a person living in a common political world. Thus from its inception the ideal of the public sphere, or political realm protected by the state, embodied an attempt to create a unity out of diversity. The opening line of the Toleration Act of 1689 asserts: "Forasmuch as some ease to scrupulous consciences in the exercise of religion may be an effectual means to unite their Majesties Protestant subjects in interest and affection" and then continues by delineating the penalties lifted (along with other provisions as well as stipulations) for those Dissenting religious groups previously suppressed. The purpose of the act is explicitly stated as *uniting* citizens in interest and affection.[24] It is quite natural to ridicule the rhetoric of this Act and others like it, exposing the underlying interests served, and the fact that parties were left unprotected by it. Nevertheless, the historical and ethical meaning of such legal documents is larger than the self-interest of the persons who framed it. We cannot reduce that meaning to the level of individual calculation because of the concrete consequences such proclamations of "unity" eventually enabled.

In the early modern period, basic norms of liberal politics began to be institutionalized by political leaders and activists. To emphasize, these norms did not develop out of altruism or dreams of universal justice. We cannot explain ethical public policy as a direct result of any group's, writer's, or actor's direct moral intention but rather as the result of the imperatives of constructing a common existence that is stable and acceptable between persons divided by religion, culture, interests, and so forth. The normativity comes out of the collective necessity. Because diverse believers at this time (often bitterly) disagreed with one another, their capacity to move on together depended on growth in their political identifications, to include state institutions and more "impartial" political norms.

My brief look at the logic of the origins of toleration in post-Reformation Europe argued for the importance of an independent political realm as the solution to the problem of mutual impassability. We begin with the problem of newly politicized groups challenging a status quo and calling into question the will to relationship. Political rulers and theorists asserted the basis of continuing in a common life rather than secession. To achieve this persons and groups take up the perspective of a public realm.

Toleration establishes as an ideal the concept of an arena of accommodation between groups who had previously attempted forcible conversions or ejection of others. To be able to occupy this space of mutual existence, a majority of persons must be able to identify with this political sphere. The process of creating an allegiance to the political realm was the work of theorists such as Bodin, Hobbes, Locke, and others who did so in more indirect ways.[25] The extent to which politics can become secure in part depends upon people's willingness to transfer allegiance to it, to identify with it as a realm in which norms of non-particularist justice and of accountable government are in theory aspired to. These aspirations are not meaningless and morally hypocritical; they constitute a unifying process which enables the protection of the diverse groups within a political community.

III. Deciding Conflicts: Mutuality as an Innovative Norm

The story of toleration's beginnings as a conscious political idea shows how the demands of negotiating relationships in a context of politicized differences necessarily pulls all parties, the stronger and the weaker, to an acknowledgment of a form of mutuality, which had ethical consequences. I now shift to consider whether and how the role of mutuality assists us in addressing continuing contemporary conflicts. The issue of the imposition of religious uniformity may have been taken off the table but religion continues to be a divisive force in other ways. In addition, new issues and claims raise other divisions. Immigration, emigration, and population changes shift balances of interest and identity; growing awareness of social problems (e.g., environmental and economic) and cultural transformation (e.g., gay rights and growth of fundamentalist religions) also generate contention. In the face of these contentions, how does mutuality serve to guide how we ought to balance relations and demands between conflicting claims? In this section, I want to unpack more fully the nature of the ethical imperative that toleration brings in deciding conflicts.[26] Moreover, in looking at some persistent problems, we get a better sense of what mutuality means in more concrete terms.

The fact of deep conflict not resolvable by strategic bargains is the context in which toleration becomes important. The ideal of toleration does not give us a blueprint or a decision-rule for deciding a particular case in accord with some metric. It does not for instance demand that in all cases of conflict the logic of equality or of autonomy ought to apply (as noted, the definitions of "equality" or "freedom" are themselves up for contention). But in deciding conflicts it does say: act so that you acknowledge the presumptive worthiness of your opponent's position in the face of your own, and sustain the mutual benefit of your common lives. Or in other words: adopt public policy that most fully enables a common life cognizant of people's pursuit of meaningful differences.

We need to distinguish here between two lines of addressing conflicts. One line deploys principles or decision-rules such as "maximize" equality, individual rights, or order/security; or tradeoff between order and freedom in the ratio of x; and other direct decision-rules. Toleration is not reducible to this direct decision-rule, which yields a specific tradeoff. It does not for example insist that individual rights must always be maximized, because this would not be a sustainable rule in a society in which communal goods (capacities to sustain minority group integrity) must also be protected. Rather, it directs us to choose a decision-rule so that two things are balanced: the capacity for diverse persons to lead meaningful lives (particularity is taken into account) and the value of the common political life is sustained (for all to agree, basic freedoms and rights are essential). Toleration here is a meta-level attitude one ought to have in deciding conflicts, not the metric that will decide between those in contention over specific policies; nevertheless, it is of intrinsic, not derivative, value because the guiding, overarching attitude it fosters is necessary for justice and social unity in a diverse society.

Given the redefinition of the logical structure of toleration with which I began this paper, we can now see its characteristic ethical core. It explicitly supports the capacity of persons to adopt a complex moral attitude: stand for principles, respect others who do not share those same principles, and sustain a common life. While persons have in effect done this implicitly and on various scales since moral consciousness began,[27] the unique quality of toleration is its direct justification of this capacity for sustaining a complex social morality. This attitude does not say: accept all differences regardless of their consequences. Rather it says: make policy decisions to resolve conflicts so that the reasoning and results sustain the mutual benefit of your common but diverse lives. The fact is that in many conflicts public policy must be made in which some will win and some lose. That this social fact exists does not mean that toleration does not. It may help to indicate a legal analogy here: the institution of the courts themselves or the idea of "due process" stand for the meta-level attitude of willingness and need to sustain a common life, in the face of the fact that there will be conflicts which will sometimes lead to what appear to be zero-sum outcomes.

I have called the explicit commonality-supporting feature of toleration "mutuality" as distinct from the initiating will to relation. Mutuality is the norm-guided disposition that others who disagree or maintain different practices have a presumptive claim to their differences, and to being our interlocutors in the common political project. Ideally, all groups in society accept this about one another and are aware of these interdependent presumptive claims. For toleration to be a long-term guiding feature of a just society, it must be supported by mutuality as an end, enabling continuous adjustment and negotiation without expecting a conflict-free consensus. These norms are embodied in society in an ethos that values engagement with one's opponents, the role of government and the moral and constitutive worth of the public sphere precisely because it mediates contention. Persons in a diverse society value politics because of their recognition of the structure of human life in the contemporary world. It is diverse and conflict-ridden (even conflict-producing). And, therefore, no one's particular objectives can be conceived as if they existed in isolation from another's, and thus a liberal, tolerant regime is not one in which each separate group will be able *to live life as if the presence of different others were not an enduring reality*. This goes beyond the classical view of a liberal society in stressing that members cannot only care about the terms separating and keeping them safe from one another, but must as strongly and directly care about what binds them together. In this way, mutuality adds to what people care about: they care about their particular cultures and beliefs and also about what enables them to live peacefully and justly with those who don't share these. Persons, individually and as members of groups, accept this about their society and acknowledge the importance of their interdependency. Such a perspective forces individualists on one side and communalists on the other to modify exclusionary, categorical objectives.

In order to flesh out in a cursory, preliminary way what mutuality amounts to concretely, I take up three perspectives from which the core problem of toleration is attacked. All three lines of criticizing toleration do so from the same objection: toleration purports to allow differences to coexist but this core objective is bound to fail. These important challenges are: incompossibility; hegemony and cultural loss; and illiberal minorities.

Incompossibility: One view of liberal toleration holds as its objective the coexistence of radically diverse beliefs and practices. Jeremy Waldron argues that such a place—the condition of "compossibility" as he terms it—cannot exist. He concludes that liberals must accept having reached an impasse: "It seems more honest to admit defeat in the long search for a solution to the algebra of compossibility."[28] Waldron has constructed a powerful case for liberal society's failure to accommodate, without bias, all (reasonable) alternative aims. Given this problem, one would think a claim of mutuality to be a charade (cynical or naïve). In order to show how conceptualizing toleration as a form of mutuality can help us think through the problem Waldron confronts us with, I want briefly to consider two examples he gives. In one situation, Waldron juxtaposes the entrepreneurial pornographer (P) and the devout Muslim (Q) and observes:

> In the example of the pornographer and the Muslim, we concluded that P and Q cannot live together in a liberal arrangement any more than our imagined slave-hunter and his victims could live together. But even if the incompatibility between P and Q is like the incompatibility between the slave-hunter and his victim, it is not clear who, in the case of P and Q, is like the slave-hunter and who is like the victim. Is P like the slave-hunter because he insists on *flaunting* his pornographic wares in a way that makes Muslim life impossible for Q? Or is P like the victim because his *exhibitionism* is crowded out by Q's imperious insistence on a certain sort of pious environment? If a liberal society cannot accommodate P and Q together, then which of them should it throw out? P or Q or both? And what is the principle on which that is to be decided?[29]

Waldron compares this situation to that of the impasse reached between Salman Rushdie and the devout Muslims insulted and disturbed by his publication of *The Satanic Versus.* These examples highlight the problem that no condition exists in which neither party will have to bear being imposed upon, or to have their chosen ends denied. Often sustaining both sets of chosen ends will be impossible in a common world.

Waldron throws a spotlight on the problem intrinsic to liberal toleration: for it to offer a true approach to real differences it must be able to acknowledge and somehow accommodate nonliberal communities and beliefs. But it is impossible that the differences in a society of toleration will remain wholly "protected" in the sense of unconstrained or unrestricted through their having to come into contact with others very unlike them. The objective of toleration as mutuality, however, does not pretend to achieve a "sort of Kantian algebraic liberalism."[30] It directs us toward establishing lines of communication rather than toward securing a space of coexistence that protects each from impingement by others. All societies as systems of *interaction* and imposition require rules of interaction, and as I have stressed toleration must take the nature of interaction, not simply the possibility of coexistence on parallel tracks, into account. What will the terms of that interaction be? What principles might guide our judgment about when one party rather than the other ought to bear the brunt of hard interactions? What can be said to the constrained party that might justify their constriction in any particular conflict?

While the case of P and Q and the Rushdie case are similar in their demonstration of the impossibility of achieving an uncoerced coexistence of ends, they are not similar in how we argue about where the burden of impingement ought to fall. I would suggest that those "proponents of communal or militantly sensitive religions"[31] must always be taken into account: on the one hand, not forced to become liberals, nor on the other, permitted a veto over the direction of public policy. The fact is, if a society is to be defined in part by its capacity for toleration, then at its foundation is a predisposition toward allowance of a broad range of human existence and meaning. This foundation is antithetical, therefore, to those persons who seek to live in a condition of communal and religious uniformity. Toleration cannot characterize their world. Nevertheless, toleration would not exist if it were not sensitive to persons who are "sensitive." It is not present in a purely procedural, callous world of indifference.

In the examples given, we can justify denying protection to the pornographer's ends and justify Rushdie's right to publish. A perhaps too-easy retort to the pornographer is that his desires are of an intentionally offense-producing nature. He desires to *impose* his taste for pornography on "unwilling passers-by": he wants more than just to enjoy pornography in the privacy of his own home, or even to sell it in brown wrappers on the street. If we care about the nature of our intersubjective existence, then it would seem to be relevant whether one's aims rest upon directly causing offense to others. We might say that schadenfreudian aims are not equally worthy of protection, as non-intentionally offensive objectives might be. The pornographer would defend his right to offend others as a right to freedom of expression. But we can object that graphic depictions of sex in the public sphere are a confrontation, an attempt to stop communication rather than maintain it. Interaction is halted: the pornographer's act is a one-time or iterated series of shocks. His is a desire to impinge on others for narcissistic gratification without having to filter this through any norms of artistic expression.

On the other hand, while it is not integral to Q's aim to *cause* offense to others, the devout Muslim's desire *not* to be bombarded with pornographic images on the street might be seen as just as imperialistic as the pornographer's. Where will this desire not to be imposed upon stop? Does acknowledging its power here commit us to its power in the Rushdie case? Salman Rushie is not like the pornographer insofar as Rushdie's aims were not essentially meaningful because they brought pain to Muslims, even though the publication of *The Satanic Versus* certainly had the effect of causing great alarm and shock. For Rushdie, the right to publish what others consider blasphemy is integral to his artistic freedom. The long history of artistic expression, which enables artists to push boundaries beyond the confines of conventional society, is a valuable heritage with political consequences that must be protected in a liberal, tolerant society. What goes on under the aegis of artistic expression will often be offensive to those who reject such experimentation with taste, form, and ideas. Nevertheless, the sensitivity of a community cannot justify the repression of exploration in this realm of human experience. We might argue that the discipline of attempting to present expression in forms of "art" justifies the artist's experimentation. These bounds allow an artist to transgress the tastes of the sensitive persons in the larger society. Clearly, this dichotomy between a purely offensive act and an artistic act that offends deserves much more discussion, which I cannot provide here. What the conception of toleration in terms of mutuality enables us to focus on in these difficult tradeoffs is the way in which the burden of impingement can be justified between those in conflict. In the Rushdie case, the conditions for interaction are maintained when we locate artistic freedom within a protected domain, even as the content is disturbing.

Thus, denying the pornographer and justifying Rushie both result from the need to protect the broad grounds for communication and interaction that make up the background of toleration. These grounds are protected by a commitment to the exploration of language, communication, and ideas generally. This commitment is not reducible to a Millian marketplace of ideas, because not all ideas contribute to the practices of language development. But the domain of artistic experimentation can be conceived as a hard-won political innovation, one contributing to the good of a free and tolerant society.

Hegemony and cultural loss: One of the more persistent attacks on the liberal theory of toleration is that it is itself a hegemonic discourse,[32] which does not resolve but hides (indeed reinforces) power. This is simply the incompossibilty thesis presented with an indictment of the liberal structure. Stanley Fish gained notoriety in arguing that all acts in the public sphere are inevitably acts of domination: to label some beliefs and practices as "intolerant" is itself an arbitrary imposition of power perpetrated by those who happen to be in the majority and get to decide the boundaries of the intolerable for the time being.[33] Because there can be no impartial, absolute standard of acceptability (this we know because of the very need to have toleration), we cannot impose a line between the tolerable and the intolerable that will not have bias built into it. The problem with this line of attack is that to claim that the meaning of all acts in the public sphere can (and therefore should) be reduced to a story about domination makes ethical discourse and intention an absurd undertaking. It is logically and indeed morally wrong to assert that because there is no absolute standard, every attempt to draw a line between the tolerant and intolerant is equally biased, as I argued in discussing incompossibility.

As a standpoint from which to address the problem of cultural loss, however, it must be taken seriously. A major problem in diverse, pluralist societies is the degree to which some groups' practices and beliefs are undermined by the larger, more powerful culture. This issue (along with that of illiberal minorities) has generated a large literature on group rights, which I shall not address here. But the alternatives may to some degree be put succinctly. Defending a version of cultural rights, Charles Taylor has argued that the state ought to positively protect the survival of threatened groups and culture from absorption and dissolution into the larger culture, which inevitably happens when "neutrality" prevails in the application of rights. The curious feature of his argument is his failure to justify singling out as the subject of protection *a culture* as distinct from *a people* holding a culture. He writes:

> It is not just a matter of having the French language available for those who might choose it. . . . [I]t also involves making sure that there is a community of people here in the future that will want to avail itself of the opportunity to use the French language. Policies aimed at survival actively seek to create members of the community, for instance, in their assuring that future generations continue to identify as French-speakers.[34]

But generalizing such a principle raises many difficulties. Which cultures are worth preserving via policies to insure the existence a community of people who will want to carry this culture forward into the future? In this view, people become carriers of culture, rather than culture being worthwhile because it remains a vibrant tool sustaining people who live in a world they want to carry on. Jürgen Habermas makes the right argument, I believe, against this line when he claims that "the protection of forms of life and traditions in which identities are formed is supposed to serve the recognition of their members; it does not represent a kind of preservation of species by administrative means."[35]

On the other hand, writers such as Brian Barry opt for what he calls the rule-and-exemption approach. This is a pragmatic, not a principled political recourse, he insists, asking which legal mechanisms for accommodating and protecting various salient or vulnerable groups within liberal societies should be pursued. He modifies a purist stance of identity-blind liberal justice in order to account for the differential effects of laws on minorities, which can have an eroding effect on the capacity of a people to engage in their distinctive practices. A rule-and-exemption approach "avoids the invidiousness of having different rules for different people in the same society."[36]

In contrast to Barry, who sets the bar high for group exemption, I have stressed that toleration is predisposed to acknowledge the claims of distinctive groups for protection of practices to which they are deeply committed. This version of toleration cannot be reduced to a *carte blanche* for group rights. It begins with the aim of balancing sensitivity to diversity with an aim to mutuality. But it does not see mutuality as guaranteed only through difference-blind neutrality. Mutuality as the acceptance of difference within the rubric of relationship must protect those persons' ability to maintain constitutive practices. In some situations, governmental concessions may be required because of the nature of the threats to the groups (Sikhs being prevented from wearing turbans on motorcycles; the Amish being allowed to take their children out of public schools before the age of 16). In others, the cultural practices will not be justified in seeking exemptions and persons will have to modify their ways of practicing or their beliefs (female genital cutting is a famous example). One might argue that this is a recipe for fragmentation rather than mutuality,[37] but that does not have to be the case.

First, the background condition is always present: objectives cannot be justified in isolation from others. Because we are talking about a society in which there will necessarily be at least public interaction, there can be no claim to isolation from the effects of natural influence and transformation. Protection of groups does not apply to the natural movement of cultural change but rather to the effects of legal restrictions on constituted groups, that is, to the effects produced on particular persons who may be prevented from being able to be who they are because of neutral legal application. Thus, protections apply when practices are eroded owing to legal neutrality rather than simply to cultural shifts, when these practices are constitutive of oneself, and when these constitutive practices are not objectionable according to certain standards, a point I will discuss shortly.

These restrictions may not seem to be enough in the minds of some critics of group exemptions. There will be cries of reverse discrimination that may lead to an unraveling of public engagement by those not given group rights. Instead of mutuality we have particularism spreading on all sides. But this political psychology is not inevitable if a commitment on all sides to political engagement is secured. It can be argued that in being granted distinctive rights, those receiving recognition will find themselves more invested in (rather than resentful and withdrawn from) the polity that has carved out a space for them to continue to uphold important practices and beliefs. In order to address the legitimate demand that the state play a role in protecting groups from dissolution by an overpowering majority without this leading to public policy artificially propping up group preservation, we might make a distinction between what could be called activist identity claims and preservationist identity claims. An active orientation to their own members and an engagement with the public political realm would be important as preconditions for protection. We can directly make room for group differences (wearing religious dress or articles, acknowledging gay rights) because and insofar as in doing so we maintain a vital and engaged public sphere. Thus, there is room for protection of groups from dissolution in this view of toleration, but the nature of the threats to the group's survival, the vitality of the group, and the engagement in a public political realm are important considerations.

Public debate must pose the question: can it be justified to require of some people that they lose the legal and social ability to maintain constitutive practices? Can those who lose nothing face those who lose much of their distinctive nature and claim that this is fair? Ultimately, the principle governing when or when not to recognize a group's distinctive demands must depend on a balance between considerations of political vitality and ethical sustainability. Most important practices of particular believers or cultural groups are not unconscionable (and hence are ethically sustainable) to those with whom they come in contact, even if they are foreign or different. If these beliefs and practices are indeed central to the identity of a group and the application of laws will harm them, then they ought to be allowed. But this will also require reciprocal acknowledgment by the exemption-receiving group to maintain and carry forward their commitment to the vitality of the political realm. Recognition of diverse core beliefs and practices should contribute to the building up of a store of investment in the public good, and will do so as long as these are important core beliefs and as long as those not receiving exemptions recognize the fairness of the policies. Frivolous or purposely divisive identity claims are not a basis for receiving recognition given that such expenditure of public policy detracts from the purpose of the political realm as sustaining mutuality.

Illiberal minorities: Issues raised by the existence of illiberal minorities in a liberal society present in a stark way some of the most important problems facing toleration. The problems they are usually thought to pose are either that such groups demand the right to maintain practices which are antithetical to freedom and equality: how could toleration concede this without transgressing its core values? Or on the other hand, they force toleration to reveal its hidden biases—toleration is displayed to be incapable of neutrality toward such groups and must impose limitations. In the next section, I discuss principles according to which the line between acceptable and unacceptable differences might be justified. Here, I want to focus on alternative approaches to managing relations with illiberal minorities. In some sense, these are the true test case of the logic of toleration as a capacity to maintain relationships of moral significance among persons and groups who are radically different.

Two well-known, contrasting defenses of toleration have been offered by Will Kymlicka and Chandran Kukathas in a lengthy and rich debate that I shall not rehearse. But a couple of observations are in order. Kymlicka insists on the imposition of liberal norms to members of minority groups: "a liberal view requires *freedom within* the minority group."[38] As he writes, "Minority rights will not justify . . . 'internal restrictions'—that is, the demand by a minority culture to restrict the basic civil or political liberties of its own members."[39] The reason for the guarantee of civil and political liberties, he states, is the promotion of individual freedom and personal autonomy. One problem with this argument is that civil and political liberties, while an indispensable structural condition, do not necessarily insure Millian autonomy of the type that enables one to "revise one's plan of life." Certainly, the capacity for individual choice is not guaranteed by most child-rearing practices or most norms of marital relations in the larger, majority "free" culture of individualism, which is accompanied by a highly conformist and consumerist American culture. We may grant the need for civil and political liberties without grounding it in the cause of autonomy. An even more obvious problem with this approach is that to insist on freedom *within* minority groups is to transform them from being illiberal into liberal groups, and the problem of tolerating them disappears. Kymlicka's aim is to defend the principle of liberal tolerance (as opposed to nonliberal tolerance as exemplified in the Ottoman millet system)[40] which integrates nonliberal groups more fully into the norms of a liberal society by making sure that an individual is "free to assess and potentially revise their existing ends."[41] Yet, such groups very often reject this attempt to integrate them into the broader political and social community.

In contrast, Chandran Kukathas makes a virtue out of separatism, beginning with his argument that standard liberal tolerance "does not give any independent weight to toleration at all. This is so because all dealings with illiberal communities are conducted on the basis of settled principles of liberal justice."[42] Kukathas believes another version of toleration could in principle prevent this distortion or constriction of illiberal minority groups (or points of view). Cultural toleration means that we must allow the development of any and all distinctive groups that do not "directly harm the interests of the wider community." Kukathas takes as his starting point the radical incommensurability of cultural differences. Toleration must permit these to flourish—no "we" can judge them to be unacceptable for inclusion in "our" society, because if we take toleration as the core of liberalism, we begin with radical difference and must protect it. The resulting "wider community" is really a loose federation of locally settled groups, and the state merely serves to protect order. Kukathas wants to justify the independent value of toleration in this view by arguing that it enables "free discussion and criticism of all standards and judgments"[43]—a Kant-inspired idea of free public reason. But Kukathas's solution to the question of illiberal groups is not satisfactory either. In coming to this point, he has committed the same evasion as the autonomy-based liberals he criticizes. He writes: "In the world of human settlements, relations between liberal majorities and illiberal minorities amount to a dispute about the nature of the good life to the extent that none is prepared to forsake its own ways and embrace one of the alternatives. For as long as toleration prevails, and no one tries to compel or manipulate the other to live differently, reason also prevails."[44] The crucial clause is: "no one tries to compel or manipulate the other to live differently," which seems a major hurdle to have scaled! Given the interaction over the nature of the public good, not to mention the intolerance of the contemporary world, it is hard to imagine this being more than a utopian ideal of libertarian localism. How could a world of separate peoples manage the claims for authority that inevitably arise? The problem is not just a matter of transitioning from a world in which diverse groups are now interconnected and often in conflict to a world in which each group is partitioned into a separate space and relations have become purely reasonable or disinterested.

Kukathas' implicit view of the nature of culture and of group integrity is misconceived. Intersubjective appraisal and judgment are integral to cultural distinctions, to the basic premises constructing a "people" or group in the first place. A majority culture necessarily "goes inside" a minority to judge the sustainability of the goals of the minority. And the minority is itself—in its very being—a judgment of having chosen an alternative to the majority (at least of the specific beliefs or practices which constitute the majority/minority split). This process of intersubjective, mutual judging does not simply exist at the level of ideas to be debated but at the level of beliefs/practices to be sustained within the boundaries of common life. That is, one would have to hold that it is not unbearable to one's sense of self to live a life cognizant of, and in the same ethical and political universe as someone of a very different way of being. A principle of toleration cannot be founded upon a view of human judgment and value as mutually disinterested or autarkic.

Brian Barry rejects this entire dichotomy of approaches to illiberal groups, arguing instead that liberal theory defends the right to association, which would include a right to associate with groups whose (illiberal) norms we would not want the state to enforce. There is no need to dwell on respecting diversity on the one hand, or protecting autonomy on the other, because the principle is purely about rights to association and exit.[45] Is this enough for a theory of toleration? Specifying decision-rules about the costs of association and exit yields a particular metric of win/lose. But as I have emphasized toleration must attend to the attitudinal level of commitment to forming and abiding by decision-rules that leave some worse and some better off. If we care about the degree of alienation and separatism of illiberal groups in a society, then just specifying rights of association as bulwarks against the state is not enough.

The problem that illiberal minorities pose is not only that they support values contrary to core commitments of freedom and equality for all persons. Indeed, is that really the main issue? The

Catholic Church is based upon hierarchical and gender-biased norms, and there are real costs for those who wish to rescind their membership. But this case is illustrative of the other main issue that illiberal groups pose, which is their insularity from engagement with the majority political and social culture. The Catholic Church does not sequester itself, hence it is not seen as an "illiberal group" even though norms internal to it run contrary to equality for women and complete freedom of choice. In contrast, many of the illiberal groups that serve as examples—Pueblo Indians, the Amish, the Hutterite Church, etc.—seek to maintain a distant, unintegrated relationship with the larger society. Illiberal minorities challenge toleration not simply because they are so different from those usually welcomed by regimes of equal freedom but, importantly, because they seek to remove themselves from practices of a common life. Political engagement is precisely what they do not seek; rather they desire to be allowed a separate space from the majority culture and society. So the demand for toleration in cases of majority versus illiberal minority appears to be a one-way street. This is a structural and an attitudinal situation that must be changed if toleration is to mean anything. How to inject the element of mutuality into the imbalance between the majority and minority? What kinds of arguments can be made to bring these reclusive groups into a sufficiently engaged stance? The objective here is not forced incorporation into the larger society.

We might make the following argument: allow illiberal groups to practice nonegalitarian, restrictive practices within the domain of their membership, but insist on the capacity of persons to enter or exit without prohibitive costs. A person may choose to become a member of a group in which choices are limited and there may be little equality between persons. A person may have spiritual reasons to find this structure of existence attractive and meaningful. The limitation on such groups, however, is that they must secure their membership through the meaningfulness of their practices and ideals and not through coercive techniques in which individuals are forced to enter or kept within the group. The importance of the rules of entrance/exit, therefore, is not simply that they provide freedom of association for individuals, but that these rules are a tangible link between the minority and majority society to prevent minorities from becoming isolated islands. We must guarantee civil and political liberties to enter and exit the group, while we cannot insist on equality and free choice within the group. They serve as a bridge, channel, or corridor to maintain ties and to insure that the basis of membership is meaning and preference rather than fear and coercion.

The solution to the problem of illiberal minorities is not to begin with radical difference and construct public policy to maintain it as an end of political life, as Kukathas argues. Rather, the limits of sustainability of illiberal minorities must be specified through values that are rooted in thinking about why we seek to sustain (and not suppress) such differences in the first place: life, bodily integrity, and protection of meaning. When and if the practices of minority groups trespass these, the state should be called on to intervene. But in order to prevent this from verging in that direction, we ought to experiment with languages and processes of mutuality.

IV. Which Differences: Finding a Common Ethical Language

I have so far focused on toleration as an ideal about relationship that becomes an issue in a context of conflict and disagreement. In this context, it is the disposition to allow differences in order to end violence or coercion, to overcome the insuperability of conflict and to establish and continue a mutually acceptable basis of relationship. I examined this aspect of toleration through its initiating role and in its sustaining role as relations continue to develop and generate new conflicts. My purpose has been to make the relational aspect of toleration clearer, in both its causal and normative functions. But this refocusing of the meaning of toleration has left a crucial question unaddressed. Given that it is impossible to allow all differences, how are the boundaries of the acceptable and unacceptable drawn? A regime that purports to uphold toleration cannot build engaged political relations with persons who practice slave-holding or human sacrifice. But these are not hard cases any longer. What should the argument be against those who perform female genital cutting as a rite of passage? Or what does toleration as mutuality determine about hate speech and wearing the veil in public schools in France? The maintenance of relationship assumes some measure of substantive value, a certain threshold of conceivable ends that determines the range of differences a society can sustain. Toleration begins by taking relationality as a starting point: one must accept the moral immediacy of relationships. One cannot just pronounce in the face of opposition: "this is the truth and I am utterly indifferent to what you believe." One is not just a place-holder for a set of beliefs or cultural practices, rather one is a person always in a context of other persons.

So much may be granted and yet, why would this not simply mean that one must therefore make *every effort,* for the sake of other souls or the sake of the perpetuation of the right practices and beliefs, to convince others of the truth, and to win them to one's side? Relationality may lead to an imperative to convert. We must therefore add to this starting point an acceptance of plurality as part of human existence. The world is made up of ineradicable differences and the pragmatic fact is that this is inescapable. Moral arguments claiming that "harm" is done when a group is "forced" to accept a pluralist society around it are specious. The ever-present reality of differences would require that the imposition of uniformity be an unceasing production of pain, and a human point of view in which relationality plays a recognized part would deny the impossible objective of the conversion of all others. In addition, differences of ethnicity, race, and language—often a focus of calls for toleration—always remain as sources of ever-present plurality.

How do these abstract starting points help determine acceptable differences and those we can justifiably reject? One simple principle might be: reject those differences that inherently reject relationality and plurality (don't tolerate the intolerant). But this is not sufficient, because there are occasions in which the intolerant will be allowed and cases in which discrimination has to be made, and as we've acknowledged a blanket call for pluralism will not work.

We—by this I mean myself and those engaged in this effort, as persons attempting now to defend toleration—want to begin with a language (which may not yet be a set of worked out substantive principles) that has as broad an appeal as possible in the contemporary world, not to set aside concrete ethics in the cause of neutrality. I am not presupposing the principles of toleration as mutuality but arguing for their good, on the assumption that they are human values that persons of all cultures could find meaningful and within which cultural diversity could still be protected. (This disposition is itself not devoid of "bias": some persons or groups may not seek to find a basis for what is ethically shared.) If we look at ethical beliefs across the world, we can find some grounds for a human point of view. Public policy should aim at human well-being, which would be realized by protecting physical and psychological integrity. If a primary aim of politics is to make possible the well-being of persons (even those who emphasize order do so ultimately for the purpose of flourishing life, as Hobbes pointed out), how should we define the criteria of such well-being? The main components would include: that persons not suffer pain and constriction from malevolent or systematic human sources, which could be made otherwise; that persons develop to have a capacity to experience meaning and pleasure in existence and in others; finally, that the sources of meaning and pleasure are not in others' harm or misfortune.

To make use of these basic assumptions, I suggest an idea of physical and psychological integrity. Toleration as mutuality uses a standard to judge where the boundaries of a common life are found. The limits reject practices that prevent physical and psychological integrity. The concept of integrity invokes a state of wholeness and soundness of body, mind, and emotion. Such a notion, as descriptive of an ontological fact is certainly controversial and challenged by psychologists, sociologists, and philosophers, but I believe it provides an important term for a political language of the person, in that it protects the sanctity of human life. Toleration's aim cannot be to guarantee integrity through proactive means, but it ought to preclude actions that one expects will lead to violations of it. Acknowledging the integrity of persons is the only basis for maintaining an ethical relationship with them, and I believe it has an advantage over the idea of the "individual" in that it protects persons as creatures who live sentient and meaningful lives without presuming meaning to be individualized.

Physical integrity is easier to define—systematic norms and acts of bodily violence and coercion are unacceptable.[46] Psychological integrity is much more difficult to specify and must be determined according to prevailing standards of what it means to be a person, with a self and a character, who can think and participate in a cogent, responsible way in the workings of social, cultural, and political life. Protection of integrity precludes systemic denigration of the person, and it precludes denying persons access to prevailing sources of emotional and cognitive fulfillment. The standard of integrity is to some extent relative to a society and the expectations of its citizens, and conflicts derive from this fact.

The logic of relationship and plurality leading to a notion of integrity might run like this: all encounters are occasions of moral immediacy. The basis for interaction must be to recognize the integrity (physical and psychological) of other persons. Toleration prevents or rejects practices that abuse this. The idea of integrity seems naturally linked to relationality in that it enables us to conceive of persons as separate and yet also inherently connected to others through intersubjective norms of action and value.

Does the principle of preventing harm to physical and psychological integrity enable us to draw clear distinctions? Obviously, much more would need to be said about its meaning. It might be helpful to consider as an example the clash between fundamentalist Christians defending the *integrity of marriage* and gays seeking the right to marry. Here one side seeks to gain rights that others already have, while the other seeks to preserve a view of the sanctity of marriage that it genuinely believes to be moral and based upon God's law. If toleration is about protecting the *integrity of the person,* and instrumental to that integrity is access to important sources of economic, political, social, and cultural well-being, then society must give homosexuals access to marriage rights. Preventing access to this form of social recognition of the relationship of marriage insures that those gays who would choose it suffer concretely in terms of not being able to realize an integral psychological, social, and indeed physiological value (given the connection between the body and marriage). Fundamentalists may claim that they suffer as well from mental and spiritual discomfort by having to live in a society that enables this transgression of the sacred relationship of marriage. But their "harm" is not equivalent to that of disenfranchised gays because their own bodies and minds are not forced to be incomplete. Fundamentalists lose out here because their particular values are denied realization as the common good, yet toleration asks that even if they consider homosexuality to be antithetical to their deep, religious sense of self, they must recognize that preventing access to it for millions of gays greatly harms the well-being of their fellow citizens.

In order to continue to live with this other group who want to participate in marriage, the substantive and particular reasons for disagreeing with toleration here are not sufficient grounds for precluding the availability of this important social practice. This reasoning, of course, will not convince those who want to pass the Marriage Protection Amendment to the Constitution, thus, deploying arguments for toleration here based on mutuality and personal integrity will not be a silver bullet. Yet the virtue of the ideal cannot rest on its capacity to accomplish the impossible sleight of hand where both sides win out and determine the common good in accord with their particular view. What it does is to pose the problem in terms of the relationship between both sides: the objective of public policy must be what is most conducive to a *common* existence in which persons who disagree can find a standpoint of mutual justice. Therefore, both must acknowledge a commitment to not prevent access to the most important sources of meaning and value in a society, that is, a commitment to protect all citizens' integrity. Importantly, the point of mutuality is to continue to build a language, terms of communication about such issues. Once discussion ceases, there are no avenues to prevent hardening of the sides.

In this situation, the debate is precisely over the very parameters of social and moral norms and the kind of society that people want to live in. If the norms overridden are of such constitutive importance, the groups losing the capacity to define the common good may believe their own integrity to be severely compromised, and they may seek to withdraw from active participation in collective life and isolate themselves, given that secession is not usually feasible. This is always a possibility and it points again to the importance of politics. In the last analysis, we come down to the question of why would those who believe fundamentally different things desire to live in a society together? Why would they accept that political system as legitimate and trust it to protect the value of all life, if that system protected values with which they fundamentally disagreed?

Conclusion: Politics as Innovative and Transformative

The greatest security we have that people will be drawn to policies and acts protecting openness and respect for others in their differences is through simultaneously reinforcing the distinctive values of a political sphere. These values include the search for justice (through ideas of equality and fairness) and engagement through communication, argumentation, and negotiation of conflict. The political sphere must be valued in its own right precisely and insofar as it is the only realm in which conflict and difference can be acknowledged and overcome, not to reach a consensus, but as a continuing constitutive activity of moral existence. The great benefits and virtues of a common history, contemporary life, and future have to be a focus of politics.

The coercive strength of the state is not enough to ensure allegiance; its moral aspirations have to be genuinely acknowledged and pursued. This active normative side of the state is not only institutionalized through a rule of law, and embedded in civil society, but also realized through a public sphere in which the presence of different groups is acknowledged in full awareness as a condition of interaction.[47] Fragmentation and alienation can be guarded against if the political realm remains an innovative and transformative area of interaction. Groups cannot be written off. Principles guiding this sphere must be first, that no one can explicitly and by right control public culture and public norms. Arguments that justify intentional control of collective norms through legal action are to be rejected. Secondly, following this will no doubt require some element of substantive value change insofar as the political public life will have to become a primary, though by no means the main, orientation of all persons. Against those who believe this to be impossible because of the total commitment of the traditionalist to his/her group, I would argue that such a view of group commitment must be wrong about the ties modern persons have to particularist communities.[48] It is a myth that "groups" are incapable of engaging and articulating particularist ties and reasons for their values. Because of the nature of modern society, which constantly forces a comparison between forms of life, ideals, and cultures, all persons can—and the political process must be conducive to this—express what about their lives is worth living, even if the ideals remain ones that others would not want to take up themselves. Cultural practices and beliefs that cause division can be made sufficiently less threatening, so that a process of continuing to live together is conceivable and desired.

Furthermore, an ideal of toleration must infuse citizens' commitment to upholding this type of society. Thus attitudes of citizenship support the value of public life: an ethos of a common world requires that all persons in the interaction are aware, open, and respectful of one another's differences and the potential for conflict. The point of public interaction is to act out a will to find a sharable point of view—that simply is what impartiality consists in: the conscious recognition of a common world in which one's actions have consequences. And fourth, the vitality of the public sphere requires leadership, particularly in times of transition. The leadership of a state must not only explicitly support the cultural and ideological underpinnings of a tolerant society, it must also try to encourage social and moral values conducive to an active and engaged public life for all citizens. It must do this through leadership about the value of public interaction itself. The main contention of this essay is that toleration rests upon a capacity—constructed through public language, individual ethics, cultural ethos, public policy, and the vitality of political institutions—to maintain ongoing relationships of negotiation, compromise, and mutuality.

Discussions of toleration today often seem lodged between a rock and a hard place—on the one side it is claimed by moral reason, on the other, by politics as war by other means. Each side enlists toleration as essentially its own. But toleration shares with moral reason an aspiration to establish a basis for relationships beyond coercion, and it shares with politics as war an abiding recognition of the inevitable conflicts and alienness between persons or groups and the tradeoffs these involve. The kind of relationship or form of mutuality that toleration consists in is grounded neither solely in abstract moral reason nor in a pure self-interested balance of power. This in-between status, I hope to have shown, does not leave toleration in a contradictory, untenable, or hypocritical position, but offers a robust and attractive vision of what is entailed by it. It is precisely a capacity to maintain distinctions and to live fairly with others in recognition of them that characterizes the unique ethical nature of toleration. Against communalist identity, toleration asserts: when you build a politics that asks for only a part of yourself, you build a stronger polity because you build it out of the commitment of a vast array of persons, each one of whom can bring to it the vibrancy of particular knowledge, aesthetics, ethics, and experience. Against the rational strategist, the *laissez faire* liberal, or the cultural separatist, toleration as I have interpreted it asserts that the involvement of persons in the public sphere, in the realm of their common world, must be a primary commitment and not a derivative and functional one. While the self does not become subsumed in the public, its identification must be a core part of its identity.

A final observation: I have focused on politics in its role of upholding relations of toleration. But "politics" itself is protean and changes in it today lead us to rethink how it can serve this purpose. In the early modern period, toleration was in part brought about through a justification of the nation-state as a realm of justice and accountability. The boundaries of the sovereign state stabilized the realm of politics as a focus of normative obligation. Today, the destabilization of political boundaries presents us with new and urgent problems. One of the causes of contemporary intolerance is the threat to assumptions about allegiance, loyalty, and the parameters of obligation. Changes in politics have also led to prevalent outbreaks of great intolerance and violence. To reassert the primary value of toleration between diverse people we need to continue the positive innovative rather than coercive and domination-seeking work of politics.[49]

NOTES

1. Instances are too numerous to count. Amy Gutmann and Dennis Thompson contrast it unfavorably with "mutual respect" (see *Democracy and Disagreement* [Cambridge, MA: The Belknap Press of Harvard University Press, 1996], 79). According to David Heyd, it might in the future be recognized to have been "an interim value," useful between an age of imposition of uniformity of value and that of complete acceptance and

openness toward beliefs and cultures. David Heyd, "Introduction," *Toleration: An Elusive Virtue* (Princeton, NJ: Princeton University Press, 1996), 5. Notable denunciations of the nature of the tolerant relationship have been those of Goethe who found it insulting; Kant's view of it as a paternalistic, haughty form of *noblesse oblige*; T. S. Eliot who believed the Christian did not wish to be tolerated; and Marcuse's rejection of it as repressive.

2. See Brian Barry's critique of this trend in *Culture and Equality* (Cambridge, MA: Harvard University Press, 2001), 118ff. Anna Galeotti (*Toleration as Recognition* [Cambridge: Cambridge University Press, 2002]) argues for a view of toleration as recognition, which moves in this direction.

3. I thank Melissa Williams for emphasizing the usefulness of the locution "will to relationship."

4. See for example, John Horton's entry in *The Blackwell Encyclopaedia of Political Thought*, ed. David Miller (Cambridge, MA: Blackwell Publishers, 1991), 521; Glen Newey, *Virtue, Reason and Toleration* (Edinburgh: Edinburgh University Press, 1999), 18ff. Many moral philosophers restrict their application of the idea of toleration strictly to moral disagreement or conflicts of belief and stipulate that toleration does not apply to questions of racism or homophobia and so on, thereby severely curtailing the relevance of a theory of toleration to contemporary conflicts. Peter Nicholson takes this position:

> Sometimes "dislike" is added to "disapproval" . . . for instance, Cranston argues that unless we include 'dislike' we cut out such matters as racial prejudice. . . . A definition of the moral ideal, however, must exclude "dislike." Raphael correctly stresses that we must see the moral ideal of toleration solely in terms of disapproval, i.e. of the making of judgements and the holding of reasons over which moral argument is possible.

Peter P. Nicholson, "Toleration as a Moral Ideal" in *Aspects of Toleration*, eds. John Horton and Susan Mendus (London: Methuen, 1985), 160. Where does the necessity—the "must"—in this description of toleration come from? It is a rational must derived from the dictates of moral argument. The problem with this is that in maintaining toleration on grounds of pure moral reason, we loose the applicability of toleration to the ethics of life, the essential *raison d'etre* of a language of toleration in the first place. This neglects some of the most urgent issues in which the language of toleration is now used.

5. Glen Tinder in his book *Tolerance: Toward a New Civility* (Amherst: University of Massachusetts Press, 1976), takes as his epigraph a quotation from Simone Weil: "Attentiveness is the rarest and purest form of

generosity." This captures a quality of toleration that is too often overlooked in the conventional definition of it. Note Mill's discussion of Mormonism: "they have been chased into a solitary recess in the midst of a desert" (J. S. Mill, *On Liberty* [Cambridge: Cambridge University Press, 1989], 91)—not exactly an example of toleration. I thank Andy Altman for mentioning this example.

6. See Barry Barnes "Tolerance as a Primary Virtue," *Res Publica* 7, No. 3 (2001), for a discussion of this essentially human capacity.

7. Thomas Nagel, "Moral Conflict and Political Legitimacy," *Philosophy and Public Affairs* 16, No. 3 (Summer 1987), 229. Its importance is also brought out through the extent to which it helps us rethink some persistent questions such as the "paradox" of toleration, which asks how it is that one could fundamentally believe a practice to be wrong and yet not stop it. Disapproving too strongly, one could not tolerate at all (e.g., child pornography), but if one does not disapprove enough, why call the attitude or act toleration? We are then merely indifferent or alternatively even welcoming of difference. Toleration is a paradox if we see it as merely a matter of unilateral individual moral calculation. Then, indeed we wonder how this could be possible. But if we recognize that the demand of toleration to restrict oneself is motivated by a need for mutuality of some sort, then the paradox lessens, because another source of motivation comes into view. Additional considerations beyond those of protecting one's moral judgments about belief X or cultural practice Y are at work in one's motivation to be tolerant. Thomas Scanlon highlights this interpretation as well: "What tolerance expresses is a recognition of common membership that is deeper than these conflicts, a recognition of others as just as entitled as we are to contribute to the definition of our society" (Scanlon, *The Difficulty of Tolerance,* [Cambridge: Cambridge University Press, 2003], 193) and "the case for tolerance lies in the fact that rejecting it involves a form of alienation from one's fellow citizens" (ibid., 194).

8. Nagel, 231.

9. Ibid., 229.

10. Ibid., quotes on 230.

11. Ibid., 229–30.

12. Furthermore, in situations of moral conflict over issues like abortion, it may be the case that when we justify "allowing" abortion or "allowing" freedom of sexual conduct because of the fact that conflicting points of view on these issues are not amenable to open, public debate, but instead rest on deeply personal, often inaccessible reasons—when we "justify" allowance of these for these reasons—this in itself is a different political act than one in which we allow them because we support them as conducive to a liberal lifestyle.

13. John Locke, *A Letter Concerning Toleration* (Indianapolis: Hackett, 1983), 23.

14. Melissa Williams's essay "Tolerable Liberalism" clearly lays out the relationships among arguments for toleration. The main arguments she considers are those founded on reasons of freedom, equality, and peace. She notes: "What I find is that despite the marginalization of peace-based considerations in the liberal theory of toleration, in practice such considerations creep in constantly to temper the judgments that freedom or equality would dictate." "Tolerable Liberalism," in *Minorities within Minorities,* eds. Avigail Eisenberg and Jeff Spinner-Halev (Cambridge: Cambridge University Press, 2005), 22. Her conclusion that "giving deliberative priority to peace-as-social-concord is likely to lead to a more creative liberalism" (ibid., 40) supports my focus on relationship as part of the core of toleration.

15. What then is the connection between the reasons usually given in defense of toleration and the role of mutuality? We might picture the two versions as follows. Version 1 would be constructed as $D + C (R^1, R^2, R^3) = T^1$, where D is disagreement/difference; C is constraint; and R is reason. Version 2: $D + M + C (R^1, R^2, R^3) = T^2$, where M is mutuality. My argument is that as a political, public practice and ideal, toleration only makes sense as T^2.

16. The fact that these differences cannot be eradicated is itself a significant cultural point which limits what politics must or can become. Indeed one of the lessons of the religious wars was the power of ideas and the insufficiency of violence to eradicate them. Or perhaps it was the case that the stomach for decimation of an intransigent population was becoming less hardened, again this would indicate a major cultural change.

17. Some writers deny the applicability of the story of the emergence of "classical" toleration to contemporary conflicts. Antoine Garapon, for instance, in "The Law and the New Language of Tolerance" in Paul Ricoeur, *Tolerance Between Intolerance and the Intolerable* (Providence, RI: Berghahn Books, 1996), 71–89, argues that the original type of conflict over religious beliefs was a clash of definitions of societal good, beliefs that constituted "conflicting institutionalized cultures" while contemporary issues of toleration pertain to diversity of lifestyles, between individuals emancipating themselves from a dominant culture. A different critique focuses on the inapplicability of the logic of toleration because it relegates differences of conscientious belief beyond the scope of public power—privatizing them—while today's "differences" are inherently constituted by public power—and hence cannot be privatized as religious beliefs were. See Kirstie M. McClure, "Difference, Diversity and the Limits of Toleration," *Political Theory* 18 (August 1990), 361–91.

18. James Tully, writing about Skinner's work on the early modern period, notes: "Effectual changes in European political thought and action in this period are the consequences of wars and practical struggles and, secondarily, the outcome of the ideological response to the legitimation crises engendered by the shifting power relations that give way to battle." See *Meaning and Context, Quentin Skinner and His Critics,* ed. James Tully (Princeton, NJ: Princeton University Press, 1988), 23–24. See also John Horton and Susan Mendus, eds., *Aspects of Toleration* (London: Methuen, 1985), 1–2.

19. John Rawls, *Political Liberalism* (New York: Columbia University Press, 1993), 159.

20. Perez Zagorin, *How the Idea of Religious Toleration Came to the West* (Princeton, NJ: Princeton University Press, 2003), 13, 289.

21. I examine these questions and the aspects of value change integral to this shift toward toleration at length in *Toleration and Identity.*

22. Quoted in Joseph Lecler, *Toleration and the Reformation,* Volume II, trans T. L. Westow (London: Longmans, 1960), 45.

23. Anthony Marx in *Faith in Nation: Exclusionary Origins of Nationalism* (Oxford: Oxford University Press, 2003) makes the argument that policies of toleration were part of state-building as an inclusive project, but that public passions often proved too powerful to accept the construction of order in this form. Hence rulers resorted to exclusionary forms of nationalist state-building as well as the inclusive toleration-based form.

24. The fact that "unity" was premised upon excluding Catholics might be taken to undercut the moral significance of this partial universalism. But normative change happens in different ways. The language of impartiality eventually came to be used to critique the partiality of the initial settlement.

25. In *Toleration and Identity: Foundations in Early Modern Thought* (New York: Routledge, 2003), I have looked at Montaigne and Defoe in this regard; the works of Spinoza, Grotius, and Bayle, are also crucial.

26. Note Glen Newey's view that its conceptual structure renders toleration *ex ante* empty. For Newey, the principle of toleration reduces to a balancing of (a) reasons for disapproving an action/belief and (b) reasons for (however) not preventing the (disapproved of) action/belief. A person who disapproved of gay marriage and yet allowed it exemplifies toleration whereas a person who did not disapprove and allowed it, or a person who did disapprove and did not allow it would not exemplify toleration. This purely analytical definition of toleration is not intrinsically admirable because it may be the case that we are unjustified in our initial disapproval, or that the reasons given to nevertheless not prevent it are not morally robust. Thus, he emphasizes the limited and contingent na-

ture of toleration. Things we may have tolerated in the past are now accepted and cannot therefore be "tolerated" any longer. Examples of past toleration, e.g., between Catholics and Protestants in France, or Anglicans and Dissenters in England, display the inherently asymmetrical element of power in toleration and indicate its only contingently liberal character. But tendentious examples like smoking display the purely formal rendition of Newey's understanding of this "value," and leave us wondering why the discourse of the modern world keeps using "toleration" if its resonances are as empty as he asserts. Newey is right on one level, insofar as he correctly describes toleration as dependent on competing definitions of public policy for directing the application of toleration, but I would contend that this does not exhaust the content of its ethics.

27. See note 6 above.

28. Jeremy Waldron, "Toleration and Reasonableness" in *The Culture of Toleration in Diverse Societies,* eds. Catriona McKinnon and Dario Castiglione (Manchester: Manchester University Press, 2003), 33.

29. Ibid., 20 (my emphasis).

30. Ibid., 19.

31. Ibid., 33.

32. See Newey's contribution to this volume.

33. He writes: "[A]ny regime of tolerance will be founded by an intolerant gesture of exclusion. (This is a criticism only from the perspective of the impossible goal a regime of tolerance sets for itself.) And those who institute such a regime will do everything they can to avoid confronting the violence that inaugurates it and will devise ways of disguising it, even from themselves." Stanley Fish, *The Trouble with Principle* (Cambridge, MA: Harvard University Press, 1999), 167. One wonders how those who lived through purges in Stalinist Soviet Union, the cultural revolution in China, Pol Pot's Cambodia, Khomeini's Iran, or lynching in the American south would equate the "violence" of liberal toleration to their experience.

34. "The Politics of Recognition," *Multiculturalism and "The Politics of Recognition,"* ed. Amy Gutmann (Princeton, NJ: Princeton University Press, 1994), 58–59.

35. He continues:

> the ecological perspective on species conservation cannot be transferred to cultures. Cultural heritages and the forms of life articulated in them normally reproduce themselves by convincing those whose personality structures they shape, that is, by motivating them to appropriate productively and continue the traditions. The constitutional state can make this hermeneutic achievement of the

> cultural reproduction of life-worlds possible, but it cannot guarantee it.

Jürgen Habermas, "Struggles for Recognition in the Democratic Constitutional State," in *Multiculturalism and "The Politics of Recognition,"* 130.

36. Ibid., 39.

37. For a typical objection to it in principle, see e.g., Barry, *Culture and Equality* (Cambridge, MA: Harvard University Press, 2001), 4–8.

38. Will Kymlicka, *Multicultural Citizenship* (Oxford: Clarendon Press, 1995), 152.

39. Ibid.

40. Ibid., 156.

41. Ibid., 158.

42. Kukathas, "Cultural Toleration," *Ethnicity and Group Rights,* NOMOS XXXIX, ed. by Ian Shapiro and Will Kymlicka (New York: New York University Press, 1997), 78.

43. Ibid., 80.

44. Ibid., 82.

45. Barry argues that the real issue in deciding upon principles to govern illiberal groups is freedom of association and freedom to exit such associations. There must be a balance between groups being able to decide on membership and exclusion in order to be able to maintain their own affairs, and prevention of costs to individuals who may wish to exit such groups. See Barry, *Culture and Equality* (Cambridge, MA: Harvard University Press, 2001).

46. Judith Shklar, through her idea of a liberalism of fear, eloquently defended the worth of toleration as a rejection of intolerance: "liberalism's deepest grounding is in . . . the conviction of the earliest defenders of toleration, born in horror, that cruelty is an absolute evil, an offense against God or humanity," in "The Liberalism of Fear," *Liberalism and the Moral Life,* ed. Nancy L. Rosenblum (Cambridge, MA: Harvard University Press, 1989), 23.

47. This notion is in line with Rawls's depiction of public reason. His approach to the function of the public sphere however tends to assume reason as already operative in the coming to negotiate differences, whereas I have sought to portray the aspirational nature of the public sphere as a means of bringing about effective political identity formation between those in conflict. See, e.g., Rawls, "The Idea of Public Reason Revisited," *The Law of Peoples* (Cambridge, MA: Harvard University Press, 1999).

48. Even in the proverbial case of the Amish, they cannot seek to protect a complete purity of culture. Indeed the Amish have adapted insofar as they have had to learn to argue their rights/interests in a secular court

of law, and they have had to take up new economic activities as their farming has been undercut by market forces (now entering the woodworking industry and arguing that their 14 year olds ought to be exempt from child labor laws that will not allow children under 18 to work in factories with heavy machinery). See George Simmel's classic analysis of the types of ties characterizing modern group affiliations versus medieval group locations, *Conflict and the Web of Group Affiliations* (New York: The Free Press, 1955).

49. I thank the following people for comments on this chapter: Andrew Altman, Dario Castiglione, Noah Feldman, John Ferejohn, Steven Kelts, Glen Newey, Melissa Schwartzberg, and Melissa Williams.

14

TOLERATION, POLITICS, AND THE ROLE OF MURALITY

GLEN NEWEY

I. Introduction

Ingrid Creppell's essay "Toleration, Politics, and the Role of Mutuality" offers a rich and wide-ranging reinterpretation of toleration. In contrast with some writers, Creppell displays an admirable feel for the intractability of modern disputes over toleration. She is also right to argue that justifying toleration by appeal to "pure moral reason" is self-defeating because it cannot show clearly how toleration applies to the attitudes involved in real-life conflicts, which is "the essential *raison d'être* of a language of toleration."

In controversies over toleration the futility of moralizing *in vacuo,* or wishing that the protagonists were differently motivated, is more than usually obvious, and Creppell avoids this pitfall. The principal virtue of her paper, however, is its salutary emphasis on *politics* (rather than, say, judicial processes) as the primary and inescapable medium through which real disputes involving toleration are conducted. I shall however argue that the political basis of conflicts about toleration, once properly understood, supports a less normatively ambitious account of toleration than hers. This scaling down of normative ambitions becomes the more compelling if we keep in mind the peculiarity of toleration as a concept.

This chapter falls into two main parts. First, I offer a critique of Creppell's mutuality-based account of toleration. Second, I develop from this critique an alternative approach, *toleration as murality,* which emphasizes the importance of securing the civic peace on which toleration depends. I shall argue that in fact this can create greater scope for toleration than Creppell's theory, or those of other liberals.

II. Toleration as Mutuality

(a) Exposition

It is central to Creppell's argument that mutuality is "part of the core meaning of toleration,"[1] in contrast with "conventional"[2] theories which focus on toleration as non-interference or non-coercion in the face of (moral or other) disapproval. She argues that the conventional view must be supplemented by the "crucial" claim that "one remains in a relationship with the person or group with whom one is in conflict. We do not call an act toleration if disapproval and restraint are followed by a retraction of contact, or by ignoring or making the other invisible."[3] The commonality or mutuality of the relationship is an "essential"[4] condition of toleration; thus the accommodation required by acts of toleration occurs within the context of a continuing relationship between tolerators and tolerated.

Creppell argues that there are historical reasons underlying the conventional theory's stress on self-restraint. During the early modern period in Europe toleration arose in "situations of asymmetrical power,"[5] e.g., between the monarchical state and heterodox religious minorities such as the Huguenots in France, or Dissenters in England. Because the paradigmatic context of toleration involved asymmetries of power, theories have mistakenly inferred that toleration can be exhaustively analyzed as self-restraint on principled grounds by the relatively powerful towards the relatively impotent. Now that we "live in conditions of relative equality," she contends, "different aspects of its normative force come to the foreground."[6] These aspects are held to explain both why restraint is seen as appropriate, and also why, for modern-day tolerators, it is insufficient.

"[R]estraint is motivated because of a pre-existing will to relationship" which "set[s] the stage" for "norms of political mutuality."[7] It is not the "initiating will to relationship" which supports toleration directly, but the commitment to mutuality which is held to result from it. To accept mutuality is to accept that others "have a presumptive claim to their differences, and to being our interlocutors in the common political project."[8] Thus mutuality is not simply an adventitious condition of political life, but rather an explicit end in itself.

Creppell goes on to argue that with mutuality *qua* "will to relationship" in the foreground, it becomes clear that modern liberal theory's answer to toleration—public neutrality between conceptions of the good life—is "strained."[9] Nor, however, should we react, like such advocates of "difference" as Iris Young, by endorsing a form of balkanization in which minority groups are offered wholesale opt-outs from the public sphere. Creppell's third way between neutrality and difference sides with difference theorists in giving due weight to "identity" as a bargaining-chip in political conflicts, while insisting, against these theorists, that identity-groups cannot simply secede from the public sphere as a realm of mutuality.

This sphere is transactional and transformative: it sets the stage for encounters between identities, but the very fact of political encounter is liable to transform the identities in an open-ended way. Creppell's concession to liberal neutralists lies in her demand that mutuality sets an impartial standard by which specific issues involving toleration can be judged: we should "make policy decisions to resolve conflicts so that the reasoning and results sustain the mutual benefit of [our] common but diverse lives."[10]

(b) Critique

At the outset of her chapter, Creppell argues that the concept of toleration is *essentially* characterized by mutuality. There appears, first, to be a certain tension between the conceptual analysis of toleration which Creppell offers, and her historical-cum-genealogical argument about the origins of the "conventional" picture. Arguments about what is "essential" to the conceptual structure of toleration are arguments about those properties of toleration without which it would not be the concept that it is—that is, without which the concept under examination would not be toleration at all. Mutuality is such a property, on Creppell's analysis. But then we cannot say of the early modern period, with its asymmetries of power and consequent lack of mutuality, that it met the conditions required for the exercise of toleration. It merely met the conditions for principled self-restraint.

But *is* mutuality essential to toleration? It depends, obviously, on how mutuality itself is characterized. It is clear that Creppell's "mutuality" builds upon, and is not itself an implication of, the "will to relationship" idea. After all, the mere will to relationship is consistent with a lack of mutuality, at least if mutuality entails equality: a relationship may for example be willed from either side as dominating or dependent. Creppell highlights ostracism, the withdrawal of relationship, as the antithesis of toleration. But some relationships continue, and are willed to continue, as embodiments of shame, humiliation, or other forms of degradation. This suggests that the idea of relationship will not by itself do the normative work which she wants from it.

Creppell contends that demands for toleration have historically taken the form of demands for equality: excluded groups demand inclusion as full citizens, co-equal with others.[11] However, Creppell argues, the reason those calling for toleration have demanded equality is because this is the only way in which "relationships [can be] maintained."[12] The demand for equality is thus "subsequent to a will to relationship."[13] Thus, for Creppell, the "will to relationship" characterizes what I call the *circumstances of toleration*—that is, the conditions in which it becomes a practical question whether or not something should be tolerated.

If mutuality requires equality, as Creppell's contrast with the asymmetries of power in early-modern conditions suggests, then cases of toleration will be much harder to come by than if mutuality allows for hierarchical roles. The circumstances of toleration will only arise when the practical issue involves a demand for mutuality. This is not an objection in itself, but it does underline an important, if obvious, fact which is sometimes ignored in theoretical writing on the subject: what counts as toleration, and hence its scope as a value or virtue, will be shaped by explicit or tacit assumptions about the nature of toleration as a concept. Any philosophical theory of toleration will analyze the concept in a certain way, and that analysis, in conjunction with relevant values or norms, will determine not only which policies count as tolerant, but also when the circumstances of toleration arise in the first place. Thus to adopt an account of toleration is to decide, at least broadly, when a political issue involves *toleration,* rather than some other consideration. When someone adopts an account of toleration, it *shapes* her view of when the circumstances of toleration arise. Thus Creppell's view of toleration is shaped by mutuality,[14] so that only those political relationships which display the ideal of mutuality instantiate toleration. Similarly, the circumstances of toleration will arise only when the conflicting parties are committed to this ideal.

But this analysis becomes hard to sustain when we take into account the quite specific role which Creppell envisages for mutuality. Sometimes Creppell refers to the idea of a "common world"[15] shared by tolerators and tolerated, and there is a clear, if platitudinous, sense in which all parties in the circumstances of toleration inhabit a common world: for example, the tolerators must be in a position to influence the interests of the tolerated for good or ill. Before this, there is the yet more obvious point that we all have to inhabit the same planet, or state, and this already raises questions of toleration. However, Creppell's account of mutuality goes beyond mere cohabitation, or the brute fact of influence. It seems to require, as a condition of toleration, that the parties regard mutuality—a commitment to a relationship between equals—as a substantive *goal* of their interaction. But this is very rarely the case in politics, and only intermittently the case elsewhere. It would be more plausible to treat mutuality as a side-constraint, in Robert Nozick's sense,[16] on political encounters—a condition which such encounters have to meet, rather than their goal. But even this is rarely the case with sectarian conflicts, for instance, or the other clashes of outlook which exemplify the circumstances of toleration. In these circumstances, concern for mutuality is liable to be noticeable only by its absence.

Political theorists risk distorting conflicts over toleration by shaping them in an unduly theory-friendly way. There is a strain of normative theorizing which prides itself on its blithe disregard of political realities. But the idealizing approach is peculiarly inappropriate to toleration, which, as has been pointed out,[17] only becomes politically contentious when a conflict breaks out between people who are not acting tolerantly. The danger in analyzing toleration through a partly normative concept such as mutuality is that we lose sight of what made it a political problem to start with.[18] If the concern with mutuality had been uppermost in the minds of the protagonists, they presumably would not have acted as they did.

To take an example which I have discussed at greater length elsewhere,[19] the continuing sectarian conflict in Northern Ireland between the unionist and nationalist traditions gives rise to many political clashes which, on the face of it, can be characterized as disputes over toleration. During the annual marching season, for example, sectarian tensions often arise from the desire of unionist or loyalist Orange Lodges to march through predominantly nationalist residential areas, such as Drumcree. The conflict has become inflamed when residents' leaders have refused to permit the routing of marches through their neighborhoods, while the lodge masters have on occasion refused to be diverted from what they regard as a traditional route. The deadlock thus created might be said to result from a failure of mutuality. Neither side displays much of a "will to relationship" with the other: in fact, these conflicts are so divisive in part because the marches are charged with symbolic force, as symbols of *sectarian* power. The issue is so hard to resolve precisely because each side sees the stakes as all-or-nothing, with nothing left for the vanquished. If an overriding concern with mutuality prevailed, there would be no problem to solve.

Shaping toleration by mutuality is thus liable to leave a blind spot *vis-à-vis* real political conflicts, since the lack of any commitment to mutuality is precisely what marks these conflicts. The same goes for other normative ideals which have been proposed by theorists of toleration, such as autonomy,[20] or "recognition."[21] The blind spot extends not only to theorists' proposed solution to these conflicts, but even to the characterization of them as conflicts over *toleration.* If only those with a regard for the value of mutuality (or for autonomy, recognition, etc.) are tolerant, it is a short step to the conclusion that conflicts between those who lack any regard for the value do not really involve toleration at all.

Rather they are clashes between parties whose intolerance puts them beyond the pale of a theory of toleration.

Creppell does in fact begin by imposing an extremely demanding standard for philosophical justifications of toleration. She argues that we should ask whether these justifications are such that the protagonists in fact accept them. For instance, in discussing Thomas Nagel's neutralist theory, Creppell criticizes Nagel's appeal to an epistemic division between public and private realms, whereby the standard for public justification is more demanding than for private beliefs, so I may hold private beliefs which I cannot justify publicly; Nagel's ulterior point, which has been argued by other neutralist defenders of toleration,[22] is that I should tolerate beliefs which diverge from my own if the latter cannot be publicly justified. Creppell argues that this will not provide a "necessary logic *for the devout,* from *within* their point of view."[23] That is, if there is a conflict between the secular and the devout over some issue of policy, it is pointless to appeal to a standard of political legitimacy—i.e., whether a given reason can be publicly justified—which only the secularist accepts. What is needed, presumably, is a standard of justification which is acceptable, in the strong sense of actually being accepted, by both parties.

As this passage shows, Creppell suggests that liberal attempts such as Nagel's to resolve disputes between, for example, secularists and religious dogmatists are unsatisfactory precisely because they threaten merely to repeat, rather than resolve, the conflicts of value which give rise to them in the first place—what I shall refer to as the *reiteration problem.* That is, political conflicts express clashes of value; but if liberal political theorists respond to these clashes by reaffirming a value, which by hypothesis one or other of the parties is liable to reject, the proposed "solution" merely reiterates the problem—a conflict of values—rather than solving it. As the Nagel example shows, the problem can be posed not just with substantive justifications, but with proposed methods for deriving them, such as neutrality: the devout do not want a neutral state, but one skewed in favor of their own religious doctrines. It is this which is held to show that neutrality does not provide "a necessary logic for the devout."

However, the reiteration problem arises with mutuality as well. Why should mutuality, the upshot of parties' "will to relationship," prove compelling for those who lack any such will? The truism that all parties to conflicts have to occupy the same space leaves their attitudes towards peaceful coexistence entirely open. People wage war, the ultimate rejection of relationship, precisely in order to avoid having to coexist with an intolerable other. And war has its analogue in the legal proscription of acts which the polity finds that it cannot countenance. In other words, mutuality provides a basis for coexistence—except when it does not. Like every other normative basis for toleration, mutuality has to distinguish the polity's friends—those whom the dominant party is prepared to accept—from its enemies. This is inevitable: it is a condition of political life. Another way of putting this point is to say that the reiteration problem has no solution.

Given the reiteration problem, the liberal theory of toleration threatens to become what critics sometimes call a "hegemonic discourse," which serves to supplant, rather than confront, the questions about power which prompted liberals to worry about justification in the first place. In many situations a form of hegemony is unavoidable; it certainly need not be undesirable. Liberals must agree with this, since they defend the state against anarchists, and the liberal state against anti-liberal statists. But if they ignore the role of sheer power in toleration, liberals risk deceiving themselves not only about their own motives, but about the benignity of liberal ideology in practice.

Creppell's critique of Nagel suggests that the normative thinning aims to get round the reiteration problem, by basing toleration on minimally controversial foundations. Mutuality is held to be of the essence of toleration, and at times Creppell writes as if "mutuality" were synonymous with the fact of coexistence. But once mutuality is construed as something more normatively fat, such as a relationship whose aim is mutuality, it will exclude many political relationships, and by hypothesis most of those relationships in which toleration is an issue. Where it is an issue, toleration forces polities to distinguish friends and enemies. There is no basis for toleration so thin that it can avoid excluding some groups, in the form either of direct legal proscription, or of other political, legal or social penalties. This also applies to those who, conscientiously or opportunistically, cast themselves as put-upon "identities."

Mutuality apparently precludes a possibility which is also strikingly absent from many other theories of toleration, including ostensibly liberal ones. That is the idea that toleration has to do with accepting what is unpalatable, including some things which may be unpalatable for the theorist of toleration herself. In common with other writers like Galeotti, Creppell offers a pivotal value, mutuality,[24] on which toleration is to be based. At this point, the argument often tends to be applied to resolving disputed areas of public policy such as homosexual marriage, the public status of religious symbols, pornography, and so on. As we have already seen, this necessarily runs afoul of the reiteration problem. What these applications cannot do is to dissolve the conflicts of value which first made these questions disputed: either the protagonists accept the pivotal value, but interpret it as supporting their own position, or they regard the fact that it does not as a reason for rejecting it.

However, having unearthed a value which is held to solve or sideline the reiteration problem, theorists of toleration feel free to advocate their favored solutions to political problems, which now acquire the added allure of being "tolerant." It is in keeping with this approach that the alleged implications of the value usually prove to confirm the theorist's first-order convictions; for example, that the underlying value prohibits female genital mutilation as practiced by some traditional African societies while permitting male genital mutilation as practiced by orthodox Jews. My concern is not whether these convictions are justified. It is rather that the theorists seem seldom to entertain the idea that the practical implications of the philosophical theories they espouse, especially those regarding the normative foundations of toleration, might be uncomfortable for *them.* This makes their theories, appearances notwithstanding, not really theories of toleration at all. They are rather theories of what people with other ("intolerant") convictions should have to put up with, backed up by an appeal to the pivotal value which the theorist herself accepts.

A large question underlies these divergent views about the nature of toleration. Why do we have politics? Why do we have the government of people, and not merely the administration of things? The most general answer to this question is this: because, at least a lot of the time, it is not obvious what to do. Either nobody knows what to do, or too many people with conflicting ideas claim to know what to do. Politics provides various kinds of mechanism by which to break through indecision to action. These mechanisms seldom involve the dispassionate application of pure reason to practical decisions. In fact, democratic politics contains certain fully institutionalized procedures, such as the majority vote, for reaching decisions when reason has failed to determine a course of action. This may not mean anything as dramatic as that political life is merely the blind clash of irrational forces. It may mean only that politics, with its invariable accompaniment, the use of power, comes into play when reason has played itself out. To that extent political life is irredeemably decisionistic, in the Schmittian sense.

Accordingly, if we aim, as Creppell does, for an understanding of toleration which remains applicable to "the ethics of life," we are going to have to face the fact that political conflicts over toleration very often involve asymmetries of power. I take it that a distinctive feature of power is that it can explain why a course of action was taken, when that action may be underdetermined by (other) reasons. For example, it can explain why a policy was implemented as a result of a majority vote by some executive body. There is nothing in the concept of toleration which rules it out that the protagonists are unequal in power. Indeed, in interpersonal situations, too, they are often unequal. It is too quick to say that inequalities of power mean inequalities of value—in some conflicts the parties are divided by a shared value—but often, especially in the cultural divisions which so preoccupy theorists of toleration nowadays, some values are indeed more equal than others. Even where values are shared, the division of power between conflicting groups may not be.

There is no remotely plausible representation of democratic politics which annuls asymmetries of power. This casts doubt on Creppell's very strong claim that mutuality is the goal of the public sphere, i.e., the purpose for which it exists. The trouble with this claim is that it is either false, or true only by definitional fiat. For it is untrue that we cannot characterize the public sphere without making reference, explicitly or otherwise, to the goal of mutuality. The public sphere may, on the face of it, have any number of ends, or none. To the extent that brute force characterizes public interaction, it is not aiming at mutuality as its goal; this is one reason why Kantians have so much trouble making sense of politics. Of course, it is possible to assert that only those fields of encounter which have mutuality as their end rather than, say, strategic interaction, could count as the public sphere, as for example some followers of Habermas seem to believe. But to designate the public sphere as the sphere of mutuality, simply displaces many conflicts outside that sphere, and implicitly justifies methods other than agreement, such as coercion, in dealing with them.[25]

Creppell's focus on impartiality can sometimes give the impression that a limitlessly inclusive politics is possible. This goes hand in hand with a tendency to play down the fact that toleration is non- or even anti-inclusive. Historically, beneficiaries of toleration such as religious dissenters were denied full inclusion in the polity. They were, for instance, subject to civil disabilities which debarred them from public office, as in the 1689 Toleration Act (to say nothing of other groups, such as Roman Catholics). This was no historical aberration, but a consequence of the disapproval which is integral to toleration. Disapproval may have become unfashionable or embarrassing, but toleration demands it. And a decision to tolerate always has (if only implicitly) to set limits to toleration: this necessarily means excluding some individuals or groups. Catholics suffered exclusion not merely in the 1689 Act, but also in writings by such prominent advocates of toleration as Milton and Locke.

In contemporary conditions, the appearance of inclusiveness is kept up by the notion of "identity." Its function here—as in much other work on toleration[26]—is to put off the reiteration problem, by making liberal politics look like a party open to all. In fact, as currently used, "identity" is a passport extended to those groups or interests towards whom liberals are disposed to be "inclusive." However, it was identity which set up the problem in the first place, and often the political task is to decide whether, and if so how, to accommodate identities which threaten civic peace, or civilized life. The fact, if it is one, that a person regards a certain identity as central to her sense of herself provides no overriding reason for respecting that identity.

The politics of inclusion also risks licensing a category-mistake about the nature of toleration. Inclusion seems to promise equal status for all, but in fact toleration and equality make uneasy bedfellows. Gutmann and Thompson refer to "mere" toleration, contrasting it with the parity which groups previously tolerated, such as Catholics, may eventually achieve.[27] As they rightly acknowledge, once full civic and political status has been attained, we no longer have toleration, but equality. What is needed is an acknowledgement that the process of inclusion is a dynamic one, whereby once excluded groups may pass through toleration to full inclusion. To the extent that any particular instance of toleration is seen as a halfway-house on the path to equality—a "provisional attitude" as Goethe called it—it always tends to its own annihilation. Citizens who have secured full inclusion have, as it were, outgrown toleration: for instance, in the UK and the US, most of the time, Roman Catholics are no longer merely tolerated. The understanding that civic inclusion via toleration is a dynamic process follows once we realize that the term "toleration" applies only by a kind of transference to those who benefit from it, or the policies which benefit them. Conceptually, toleration consists in a second-order relation between different kinds of value, normative attitude or disposition.[28]

III. Toleration as Murality

(a) Toleration and Conflict

Those in relationships will know that they are all too often the scene of conflict. As with any relationship involving conflict, there is always the choice whether to tolerate the conflict or to cut one's losses. This effectively sets the limits to politics, at least if it is defined as the domain where sharers of the world engage in a public "relationship." In what sense, if any, do the US political establishment and al-Qaeda, or Hamas and the Likud, participate in a *common world,* or a *relationship?* Any interpretation of these phrases which is elastic enough to make it true that these actors share a world or a relationship must also allow that they can feel, if not act on, murderous hatred towards one another. We now know that this is as true of liberal polities as of others. As the Marquess of Salisbury remarked, "the free institutions which sustain the life of a happy and united people, sustain also the hatreds of a divided people."[29] Toleration does not in itself provide any resources which rule out these implacable enmities. Given its conceptual structure, toleration *ex ante* is empty: it is devoid of implications for policy until specific values are penciled in, and even then the values have to be given practical content.[30] Indeed, conflict as an enduring fact of life continually engenders the circumstances of toleration. These circumstances would not exist if the actors did not find themselves in conflict in their practical or evaluative judgments. The need for toleration is itself evidence of conflict.

The coupling of conceptual analysis and normative commitment favored by Creppell tends to obscure this fact, because the content of toleration can always be retailored to fit whatever one now happens to believe is justified. A self-justificatory line of thought then becomes tempting: if we now prohibit what was previously permitted, that is because we have discovered that it is *justified* to prohibit it; intolerance is never justified; therefore, this new prohibition cannot display intolerance. And, since the policy is not intolerant, those who lose out through the prohibition cannot protest against it by appealing to the value of toleration, i.e., by claiming that the prohibition is intolerant.

What this leaves is, on the one side, conflicts which turn out to be illusory because they can be defused by a consensual value such as mutuality, on which the account of justification rests; and, on the other side, conflicts which are not about toleration, because one party or the other rejects the favored account of justification. Summarily put, either toleration excludes conflict, or conflict excludes toleration. But by uncoupling analysis and normative commitment, we can see that value-based conflicts often involve toleration itself. This enables us to save some of the key phenomena of toleration: that individuals or groups may find themselves in implacable conflict over toleration, even though each side may act tolerantly relative to its own values. From its own perspective each side may see its opponents as unjustifiably intolerant and its own position as tolerant—or as justifiably intolerant.[31]

Uncoupling also permits the commonsense thought that policy may *justifiably* become more intolerant rather than less so.[32] Some groups or persons previously outcast may progress to toleration and beyond, while others hitherto accepted are pushed to the margins. That is, the circumstances of toleration may obtain, but it may turn out that displaying intolerance towards a particular group is justified. By not building normative commitments into the conceptual analysis of toleration, we can describe certain changes in our own society, such as the greater restrictions now placed on public smoking, as involving a move away from toleration, without taking a view on whether these changes are justified. To this extent, the separation of analysis from normative commitment actually promotes a keener appreciation of difference.

These resources will not be available if the conceptual analysis of toleration is given direct normative content, since in that case only those actions or motives which are justified will count as tolerant, and conversely. Then it follows that, if we now marginalize smokers, for example, this shows not that we have become less tolerant, but that we have now come to believe that smokers may justifiably be marginalized.[33]

However, the other side of this coin is that there will be no monolithic value of "toleration" to which we can refer in deciding the conflicts constitutive of the circumstances of toleration. These circumstances include, of course, the fact that modern societies contain many systems of value, which are often incompatible with one another. It follows from this, on the analysis I have advocated, that when conflict arises it may be possible that each party is acting tolerantly, relative to its own evaluative beliefs. Hence the value of toleration does not, by itself, suffice to resolve these conflicts. This does not mean that when a political resolution is imposed, it cannot be regarded as tolerant—indeed, it follows from the analysis that it may well be tolerant. The state expresses specific values, on the basis of which it disapproves of certain conduct, but may also restrain itself from prohibiting that conduct.

Opposing values both trigger the initial conflict and opposing views as to how to act tolerantly with regard to it. We can take as an example the debate over the English laws on blasphemy, which protect the established Anglican religion. Muslims can and do argue that toleration requires that the laws be extended to protect all (major) religious denominations, including Islam. Secularists argue that the tolerant course of action is to disestablish religious disabilities of the kind enshrined in the existing blasphemy laws by repealing them. An Anglican can argue for the status quo, commending as tolerant a regime in which non-established faiths are granted freedom of worship despite lacking the special protection of the blasphemy laws. The state may endorse one or other of these views. It may decide, as a confessional state, to permit blasphemy despite its disapproval of profanity. Or it may decide, despite being a secular state, that it will enact blasphemy laws applicable across different religions because it believes that this will enhance mutual respect. In other words, the state could adopt any one of several policies, each of which would meet the formal requirements for toleration as principled self-restraint. Which policy it does adopt depends not only on its favored values, but also on pragmatic and political considerations.

(b) Mutuality v. Murality

Modern philosophical liberals do not have much to say about power, except insofar as a theory of justified coercion is at least implicit in their justifications of the state. However, to the extent that liberalism is not just a philosophy, but an ideology, it must countenance the use of power. This includes using power to overcome, by conciliation or otherwise, conflicts of interest and outlook. Thus liberals, in direct competition with others, have a clear interest in holding power and using it. This game is largely zero-sum, since liberals can exercise power only to the extent that non-liberals lack it. Liberals risk over-reaching themselves if they think that when they are parties to a conflict over toleration, they can offer justifications—couched for example in terms of impartiality—which will necessarily satisfy those on the receiving end of political power, rather than providing justifications which satisfy themselves. However, liberals want justifications which are, at least in theory, satisfactory to all, and not just to themselves. This is because impartiality figures prominently among the constraints modern liberals impose on justification.

The recognition that the impartiality constraint makes unfeasible demands on justification marks the point of departure for my favored alternative view of toleration, which I call, by intended contrast with Creppell, *toleration as murality*. Toleration as murality accepts the role of *walls*[34]—real or virtual—in containing antagonisms, but also in creating a secure domain in which civic conflicts can be played out. Murality sees walls first and foremost *as* walls, rather than as proxies for something normatively grander. Taken in themselves, walls are simply a concrete fact of urban topography; sometimes they are only a relic of forgotten enmities. But very often they mark the bound of civic space, and the sphere of toleration, the *de facto* space in which conflicts are contained. It is a real rather than a hypothetical or ideal space, and this is appropriate to toleration. For the conflicts which create the circumstances of toleration are real. Ideal theory, with its focus on reasonable agreement, persistently misconstrues this aspect of toleration, overlaying often insoluble real conflicts with precepts to which the protagonists would (that is, should) agree if reasonable. The heroism of Creppell's failure lies in the fact that her theory champions the actual against the ideal, while she remains in thrall to the agreement model which is ideal theory's undoing.

It is definitive of toleration as murality that it does not require consensus in moral judgments. The relevant point here is not that such consensus is in practice impossible, but rather that collective existence *is* possible regardless of whether consensus obtains. The mural synecdoche—whereby walls represent the state's protection of its citizens—is intended to bring this out. It emphasizes that the basis for collective existence may lie in a brute fact, that the polis can provide protection to its citizens against internal or external aggressors. This ability need not depend on any reasonable consensus among those protected. Fairly obviously, murality's focus on walls is also meant to highlight the central importance of one specific basis for collective existence, namely security. Walls are the preconditions of other kinds of good, including toleration. Only once these preconditions are met can there be politics, and the processes which make toleration possible. For the polis to exercise the principled self-restraint constitutive of toleration, it needs first to be capable of self-direction, and that requires security.

By contrast with moralism, murality does not seek from justifications for toleration a political settlement which will satisfy all contending parties. The partial nature of political settlements, in disputes over toleration, is shown by the fact that walls may be internal to the polis as well as external, marking zones of indulgence in which otherwise illicit activities are bounded, but also protected. They mark not only the outermost bound of jurisdiction, but the "liberties" within which citizens may go unmolested —not just by the law, but by other citizens. Hence one function of walls is to create and protect domains of privacy, but also to delimit, as outside legitimate intervention, spheres in which actions disapproved of by others, including the state, may nonetheless proceed—in other words, to protect the space for toleration. Equally, walls may mark the limit of toleration. The ancient Athenian polis illustrated this coincidence graphically by depositing the bodies of convicted criminals outside the city walls, as Creon demands be done with Polyneices in Sophocles' *Antigone.*[35]

Walls suggest not only the necessary limits of inclusion, but also *degrees* of inclusion. Polities confine many activities *intra muros,* as accepted but not fit or appropriate for public space: indeed, this is one way to understand the division between public and private spheres. Some tolerated activities occupy an intermediate space between the two, as with the zoned availability of pornography, gambling, or alcohol.[36] The goods of protection conferred by a functioning polity create the possibility of toleration, by staking out zones of civic peace within which the enmities which mark the circumstances of toleration can be contained, and this includes protected areas within the polity as well as without.

A good example is the creation of *eruvs* in London's Hampstead Garden Suburb and other cities with significant Orthodox Jewish populations, within which laws restricting behavior on the Jewish Sabbath are relaxed. The fact that the relevant space was marked purely symbolically, by suspending wires above head-height, indicates that the *eruvs* exist within a space of civic peace. The *eruvs* show not only the attainment of civic peace which first made possible the toleration of Jews within the wider population, and subsequently their acceptance (if not assimilation) as full citizens. The *eruvs* also show that the civic peace which is a prerequisite of toleration itself permits Orthodox Jewry to act tolerantly towards co-religionists.[37]

One does not have to be an Orthodox Jew, or even to approve of the *eruv,* to regard it as tolerant. It is possible to recognize an act as showing principled self-restraint even if one rejects the principles or values on which the act is based. The *eruv* permits actions contrary to strict orthodoxy, such as carrying infants on the

Sabbath, while marking orthodoxy's disapproval of such actions by confining them within a *cordon sanitaire.* It marks an island within an island—a locus of toleration or easement within the orthodoxy of a tolerated sect, as one of the benefits of civic peace.

Murality permits a varied and nuanced approach to the practical problems of toleration, where liberal egalitarianism tends to apply a uniform template. This tendency results from liberals' search for a foundational justifying value which will bind disputing parties into a political relationship, including that of toleration. Creppell finds the value in mutuality. As we have seen, she takes the very demanding view that the justification must be such that all parties actually accept it. By contrast, Creppell's fellow moralists such as Brian Barry and T. M. Scanlon rely on hypothetical or counterfactual agreement to provide the overarching justification to which, it is held, citizens in good standing should subscribe. Barry and Scanlon argue that political arrangements are justified only if nobody *could* reasonably reject the norms or values supporting them (regardless of whether particular individuals in fact *would* reject them).

What Barry, Scanlon, and Creppell share is their belief that the normative basis for political existence lies in consensual moral justification. They endorse a permanent politico-juridical order enshrining the paramount moral value, which can bind disparate groups to that order. It is of course a familiar idea in modern liberalism that political justification has to contend with sharp moral disagreements. But the standard liberal response—exemplified by Rawls' "overlapping consensus"—seeks to show that the appearance of disagreement masks a deeper underlying agreement, which forms the basis for political justification. On this view, the polity is divided against itself if it lacks fundamental agreement in normative judgments. In order to be legitimate, a polity requires such agreement.[38] Although Rawls begins from disagreement, in the form of "reasonable pluralism," it is central to the project of *Political Liberalism* that the parties can reasonably agree about fundamental political principles. In the work of other liberals, such as Barry and Scanlon, the imperative for agreement surfaces in the demand that political outcomes cannot reasonably be rejected. Similarly it is very important for moralists that the philosophical theory of justification furnishes reasons which will be acceptable

—whether in fact, as for Creppell, or merely in principle, as for Barry and others—to the tolerated.

But disagreement may go all the way down. Usually in liberal theory the relevant agreement is counterfactual, or hypothetical, as with the theories of Rawls, Scanlon, and Barry. These approaches always leave it open to question what secures the truth of the relevant conditional claims—that persons would agree under certain imagined conditions. Even if it is true that they would agree under the relevant conditions, it still has to be shown why that matters here and now. As Ronald Dworkin argued in response to the hypothetical contract of Rawls' *Theory of Justice,* we need to know why the fact that parties in the Original Position hypothetically would reach agreement means that we are bound as if we really have made such an agreement.[39]

In fact toleration poses a particularly thorny problem for moralists, given their emphasis on consensus in moral judgments. The circumstances of toleration arise only when this consensus is absent, or has broken down. Hence the attempt to forge political relationships on the basis of moral consensus comes to seem quixotic, and creates the blind spot over toleration noted earlier: if one or other party fails to join the reasonable consensus, it is therefore unreasonable, and so beyond the pale of toleration. Hence the conflict is not really one of toleration to begin with. Moralists will respond that normative consensus is aspirational, an ideal constraint on less than ideal political realities. But there is no single coherent ideal in the face of irreducible conflict. Vying groups may each forward their own visions of the best policy, or polity in general, without reaching agreement, and then a political resolution becomes necessary which resorts to the use of power. For this reason, much liberal theorizing about toleration aims not to establish what the state should tolerate, but to give reasons why one group of citizens who disapprove of another should be restrained from acting on their disapproval. So, for example, theorists may argue that homosexual marriage should be tolerated—that is, it should be legally permitted despite the fact that some people disapprove of it.[40]

Muralists, by contrast, do not regard normative agreement as necessary to justify toleration. They believe that once the basis for collective coexistence is in place,[41] the question of how to justify toleration may be decided without making any reference to normative agreement, even in principle. Instead, muralists contend that the provision of the basic political good of security is needed for toleration, and this provision, coupled with local and contextual factors, can be sufficient to justify it, in the sense that it meets the formal conditions of toleration and fulfils local conditions for political legitimacy.[42] These local factors will include, very importantly, the things which those in power regard as goods. These goods may command enough local support to yield consensus,[43] and where this is so, the consensual goods will figure in the justification. For example, there may be a consensus that certain forms of behavior are acceptable if conducted in private. What is important for toleration, however, is that these local goods determine policy in the way needed for toleration: in other words, the local goods have to justify a policy of principled self-restraint.

A convergence on values could be one way in which the basis for collective coexistence could be secured. That is, if the basis for trust somehow existed of its own accord, it might be possible for citizens to deal with each other on the basis of shared values; such a model has inspired some Christian communities, for example. But there is no need for such convergence in general, and even where citizens converge on values, the basis for trust still lies in brute facts about security. In Palestine, for instance, toleration is impossible if political conflict is so virulent that security is threatened. The threat to peace explains, obviously, the construction of the "peace wall," in order to create a space within which democratic institutions and civic life generally can continue. Without the wall, the Israeli state would find it difficult or impossible to stabilize expectations to the degree needed for collective coexistence.

Here it is important to see the distinction between the actual basis on which collective coexistence rests—whatever this may be—and the reasons which citizens may be thought to have for supporting the polity which secures that coexistence. It would indeed be strange if there were no linkage at all between the actual basis for collective coexistence and the reasons which may motivate citizens to give the polity their support: the lack of such a linkage is in fact a template of some kinds of despotic rule. But this relationship is, for muralists, complex and multi-faceted, and the basis for collective coexistence need not be reduced simply to citizens' disposition to act on reasons which may be normatively compelling.[44] The basis may lie instead in the simple fact that the state can concert the conditions needed for collective coexistence, by main force.

Given the muralist emphasis on securing the basis for collective coexistence, neither the practical content of toleration nor the guiding principles on which policies of toleration may be based are determined in advance. The defining feature of toleration is principled self-restraint, but it is not given in advance what the substantive principles are. Nor is it specified why there are certain kinds of action which call for self-restraint in the first place, i.e., actions which by affronting certain values are *prima facie* targets for prohibition, or other kinds of disability. Indeed, one and the same value may support a principled self-restraint for one person, and principled prohibition for another. For example, one individual might see liberty as a reason for permitting smoking, despite harboring a personal dislike of the habit, while a second sees permitting smoking as an affront to the liberties of "passive" smokers.

It may be said that murality, as I have presented it, requires political amoralism or relativism which could, in principle, justify a Hitler or Stalin. The charge of relativism gains color from the fact that murality allows for local and contextual factors to influence justification. However, while murality is consistent with relativism about values, it is also consistent with the rejection of relativism. Murality applies the general form of toleration as a relation between reasons for action—reasons for disapproval and reasons for restraining oneself in expressing or acting on that disapproval—but allows for local variability in what agents regard as valid reasons for action. A person can act tolerantly relative to her beliefs, even though the beliefs may not be objectively true, or may be objectively false—just as someone can act rationally relative to untrue beliefs. Thus muralists can argue that even if an objectively true theory of value showed that an agent's evaluative beliefs were false, that agent could act tolerantly relative to those false beliefs. Since the beliefs can be false, murality is consistent with rejecting relativism.

The second charge, of political amoralism, states that because toleration as murality eschews a general theory of justification of the kind offered by liberal moralists, it lacks the resources to deny that a totalitarian regime may be justified. So murality may find itself endorsing totalitarianism. The first, obvious, point in response is that totalitarian regimes have not in general practiced toleration, as murality understands the term. They have not engaged in the principled self-restraint which marks the tolerant polity. Second, murality stresses the central importance of *security* to toleration. In common with other totalitarian regimes, Nazism and Stalinism both subjected their citizens to radical insecurity. It was precisely these regimes' denial of security to political opponents which showed them up as intolerant. Finally, security is a genuine political good, which consists in making available to citizens other kinds of good, rather than failing to provide them or actively withholding them.

There is nothing especially liberal about toleration as murality. Muralists are clear that many tolerant regimes will be non-liberal ones. While providing the good of security to their citizens, these regimes will not provide some goods which liberals regard as necessary for political legitimacy. The non-liberal regimes may wholly or in part withhold such goods as the franchise, freedom of religion, or freedom of expression. Of course liberals may say in response that these goods are themselves required for toleration. But this claim needs to be argued for. The general form of toleration places no preconditions on the content of the reasons which ground disapproval and restraint. An authoritarian regime may provide security and other goods to its citizens without providing the liberal goods, and it may act tolerantly by its own lights. The Millet system under Ottoman rule is an often-cited example. So is the Edict of Nantes issued by Henri IV at the end of the French wars of religion. Equally, liberal regimes often derogate from commitment to the franchise,[45] free expression,[46] or freedom of religion.[47]

Creppell finds the normative basis for common political existence in mutuality, as a way of binding disparate groups or "identities" into the polity. As her critique of Nagel suggests, she interprets this basis in a strong sense, requiring its actual acceptance by vying groups. Moralists are troubled by the reiteration problem, since it raises the specter of a political life made unlivable by the failure to find a consensual value. However, as we have seen, insofar as conflict prevails, the consensual value is very unlikely to command universal assent, and for this reason the reiteration problem has no solution. Moralists respond to its insolubility by demarcating a zone within which the toleration-supporting value can be respected, but this leaves outside the zone those who reject or flout the value, such as some religious fundamentalists, racists, and so on.

Hence for moralists there is still an absolute friend/enemy distinction to be observed, marked precisely by groups' acceptance or rejection of the relevant value. But among friends—those within the ambit of toleration, as defined by the value—equality of respect prevails. This lands us with the dilemma which Gutmann and Thompson identify, whereby the prevailing egalitarian ethos demands either full inclusion, in which case "mere" toleration seems an unjustifiable halfway-house, or else it demands full exclusion, with the civic and other penalties to which enemies of state or society have historically been subjected. What is missing, accordingly, is precisely the space for mere toleration, where the behavior tolerated is indeed seen as second-best, but not as meriting outright prohibition.

By contrast, because muralists regard security as the basis for collective coexistence, they are unabashed in accepting that political toleration rests on specific values which may not be shared among all members of the polity. They are thus happy to accept that toleration is usually a matter of how *we* treat *them,* for some relatively powerful *we* and relatively powerless *them.* To this extent, hegemony is unavoidable within the politics of toleration.[48] Once security is in place, there is no univocal question as to how to approach toleration, let alone a unique answer to the question. At the most abstract level, there is only the flux of political relationships, which may be more or less strongly marked by normative consensus at different places and times.

How far it matters politically whether there is a normative consensus may also vary. But what tends to mark off the circumstances of toleration from other kinds of political relationship is that this consensus is relatively weak. This is, indeed, the point at which "agreement in judgments"[49] breaks down. Even where the parties share at least a nominal commitment to some value, the practical interpretations they place upon it may diverge, or conflict sharply. The fact that the consensus is often weak or non-existent is not a matter for regret; it is implicit in the very fact of having contestable normative commitments.

Thus murality faces head-on the fact that the reiteration problem has no solution. Given that conflicts over toleration arise from different views about what should be tolerated, the conflicts of value which constitute the circumstances of toleration often defy resolution by appeal to common values. Then those in power have to decide whether a group with whom they are in conflict poses a danger to the state. Even if they decide that the group does not, there is still a question about whether to tolerate the group, and there may be good reason not to do so. Laws on public decency are one example.

The circumstances of toleration mean that agreement in judgments is not available. Given this disagreement, the political question is how to treat those whose ways of going on make them resident aliens within the polity. Their presence marks a decisionistic vacuum in the life of the polity, one which recent political theory has tended to ignore or remove. For once the question of toleration has arisen, those in power have to decide whether or not to invoke the dominant values in extirpating deviance, or whether to accommodate it by a suitable reinterpretation of their usual procedures. Partly this decision will involve questions of security itself, but beyond this, it is liable to draw on pragmatic and other considerations in non-systematic ways.

This bricolage of reasons corresponds to similarly various modes in which a policy of toleration may be pursued. For example, one issue for tolerators is always the *comprehension* question, vigorously debated at the time of the 1689 Act: whether to relax orthodoxy so as to include aliens, or to opt for balkanization by reaffirming it, while permitting diversity outside it. The alien may be dealt with on terms of equality, or near-equality, as Roman Catholics now are in the UK;[50] or the equality may be more radically qualified, as is currently true of homosexuals. Again, certain groups, not necessarily posing any threat to social stability, may find themselves excluded entirely, or subject to burdens not laid on the population at large.

As an illustration of the contrast between moralist and muralist approaches, consider the 1998 Belfast Agreement in Northern

Ireland. A key aspect of the Agreement was its amnesty on terrorist convicts of both sides in the name of including the political representatives of previously excluded political groups—notably the republican party Sinn Fein—in the political process. However, since 1998, Sinn Fein's paramilitary wing, the IRA, has continued its involvement in punishment beatings, alleged espionage and organized crime, including (in the judgment of both the British and the Irish governments) responsibility for the largest bank raid ever conducted in Britain in December 2004. The decommissioning of illegal weapons called for by the Agreement has not been accomplished. Partly for these reasons, the Northern Ireland Assembly created under the Belfast Agreement has been repeatedly suspended.

One way to view the Agreement is as a gesture of inclusion, and indeed of mutuality, expressing a will to relationship with former outcasts. The Agreement itself mentions the parties' shared commitment to the democratic and peaceful resolution of conflicts, and thus implicitly to the salience of continuing political relationships. This shared commitment is, for moralists, the sole basis on which common political existence can rest—that is, normative agreement on the value of a continuing relationship. What should be said then about IRA training of FARC guerrillas in Colombia, Sinn Fein's espionage activities against fellow Northern Ireland Assembly members in Stormont, its non-disclosure of weapons caches and the IRA's presumed responsibility for the Northern Bank robbery? The alternatives for the moralist, or specifically for Creppell's mutualist, seem to be these: either to decide that condemning these actions is less important than is maintaining political relationships, despite the fact that the breaches of the Agreement indicate republicans' lack of commitment to mutuality; or to remove republicans from the political process, precisely because these actions destroyed the mutuality which provides the sole basis for toleration.

For muralists, there is no problem in saying that the 1998 Agreement *tolerated* republicanism,[51] and that the gains in security since the 1994 ceasefire made this possible. The question remains whether to tolerate republicans within the devolved structures *despite* their abandonment of mutuality. Indeed, it can be said that this abandonment is what makes it a question of *toleration*. The authorities decided that despite its manifest and continued links with paramilitary violence, Sinn Fein could be drawn into the political settlement. That settlement was premised on the assumption that the republican leadership—who, notoriously, figured both in the political leadership of Sinn Fein and of the IRA Army Council—had come to realize that "the armed struggle" had failed. Hence collective security was not necessarily jeopardized by overt negotiation with Sinn Fein and its inclusion in the eventual Northern Ireland Executive. There need be no core value binding the parties to the Agreement together. Indeed, it has been widely observed that the wording of the Agreement allowed each faction to draw its own conclusions about the long-term future of the province.

Muralists accept that any set of political values will exclude as well as include, and hold that there is no coherent standpoint from which this fact should cause regret. To acknowledge the finitude of political space is not to embrace nihilism, or even pessimism. It is to celebrate the political benefits of estrangement and withdrawal, graphically illustrated by "peace walls" such as those which protect the warring communities in the Short Strand area of north-east Belfast from each other. No doubt it would be for the best in some respects if these communities found that they were able to live together in harmony. But the best may be unattainable, and the most that can realistically be attained is the bearably bad.

Conclusion: Murality as optimism

What is the positive value that muralists celebrate? It is that of coexistence, unquiet but not murderous, with the Hobbesian goods with which are all familiar. It might be thought that the world of the enclave—of the laager, the ghetto, or the gated compound—was a political singularity. But it does not belong only to the world where what we call politics began, that of the polis, walled and gated against outsiders. It is also, inescapably, our own world. A recurrent meliorist fantasy has it that the barriers can be thrown down, as in the *décloissonnements* of 1968. That this really is a fantasy, itself follows from the anti-perfectionism to which most philosophical liberals today subscribe. It is only within the security of the laager that questions of toleration can even be asked.

To accept the constant presence of withdrawal and entrenchment—at least as possibilities—also suggests a broader image of politics than is usual within liberalism. To invert Clausewitz: politics is war by other means. This does not mean that it is a mere playground for psychopaths. Politics occupies the no man's land between reason and pugilism. But, as struggles over toleration show all too clearly, politics often gets going precisely when reasonable consensus fails. Political philosophy in its standard liberal form aims to show how things would be if political life were governed by reason or consensus. In Creppell's argument, political consensus seems at first to disappear when conflict enters the picture, only to reappear once the "common world" is colored in. But in the circumstances of toleration there is a limited point in asking how things would be if reason resumed its sway, and to the extent that it ignores this fact, the political philosophy of toleration rests on a mistake.

Oddly enough, once we understand that the space which politics occupies is unstable and fluid, we can envision a brighter future for toleration. If we see that tolerating somebody does not require us to think of them as better than they really are,[52] we can also get a more realistic grasp of what is at stake in the circumstances of toleration. Its peculiar value can be recovered by abandoning conceptual tinkering—in particular, the attempt (so to speak) to naturalize toleration by converting it into respect, equality, recognition or some other trumping value. Instead, we should allow it to become what it is: a concept which, by signaling the presence of what is alien in our midst, marks the shifting frontier between politics and war.

As so often, the best safeguard against future disappointment lies in abandoning hopes—the hope, for example, that history will at some point usher in the universal accommodation of difference. For, on any view, some differences should not be accommodated at all. The mistake is to infer from this, as writers such as Galeotti seem to do, that the polity must either embrace the alien or cast it out. This is, indeed, the mentality of *die Mauer im Kopf*.[53] That toleration is politically possible, shows that this need not be so: the secure polis can indeed endure some difference without courting disaster. The merely tolerant state does not—at least, not necessarily—risk the fate of Troy or Jericho.

NOTES

1. Creppell, "Toleration, Politics, and the Role of Mutuality," 316.
2. Ibid.
3. Ibid., 317.
4. Ibid.
5. Ibid.
6. Ibid.
7. Ibid.
8. Ibid., 332.
9. Ibid., 317.
10. Ibid., 332.
11. Ibid., 320.
12. Ibid., 321.
13. Ibid., 322.
14. It is a further question, which I shall not explore in detail, how far mutuality in Creppell's account coincides with the familiar liberal value of equal respect for persons. At times, Creppell seems sympathetic to the critique of equal respect made by some other recent writers on toleration (such as Elisabetta Galeotti), that giving formal effect to equality through the law may leave certain kinds of (unjust) disadvantage intact. But it is hard to see what can motivate a concern for mutuality if not an antecedent notion of equal respect, which is embodied in a relationship of mutuality.
15. Creppell, "Toleration, Politics, and the Role of Mutuality," 320, 329, 334, 351, 352.
16. R. Nozick, *Anarchy, State, and Utopia* (Oxford: Basil Blackwell 1974).
17. B. Williams, "Toleration: An Impossible Virtue?" in D. Heyd (ed.), *Toleration: An Elusive Virtue* (Princeton, NJ: Princeton University Press 1996).
18. The other side of this coin, admittedly, is if we focus on the enduring elements of conflicts such as sectarian divisions in Northern Ireland, they may come to seem insoluble.
19. G. Newey, "Discourse Rights and the Drumcree Marches: A Reply to O'Neill," *British Journal of Politics and International Relations* IV (i) (2002), 75–97.

20. See, e.g., J. Raz, *The Morality of Freedom* (Oxford: Oxford University Press 1986).

21. E. Galeotti, *Toleration as Recognition* (Cambridge: Cambridge University Press 2002).

22. For this line of argument, see, e.g., P. Jones, "Toleration and Neutrality: compatible ideals?" in D. Castiglione and C. McKinnon (eds.), *Toleration, Neutrality and Democracy* (Dordrecht: Kluwer 2003); for a response to Jones see S. Meckled-Garcia, "A Reply to Peter Jones," in the same volume.

23. Creppell, "Toleration, Politics, and the Role of Mutuality," 319. Emphasis in the original.

24. In Galeotti's case the core value is recognition.

25. Creppell is surely right to contend that the public sphere requires a relationship of some sort between participants in it. This follows from the fact that this sphere is one in which the participants seek to concert *collective* action. We disagree about the broader normative commitments which ensue from the relationships involved in collective action.

26. See, e.g., Elisabetta Galeotti, *Toleration as Recognition.*

27. See Amy Gutmann and Dennis Thompson, *Democracy and Disagreement* (Cambridge, MA: Belknap Press of Harvard University Press 1996), 62; for a recantation of this position, see Gutmann and Thompson, "Democratic Disagreement," in Stephen Macedo (ed.), *Deliberative Politics: Essays on* Democracy and Disagreement (Oxford: Oxford University Press 1999), 251.

28. For more on this point, see my *Virtue, Reason, and Toleration: The Place of Toleration in Ethical and Political Philosophy* (Edinburgh: Edinburgh University Press 1999), especially ch. 1.

29. Quoted in R. Blake, *The Conservative Party from Peel to Churchill* (London: Fontana-Collins 1972), 133.

30. One arresting consequence is that, insofar as liberalism historically has been identified with specific policies such as opposition to censorship, or freedom of association, toleration is only contingently liberal, since these policies are only contingently tolerant. I expand on this point with regard to censorship in my "*Fatwa* and Fiction: Censorship and Toleration," in J. Horton (ed.), *Liberalism, Multiculturalism and Toleration* (Basingstoke: Macmillan 1993).

31. This is not to say that *all* situations in which toleration is a political issue are symmetrical, in that each side sees the other as intolerant while seeing itself as tolerant (or not unjustifiably intolerant). I discuss the symmetry phenomenon in "Is Democratic Toleration a Rubber Duck?" in D. Castiglione and C. McKinnon (eds.), *Toleration, Neutrality and Democracy.* But the circumstances of toleration do very often produce this symmetry.

These circumstances involve actions which one party finds objectionable, while the other objects to the objection. The point is not so much whether (as in the example of someone who objects to my simply reading a book) one can devise examples in which only one party's behavior seems intolerant. It is rather that in real situations someone could intelligibly be described as intolerant in ignoring the grounds of the objections to his behavior, given that others sincerely find it objectionable.

32. Creppell is wrong to infer that this analysis means that toleration is "not intrinsically admirable," "Toleration, Politics, and the Role of Mutuality," fn26. It means only that the conceptual side of the analysis is distinct from the normative theory which explains why toleration is a good thing, something which I explore in detail in chapter 3 of *Virtue, Reason, and Toleration.*

33. For reasons which are obscure to me Creppell describes the example of smoking as "tendentious," "Toleration, Politics, and the Role of Mutuality," fn24. On any theory of toleration, there must be certain acts of toleration which are regarded as justified, and others which are not so regarded, as I argue in *Virtue, Reason, and Toleration,* ch. 1.

34. For a fascinating insight into the centrality of walls in political theorists' vision of the ideal commonwealth, see R. Schaer, G. Claeys, and L. Tower Sargent (eds.), *Utopia: The Search for the Ideal Society in the Western World* (New York: Oxford University Press 2000), e.g., 123. Perhaps unsurprisingly, the incidence of the mural trope in blueprints for utopia seems to have peaked in the early modern period during the politico-confessional strife of the late sixteenth and seventeenth centuries.

35. An interesting parallel is the origins of the idiom "beyond the pale." The "Pale" was a margin of land—such as that surrounding Dublin in medieval Ireland, or Calais in France, subject to effective English control, beyond which local chieftains held sway. The "Russian pale" was that area in which Russian Jewry were permitted to live. In modern English, of course, the phrase refers to what lies beyond the limits of tolerability.

36. Though it should be added that many activities which are confined to the private sphere are not tolerated, because not, in themselves, the subject of disapproval.

37. Interestingly, however, one argument made by local opponents of the Hampstead *eruv* was that the Jewish religion was actually being treated more favorably than other religions, which had not sought to demarcate tracts of civic space in this way.

38. It is a further question for moralists, whether or not the polity can *survive* in the face of radical disagreement.

39. R. M. Dworkin, "The Original Position," in N. Daniels (ed.), *Reading Rawls* (New York: Basic Books 1974).

40. For this claim see, e.g,. Galeotti, *Toleration as Recognition,* ch. 6.

41. This demands an account of security, a subject which has received insufficient attention from political philosophers. I attempt to provide one in a paper, "What Good Is Security?" forthcoming in a volume edited by Melissa Lane and Glyn Morgan. It is fully compatible with this position that one way in which collective security can be achieved is by terms of political engagement which encompass principled or other grounds for buying off dissenters.

42. Here I rely on the notion of a *justificed* outcome as sufficient for political legitimacy. The term *justificing* is coined on analogy with the economist's notion of *satisficing.* A justificed outcome is one such that no alternative is demonstrably better than it (so there may in any situation be an indefinite number of justificed outcomes). It may thus be that a justificed outcome is one which there is insufficient reason to endorse, as part of a set of such outcomes, each or some of which excludes others in the set. Hence, if it follows from there being insufficient reason to endorse an outcome that it is not justified, there can be justificed outcomes which are not justified. My argument regarding local variability in standards of legitimacy or political justification is also indebted to John Gray, *Two Faces of Liberalism* (Cambridge: Polity 2000), esp. ch. 3.

43. The local normative environment may, of course, treat consensus itself as a good. But, again, there is no necessity about this.

44. In common with most modern liberals, moralists impose the quasi-Kantian requirement that the moral judgments on which the state's justification rests be such that all reasonable persons can freely assent to them. But this condition becomes empty if the test of "reasonableness" is whether one assents to the judgments. This problem is particularly sharp for those liberals who, like the Rawls of *Political Liberalism,* maintain that there is a "reasonable pluralism" of "comprehensive doctrines," i.e., of ideals of the good life.

45. This is often achieved, of course, by means other than the straightforward denial in law of the franchise to individuals or groups. Intimidation, or placing insuperable obstacles in the way of voters, or disqualifying ballots (as in Florida in the disputed US presidential election of 2000) are all ways in which the vote can be denied to citizens. Another is to impose citizenship restrictions on resident aliens or incomers.

46. Free expression is often limited in the name of promoting security or public decency, or of preventing defamation.

47. The French notion of *laïcité,* invoked in the *affaire foulard* over religious dress in French state schools, is an example.

48. Does the fact of hegemony make murality "repressive" in Marcuse's well-known sense of the term ("Repressive Tolerance," in R. P.

Wolff, B. Moore Jnr., and H. Marcuse, *A Critique of Pure Tolerance* [Boston: Beacon Press 1969])? It depends how high the demand for justification is pitched. If it has to solve the reiteration problem in order to avoid being "repressive," then it certainly counts as repressive, as do all liberal theories. But insofar as hegemony is inevitable, the muralist theory need be no more repressive than any other.

49. In Wittgenstein's well-known phrase: see *Philosophical Investigations* (Oxford: Basil Blackwell 1951), sects. 217–18.

50. Near-equality, because for example the sovereign still cannot be, or marry, a Catholic.

51. Whether it was a good idea to tolerate republicanism is, of course, an entirely different matter.

52. A good example is prostitution, which was the subject of a radio discussion (BBC Radio 4 *PM* program, 30.12.03); the interviewee made it clear that prostitution was tolerated in the UK precisely because, though distasteful, it is not legally proscribed.

53. This term—"the wall inside one's head"—has come to describe the attitude among Germans that despite the fall of the Berlin Wall and reunification, an impenetrable wall remains between the former inhabitants of East and West Germany.

15

MORALITY, SELF-INTEREST, AND THE POLITICS OF TOLERATION

NOAH FELDMAN

1.

More than other facets of contemporary liberal theory, discussion of toleration tends to combine historical inquiry with philosophical analysis. The reason may be that toleration—both as concept and practice—is evidently historically prior to full-blown liberalism; this opens the door to a Whiggish inclination to see in seventeenth-century toleration the roots of the liberal thought that followed it by a century and half. A further reason to bring history into our analyses of toleration may lie in the availability of a convenient just-so story about why government adopted a theory articulated by philosophers: "sheer exhaustion brought about by incessant religious war."[1] If we are to see the rise of political liberalism as a process of gradual enlightenment in which peoples, countries, and eventually—one hopes—the world come to see the evident benefits of putting aside violence as a mechanism for resolving disputes, then there is something very appealing about identifying the conditions under which real, power-wielding institutions actually make progress toward the desired goal. For professional intellectuals, especially, the progressive story affords inspiration and hope: ideas really can make a difference! All you need are some wars of religion, and the politicians will come to see the inevitable attractions of reasoned discourse.

Let me hasten to insist that the turn to history in discussions of toleration is, on the whole, an excellent thing, not because it provides a how-to guide for getting power to listen to truth, but because it really can illuminate the relationship between political institutions and political theories. In fact, as I shall suggest, the different motivations of philosophers and politicians that emerge clearly in an account of the history of toleration can shed light on similar divergences in our own intellectual and political worlds, and can do much to chasten the aspiration to see a convergence between what morality requires and what the dynamics of power allow. By all means, let us explore the relationship between the Act of Toleration of 1689 and the *Letter Concerning Toleration*[2] of the same year.

But a word of warning is in order, if it can be urged by an academic who has spent considerable time trying to negotiate between liberal ideas and political realities in Iraq: their ways are not our ways. It is not that politicians (statesmen and stateswomen, if you prefer) are deaf to the power of moral reasoning. To the contrary, many of them can deploy moral arguments with an astonishingly nuanced ear for how they will be heard and received. Rather, the conditions for the exercise of political power—namely that the politician can never completely forget that his authority rests on the ability to direct and control violence—relentlessly ensure that moral arguments acknowledge and respond to pragmatic ends.

Moral values can nonetheless play a crucial role in shaping what people understand as pragmatically possible. I am *not* saying that in the political realm morality is purely subordinated to power politics, or condemned to the status of empty rhetoric. But in the sphere of politics, morality also never trumps or transcends the basic reality that the state exists through its coercive force and the popular beliefs legitimating that coercion. If morality did have that transcendent capacity, we would no longer be dealing in politics. We would have entered the messianic realm of pure moral reasoning, in which each person conceives of her self-interest solely in terms of what is morally right for all. Only in such a world would we not need to fear the backsliding of the bad man who will get away with anything he can so long as he can avoid punishment that costs him more than what he stands to gain.

2.

It is possible and maybe even conventional to distinguish a moral conception of toleration from a pragmatic or expedient one.[3] Toleration by definition relates to beliefs or conduct which one believes to be wrong. According to this view, if I tolerate your beliefs out of the pragmatic or expedient hope that you will tolerate mine in return, or if a government tolerates your beliefs on the assumption that it will function more efficiently if it does, this would not count as moral toleration.[4] To qualify as moral toleration, there must be some principled reason to tolerate beliefs or conduct considered wrong: a concern, say, for the victims of persecution considered in themselves,[5] or for the wrongfulness of trying to coerce people to give up certain beliefs or conduct to which they are deeply committed.

Which came first? If we look to the early history of toleration, there is reason for uncertainty. Consider the Act of Toleration of 1689. It states that, "Forasmuch as some ease to scrupulous consciences in the exercise of religion may be an effectual means to unite their majesties' protestant subjects in interest and affection," various requirements of church attendance shall be lifted by the Act. The text of the preamble gives as the reason to ease "scrupulous consciences in the exercise of religion" *not* the value or importance of conscience, but the political goal of uniting political subjects in common interest.

Each carefully chosen word of the Act underscores the sense that no fundamental right to liberty of conscience is being created or acknowledged, but that the Act instead advances the interests of successful coercive government. Consciences are not "protected" here; they are simply "eased." The consciences in question are not ordinary but "scrupulous," which is to say particularly sensitive, and therefore not so much deserving of being eased as being granted easement as a boon. The gracious conferral of toleration is restricted to "protestant subjects" and by no means expanded to Catholics or to dissenters unwilling to swear to a test oath also prescribed by statute. What is more, conscience is eased "in the exercise of religion"—a phrase which made its way into the First Amendment to the U.S. Constitution a century later—

and not generally, which is to say that a claim of conscience would offer no protection against coercion in any non-religious realm.[6]

This entire formulation is a classical statement of the expedient or pragmatic conception of toleration. The justification for toleration offered by the Act is a *reason of state* in the classic, Florentine and French[7] sense: scrupulous consciences will be eased for the pragmatic reason that it will enable their majesties' subjects to get along, and thereby benefit the stability of the state and the viability of William and Mary's revolutionary rule. The state deliberately refuses to acknowledge the liberty or the right of the individual or indeed any moral reason at all for tolerating, and opts instead to tolerate only in order serve its own interests in avoiding civil discord.

It is not that more expansive conceptions of the protection of conscience were unavailable to the drafters of the Act. Fifty years before, the Westminster Confession had declared that:

> God alone is Lord of the conscience, and hath left it free from the doctrines and commandments of men which are in any thing contrary to his Word, or beside it in matters of faith on worship. So that to believe such doctrines, or to obey such commandments out of conscience, is to betray true liberty of conscience; and the requiring an implicit faith, and an absolute and blind obedience, is to destroy liberty of conscience, and reason also.[8]

That earlier formulation, to be sure, still left room for the state to regulate religious worship and teaching; but it proceeded from the assumption that conscience had its own inherent value, and required protection on that ground, not to serve the interests of government. Without quite calling for toleration, the Confession offered an argument against "requiring" faith and obedience: to do so would be to destroy the liberty of conscience that the individual holds by the grace of God. That argument may be recognized as a moral one insofar as it hints that the liberty of conscience is a God-given right that cannot be violated without harming the person who holds it.

To see clearly how the Act of Toleration stands for the pragmatic conception of toleration, not the moral one, contrast its compressed reasoning to that of Locke's roughly contemporaneous *Letter Concerning Toleration.* For Locke, the primacy of individual conscience derives, as it did for the Puritans who crafted the Westminster Confession, from the moral and religious truth that God has left the conscience free in order for the individual to form beliefs efficacious for salvation.

It is true that Locke argues that it would be irrational for the government to try to coerce people against conscience—a famous argument that Jeremy Waldron has noted might not itself be a moral one, insofar as it focuses on the irrationality of coercion, not its consequences.[9] Locke also argues, in the *Letter,* that the commonwealth exists to serve civil ends, not religious ones.[10] But both of these claims depend, I think, on the logically prior argument that it would be illogical for the individual to alienate to the state his right to form religious beliefs. The reason such alienation would make no sense, for Locke, is precisely that religious belief reached by means other than free, faithful choice has no salvific value: "No way whatsoever that I shall walk in against the dictates of my conscience, will ever bring me to the mansions of the blessed. . . . In vain, therefore, do princes compel their subjects to come into their church-communion, under pretence of saving their souls."[11] In response to Jonas Proast's argument that state coercion might in principle lead to the formation of true beliefs, Locke could offer the straightforward (and indeed traditional) response that acting against one's own conscience was inherently sinful, regardless of whether one's conscience was in error.[12]

It follows, then, that Locke's argument in favor of toleration is a moral-religious one with some pragmatic offshoots. What is ultimately wrong with coercion against conscience is that it forces the coerced individual to act against his conscience and therefore in a way that would bring him the harm of damnation and certainly could not bring him the good of salvation. Thus, the core argument of the *Letter,* as Waldron has recently acknowledged, "does have to rest on its distinctively Christian foundations."[13] Those foundations are not only religious in the sense of deriving from beliefs about the nature of salvation, but definitively moral in their concern for the well-being of the soul of the one coerced. Locke's rationale for toleration, then, differs markedly from the rationale offered by the preamble to the Act of Toleration: the moral argument imposes an obligation on the state to respect individual conscience, while the pragmatic argument suggests that tolerating conscience serves the expedient interests of the state. Juxtaposing the legislators' version of toleration with the philosopher's strongly suggests, at a historical level, that the state is promoting its own pragmatic interests in peaceful coexistence over and against a moral theory which the statesmen of the Glorious Revolution were loath to adopt.

3.

Can we imagine an actually existing state adopting a policy of toleration on moral grounds? One can perhaps imagine a Christian state tolerating on Lockean principles,[14] or an Islamic state tolerating Jews and Christians on the ground that the Qur'an prohibits coercion in religion—a variant on Locke's concern for the well-being of the souls of the tolerated person. Rawls, however, proposes a model of moral toleration not grounded in religion. In it, "toleration is not derived from practical necessities or reasons of state," but from the principle of the equal liberty of conscience.[15] Under this approach, the state adopts a constitutional scheme "that guarantees an equal liberty of conscience regulated solely by forms of argument generally accepted"[16]—roughly, what the later Rawls calls public reason.

According to Rawls's account in Political Liberalism, the overlapping consensus that provides among other things the grounds for toleration "is quite different from a modus vivendi," both because the conception of justice that is the subject of the overlapping consensus is moral, and because (more importantly for our purposes) "it is affirmed on moral grounds."[17] The moral basis for toleration on which an overlapping consensus may emerge is that every person has an equal right to form his own beliefs; and the state adopts the policy of toleration in recognition of this principle. The relation between tolerance and public reason is that non-public, comprehensive doctrines *may* give strong reasons for intolerance—Rawls mentions both Catholics and Protestants of the sixteenth century as having such reasons[18]—but public reason does not provide such reasons, according to Rawls, except in the limited case where toleration of intolerance would lead to the downfall of the tolerant state.[19]

When considered in the light of what we know about the real world, Rawls's attractive vision of a constrained politics runs against our intuitive (and arguably empirical) sense of politics as the realm in which interest groups seek to express their preferences both in shaping the way institutions of government deploy power (constitutional politics) and in distributing the resources of the state (ordinary politics). At the same time, of course, we can also observe in many instances a type of political argument that appeals to impartial interests and uses "forms of argument generally accepted"—whether in the arenas of civil rights, environmentalism, or, increasingly, international affairs. The aspiration to a politics that would replace an appeal to the common interest (or in the fashionable jargon, public choice with public interest) can thus be understood as the wish to infuse the sordid politics we know with the elevated politics we occasionally glimpse.

One standard reaction to this aspirational vision of common-interest politics is simply that it is unrealistic—that politics in this world can never achieve the goal of impartiality, because nothing short of a transformation in human nature can ensure that citizens will not band together to seek their partial self-interest and will not make arguments for it in terms that are less than generally acceptable or accepted.[20] Without active state regulation of political culture, what is to stop interest groups from making arguments that rely not on impartiality but naked particularism and on assumptions not generally acceptable? In a moment, I intend to make just such a realist (or maybe cynical) response, although I hope to add to it at least a brief distinguishing account of why moral aspirations in politics nevertheless can bring about practical consequences even in a universe of living, breathing, self-interested, power-seeking humans. Before I do, however, I first want to pause and consider a possible *moral* objection to the argument that the right way to instantiate moral toleration lies through a political sphere characterized by an overlapping consensus that nevertheless is not a comprehensive conception of the good.

First, consider the position of persons who believe as a matter of their comprehensively held doctrine that toleration is only appropriate on expedient, modus vivendi grounds. Rawls says that "so long as such views . . . are very much in the minority, and are likely to remain so, they do not significantly affect the moral quality of public life and the basis of social concord."[21] Of course, if they were to become something more than a small minority, "the moral quality of political life will also change in ways that are obvious and require no comment."[22]

What is the tolerant state to do with the peaceful efforts such minorities will make to use the apparatus of the state to convince the rest of the citizens of the state to adopt their comprehensive conceptions of the good? I am not now speaking of the intolerant, whose claims may plausibly be dealt with—as Rawls deals with them—by noting both the practical necessity of limitation and also their weakened claim to toleration.[23] I am speaking, rather, of those who tolerate and favor toleration, but who as a matter of principle can do so only on non-moral grounds. Such people do not participate in the overlapping consensus insofar as they cannot adopt the state's policy of toleration on moral grounds without compromising their comprehensive beliefs.

In the real world of democratic politics, such minorities, like everyone else, will vie to use the state's institutions, including its schools, to teach children their version of the good life. If the state were to prohibit them from trying to achieve this goal, then the state's moral version of toleration would in effect function as a limit on the conscientious political participation and action of people *who are themselves committed to toleration,* albeit on expedient grounds. This is a troubling result, for reasons that, as Rawls would say, "are obvious and require no comment."

Alternatively, the state could simply allow such minorities to try to use the state's institutions to promote comprehensive views that include the view that one may tolerate only for expedient reasons. This approach, however, opens the door to the abandonment of the moral ground for toleration. The problem is especially acute in democracies, where the plurality of interests will drive each sub-group to seek to benefit itself proactively, lest other groups take advantage. In the modern state, with its plethora of incommensurable interests, taking the morally tolerant position in politics may well mean losing out to alternative visions. Moral toleration, it turns out, is far easier to accomplish when an absolute ruler exclusively occupies the political field and in that capacity takes moral account of the interests of all his subjects. Although Rawls in *Political Liberalism* tells a genealogical story in which expedient toleration gives rise to constitutional consensus and then genuine overlapping consensus, it is at least possible to tell a story that eventually runs in the other direction—from moral toleration to the growth of minorities who eventually capture the state and return it to toleration on expedient grounds alone.

4.

Recognizing that the democratic state with its plural values and identities is a historically contingent mode of organizing political power leads the way to describing the serious practical problems with grounding toleration in a moral theory. The most basic problem is that, in practical terms, we have little reason to expect that either individuals or groups who would like to pursue their own interests will refrain from seeking to advance those interests in constitutional or ordinary politics.

If we do not want to regulate the political realm to restrict forms of discourse that embrace toleration on expedient grounds only, how we are to expect moral toleration to emerge? Leaders and their states may condemn the worst excesses of intolerance. But this is not enough to make the goal of moral toleration seem more than utopian. Politicians' incentives are structured by the way they get their bread. In an established democracy, that means they will need to get reelected; in a more fluid, non-state situation (for example, a transitional occupation), politicians make their living by asserting that they can command constituencies capable of shaping the affairs of the country. In either case—the latter more obviously than the former, of course—politicians deploy a certain type of power, power derived from their capacity to shape and direct violence. The legislator passes laws that crystallize the coercive power of the state into a command potentially backed by violence, while the communal or religious leader may have to put bodies on the streets to create a coercive threat to other groups or institutions. But the business is the same for each. In both cases, actual violence is a last resort and leaders matter precisely because they coordinate popular action in a way that reduces coordination costs and legitimates the exercise of power.

From political leaders' function one can deduce the mechanism for getting them to adhere to principles of toleration: in a word, self-interest. In general, politicians will negotiate solutions that seem to them mutually advantageous, just like any other relatively rational actors.[24] This is the historical explanation for the emergence of toleration in the wake of the wars of religion: not exhaustion or enlightened proto-liberal revelation, but rather a complexly negotiated settlement in a situation where statesmen calculated that their states' interests (and their own) would be served better by coexistence than coercion. The Act of Toleration has more in common with the Peace of Westphalia than with the philosophy of John Locke. Iraqis in their constitutional negotiations settled on a principle of toleration to the extent that Shi'i, Kurdish, and Sunni Arab leaders concluded that their particular interests would be better served by avoiding the political turmoil that would follow from intolerance. (As it turned out, the best pragmatic intentions of the politicians have not been enough in the Iraqi case.) To hear Rawls tell it, expedient reasons are replaced by moral ones because people see the success of the expedient model, begin to trust their fellows, develop a constitutional consensus,[25] and then, most important to the transformation, develop political conceptions to appeal to others. But why, exactly, should the institutionalized self-interest of the last stage give rise to moral reasons for toleration? The reason there is something dissatisfying about a morally-based account of toleration that focuses on the creation of political sphere of overlapping consensus is that such an account slights the role of self-interest in making toleration into a practice of continuing utility *at every stage in its existence.*

From the self-interest story, I propose, though, it does not follow that there is no room for a moral account of the value of toleration in shaping political reality. It is just that in such a story, morality will not provide a transcendent basis for toleration within the self-interested activity of politics. Politicians are people like any others (only more so, one is tempted to add). That means they, and the people whom they govern or represent, form beliefs that guide their conceptions of their own self-interest. Here morality, whether individual or collective, enters the picture, shaping the norms that politicians promote, and occasionally even the means they consider legitimate for promoting them. Martin Luther King, Jr.'s political morality need not be seen solely as a self-interested attempt to advance the interests of African-Americans; it can be seen as part of a sincerely motivated moral project of advancing universal interests. The same can even be said of Lyndon Johnson's advocacy of the Civil Rights Act of 1968. No matter how well-deserved Johnson's reputation for political cynicism, there is reason to think that the civil rights movement changed his moral evaluation of segregation. What cannot plausibly be asserted, however, is that the political strategies of King in Selma or Birmingham or of Johnson in manipulating Congress depended solely or even primarily on the deployment of impartial public reasons. To get what they wanted, these statesmen played politics. What they did was no different than what corporations do when they want environmental laws weakened, or for that matter what environmentalists do when they want the same laws strengthened. They play the game of politics: they appeal to self-interest and they manipulate the levers of power.

5.

What is then so appealing about a moral conception of toleration, in which I tolerate you or your views on principle, rather than because I hope you will tolerate me, as well? Rawls seems to suggest that the principle seems more likely to be durable than the contingent fact that I seek to be tolerated myself: unlike overlapping consensus, he says, the stability of a modus vivendi toleration "does depend on happenstance and a balance of relative forces." This view, however, if intended normatively, would seem to place the moral argument in the service of (expedient) self-interest in stability. Furthermore, self-interest would seem to be at least as durable as abstract principle; so even if we were after the theory of toleration most likely to protect us, it seems entirely possible that we would prefer the reassurance of mutual self-interest to the shaky guarantees of moral commitment.

To put the question the other way around, what would be dissatisfying about concluding that, in the end, self-interest and expediency are the only basis we have for being tolerant? The answer seems to be twofold. First, there is the problem of cheating.

If we adopt a general scheme of toleration because it serves our interests, circumstances will arise in which we think we can get away with an occasional defection from the principle without endangering our own right to be tolerated. (Perhaps our exception will not be much noticed, or the party bearing the brunt of our intolerance will lack the capacity to get revenge.) This consequence of a game theoretic approach could perhaps be obviated if we were guided by principled moral toleration, which ought to have few exceptions, or none.

From this perspective, a moral theory of toleration might turn out to be a useful supplement to an expediency theory: suspenders *and* a belt to make sure that our arrangements hold up. Pragmatists might want not only to be tolerant, but to promulgate a moral theory in support of their toleration, in order to assure that toleration would exist as much of the time as possible. The idea might be that convincing people to internalize a belief is far more efficient than enforcing a social practice like toleration against self-interested potential back-sliders. One vision of the relation between moral and pragmatic toleration, then, would be that the moral approach does indeed ultimately serve pragmatic ends.

Alternatively, expedient toleration might take a shape that would turn out to be morally unjustifiable under some set of conditions; and if we want our political arrangements to satisfy the demands of morality, we might discover that we had to reimagine toleration in moral terms in order to justify it. According to this approach, it is not enough for toleration to be useful to everybody —it must actually *be* morally just. If we were to assume that toleration was morally neutral, perhaps we could allow it on that basis. But it seems relatively unlikely that a practice which permits the maintenance of morally reprehensible beliefs and actions would turn out to be morally neutral. On this view, we want a moral theory of toleration precisely because we suspect, as a matter of initial intuition, that toleration is immoral.

To follow this possibility where it goes, one might be tempted to argue that toleration could be found conclusively moral if we were to follow some sort of a veil-of-ignorance procedure and conclude that reasonable persons would agree to it. This raises a puzzle: would our toleration be of the moral variety if we adopted it because reasonable people would agree to it behind a veil of ignorance—but on purely self-interested grounds? Or would it be expedient merely?[26]

I will not try to solve this puzzle here; rather I would like only to suggest that the categories of moral and pragmatic toleration can be made to collapse into one another in ways that call into question both the practical and theoretical consequences of the distinction. The interplay of pragmatic politics with moral theory has a long enough history to make one doubt that either side of the equation will soon disappear. The social practices of politics run on non-moral fuel; but despite the fond hopes of rational choice theorists, people keep doggedly asserting and believing in moral arguments. Occasionally they even change their behavior as the apparent result of some change in moral belief. Why, then, should it matter so much whether we tolerate despite ourselves or out of self-love? If toleration did not serve self-interest, it would probably not be sustained for long. If, on the other hand, toleration served only self-interest, it seems unlikely that so many people would care so passionately about it.

NOTES

1. Ingrid Creppell, "Toleration, Politics, and the Role of Mutuality," this volume at 324.

2. John Locke, "A Letter Concerning Toleration," reprinted in *John Locke: A Letter Concerning Toleration in Focus,* John Horton and Susan Mendus eds. (London: Routledge, 1991) [hereinafter *Letter*].

3. Ingrid Creppell, *Toleration and Identity: Foundations in Early Modern Thought* (New York: Routledge, 2003). See also "Toleration, Politics, and the Role of Mutuality," this volume at 315–59. References below are to this essay, not to the book.

4. Ibid., 325.

5. See Waldron, "Locke, Toleration, and Persecution," *Letter,* 113.

6. Conscientious objectors, for example, would have no claim to be exempted from the nominally secular activity of making war by this language, which protects only religious activities.

7. *Ragione di stato, raison d'état.*

8. *The Confession of Faith, Together with the Larger and Lesser Catechismes,* composed by the Reverend Assembly of Divines, Sitting at Westminster, Presented to Both Houses of Parliament (London: Co. of Stationers,

1658). The Westminster Confession was collectively authored by the Westminster Assembly (1643–52).

9. Waldron, "Toleration and the Rationality of Persecution," *Letter,* 120.

10. Locke notes, on scriptural grounds, that although the Hebrew Bible did establish a religious state, "there is absolutely no such thing, under the Gospel, as a Christian commonwealth." *Letter,* 30. The difference is significant for the history of liberty of conscience, which derives in part from the doctrine of Christian liberty according to which Christ liberated the conscience from the duty to obey the laws of the Old Testament. See Noah Feldman, "Intellectual Origins of the Establishment Clause," 77 N.Y.U. L. Rev. 346 (2002) 354–72.

11. See *Letter,* 32.

12. See Richard Vernon, *The Career of Toleration: John Locke, Jonas Proast, and After* (Montreal: McGill-Queen's University Press, 1997), 17–34 (presenting Locke's argument from belief and Proast's critique of it); Jeremy Waldron, "Locke: Toleration and the Rationality of Persecution," *Letter,* 98, 115–19.

13. Jeremy Waldron, *God, Locke, and Equality* (Cambridge: Cambridge University Press, 2002), 210.

14. Compare John Rawls, *Political Liberalism* (New York: Columbia University Press, 2005), 145, n.12.

15. Rawls, *A Theory of Justice* (Cambridge: Harvard University Press, 1973), 214.

16. Ibid., 215.

17. Rawls, *Political Liberalism,* 147.

18. Ibid., 148.

19. Rawls, *A Theory of Justice,* 215–21.

20. Rawls himself is concerned to refute the view that overlapping consensus is "utopian." *Political Liberalism,* 158–64.

21. Ibid., 148.

22. Ibid., 149.

23. Cf. Rawls, *A Theory of Justice,* 218–20.

24. There is a growing rational choice literature on this subject, much of it painfully full of truisms about people agreeing to things just when they decide to agree to them. But the truism is still true.

25. Rawls, *Political liberalism,* 163.

26. Rawls says that the denizens of the original position "cannot take chances with their liberty by permitting the dominant religious or moral doctrine to persecute or to suppress others if it wishes." *A Theory of Justice,* 207.

16

TOLERANCE AS/IN CIVILIZATIONAL DISCOURSE

WENDY BROWN

. . . alongside an infinite diversity of cultures, there does exist one, global civilization in which humanity's ideas and beliefs meet and develop peacefully and productively. It is a civilization that must be defined by its tolerance of dissent, its celebration of cultural diversity, its insistence on fundamental, universal human rights and its belief in the right of people everywhere to have a say in how they are governed.[1]

—UN Secretary Kofi Annan

We meet here during a crucial period in the history of our nation, and of the civilized world. Part of that history was written by others; the rest will be written by us . . . And by acting, we will signal to outlaw regimes that in this new century, the boundaries of civilized behavior will be respected.[2]

—President George W. Bush

. . . America and the West have potential partners in these [Islamic] countries who are eager for us to help move the struggle to where it belongs: to a war within Islam over its spiritual message and identity, not a war with Islam . . . a war between the future and the past, between development and underdevelopment, between authors of crazy conspiracy theories versus those espousing rationality . . . Only Arabs and Muslims can win this war within, but we can openly encourage the progressives. . . .

> The only Western leader who vigorously took up this challenge was actually the Dutch politician Pim Fortuyn . . . Fortuyn questioned Muslim immigration to the Netherlands . . . not because he was against Muslims but because he felt that Islam had not gone through the Enlightenment or the Reformation, which separated church from state in the West and prepared it to embrace modernity, democracy and tolerance.
>
> As a gay man, Fortuyn was very much in need of tolerance, and his challenge to Muslim immigrants was this: I want to be tolerant, but do you? Or do you have an authoritarian culture that will not be assimilated, and that threatens my country's liberal, multicultural ethos?[3]
>
> —*New York Times* editorialist Thomas Friedman

> The War on Terrorism is a war for human rights.[4]
>
> —Secretary of Defense Donald Rumsfeld

> Every terrorist is at war with civilization. . . . And so, America is standing for the expansion of human liberty.
>
> —President George W. Bush, 18 May 2004

In the modern West, a liberal discourse of tolerance distinguishes "free" from "fundamentalist" societies, "civilized" from "barbaric," and individualized from organicist or collectivized. These pairs are not synonymous, are not governed precisely the same way by tolerance discourse, and do not call up precisely the same response from that discourse. However, they do assist in each other's constitution and in the constitution of the West and its Other. Whenever one pair of terms is present, it works metonymically to imply the others, in part because these pairs are popularly considered to have an organic association with one another in the world. Thus, the production and valorization of the sovereign individual is understood as critical in keeping barbarism at bay, just as fundamentalism is understood as a breeding ground of barbarism, and individuality is what fundamentalism is presumed to attenuate if not cancel. But there is a consequential ruse in the association of liberal autonomy, tolerance, secularism, and civilization on the one hand, and the association of group identity, fundamentalism, and barbarism on the other. This essay seeks to track the operations of that ruse.

Civilizational Discourse

If tolerance as a political practice is always conferred by the dominant, if it is always a certain expression of domination even as it offers protection or incorporation to the less powerful, tolerance as an individual virtue has a similar asymmetrical structure. The ethical bearing of tolerance is a highminded one, while the object of such highmindedness is inevitably figured as something more lowly. Even as the outlandish, wrongheaded, or literal outlaw is licensed or suffered through tolerance, the voice in which tolerance is proffered contrasts starkly with the qualities attributed to its object. The pronouncement, "I am a tolerant man," conjures seemliness, propriety, forbearance, magnanimity, cosmopolitanism, universality, the large view, while those for whom tolerance is required take their shape as improper, indecorous, urgent, narrow, particular, and often ungenerous or at least lacking in perspective.[5] Liberals who philosophize about tolerance almost always write about coping with what they cannot imagine themselves to be: they identify with the aristocrat holding his nose in the agora, not with the stench.

Historically and philosophically, tolerance is rarely argued for as an entitlement, a right, or a naturally egalitarian good in the ways that liberty generally is. Rather, one pleads for tolerance as an incorporative practice that promises to keep the peace through such incorporation. And so the subterranean yearning of tolerance for a universally practiced moderation that does not exist, a humanity so civilized that it would not require the virtue of tolerance, sits uneasily with the normative aspect of tolerance that reaffirms the characterological superiority of the tolerant over the tolerated.

Attention to these rhetorical aspects of tolerance suggest that it is not simply asymmetrical across lines of power but carries caste, class, and civilizational airs with it in its work. This essay scrutinizes that conveyance through consideration of the logic of tolerance as a civilizational discourse. The dual function of civilizational discourse to mark in general what counts as "civilized" and to confer superiority on the West produces tolerance itself in two distinct, if intersecting, power functions: 1) as part of what defines the superiority of Western Civilization, and 2) as that which marks certain non-Western practices or regimes as "intolerable." Together, these operations of tolerance discourse in a civilizational frame legitimize liberal polities' illiberal treatment of selected practices, peoples, and states. They sanction illiberal aggression toward what is marked as intolerable without tarring the "civilized" status of the aggressor.

Remarks by George W. Bush emblematize the material of my argument. Shortly after September 11th, the President asserted: "Those who hate all civilization and culture and progress . . . cannot be ignored, cannot be tolerated . . . cannot be appeased. They must be fought."[6] Tolerance, a beacon of civilization, is inappropriately extended to those outside civilization *and* opposed to civilization; violence, which tolerance represses, is the only means of dealing with this threat and is thereby self-justifying. Paired with remarks in February 2002, in which Bush declared the United States to have a "historic opportunity to fight a war that will not only liberate people from the clutches of barbaric behavior but a war that can leave the world more peaceful in the years to come," it is not difficult to see how an opposition between civilization and barbarism, in which the cherished tolerance of the former meets its limits in the latter (limits that also give the latter its identity) provides the mantle of civilization, progress, and peace for imperial militaristic adventures.[7]

"Civilization" is a complex term with an even more complex genealogy. The *Oxford English Dictionary* describes civilization since the eighteenth century as referring to the "action or process of civilizing or being civilized" and also as denoting a "developed or advanced state of human society."[8] In *Keywords,* Raymond Williams notes that while "civilization is now generally used to describe an achieved state or condition of organized social life," it pertained originally to a process, a meaning which persists into the present.[9] The static and dynamic meanings of civilization are easily reconciled in the context of a progressivist Western historiography of modernity in which individuals and societies are configured as steadily developing a more democratic, reasoned, and cosmopolitan bearing. In this way civilization simultaneously frames the achievement of European modernity, the promised issue of modernization as an experience, and crucially, the effects of exporting European modernity to "uncivilized" parts of the globe. European colonial expansion from the mid-nineteenth through the mid-twentieth century was explicitly justified as a project of civilization, conjuring the gifts of social order, legality, reason, religion, regulating manners and mores.[10]

However, civilization did not remain a simple term of colonial domination in which all the subjects it touched aspired to European standards. Not only did non-European elites and various anti-colonial struggles reshape the concept to contest and sometimes forthrightly oppose European hegemony, the idea of civilization was also pluralized in both scholarly and popular discourses during the last century. From Arnold Toynbee to Fernand Braudel to Samuel Huntington, there has been a concerted if variously motivated effort to pry civilization apart from Europe and even from modernity to make it more widely define structured "ways of life" comprising values, literatures, legal systems, and social organization.

Plural accounts *of* civilization, however, do not equate to a pluralist sensibility *about* civilization. Samuel Huntington's thesis (best known as an argument about the mutual sparking points among what he designates as the world's distinct and incommensurate civilizations) makes abundantly clear that such pluralization can cloak rather than negate the Western superiority charging the term. Although Huntington insists that Western Civilization "is valuable not because it is universal but because it *is* unique" (in its cultivation of the values of individual liberty, political democracy, human rights, and cultural freedom), this apparent gesture toward cultural relativism does not materialize as a principle of mutual valuation.[11] This is not only because Huntington's argument about Western Civilization's uniqueness forms the basis for intolerance of multiculturalism *within* the West (famously, Huntington argues: "a multicultural America is impossible because a non-Western America is not American . . . multiculturalism at home threatens the United States and the West").[12] Equally important, *The Clash of Civilizations and the Remaking of World Order* concludes with a warning about the current vulnerability of what Huntington calls "civilization in the singular": "on a worldwide basis Civilization seems to be in many respects yielding to barbarism, generating the image of an unprecedented phenomenon, a global Dark Ages, possibly descending on humanity."[13] This danger is evident,

Huntington continues, in a worldwide breakdown of law and order, a global crime wave, increasing drug addiction, a general weakening of the family, a decline in trust and social solidarity, and a rise in ethnic, religious, and civilizational violence. And what is occasioning this dark specter of what Huntington terms "a global moral reversion?"[14] Nothing less than the decline of Western power, that which established the rule of law as a civilizational norm and decreased the acceptability of "slavery, torture and vicious abuse of individuals."[15] So even as Huntington argues for all civilizations to bond together in fighting barbarism, the intolerable, only the values of the West can lead this fight: what will hold barbarism at bay is precisely what recenters the West as the defining essence of civilization and what legitimates its efforts at controlling the globe.

When these two arguments of Huntington's are combined—the argument for mutual accord among civilizations governed by what Huntington sets out as the distinctly Western value of tolerance, and the argument that the barbarism into which the world now threatens to slide is attributable to the decline of the West—there appears an unmistakable chain of identifications of the West with civilization ("in the singular"), of civilization with tolerance, and of the intolerant and the intolerable with the uncivilized. That these identifications occur despite Huntington's sincere effort to disrupt them is only a sign of how powerful civilizational discourse is in liberal theories of tolerance, even (and perhaps especially) when that discourse is most thoroughly inflected by political realism.

Huntington's work also makes clear that even when civilization is rendered in the plural, its signifying opposite remains barbarism. "Barbarian," it will be remembered, derives from the ancient Greek term denoting all non-Greeks. With the rise of Rome, its meaning shifted to refer to those outside the Empire; with the Italian Renaissance, barbarian defined all those imagined unreached by the Renaissance, that is, non-Italians. A barbarian is thus technically "a foreigner, one whose language and customs differ from the speaker's" but crucially, this foreignness has been continually established *vis-à-vis* empire and imperial definitions of civilization. And so the OED provides the second meaning: a condition of being "outside the pale of civilization." Outside the pale (an English phrase for measuring its colonial jurisdiction in Ireland in the sixteenth century) is not merely beyond geographical bounds but unreached by civilization without its canopy. It is not difficult, then, to see the path from the ancient meaning of barbarian as foreigner to its contemporary signification, the third listing in the OED: "a rude, wild, uncivilized person . . . an uncultured person, or one who has no sympathy with literary culture."[16] As we shall see shortly, Susan Okin's designation of selected non-liberal cultural practices as barbaric, and her inability to see "barbaric" practices anywhere within liberal orders perfectly mimics the etymological slide of barbarian from *foreigner* to *uncivilized* to *wild brute,* and inhabits as well the blindness to colonial or imperial domination that this slide entails. Again, this slide also underwrites George W. Bush's routine accounts of his military engagements in the Middle East as a struggle of the civilized world against barbarism: "Now is the time, and Iraq is the place, in which the enemies of the civilized world are testing the will of the civilized world."[17]

If being beyond the pale of civilization is also to be what civilization cannot tolerate, then tolerance and civilization not only entail one another, but mutually define what is outside of both and together constitute a strand in an emerging transnational governmentality. To be uncivilized is to be intolerable is to be a barbarian, just as to declare a particular practice intolerable is to stigmatize it as uncivilized. That which is inside civilization is tolerable *and* tolerant; that which is outside is neither. This is how, even amidst plural definitions of civilization, the discourse of tolerance re-centers the West as the standard for civilization, and how tolerance operates simultaneously as a token of Western supremacy and a legitimating cloak for Western domination. This is also why Kofi Annan, in one of the epigrams for this essay, had to bring all the world's cultures into a discursive meeting place governed by a liberal political idiom named "global civilization." In no other way could these diverse cultures attain or keep their status as civilized.

Teaching Tolerance

According to Huntington, the West will save itself by valuing itself and will save the world through developing global practices of civilizational tolerance, but the latter requires enlightening others about the value of tolerating difference and eschewing fundamentalism. This formulation renders tolerance as pedagogically achieved, a rendering inscribed in the very name of the "Teaching Tolerance" project of the Southern Poverty Law Center.[18] Or, in the words of K. Peter Fritzsche of the International Tolerance Network, ". . . tolerance has to be learned. One has to be made capable of tolerance, and it is one of the utmost tasks of tolerance education to promote the elements of this capability."[19] And Jay Newman, a contemporary philosopher of tolerance, introduces his volume on religious tolerance with a similar invocation: "intolerance is the most persistent and the most insidious of all sources of hatred. It is perhaps foremost among the obstacles to civilization, the instruments of barbarism."[20] Newman's cure for intolerance? Education, which he equates with "a process of civilizing." So strongly does the binary of the ignorant and parochial hater and the cosmopolitan sophisticate govern Newman's argument that he does not even feel compelled to specify what *kind* of education is needed; knowledge and thinking are themselves the engine that dispel tribal enthusiasms and replace them with reflective individuals.[21]

The notion that tolerance must be taught articulates intolerance as the "native" or "primitive" response to difference, an articulation consonant with an equation of tolerance and individuation. The rhetoric of "teaching tolerance" relegates enmity or intolerance to the construed narrow-mindedness of those more childlike, less formally educated, and above all, less individuated than enlightened moderns. Hence, the equation of the "bigot" with "ignorance," and also the popular journalistic tropes of "primitive blood feuds" or "archaic enmity" to frame contemporary ethnic conflict in eastern Europe, Rwanda, or Ethiopia. Hence, too, another popular journalistic trope that Islamicist violence is the consequence of a premodern sensibility. At work here is a familiar Orientalist narrative of the cosmopolitan Westerner as more rational and peaceful because more enlightened than the native, a rationality, cosmopolitanism, and peaceability understood to derive from and generate tolerance. This is a narrative in which, as Barry Hindess argues, difference itself is temporalized, and in which progressivism tied to Western notions of the individual, as well as of knowledge and freedom, are fundamentalized.[22]

The native, the fanatic, the fundamentalist, and the bigot are what must be overcome by the society committed to tolerance; from the perspective of the tolerant, these figures are pre-modern or at least have not been thoroughly washed by modernity, a formulation endlessly rehearsed by Thomas Friedman in his *New York Times* editorials on Islam.[23] This reminds us that it is not really Western Civilization *tout court* but the identification of modernity and, in particular, liberalism with the West, indeed the identification of liberalism as the telos of the West, that provides the basis for Western civilizational supremacy.

What wraps in a common leaf the native, the fanatic, the fundamentalist, and the bigot—despite the fact that some may be religiously orthodox or members of an organicist society while others may be radical libertarians—is a presumed existence in a narrow, homogeneous, unquestioning, and unenlightened universe, an existence that inherently generates hostility toward outsiders, toward questioning, toward difference. "Learning tolerance" thus involves divesting oneself of relentless partiality, absolutist identity, and parochial attachments, a process understood as the effect of a larger, more cosmopolitan worldview and not as the privilege of hegemony. It is noteworthy, too, that within this discourse the aim of learning tolerance is not to arrive at equality or solidarity with others but, rather, to learn how to put up with others by weakening one's own connections to community and claims of identity, that is, by becoming a liberal pluralist, one who, according to Michael Ignatieff, can "live and let live" or "love others more by loving ourselves a little less."[24] Tolerance as the overcoming of the putative natural enmity among essentialized differences is the issue of education and repression, which themselves presume the social contract and the weakening of nationalist or other communal identifications. Formulated this way, the valuation and practice of tolerance simultaneously confirms the superiority of the West, de-politicizes (by recasting as nativist enmity) the effects of domination, colonialism, and Cold War deformations of the Second and Third Worlds, and portrays those living these effects as in need of the civilizing project of the West.

Undergirding this conceptualization of enmity toward difference as natural and primitive is the conceit that the rational individual is inherently more peaceable, civil, far-seeing, and hence tolerant than are members of "organicist societies." If Thomas Friedman is one of the most widely read and unabashed promulgators of this view, Michael Ignatieff is one of its most subtle exponents. For Ignatieff, racism and ethnically based nationalism are the effects of being "trapped in collective identities," the cure for which is "the means to pursue individual lives" and especially individual routes to success and achievement.[25] Thus, it will be recalled, Ignatieff argues that "the culture of individualism is the only reliable solvent of the hold of group identities and the racisms that go with them" and that the "essential task in teaching 'toleration' is to help people see themselves as individuals, and then to see others as such." Ignatieff also understands this way of seeing as bringing us closer to the truth of "actual, real individuals in all their specificity" as opposed to the "procedures of abstraction" constitutive of group interpellation; it brings us closer, in other words, to the truth of what human beings really are.[26] This makes the individual a distinctly Hegelian *a priori* in Ignatieff's analysis—ontologically true yet historically achieved. And the more developed and rewarded this individual is *as* an individual, the more that collective identity is eroded or undercut by individualism and especially individual ego strength, the greater the prospects for a tolerant world. This is the equation that not only posits liberalism as superior because true and posits tolerance as the sign of a fully and rightly individualized society (one that has arrived at the core truth of human beings) it also invokes a representation of liberalism as both a-cultural and anti-cultural, beyond culture and opposed to culture.

Conferring and Withholding Tolerance

Tolerance is generally conferred by those who do not require it upon those who do; it arises within and codifies a normative order in which those who deviate from rather than conform to the norms are eligible for tolerance. The heterosexual proffers tolerance to the homosexual, the Christian tolerates the Muslim or Jew, the dominant race tolerates minority races . . . each of these only up to a point. However, the matter is rarely phrased this way. Rather, power discursively disappears in an action in which a hegemonic population tolerates a marked or minoritized one. The scene materializes instead as one in which the universal tolerates the particular in its particularity, which also means that the putative universal always appears superior to that unassimilated particular, a superiority itself premised upon the non-reciprocity of tolerance (the particular does not tolerate the universal). It is the disappearance of power in the action of tolerance that convenes the hegemonic as the universal and the subordinate or minoritized as the particular. The mechanics of this are familiar: homosexuals discursively appear as more thoroughly defined by their sexuality and hence less capable of participation in the universal than heterosexuals, just as Jews, Catholics, Mormons, and Muslims appear more relentlessly saturated by their religious/ethnic identity than other Americans. (Thus, vice presidential candidate Joseph Leiberman's orthodox Judaism became a significant campaign issue, as did John F. Kennedy's Catholicism, while the born-again Christianity of Jimmy Carter, Ronald Reagan, and both Bushes did not.) This quality of saturation is consequent to a normative regime and not to some quality inherent in the identities or practices. However, in aligning itself with universality and relative neutrality, the unmarked-because-hegemonic identity also associates tolerance with this standing, and conversely, associates objects of tolerance with particularity and partiality.

When the heterosexual tolerates the homosexual, when Christians tolerate Muslims in the West, not only do the first terms *not* require tolerance, but their standing as that which confers tolerance is their superiority over that which is said to require tolerance; the tolerating and tolerated are simultaneously radically distinguished from each other and hierarchically ordered according to a table of virtue. That which tolerates is not eligible for tolerance; that which is tolerated is presumed roughly incapable of tolerance. It is this aspect of the binary structure of tolerance discourse that circulates not just power but the superordination of a group with the term. Through the alignment of the object of tolerance with *difference,* its inferiority to that which is aligned with sameness or universality is secured. The inflection with difference places the object of tolerance outside the universal, positioning it as needing tolerance but unable to tolerate, and hence casting it as a lower form of life than the host. But this positioning is a discursive trick, one that disguises the extent to which it is power, and not inherent qualities of openness or rigidity, moral relativism or orthodoxy, that produces the universal and the particular, the tolerant and the tolerated, the West and the East, the pluralist and the fundamentalist, the civilized and the barbaric, the same and the other. This discursive trick also purifies the first term, the tolerant entity, of all intolerance; and it saturates the second term, the tolerated, with intolerance nearly to (and sometimes arriving at) the point of intolerability.

In liberal theories of tolerance concerned with liberalism's orientation toward putatively non-liberal cultures, or practices, liberalism acquires moral superiority through its ability to tolerate in its midst those thought not to be able to tolerate liberalism in their midst. This superiority is sustained by the conceit that liberalism can tolerate religions without being conquered by them, or tolerate certain fundamentalisms without becoming fundamentalist. Liberalism tolerates fundamentalism, it can incorporate it, so the logic goes, while fundamentalism cannot tolerate or incorporate liberalism; the superior entity is the more capacious one, the one that can harbor difference and not be felled by it. In this regard, tolerance valorizes both size and strength; its virtue rests in a presumption about the value of being large, and that which cannot be large is its inferior. This is how tolerance discourse rewards power's potential for capaciousness with the status of virtue.[27]

Politically, then, the capacity for tolerance is itself an expression of power and of a certain security in that power. At the collective and individual levels, the strong and secure can afford to be tolerant; the marginal and insecure cannot. A polity or culture certain of itself and its hegemony, one which does not does not feel vulnerable, can relax its borders and absorb otherness without fear. Thus the Ottoman Empire could be modestly tolerant and so could Euroatlantic liberalism, though the latter has reified tolerance as a continuous principle while the actual practice of tolerance in liberal societies varies dramatically according to perceived threats and dangers. Indeed, liberal commitments to tolerance are always modified by anxieties and perceived dangers—from the effect of racial integration on neighborhood property values to the effect on schoolchildren when open homosexuals are teachers. If tolerance is an index of power, it is also a practice of vulnerability within this power, an instrument of governance that titrates vulnerability according to a variety of governmental aims.

This suggests that tolerance is also crucial to the shell game that liberal political thought plays with Christianity and with liberal capitalist culture more generally, the ways it denies its involvement with both while promulgating and protecting them.[28] A homely example: the University of California academic instructional calendar, like that of most state schools, is prepared without deference to major religious holidays for Jews, Muslims, or eastern Orthodoxy. One year, a faculty member complains that the first day of fall instruction, when students risk losing their place in over-subscribed courses if they are not present, falls on Yom Kippur. The Registrar responds that the academic calendar honors no religious holidays but that faculty are urged to tolerate all recognized religions by offering make-up exams and other non-punitive accommodations for students whose religious commitments require them to miss selected classes. The faculty member notes that classes are never held on Christmas, Easter, or for that matter, the Christian sabbath. The Registrar replies that this is a coincidence of the timing of "winter break" and of Easter and Sundays always falling on a weekend.

Liberal tolerance discourse not only hides its own imbrication with Christianity and bourgeois culture, it sheaths the cultural chauvinism that liberalism carries to its encounters with nonliberal cultures. For example, when Western liberals express dismay at (what is perceived as mandatory) veiling in fundamentalist Islamic contexts, this dismay is legitimized through the idiom of women's choice. But the contrast between the nearly compulsory baring of skin by American teenage girls and compulsory veiling in a few Islamic societies is drawn routinely as absolute lack of choice, indeed tyranny, "over there" and absolute freedom of choice (representatively redoubled by near nakedness) "over here." This is not to deny differences between the two dress codes and the costs of defying them, but rather to note the means and effects of converting these differences into hierarchicalized opposites. If successful American women are not free to veil, are not free to dress like men or boys, are not free to wear whatever they choose on any occasion without severe economic or social consequences, what sleight of hand recasts this as freedom and individuality contrasted with hypostasized tyranny and lack of agency? What makes choices "freer" when they are constrained by secular and market organizations of femininity and fashion rather than by state or religious law? Do we imagine the former to be less coercive than the latter because we cling to the belief that power is only and always a matter of law and sovereignty, or, as Foucault put it, because we have yet to "cut off the king's head in political theory"? A less politically innocent account of this analytic failure would draw on the postcolonial feminist insight that the West encodes its own superiority through what Chandra Mohanty identifies as the fantasy of Western women as "secular, liberated, and having control over their own lives," an identity derived in part from the very figure of an oppressed Third World opposite.[29] To acknowledge that we have our own form of compulsory feminine dress would undercut this identity of superiority: we *need* fundamentalism, indeed, we project and produce it elsewhere, to understand ourselves as free.[30]

One of the most crucial mechanisms of this projection is the reification and totalization of "intolerant societies," the representation of such societies as saturated by intolerance and organized by the very principle of intolerance. Conversely, the political principle is almost always imagined to exhaustively define the polity that harbors it, even as the question of the limits of tolerance may be hotly debated within it.[31] This division of the world into the tolerant and the intolerant, the fundamentalist and the pluralist, the parochial and the cosmopolitan, allows the political theoretical and philosophical literature on tolerance to repeatedly pose the problem, "what should be the attitude of the tolerant toward the intolerant," as if these were true and dire opposites hosted by radically different entities. The point, again, is not that there are no differences between regimes that expressly advocate tolerance and those that do not, but that civilizational discourse converts these differences into opposites and attributes a distorting essence to each—"fundamentalist/intolerant/unfree" on one side and "pluralist/tolerant/free" on the other—as it aligns liberalism with civilization.

It is not only liberal advocates of tolerance who participate in this Manichean rhetorical scheme. Liberal anti-relativists, on the right and the left, who seek to limit tolerance, indeed who regard current deployments of cultural tolerance as abetting a loathsome relativism, also depict the world as divided between the tolerant and free (West) and the fundamentalist and oppressive (non-West). In a special issue of *Daedelus* entitled "The End of Tolerance: Engaging Cultural Difference" and in Susan Okin's *Is Multiculturalism Bad for Women?* a concerted argument emerges for articulating standards of the humane and acceptable and limiting tolerance to those cultural practices or even to those cultures that meet such standards.[32] Western refusals to condemn and legally ban practices such as genital mutilation, widow suttee, or polygamy are treated as relativism run amok (tacitly, if not expressly attributed to something called "postmodernism") and as thoroughly compromising liberal values of autonomy and freedom. Tolerance is not here repudiated as a value but rather is practiced as a line drawing activity where the line is drawn at the "barbaric" or the coerced.

Intrinsically unobjectionable as this argument may sound, the problem is that all instances of the barbaric and the coerced are found on the non-Western side of the line, that is, where culture or religion are taken to reign and hence where individual autonomy is unsecured. No legal Western practice is marked as *barbaric* (which is only to say that it is a culture that, like all cultures, affirms itself), including feasting upon a variety of animals except those fetishized as pets, polluting the planet and plundering its resources, living and dying alone, devoting life to the pursuit of money, making available human eggs, sperm, and infants for purchase by anonymous strangers, abortion, nuclear weapons, sex clubs, indigency and homelessness, flagrant luxury enjoyed in the presence of the poor, junk food, imperialist wars—any one of which might be considered violent, dehumanizing, or degrading from another cultural perspective. But what Okin and others consider beyond the pale of tolerance are selected non-Western practices, each of which is taken to be promulgated by culture, religion, or tradition, three terms from which Okin imagines liberal legal categories to be immune. The effect is to tar the non-West with the brush of the intolerable for harboring certain practices that are not only named barbaric, that is, uncivilized in contrast to our practices, but coerced, that is, unfree compared to our practices.

The limits of tolerance are thus equated with the limits of civilization or with threats to civilization. Indeed, their common invocation of a civilizational discourse for brokering the tolerable is where those who worry about tolerating what portends the unraveling or decline of Western civilization (Samuel Huntington, the Neoconservatives, rightwing Christians) ideologically converge with those who worry about tolerating non-Western practices that are outside civilization's pale (Susan Okin, liberals, human rights activists). Conservatives and liberals alike are captured by this colonially inflected discourse to establish a civilizational norm by which the tolerable is measured, a norm that tolerance itself also secures.

Moreover, for purposes of distinguishing the civilized from the uncivilized, the discourse of tolerance at its limits is as effective as the discourse of tolerance in a more capacious mode, where it demeans what it abides by making it an object of tolerance. The former marks the barbaric, the latter the abject or deviant. Together, they figure the West *as* civilization and produce liberalism itself as uniquely generative of rationality, freedom, and tolerance; at the same time, they designate only certain subjects as rational and free, and only certain practices as normative. A closer examination of Susan Okin's argument in *Is Multiculturalism Bad for Women?* will allow us to grasp this logic.[33]

Okin's basic claim is that multiculturalism, which she takes to be a relatively unqualified respect for various cultures and which may assume the juridical form of group rights or cultural defenses of particular practices, is in high tension with feminism, the opportunity for women to "live as fulfilling and as freely chosen lives as men can."[34] Reduced further, Okin's argument is that respect for culture collides with respect for gender equality, even that culture *tout court* is in tension with feminism. If culture and sex difference are something that all peoples everywhere have, there is, of course, no logical reason for culture and gender equality to be antagonists, especially when one considers that the gender equality Okin values itself emerges from within some culture.[35] Or does it? What Okin mostly means by culture is not the conventions, ideas, practices, productions, and self-understandings that bind and organize the lives of a particular people. Rather, for Okin, culture comprises ways of life that are not markedly liberal,

Enlightenment bound, rational-legal, and above all, secular. Culture is implicitly pre-modern or at least incompletely modern in her account. For Okin, non-liberal societies *are* cultures; liberal societies are . . . states, civil societies, and individuals. Culture appears when a collectivity is not organized by individual autonomy, rights, or liberty. Culture is non-liberal; liberalism is *kulturlos*.

Okin does not argue this explicitly; to the contrary, she manages to utter the phrase "liberal culture" when acknowledging and lamenting that Western democracies harbor some sexist practices; in other words, culture makes an appearance in the West whenever Okin has to explain how sexist practices have persisted into a time and place formally governed by individual rights. But this only confirms the pejorative standing of "culture" in her analysis —culture is what a complete realization of liberal principles will eradicate or at least radically subdue. Moreover, the gesture of recognizing liberalism as bearing culture seems disingenuous when one notices the incessant slide from culture to religion in Okin's argument. Not only does she repeatedly pair "culture and religion," but she begins a paragraph with a claim about the drive of most *cultures* to control women and ends that same paragraph with a series of examples from Judaism, Islam, and Christianity.[36] And that paragraph is followed by one that treats together orthodox monotheism and "Third World cultures" for their shared patriarchal tendencies. For Okin, the link between what she calls culture and religion is their common occupation with the domestic life which she takes to be a crucial site for women's oppression and the transmission of gender ideology: "obviously culture is not only about domestic arrangements, but they do provide a major focus of most contemporary cultures. Home is, after all, where much of culture is practiced, preserved, and transmitted to the young."[37] So culture and religion both organize domestic life patriarchically and are transmitted through domestic life. What is the standing of liberalism in this regard? Its sharp ideological and political-economic divide between public and private (which other feminists have spent the past thirty years subjecting to critique both for its structural production of women's economic dependence and for its depoliticization of women's subordination) is here affirmed by Okin for the dam it ostensibly erects between gendered family values and gender-neutral civic and public law.

If the private realm in liberal societies harbors gender inequality, Okin tacitly suggests, if this is where sexist culture lingers and is reproduced, this is offset by the public and juridical principles of abstract personhood and autonomy. In liberal democracies, the formal commitment to secularism and to individual autonomy can be mobilized to erode sexist culture, and this is what Okin wants for the rest of the world.

"Most cultures," Okin writes, "have as one of their principal aims the control of women by men."[38] But "Western liberal culture" (her phrase) is a little different. "While virtually all of the world's cultures have distinctly patriarchal pasts, some—mostly, though by no means exclusively, Western liberal cultures—have departed far further from them than others."[39] What distinguishes Western cultures, which "still practice many forms of sex discrimination," from others is that in them women are "legally guaranteed many of the same freedoms and opportunities as men."[40] In other words, it is not the law or the doctrine of liberalism that is sex discriminatory but some kind of cultural remainder that the law has not yet managed to reform or extinguish. Whatever the remains of culture in Western liberal orders, and whatever the remains of sexism within those cultures, liberalism as a political-juridical order is, or has the capacity to be, gender-clean. This, of course, is warmed over John Stuart Mill: in a progress narrative led by liberalism, indeed, by the bourgeoisie, male dominance is the barbaric stuff of the old regime, of a time when might, custom, and religion rather than the law of equality and reason ruled the world, and of a time before the individual reigned supreme. Thus, if liberal regimes continue to house deposits of misogyny and female subordination, this must be the result of something other than liberalism which, with its legal principles of autonomy, liberty, and equality, constitutes the remedy to such ills within the societies it orders.

But what if liberalism itself harbors male dominance, what if male superordination is inscribed in liberalism's core values of liberty, rooted in autonomy and centered upon self-interest, and equality, defined as sameness and confined to the public sphere?[41] Many feminists have argued that liberal categories, relations, and processes are inseparable from a relentlessly gendered division of labor and a far-reaching public/private distinction, in which everything associated with the family—need, dependence, inequality, the body, relationality—is identified with the feminine and constitutes both the predicate and the opposite to a masculinist public sphere of rights, autonomy, formal equality, rationality, and individuality. In this critique, masculinist social norms are part of the very architecture of liberalism; they structure its division and population of the social space and govern its production and regulation of subjects. These are norms that produce and privilege masculine public beings—free, autonomous, and equal —while producing a feminine other as a familial being—encumbered, dependent, and different.[42]

Okin does not simply elide such feminist critiques of liberalism.[43] The presumption of ungendered liberal principles counterposed to gendered cultural ones is necessary to the argument that liberalism is the best cure for the patriarchal ills of culture. Okin perfectly expresses an ideology of the autonomy of the liberal state and individual from (what is named) culture, an autonomy that positions the liberal state as singularly freeing and the liberal individual as singularly free. Culture is not only historically sexist in her account, it is corrosive of autonomy and corrupting of juridical universalism. For Okin, individual autonomy prevails only when culture recedes.[44] And where there is autonomy, there is choice and where there is choice, there is freedom, especially women's freedom. This is how Okin positions both culture and patriarchy (as opposed to mere "sexist attitudes or practices") as always elsewhere from liberalism. Culture and religion perpetuate inequality by formally limiting women's autonomy while the constraints on choice in a liberal capitalist order—say, those of a single mother with few job skills—are either not cultural or not significant. The formal existence of choice is the incontestable (hence non-cultural?) good, regardless of its actualizability. Thus, Okin concludes:

> In the case of a more patriarchal minority culture in the context of a less patriarchal majority culture, no argument can be made on the basis of self-respect or freedom that the female members of the culture have a clear interest in its preservation. Indeed, they *might* be much better off if the culture into which they were born were either to become extinct (so that its members would

> become integrated into the less sexist surrounding culture) or, preferably, to be encouraged to alter itself so as to reinforce the equality of women—at least to the degree to which this value is upheld in the majority culture.[45]

This passage involves several remarkable claims. First, in arguing that women who have self-respect and want freedom will necessarily oppose (not simply be ambivalent about) their culture, Okin rehearses a false consciousness argument always reserved today for the practices of women: a woman who defends cultural or religious practices that others may designate as patriarchal cannot be thinking for herself, and so cannot be trusted to think well about her attachments and investments. Consequently, self-respecting liberals like Susan Okin must think for her. Second, it implies that female subordination is sufficient grounds for wanting one's culture dead, an extraordinary claim on its own but made more so when coming from one as wedded to Western culture as Okin is. Third, it argues that the standard against which minority cultures are to be measured is not an abstract standard of freedom, equality, and self-respect for women but rather that superior *degree* of these things found in the majority culture and measured by the values of the majority culture. In this strict quantification of sexism—more there, less here—and inattention to the *varieties* of male superordination, it is hard to imagine a more naked version of Enlightenment progressivism and the brief for liberal imperialism it entails.

Where does tolerance fit into this picture? In Okin's view, liberal orders and liberal legalism should *not* stretch to accommodate the overtly misogynisitic or sexist practices of minority cultures—e.g., child brideship, polygamy, clitoridectomy—and should not permit cultural defenses any standing in criminal trial cases concerned with rape, wife-murder, or infanticide.[46] Okin draws the line for tolerance at the point of what she calls not simply "sex inequality" but the "barbaric" treatment of women. Tolerance is for civilized practices: barbarism is on the other side of the line, "beyond the pale."

But consider this: American women spend upwards of nine billion dollars annually on plastic surgery, cosmetic implants, injections, and facial laser treatments, and untold more on over-the-counter products advertised to restore youthful looks. In the last half-decade, tens of thousands of women have opted to smooth their forehead lines with regular injections of Botox, a diluted version of what the American Medical Association has identified as "the most poisonous substance known"; far more deadly than anthrax, "a single gram, evenly dispersed, could kill more than one million people, causing 'symmetric, descending, flaccid paralysis' and eventually cutting off its victims' power to breathe, swallow, communicate, or see."[47] How many noses have been cut, flattened, or otherwise rearranged to fit an Aryan ideal of feminine beauty? How many breasts reduced? How many enlarged? How many submissions to painful electrolysis and other means of removing body hair? What of the rising trend among well-off American women to have their feet surgically reconfigured to fit high-fashioned shoes or their labia surgically "corrected" to be symmetrical? Or the popularity of plastic surgery—for noses, lips, breasts, and hips—among high school girls?[48] Are these procedures less culturally organized than the procedures Okin cites to condemn? Is their "voluntariness" what spares them from being candidates for her attention? Does a liberal frame mistake elective surgery for freedom from coercive power, as it tends to mistake elections for political freedom? What is voluntary about treatments designed to produce conventional ideals of youthful beauty for an aspiring Hollywood actress, a trophy wife on the verge of being traded in for a younger model, or an ordinary middle-aged, middle-class woman in southern California?

Similarly, why is Okin more outraged by clitordectemy than by the routine surgical "correction" of intersexed babies in the United States—babies whose genitals are sexually ambiguous and who have no say whatsoever in these surgeries but are condemned to live the rest of their lives with the (often botched) outcome?[49] Is Western anxiety about sexual dimorphism, and in particular about female availability for penile penetration, any less cultural than the anxieties about female sexual pleasure she condemns in parts of Africa and the Middle East?[50] Why isn't Okin alarmed by the epidemic of eating disorders among American teenaged girls or the epidemic of American women being pharmaceutically treated for depression? Why doesn't Okin find drugging such women rather than transforming their life conditions barbaric and intolerable? In sum, why is Okin more horrified by the *legal* control of women by men than by the controlling cultural norms and market productions of gender and sexuality, including norms and productions of beauty, sexual desire and behavior, weight and physique, soul and psyche, that course through modern Western societies?

When individual rights and liberties are posited as the solution to coercion, and liberalism is the antidote to culture, women's social oppression or subordination (as opposed to their contingent or domestic violation or maltreatment) appears only where law openly avows its religious or cultural character, that is, where it has not taken the vow of Western secularism. But as the examples above suggest, liberalism's formulation of freedom as choice and its reduction of the political to policy and law sets loose, as a depoliticized underworld, a sea of social powers nearly as coercive as law, and certainly as effective in producing subordinated subjects. Indeed, as a combination of Marcusian and Foucauldian perspectives remind us, choice can become a critical instrument of domination in liberal capitalist societies; insofar as the fiction of the sovereign subject blinds us to powers producing that subject, choice both cloaks and potentially eroticizes the powers it engages.[51] Moreover, Okin's inability to grasp liberalism's own cultural norms, in which, for example, autonomy is valued over connection or the responsibility for dependent others (with which women are typically associated), liberty is conceived as freedom to do what one wants (for which women are often faulted), and equality is premised upon sameness (while women are always conceived as different), eliminates the possibility for discerning deep and abiding male superordination in liberalism itself—not just in "liberal cultures" but in liberal legalism and political principles.

In sum, the putative legal autonomy of the subject, along with the putative autonomy of the law itself from gendered norms and from culture more generally, combine to position women in the West as free, choosing beings who stand in stark contrast to their sisters subjected to legally sanctioned cultural barbarism. From this perspective, liberal imperialism is not only legitimate but morally mandated. "Culture" must be brought to heel by liberalism so that women are free to choose their anti-wrinkle creams.

There is a final irony in Okin's formulation of "culture" as the enemy of women. This focus sustains an elision of the conditions imposed on Third World women by global capitalism, conditions to which Western critics could be responsive without engaging in cultural imperialism or endorsing political and military imperialism. These range from labor hyper-exploitation in export platforms and free trade zones to global capitalism's often violent disruptions and dislocations of family and community. If the aim is to secure possibilities for modest self-determination for Third World women, what could be more important than addressing and redressing these circumstances? Instead, in the obsession with culture over capitalism, indeed in her apparent indifference to the economics of poverty, exploitation, and deracination, Okin repeats a disturbing colonial gesture in which the alleged barbarism of the native culture, rather than imperial conquest, colonial political and economic deformation and contemporary economic exploitation, is made the target of progressive reform. As the final turn of this essay suggests, this gesture is characteristic of tolerance discourse in its civilizational mode.

There is a second colonial gesture in a Western feminism that targets "culture" as the problem. The liberal construction of tolerance as respect for individual autonomy secured by a secular state, a construction shared by liberal theorists on both sides of the "group rights" debates, means that the practice of tolerance is inconceivable where such autonomy is not a core political principle and juridical norm. Such an account of tolerance not only consecrates liberalism's superiority but reiterates liberalism's obliviousness to social powers other than law and thereby sustains the conceit of the thoroughgoing autonomy of the liberal subject. At the same time, in its dependence upon legally encoded autonomy—rights—this definition rules out the possibility of non-liberal political forms of tolerance. But what if tolerance of differing beliefs and practices can and does attach to values other than autonomy, for example, to formulations of plurality, difference, or cultural preservation that do not devolve upon individual liberty?[52] Conversely, what if individual liberty were decentered (without being rejected) as the sign of civilization, grasped as but one way of gratifying the richness and possibility in being human and also as fictional in its absolutism? That is, what if autonomy were recognized as relative, ambiguous, ambivalent, partial, and also advanced by means other than law?[53] This would not only make non-liberal tolerance practices conceivable, it would serve as a vantage point for a more critical understanding of liberal practices than is permitted by its self-affirming vocabulary and dubious syllogisms.

Tolerance, Capital, and Liberal Imperialism

In considering the place of tolerance in civilizational discourse through the entwining of liberalism and postcolonial discourse, I have dwelt upon Okin at length. This is not because she is its most sophisticated exponent but because she is among the most openhanded. But other liberal theorists make similar moves. Recall Michael Ignatieff's argument that tolerance is the fruit of individuation and hence the achievement of societies governed by individualism. Recall, too, that Ignatieff portrays such individualism as the primordial truth of human beings—who we really are—as opposed to the abstract human being entailed in collective conceptions of identity. This positing of the individual as *a priori* not only renders collective identity as ideological, deformative, and dangerous, it tacitly assigns culture and all other forms of collective identification unconquered by liberalism to a premodern past and nonhuman elsewhere. This depicts liberal democracy as representing the truth of human beings and depicts those mired in collective identity, or as Fukuyama would have it, "mired in history" as at once misguided, irrational, and dangerous.

On a closer reading of Ignatieff, however, tolerance is not simply the fruit of individualism but of prosperity—it is not the individual as such but individual success that breeds a tolerant moral psychology. On the one hand, "the German man who can show you his house, his car, and a family as measures of his own pride rather than just his white skin may be less likely to wish to torch an immigrant hostel." On the other hand, "if the market fails, as it is failing upwards of twenty million unemployed young people in Europe alone, then it does create the conditions in which individuals must turn to group hatreds in order to assert and defend their identities."[54] Here, tolerance appears less a moral or political achievement of liberal autonomy than a *bourgeois* capitalist virtue, the fruit of power and success . . . even domination.

As the passage above suggests, while affirming the value of economic prosperity in generating a tolerant outlook, Ignatieff is fully confident that globalization brings with it a more tolerant world. He worries that its economic depression of certain populations may incite racial or ethnic nationalisms as a kind of last-gasp source of supremacy or privilege.[55] However, moral philosophers Bernard Williams and Joseph Raz have no such anxieties; for them, the market inherently attenuates fundamentalism, puts the brakes on fanaticism, and "encourages scepticism about religious and other claims to exclusivity." In short, it erodes cultural, nationalistic, and religious forms of local solidarity or belonging.[56] Williams and Raz, however, themselves differ in their accounts of how neoliberal globalization enriches the ground from which tolerance grows. For Raz, market homogenization counters the fragmenting effects of multiculturalism in the era of global capitalism. That is, the market helps to dampen the "culture" in the multicultural civic and national populations produced by globalization *because* it tends to brings liberal democratic politics along with it, thereby producing a common (cultureless) political and economic life to attenuate the substance and contentiousness of (culturally based) claims of difference. Williams, though, does not need the globalized market to import liberal democracy as a political form for it to effect an increase in religious and ethnic tolerance. For him, the market itself loosens the grip (by greasing the palm?) of the fundamentalist, thereby reducing intolerance through recourse to the principle of utility rather than by any other moral or "civilizing" principle. In Williams's words,

> when such scepticism [induced by international commercial society] is set against the manifest and immediate human harms generated by intolerance, there is a basis for the practice of toleration—a basis that is indeed allied to liberalism, but is less ambitious than the pure principle of pluralism, which rests on autonomy. It is closer to the tradition that may be traced to Montesquieu and to Constant, which the late Judith Shklar called "the Liberalism of Fear.[57]

Indeed, not only the politics of fear configured by the rightest liberal tradition of Hobbes, Montesqueiu, and Constant but a forthright neoliberal political rationality appears on Williams's pages, as unfettered capitalism is imagined to produce a normative social order and calculating subject, neither of which need be codified in liberal law or letters. For attentive students of the history of capitalism, of course, the erosion of non-market practices and customs by capital is old news. What is striking about the enthusiasm with which political liberals such as Williams and Raz applaud this phenomenon is that they are cheering raw Western liberal imperialism and neoliberal globalization for their combined effectiveness in destroying local culture.

Other political liberals are less confident about the ease with which tolerance can be exported to non-liberal sites. Speaking about multiculturalism within liberal democratic societies, Will Kymlicka concludes that there is no way to impose the value of tolerance upon minority cultures for which individual autonomy is not a primary value other than to make it part of the deal of being tolerated by the majority or hegemonic culture. For a culture to be tolerated by liberalism, in Kymlicka's view, it must become tolerant within, even if this compromises crucial principles of the culture.[58] Thus, Kymlicka effectively advocates exploiting the power position of the tolerating culture, which means deploying Kantian liberalism in a distinctly non-Kantian way, that is, treating tolerance as a means for transforming others rather than as an end in itself, and treating individual autonomy as a bargaining chip rather than as an intrinsic value. The demand for cultural transformation, of course, also compromises the gesture of tolerance at the moment it is extended. Kymlicka's proposition for the extension of tolerance to non-liberal cultures tacitly exposes the anti-liberal aspects of this aim, along with the absence of cultural and political neutrality in tolerance itself. It reminds us that more than a means of achieving civil peace of freedom, tolerance in its liberal mode is an exercise of hegemony that requires extensive political transformation of the cultures and subjects it would govern.

There are important analytic and prescriptive differences among Okin and Ignatieff, Huntington and Raz, Williams and Kymlicka. Together, however, they paint a picture of tolerance as a civilizational discourse that draws from and entwines postcolonial, liberal, and neoliberal reasoning. This discourse encodes the superiority of the West and of liberalism by valorizing (and even ontologizing) individual autonomy, by positioning culture and religion as extrinsic to this autonomy, and by casting governance by culture and religion as individual autonomy's opposite. The cultural norms carried by the market and organizing liberal democracy are not made visible within the discourse.

That tolerance is preferable to violent civil conflict is inarguable. What this truism elides, however, is the discursive function of tolerance in legitimating the often violent imperialism of international liberal governmentality conjoined with neoliberal global political economy.[59] Not only does the practice of tolerance anoint the superior or advanced status of the tolerant. Not only does withholding tolerance for designated practices, cultures, and regimes mark them as beyond the pale of civilization. It is also the case that the economy of this offering and this refusal masks the cultural norms of liberal democratic regimes and of the West by denying their status as cultural norms. What becomes clear from considering the above named thinkers together is that the discourse of tolerance substantively brokers cultural value—valorizing the West, Othering the rest—while feigning only to distinguish civilization from barbarism, protect the former from the latter, and extend the benefits of liberal thought and practices. Insofar as tolerance in its civilizational mode draws upon a political-juridico discourse of cultural neutrality, in which what is at stake is said to be rationality, individual autonomy and the rule of law rather than the (despotic) rule of culture or religion, tolerance is crucial to liberalism's denial of its imbrication with culture and the colonial projection of culture onto the native. It is crucial to liberalism's conceit of independence from culture, neutrality with regard to culture . . . a conceit that in turn shields liberal polities from charges of cultural supremacy and cultural imperialism. This was precisely the conceit that allowed George W. Bush to say, without recourse to the infelicitous language of "crusade," that "we have no intention of imposing our culture" while insisting on a set of liberal principles that cannot be brooked without risking being bombed.

Tolerance *conferred* as well as tolerance *withheld* serves this function; both are essential in the circuitry tolerance travels as a civilizational discourse. *Tolerance conferred* upon "foreign" practices shores up the normative standing of the tolerant and the liminal standing of the tolerated—a standing somewhere between civilization and barbarism. It reconfirms, without reference to the orders of power which enable it, the higher civilizational standing of those who tolerate what they do not condone or share—their cosmopolitanism, forbearance, expansiveness, catholicity, remoteness from fundamentalism. It is only against this backdrop that *tolerance withheld* succeeds in marking the other as barbaric without implicating the cultural norms of the tolerant by this marking. When a tolerant civilization meets its limits, it does not say that it is encountering political or cultural difference but that it is encountering the limits of civilization itself. At this point, the tolerant civilization is justified not only in refusing to extend tolerance to its Other, but in treating it as hostile, both internally oppressive *and* externally dangerous, and, externally dangerous *because* internally oppressive. This hostile status in turn legitimates the tolerant entity to suspend its own civilizational principles in dealing with this Other, principles that range from political self-determination and nation-state sovereignty to rational deliberation, legal and international accountability, and reasoned justifications. This legitimate abrogation of civilizational principles can be carried quite far, up to the point of making preemptive war on the Other.

The circuitry of tolerance in civilizational discourse also abets the slide from terrorism to fundamentalism to anti-Americanism that legitimates the rhetorical Manicheanism often wielded by the Bush regime: "You're either with the civilized world, or you're with the terrorists." It facilitates the slide from Osama Bin Laden to Saddam Hussein as the enemy to civilization, and from a war *on* terrorism to wars *for* regimes change in Afghanistan and Iraq. And likewise it indulges a slide from a war justified by Iraq's *danger* to the "civilized world" to one justified by the Iraqi people's *need* for liberation (by the West). Tolerance in a liberal idiom, both conferred and withheld, serves not merely as the *sign* of the civilized and the free but configures the *right* of the civilized against a barbaric opposite that is both internally oppressive and externally dangerous, neither tolerant nor tolerable.

In these operations, tolerance has a slim resemblance to its founding impetus as a response to the fracturing of church authority, an instrument for consolidating emerging nation state power and provenance, even as a *modus vivendi* for co-habiting belief communities. That tolerance has acquired such a troubling relationship to Western empire today does not add up to an argument to scrap the term or jettison its representation of a practice for living with what is undesirable, offensive, or repugnant. Rather, it suggests the importance of becoming erudite and discerning about the ways of tolerance today and of seeking to contest the anti-political language of ontology, affect, and ethos it circulates with considerations of power, social forces, and justice. This means becoming shrewd about the ways tolerance operates as a coin of liberal imperialism, intersects with racialized tropes of barbarism or the decline of the West, and abets in legitimizing the very violence it stands for deterring. It means apprehending the ways that tolerance discourse articulates normal and deviant subjects, cultures, religions, and regimes, and hence how it produces and regulates identity. It means tracking the work of tolerance in iterating subordination and marginalization and does so in part by functioning as a supplement to other elements of liberal discourse, such as universalism and egalitarianism, associated with remedying subordination and marginalization. It means grasping tolerance as a mode of governmentality that discursively depoliticizes the conflicts whose effects it manages by analytically occluding the histories and powers constitutive of these conflicts, and by casting "difference" as ontological and inherently prickly if not hostile. It means attending to the ways that tolerance draws on its reputation as a civilizing moment in the early modern West, attenuating persecution in the field of religion, for the legitimation of its current work as a civilizational discourse that masks the violence in its dealings with the non-West. It means, in sum, grasping tolerance as a mode of national and transnational governmentality today.

The development of this kind of political intelligence does not entail rejecting tolerance *tout court,* declaring it an inherently insidious value, or replacing tolerance with some other term or practice. Becoming perspicacious about the contemporary operations and circuitries of tolerance, however, does suggest a positive political strategy of nourishing counter-discourses that would feature power and justice where anti-political tolerance talk has displaced them. We can attempt to strengthen articulations of inequality, abjection, subordination, and colonial and postcolonial violence that are suppressed by tolerance discourse. We can configure conflicts through grammars of power rather than ontologized ethnic or religious feuds. And we can labor to expose the cultural and religious norms organizing liberalism along with the ethnic, racial, sexual, and gendered norms it harbors. In short, without foolishly positioning ourselves "against tolerance" or advocating "intolerance," we can contest the depoliticizing, regulatory, and imperial aims of contemporary deployments of tolerance with alternative political speech and practices. Such work constitutes a modest contribution to the larger project of alleviating the human suffering, reducing the violence, and fostering the political justice for which the twenty-first century howls.

NOTES

This chapter was originally published in Wendy Brown, *Regulating Aversion: Tolerance in the Age of Identity and Empire* (pages 176–205, 251–58), Copyright 2006 by Princeton University Press. Reprinted by permission of Princeton University Press.

1. Address to a United Nations Meeting on Dialogue Among Civilizations, September 5, 2000, Press Release SG/SM/7526/Rev.1.

2. Address to the American Enterprise Institute, February 26, 2003.

3. "Moderate Muslim Voices Must be Heard," *New York Times*, Op-Ed, June 4, 2002.

4. NPR, June 12, 2002, Rumsfeld responding to concerns about the rights of 2,400 "terror suspects" detained at that time by the United States government.

5. The same associations are not conjured by the utterance, "she is a tolerant woman" or even "he is a tolerant person." This differential speaks volumes about tolerance as both an effect of power and a vehicle of power, an expression of domination and a means of extending and consecrating it.

6. Address to Asia-Pacific Economic Cooperation Summit in Shanghai, October 20, 2001.

7. Address to the Republican Caucus in White Sulphur Springs, West Virginia, February 1, 2002.

8. "Civilization," in the *Oxford English Dictionary, Second Edition* OED online, http://www.oed.com. Gail Hershatter and Anna Tsing remind us that the OED is "itself no minor civilizational project in its creation of

literary legacies that both set linguistic standards and define a cultural practice." Gail Hershatter and Anna Tsing, "Civilization," *New Keywords: A Revised Vocabulary of Culture and Society,* ed. Tony Bennett, et al. (Oxford: Blackwell, 2005), 37.

9. Raymond Williams, *Keywords: A Vocabulary of Culture and Society,* revised edition (Oxford: Oxford University Press, 1983), 57.

10. Hershatter and Tsing, "Civilization," 36.

11. Samuel P. Huntington, *The Clash of Civilizations and the Remaking of World Order* (New York: Simon and Schuster, 1996), 311.

12. Ibid., 318.

13. Ibid., 321.

14. Ibid.

15. Ibid.

16. The conflation of civilization with culture in this definition is paralleled by Huntington's definition of civilization as "culture writ large" (41) or "the highest cultural group of people and the broadest level of cultural identity people have short of that which distinguishes humans from other species" (43). However, in its reference to one who has "sympathy with literary culture," the OED definition clearly equates civilization with high European culture, thus referencing its class connotations and explaining why we refer to children learning table manners as a process of "civilizing" them.

17. Prefatory Remarks to George W. Bush's April 13, 2004, press conference.

18. See the Teaching Tolerance website (http://www.tolerance.org) and the Southern Poverty Law Center website (http://www.splcenter.org). The SPLC has been plagued with controversy in recent years and was compromised from the beginning by the hucksterism and opportunism of its co-founder, Morris Dees. The richest civil rights organization in the business, it raises astonishing sums that it never spends and consequently has been assigned one of the worst ratings of any group monitored by the American Institute of Philanthropy. According to Ken Silverstein, who wrote about the organization in *Harper's,* the SPLC spends twice as much on fund-raising as it does on legal services for victims of civil rights abuses. And while backing away from the kinds of cases, especially death penalty appeals, that might lower its attractiveness to wealthy white liberals, it exploits and sensationalizes steadily dwindling Klan activities in a manner designed to rake in contributions from whites. In 1986, Silverstein reports, "the Center's entire legal staff quit in protest of Dee's refusal to address issues—such as homelessness, voter registration, and affirmative action—that they considered far more pertinent to poor minorities, if far less marketable to affluent benefactors, than fighting the

KKK" ("The Church of Morris Dees," *Harper's,* November 2000). Another lawyer who resigned a few years later told reporters that the Center's programs were calculated to cash in on "black pain and white guilt," a calculation that is patently evident in the over-the-top stories and testimonials featured in the fund-raising literature. However, these kinds of *exposés* from within and without have been largely ignored by the mainstream press and both the SPLC and the Teaching Tolerance project continue to garner ringing endorsements from a range of politicians, educators, and media personnel.

19. K. Peter Fritzsche, "Human Rights and Human Rights Education," International Network: Education for Democracy, Human Rights and Tolerance, *Podium* 2/2000 http://www.tolerance-net.org/news/podium/podium031.html.

20. Jay Newman, *Foundations of Religious Tolerance* (Toronto: University of Toronto Press, 1982), 3.

21. There is a certain tension in the nativism of the popular tolerance literature. Cross-cutting the view that intolerance is primordial and tolerance is a civilizational achievement is another one that "people are not born as little haters, we learn to hate. And just as we learn to hate, we have to unlearn (sic) to hate" (Caryl Stern, Senior Associate National Director of the Anti-Defamation League, quoted in WorldNetDaily.com, January 6, 2005). While superficially opposite to the idea that bigotry is primitive while tolerance is civilized and advanced, the ADL formulation may well retain the nativism. The "learning" presumably occurs in the tribe, and may very well be transmitted and absorbed almost unconsciously or at least subrationally as part of what binds and reproduces the tribe; the "unlearning" presumably occurs in a more cosmopolitan setting, and is rational and deliberate.

22. Barry Hindess, personal communication, but see also Christine Helliwell and Barry Hindess, "Temporalizing of Difference," *Ethnicities,* 5:3, 2005. Much politically liberal talk of tolerance and multiculturalism participates in this temporalizing of difference even in describing the difference between liberals and conservatives: liberals self-characterize themselves as more enlightened, forward-looking, or advanced, and refer to conservative agendas as traditional, backward-looking, or regressive.

23. See, for example, the following editorials in the *New York Times*: "The Core of Muslim Rage," March 6, 2002; "Moderate Muslim Voices Must Be Heard," June 4, 2002; "Noah and 9/11," September 11, 2002; and "An Islamic Reformation," December 4, 2002.

24. Michael Ignatieff, "Nationalism and Toleration," *The Politics of Toleration in Modern Life,* ed. Susan Mendus (Durham: Duke University Press, 2000), 85.

25. Ibid., 101.

26. Ibid., 102.

27. Capacity as such is the measure of tolerance in many domains of its usage: at its most rudimentary, tolerance is defined by how much error, contamination, or toxicity can be absorbed by the host without damaging it, whether the element at issue is alcohol consumption for a college freshman, margin of error for a statistical inference, or ethnic nationalism for a liberal society. But within a liberal regime, this capacity is not only a measure of ability but virtue.

28. As a political rationality contoured by the Protestant Reformation, liberal tolerance not only presumes individual autonomy but the viability of privatizing fundamental beliefs. Most of the belief structures of most of the world's peoples for most of human history do not fit with these presumptions. Reformation tolerance doctrine does not work well for the faith structures of the ancient Greeks, Mediaeval Christians, or of modern Muslims, Jews, Hindus, or Catholics. It does not work well for a socialist, tribalist, or communitarian ethos or order. It was coined to solve a specific problem issuing from a specific social formation and political crisis: how to allow Protestant sectarians the right to worship God according to their own individual understanding of Him and His words without undercutting both Church and state authority, how to substitute accommodation of these sects for burning heretics alive, how to stem the tide of blood spilled over religious rebellion in early modern Europe.

29. Chandra Talpade Mohanty, "Under Western Eyes: Feminist Scholarship and Colonial Discourses," *Feminist Review* 30, Autumn 1988, 74.

30. Of the many feminist post-colonial scholars who have made this point in recent years, three of the best accounts come from Lila Abu-Lughod, Interview, AsiaSource, March 20, 2002 http://www.asiasource.org; Saba Mahmood, *Politics of Piety: The Islamic Revival and the Feminist Subject* (Princeton: Princeton University Press, 2005); and Charles Hirschkind and Saba Mahmood, "Feminism, the Taliban, and Politics of Counter-Insurgency," *Anthropological Quarterly* 75.2, 2002.

31. Thus, Bush can declare, and his neoconservative and Christian backers can agree, that America stands for the principle of tolerance, even as the Republican Party is considered the party of "intolerance" by those on the cultural left, and many conversations rebuke certain practices of tolerance as moral decline or depravity.

32. *Daedalus* 129.4, Fall 2000, and Susan Okin, *Is Multiculturalism Bad for Women?* (Princeton: Princeton University Press, 1999).

33. Anne Norton's review of *Is Multiculturalism Bad for Women?* offers a scathing critique of Okin's orientalist logic, poor scholarship, and ignorance of critiques of liberal feminism and of the debates surrounding her

instances of the "intolerable," from polygamy to clitoridectomy. See *Political Theory* 29.5, October 2001, 736–49. Most of the other reviews and receptions of this work, however, have been relatively positive.

34. *Multiculturalism,* 10.

35. A discussion of Okin's argument about multiculturalism and feminism poses a conundrum about whether to deconstruct her impoverished concept of culture and thereby refuse to enter the rest of the argument, or to provisionally accept her account as one takes up other aspects of the argument. Okin largely is impervious to the last several decades of rethinking what culture is and could mean (a rethinking undertaken primarily in anthropology and cultural studies) and is wholly unconcerned with specifying what culture is—there is a stray reference to "ways of life" on page 10 of *Multiculturalism.* However, it is also the case that her analysis could not get off the ground if she attended closely to theorizations of culture that do not isolate it from the political, juridical, and economic, if she grasped the colonial inflection in the notion of culture she deploys (in which culture is always pre-liberal and liberalism is always without culture), if she recognized that the sense of culture she uses is the coinage of both liberal strategies of depoliticization and colonial discourse.

36. *Multiculturalism,* 13–14.

37. Ibid., 13.

38. Ibid.

39. Ibid., 16.

40. Ibid., 16–17.

41. See Carole Pateman, *The Sexual Contract* (Stanford: Stanford University Press, 1988); Clarke and Lange, *The Sexism of Social and Political Theory* (Toronto: Toronto University Press, 1979); Kathy Ferguson, *The Feminist Case Against Bureaucracy* (Philadelphia: Temple University Press, 1985); Wendy Brown, "Liberalism's Family Values" in *States of Injury: Power and Freedom in Late Modernity* (Princeton: Princeton University Press, 1995); Joan W. Scott, *Only Paradoxes to Offer* (Cambridge: Harvard University Press, 1996); Catharine MacKinnon, *Toward a Feminist Theory of the State* (Cambridge: Harvard University Press, 1991); Nancy Hirschmann and Christine di Stefano, eds., *Revisioning the Political: Feminist Reconstructions of Traditional Concepts in Western Political Theory* (Boulder: Westview Press, 1996); Nancy Hirschmann, *Rethinking Obligation: A Feminist Method for Political Theory* (Ithaca: Cornell University Press, 1992) and *The Subject of Liberty: Toward a Feminist Theory of Freedom* (Princeton: Princeton University Press, 2002).

42. See "Liberalism's Family Values," op cit., and Catharine MacKinnon's essay, "Difference and Dominance: On Sex Discrimination," in *Fem-*

inism Unmodified: Discourses on Life and Law (Cambridge: Harvard University Press, 1988).

43. Okin's own feminist critique of liberalism is to be found in *Justice, Gender, and the Family* (Basic Books, 1989) which argues on behalf of treating the family as one of the "spheres of justice" articulated in Michael Walzer's book by that name.

44. This makes clear why *multi*culturalism is so bad for women: it multiplies enemies to autonomy.

45. *Multiculturalism,* 23.

46. Ibid., 18.

47. Susan Dominus, "The Seductress of Vanity," *New York Times,* May 5, 2002, 50.

48. Karen Springen, "Kids Under the Knife," *Newsweek,* November 1, 2004.

49. Information about the nature and frequency of intersex, along with the history of its treatment, can be found at the website of the Intersex Society of North America, http://www.isna.org.

50. Intersexed children, regardless of where they are on a complex spectrum of physiological sex, are more often "surgically corrected" to be anatomically female than male, since, according to the surgeons, it is "easier to poke a hole than to build a poke." This surgery, which is performed neither for the physical health or nor the future sexual pleasure of the subject, may include clitoral reduction (so the clitoris is less penile-like), invagination (production or enlargement of the vagina), and removal of undescended or "internal" testes. The post-surgical course of treatment, often lasting for years, includes stretching the vaginal cavity with successively sized vaginal inserts; the aim is to enlarge it sufficiently for penetration by an erect penis when the child reaches maturity. Since administration of these painful treatments often requires forcible restraint of the child undergoing them, it is hard to name them anything other than medically authorized rape.

51. Herbert Marcuse, *One Dimensional Man* (Boston: Beacon, 1964); Foucault, *History of Sexuality,* vol 1, *An Introduction,* trans. R. Hurley (New York: Vintage, 1980). For a somewhat different perspective on this dimension of agency and capitalism's charms, see Jane Bennett, *The Enchantment of Modern Life* (Princeton: Princeton University Press, 2002).

52. Anthropologists David Scott, *Refashioning Futures: Criticism After Postcoloniality* (Princeton: Princeton University Press, 1999) and Saba Mahmood, *Politics of Piety: The Islamic Renewal and the Feminist Subject* (Princeton: Princeton University Press, 2004) are among those who have traced the arc of colonial discourse in measuring postcolonial states against liberal formulations of tolerance and have made a compelling

case for thinking about tolerance in postcolonial settings outside of the frame of liberalism, that is, a case for refusing liberal imperialism in its academic as well as political mode.

53. Even in hyper-liberal societies, not all practices of autonomy are equally valued–consider the indigent person resistant to being managed by social services or the teenager hanging around a street corner with nothing to do. Nor are all associations and practices governed by the principle of autonomy and rights; without those governed by relationality and need, there is no basis for familial or social bonds.

54. Ignatieff, "Nationalism and Toleration," 102.

55. Ibid., 94–95.

56. The cited material is from Bernard Williams, "Toleration: An Impossible Virtue?" in *Toleration: An Elusive Virtue,* ed. David Heyd (Princeton: Princeton University Press, 1996), 172. See also Jospeh Raz, *Ethics in the Public Domain* (Oxford: Clarendon, 1984), 171–72.

57. Ibid., 26.

58. Kymlicka, "Two Models of Pluralism and Tolerance," in *Toleration,* op. cit.

59. See Wendy Brown, "Neoliberalism and the End of Democracy," *Theory and Event* 7.2, 2003.

INDEX